The Cambridge Companion to Schubert's *Winterreise*

Organized in five parts, this Companion enhances understanding of Schubert's *Winterreise* by approaching it from multiple angles. Part I examines the political, cultural, and musical environments in which *Winterreise* was created. Part II focuses on the poet Wilhelm Müller, his twenty-four-poem cycle *Die Winterreise*, and changes Schubert made to it in fashioning his musical setting. Part III illuminates *Winterreise* by exploring its relation to contemporaneous understandings of psychology and science, and early nineteenth-century social and political conditions. Part IV focuses more directly on the song cycle, exploring the listener's identification with the cycle's protagonist, text–music relations in individual songs, Schubert's compositional "fingerprints," aspects of continuity and discontinuity among the songs, and the cycle's relation to German Romanticism. Part V concentrates on *Winterreise* in the nearly two centuries since its completion in 1827, including lyrical and dramatic performance traditions, the cycle's influence on later composers, and its numerous artistic reworkings.

MARJORIE W. HIRSCH is Professor of Music at Williams College in Massachusetts. She is the author of *Schubert's Dramatic Lieder* (1993) and *Romantic Lieder and the Search for Lost Paradise* (2007) and has more recently contributed to *The Unknown Schubert* (2008), *Schubert's Late Music in History and Theory* (2016), *Drama in the Music of Franz Schubert* (2019), and *The Oxford Handbook of Faust in Music* (2019).

LISA FEURZEIG is Professor of Music at Grand Valley State University in Michigan. She is the author of *Schubert's Lieder and the Philosophy of Early German Romanticism* (2014) and has contributed editions, articles, and chapters on Schubert, the Viennese *Volkstheater*, and Viennese operetta. In 2017–18 she was Fulbright-IFK Senior Fellow in Cultural Studies in Vienna. She has co-directed and performed in cabaret-style lecture-performances emphasizing music in its historical contexts.

Cambridge Companions to Music

Topics

The Cambridge Companion to Ballet
Edited by Marion Kant

The Cambridge Companion to Blues and Gospel Music
Edited by Allan Moore

The Cambridge Companion to Choral Music
Edited by André de Quadros

The Cambridge Companion to the Concerto
Edited by Simon P. Keefe

The Cambridge Companion to Conducting
Edited by José Antonio Bowen

The Cambridge Companion to Eighteenth-Century Opera
Edited by Anthony R. DelDonna and Pierpaolo Polzonetti

The Cambridge Companion to Electronic Music
Edited by Nick Collins and Julio D'Escriván

The Cambridge Companion to the *Eroica* Symphony
Edited by Nancy November

The Cambridge Companion to Film Music
Edited by Mervyn Cooke and Fiona Ford

The Cambridge Companion to French Music
Edited by Simon Trezise

The Cambridge Companion to Grand Opera
Edited by David Charlton

The Cambridge Companion to Hip-Hop
Edited by Justin A. Williams

The Cambridge Companion to Jazz
Edited by Mervyn Cooke and David Horn

The Cambridge Companion to Jewish Music
Edited by Joshua S. Walden

The Cambridge Companion to the Lied
Edited by James Parsons

The Cambridge Companion to Medieval Music
Edited by Mark Everist

The Cambridge Companion to Music in Digital Culture
Edited by Nicholas Cook, Monique Ingalls, and David Trippett

The Cambridge Companion to the Musical, third edition
Edited by William Everett and Paul Laird

The Cambridge Companion to Opera Studies
Edited by Nicholas Till

The Cambridge Companion to Operetta
Edited by Anastasia Belina and Derek B. Scott

The Cambridge Companion to the Orchestra
Edited by Colin Lawson

Composers

Instruments

The Cambridge Companion to

SCHUBERT'S
WINTERREISE

....

EDITED BY

Marjorie W. Hirsch
Williams College, Massachusetts

Lisa Feurzeig
Grand Valley State University, Michigan

CAMBRIDGE
UNIVERSITY PRESS

CAMBRIDGE
UNIVERSITY PRESS

University Printing House, Cambridge CB2 8BS, United Kingdom

One Liberty Plaza, 20th Floor, New York, NY 10006, USA

477 Williamstown Road, Port Melbourne, VIC 3207, Australia

314–321, 3rd Floor, Plot 3, Splendor Forum, Jasola District Centre,
New Delhi – 110025, India

79 Anson Road, #06–04/06, Singapore 079906

Cambridge University Press is part of the University of Cambridge.

It furthers the University's mission by disseminating knowledge in the pursuit of
education, learning, and research at the highest international levels of excellence.

www.cambridge.org
Information on this title: www.cambridge.org/9781108832847
DOI: 10.1017/9781108966146

© Cambridge University Press 2021

First published 2021

A catalogue record for this publication is available from the British Library.

ISBN 978-1-108-83284-7 Hardback
ISBN 978-1-108-96580-4 Paperback

Dedicated to Susan Youens – cherished advisor, mentor, colleague, friend

Contents

Figures

Tables

Music Examples

Contributors

Benjamin Binder, musicologist and pianist, is Associate Professor of Music at Duquesne University. His scholarly work on German Romantic music and the German Lied has been published in *Nineteenth-Century Music Review*, *The Journal of the American Musicological Society*, *Current Musicology*, *Music Theory Online*, and the volume *Rethinking Schubert* (2016). In 2016, his script for Thomas Hampson's *Song: Mirror of the World* public radio series was broadcast in the United States on the WFMT Radio Network. His work as a collaborative pianist specializing in art song includes creative partnerships with the Carnegie Museum of Art, Andy Warhol Museum, and City of Asylum.

Lisa Feurzeig is Professor of Music at Grand Valley State University in Michigan. Her research is centered on text–music relations in vocal music. In *Schubert's Lieder and the Philosophy of Early German Romanticism*, she argues that Schubert created musical equivalents for complex abstract ideas in settings of Schlegel and Novalis. In addition to Lieder, her other research areas include musical quotation and reference and Viennese theatrical traditions: *Volkstheater* plays and operettas. As a singer, she has emphasized early music, Lieder, and music since 1900.

Rufus Hallmark is Professor Emeritus from Rutgers University. He also taught at Queens College and the Graduate Center, CUNY, the College of the Holy Cross, MIT, and Brown University. His book Frauenliebe und Leben: *Chamisso's Poems and Schumann's Songs* appeared in 2014 (corrected ppb. ed. 2018). He has also written about other Schumann Lieder, including his book *The Genesis of* Dichterliebe, as well as the songs of Schubert and Ralph Vaughan Williams. He has edited *Frauenliebe* and *Dichterliebe* for the new edition of Schumann's works. He served as Secretary of the American Musicological Society for six years, and chaired the music programs at The Aaron Copland School of Music (Queens) and at Rutgers. He has also enjoyed performing much of the repertory he has written about.

Xavier Hascher is Professor of Musicology at the University of Strasbourg. He has published *Schubert: la forme sonate et son évolution* (1996) and *Symbole et fantasme dans l'Adagio du Quintette à cordes de Schubert* (2005) as well as edited the volume *Le style instrumental de Schubert* (2007) and the journal *Cahiers Franz Schubert* (1992–2000). He has also contributed to *The Cambridge Companion to Schubert* (1997), *Schubert-Lexikon* (1997), *Schubert-Jahrbuch 1998* (2001), *Schubert und das Biedermeier* (2002), *Schubert's Late Music: History, Theory, Style* (2016), *Rethinking Schubert* (2016), and *Drama in the Music of Franz Schubert* (2019).

Marjorie W. Hirsch is Professor of Music at Williams College. She is the author of *Schubert's Dramatic Lieder* (1993) and *Romantic Lieder and the Search for Lost Paradise* (2007). Her writings appear in *The Journal of Musicology*, the *Journal of Musicological Research*, the *Journal of the American Musicological Society*,

Nineteenth-Century Music Review, *The Unknown Schubert* (2008), *Schubert's Late Music in History and Theory* (2016), *Drama in the Music of Franz Schubert* (2019), and *The Oxford Handbook of Faust in Music* (2019).

Blake Howe is Paula G. Manship Associate Professor of Music History at Louisiana State University. His research interests include German song, disability studies, and film music, and he has published on these and other topics in the *Journal of the American Musicological Society*, *Music Theory Spectrum*, *The Journal of Musicology*, *Nineteenth-Century Music Review*, and the *Journal of Music History Pedagogy*. He co-edited *The Oxford Handbook of Music and Disability Studies* and served as editor of recording reviews for *Nineteenth-Century Music Review*.

Andrea Lindmayr-Brandl is Full Professor of Music History at the University of Salzburg. She studied musicology, philosophy, and mathematics at her home university, the Mozarteum Salzburg, and the Schola Cantorum Basiliensis. Her dissertation concerns the sources for the motets of Johannes Ockeghem (1990), and her habilitation analyzed Schubert's fragments (2003). She has held the Austrian Chair Professorship at Stanford University, has been guest professor at the University of Vienna, and is an active member of several academic institutions and organizations. Her field of research comprises studies in Renaissance music as well as Franz Schubert and his time.

Kristina Muxfeldt is Professor of Music in the Jacobs School of Music, Indiana University. She has served previously on the faculties of Yale University, the University of Illinois, Princeton University, and the University of Notre Dame. Her scholarship centers on European culture in the turbulent decades near the turn of the nineteenth century. She is author of *Vanishing Sensibilities: Schubert, Beethoven, Schumann* (2011). Further writings on Schubert may be found in *Franz Schubert and His World*, the *Journal of the American Musicological Society*, *19th-Century Music*, *The Cambridge Companion to Schubert*, *Music Theory Online*, *Notes*, and the *British Association of Romantic Studies Review*.

David Romand is a researcher at the Centre Gilles Gaston Granger for Philosophy and Comparative Epistemology, Aix-Marseille University, France. As a philosopher and historian of knowledge, he focuses on the nineteenth- and early twentieth-century German-speaking context. His recent publications include contributions to the history of psychology, the history and theory of psychological aesthetics and language sciences, German and Austrian philosophy, and the history and philosophy of emotions. He is currently completing a monograph on Theodor Lipps and a book on Heinrich Gomperz's theory of language.

James William Sobaskie teaches at Mississippi State University and serves on the editorial boards of *Nineteenth-Century Music Review* and *Music Theory Online*, plus the *comité scientifique* of *Œuvres Complètes de Gabriel Fauré*. His research has focused on Franz Schubert's sacred and chamber music, in addition to the Lieder, and he co-edited the anthology *Drama in the Music of Franz Schubert*, as well as two special issues of *Nineteenth-Century Music Review* devoted to the composer. His monograph, *The Music of Gabriel Fauré: Style, Structure and Allusion*, is forthcoming.

Deborah Stein teaches at the New England Conservatory, where she received a Teaching Excellence Award in 2007. She has published on text–music relations in the German Lied, including two books: *Hugo Wolf's Lieder and Extensions of Tonality* and *Poetry into Song: Performance and Analysis of Lieder,* co-authored with pianist Robert Spillman. She also edited a book of essays for students taking analytical courses: *Engaging Music: Essays in Music Analysis.* She taught at the Mannes Institute on Chromaticism in 2006 and served as Vice President for the Society for Music Theory, 2009–2011. Stein has lectured on aspects of Lieder in the US, Europe, and São Paulo, Brazil.

Laura Tunbridge is Professor of Music at the University of Oxford. Her publications include the monographs *Schumann's Late Style* (2007), *The Song Cycle* (2010), *Singing in the Age of Anxiety: Lieder Performances in New York and London between the World Wars* (2018), and *Beethoven: A Life in Nine Pieces* (2020), and the essay collections *Rethinking Schumann*, co-edited with Roe-Min Kok (2011) and *German Song Onstage*, co-edited with Natasha Loges (2020).

George S. Williamson is Associate Professor of History at Florida State University. He is the author of *The Longing for Myth in Germany: Religion and Aesthetic Culture from Romanticism to Nietzsche* (2004), as well as articles and book chapters on myth in German idealism, philosophical theories of race, debates over the historicity of Jesus, and the assassination of the playwright August von Kotzebue (1761–1819).

Susan Wollenberg was until October 2016 Professor of Music at the University of Oxford and Fellow and Tutor in Music of Lady Margaret Hall (where she is Emeritus Fellow). Among her publications are contributions to *Schubert Studies* (1998), *Schubert durch die Brille* (2002 and 2003), *Le style instrumental de Schubert: Sources, analyse, évolution* (2007), the *Schubert Jahrbuch* (2013), *Rethinking Schubert* (2016), and *Drama in the Music of Franz Schubert* (2019). Her monograph *Schubert's Fingerprints: Studies in the Instrumental Works* was published in 2011.

Acknowledgments

Our sincere thanks to Cambridge University Press Music editor Kate Brett for her enthusiastic support of this volume. We would also like to thank Nigel Graves, Barbara Wilson, Rajeswari Azayecoche, and the production team for their dedication to the project, as well as the colleagues, family members, and friends who have helped us in many ways throughout this process.

Note on Pitch

This book follows the Helmholtz system (middle C = c′) in designating specific pitches.

Chronology

1794   Johann Ludwig Wilhelm Müller born in Dessau on October 7

1797   Franz Peter Schubert born in Vienna on January 31

1808   Schubert becomes choirboy in Imperial Court Chapel and student at Stadtkonvikt boarding school

1811   Schubert composes "Hagars Klage" (D5), his first complete surviving song

1812   Müller begins studies in philology, history, and literature at University of Berlin with financial support from Duke Leopold Friedrich of Anhalt-Dessau

1813   Müller joins Prussian army in Wars of Liberation, fighting against Napoleon's forces in battles of Lützen, Bautzen, Haynau, and Kulm; Schubert leaves Stadtkonvikt

1814   Schubert composes "Gretchen am Spinnrade" (D118); begins teaching at his father's school

1815   Müller becomes infatuated with Luise Hensel (1798–1876) and continues his university studies; Schubert composes "Erlkönig" (D328)

1816   Beethoven's song cycle *An die ferne Geliebte* (To the Distant Beloved), Op. 98 published; Müller and friends improvise *Liederspiel* about a miller maid and her various suitors at Berlin salon; Schubert ceases teaching

1817   Müller embarks on two-year journey in Austria and Italy; Schubert meets Vienna court opera singer and future collaborator Johann Michael Vogl

1819   Müller returns to Dessau

1820   Müller's first volume of poetry, *Sieben und siebzig Gedichte aus den hinterlassenen Papieren eines reisenden Waldhornisten* (Seventy-seven poems from the posthumous papers of a traveling horn player), including poetic cycle *Die schöne Müllerin*, published in October by Christian G. Ackermann (dated 1821); Müller appointed ducal librarian by Duke Leopold Friedrich of Anhalt-Dessau

1821   Müller writes first twelve poems of *Die Winterreise*; Müller marries twenty-one-year-old Adelheid von Basedow (1800–1883); "Erlkönig" published as Schubert's Op. 1

1822   Birth of Müller's daughter Auguste (1822–1868); Schubert contracts syphilis in late 1822 or early 1823

1823   *Wanderlieder von Wilhelm Müller. Die Winterreise. In 12 Liedern* published in *Urania. Taschenbuch auf das Jahr 1823;* ten additional poems of *Die Winterreise* published in *Deutsche Blätter für Poesie, Litteratur, Kunst und Theater;* birth of Müller's son Friedrich Max (1823–1900); Schubert composes *Die schöne Müllerin* (D795)

1824   Müller completes *Die Winterreise;* Müller's second volume of poetry, *Gedichte aus den hinterlassenen Papieren eines reisenden Waldhornisten II: Lieder des Lebens und der Liebe* (Songs of life and love), which includes full twenty-four-song cycle *Die Winterreise,* published by Ackermann; Müller appointed privy councilor (*Hofrat*) by Duke Leopold Friedrich of Anhalt-Dessau

1826   Müller becomes director of court theater in Dessau; Schubert discovers Part I (first twelve poems) of Müller's *Die Winterreise* in *Urania ... 1823* in late 1826 or early 1827 and begins setting cycle

1827   Schubert moves in with Franz von Schober at The Blue Hedgehog in February; autograph manuscript of Part I of *Winterreise* dated "Febr. 1827" in Schubert's hand; Schubert invites friends to hear some new compositions (possibly Part I of the cycle) in early March but does not appear; Schubert discovers full twenty-four-song *Die Winterreise* cycle in *Waldhornisten II;* Beethoven dies March 26; Schubert composes Part II of *Winterreise* in summer and fall; Schubert sings "the whole of *Winterreise*" (Joseph von Spaun; *SMF,* 138) for several friends; Müller travels down Rhine River from July 31 to September 25, then dies of apparent heart attack on September 30 at age 32; fair copy of Part II of *Winterreise* dated "Oct. 1827" in Schubert's hand

1828   First and only concert performance of a song ("Gute Nacht") from *Winterreise* during Schubert's lifetime given on January 10 by tenor Ludwig Tietze at *Abend-Unterhaltung* of Vienna *Gesellschaft der Musikfreunde;* Tobias Haslinger publishes Part I of *Winterreise* on January 14; in November, Schubert corrects proofs to Part II of *Winterreise* on his deathbed; Schubert dies on November 19; Haslinger publishes Part II on December 30

1839   Johann Michael Vogl sings complete cycle *Winterreise* at age 71

1864   Julius Stockhausen gives first public performance of complete *Winterreise* cycle, using Müller's final published order of the poems

1928   First complete recording of *Winterreise* with tenor Hans Duhan and pianists Ferdinand Foll and Lene Orthmann, using Schubert's order of songs

Abbreviations

DC	Richard Kramer, *Distant Cycles: Schubert and the Conceiving of Song* (Chicago: University of Chicago Press, 1994)
DMFS	*Drama in the Music of Franz Schubert*, ed. Joe Davies and James William Sobaskie (Woodbridge: The Boydell Press, 2019)
DW	Lauri Suurpää, *Death in* Winterreise: *Musico-Poetic Associations in Schubert's Song Cycle* (Bloomington: Indiana University Press, 2013)
FSCS	Graham Johnson, *Franz Schubert: The Complete Songs*, 3 vols. (New Haven and London: Yale University Press, 2014)
FSSMW	Arnold Feil, *Franz Schubert:* Die schöne Müllerin, Winterreise, trans. Ann C. Sherwin (Portland, OR: Amadeus Press, 1988). [Original German publication: Stuttgart: Philipp Reclam, 1975]
RS	*Rethinking Schubert*, ed. Lorraine Byrne Bodley and Julian Horton (New York: Oxford University Press, 2016)
RWJ	Susan Youens, *Retracing a Winter's Journey: Schubert's* Winterreise (Ithaca and London: Cornell University Press, 1991)
SDB	*Schubert: A Documentary Biography*, ed. Otto Erich Deutsch, trans. Eric Blom (London: J. M. Dent & Sons, 1946)
SDL	*Schubert: Die Dokumente seines Lebens*, ed. Otto Erich Deutsch (Kassel and New York: Bärenreiter, 1964, rev. ed. Wiesbaden: Breitkopf & Härtel, 1996), trans. by Eric Blom as *Schubert: A Documentary Biography* (London: J. M. Dent & Sons, 1946), and as *The Schubert Reader: A Life of Franz Schubert in Letters and Documents* (New York: W. W. Norton, 1949)
SEF	*Schubert: Die Erinnerungen seiner Freunde*, ed. Otto Erich Deutsch (Wiesbaden: Breitkopf & Härtel, 1957, repr. 1983), trans. by Rosamond Ley and John Nowell as *Schubert: Memoirs by His Friends* (London: Adam and Charles Black, 1958)
SF	Susan Wollenberg, *Schubert's Fingerprints: Studies in the Instrumental Works* (Farnham: Ashgate, 2011)
SMF	*Schubert: Memoirs by His Friends*, ed. Otto Erich Deutsch, trans. Rosamond Ley and John Nowell (London: Adam and Charles Black, 1958)

SR   *The Schubert Reader: A Life of Franz Schubert in Letters and Documents*, ed. Otto Erich Deutsch, trans. Eric Blom (New York: W. W. Norton, 1949)

SSC   John Reed, *The Schubert Song Companion* (Manchester: Manchester University Press, 1985, 2nd ed. 1997)

SWJ   Ian Bostridge, *Schubert's Winter Journey: Anatomy of an Obsession* (New York: Alfred A. Knopf, 2015)

Introduction: An Endless Winter Journey

MARJORIE W. HIRSCH AND LISA FEURZEIG

"I like these songs more than all the rest, and you will come to like them as well," Franz Schubert reportedly declared upon first singing through his haunting new song cycle *Winterreise* (D911) to a few close friends.[1] The first half of the statement is remarkable given that by 1827, the year in which this intimate premiere took place, Schubert had already composed over 550 Lieder, including countless gems. His claim to prefer these "horrifying" new songs depicting a solitary wanderer's alienation, disorientation, and despair suffered amidst a bleak, frigid landscape bespeaks a deep personal attachment to the cycle. Composing the work had been taxing, as indicated by the numerous cross-outs, rewritings, and insertions in portions of the autograph manuscript, and Schubert was plainly proud of his accomplishment.[2] In asserting "I like these songs more than all the rest," he may have intended to steer his friends toward a positive assessment of the cycle, to reassure them that it was not merely the regrettable creation of a disturbed mind.

If Schubert was proud of *Winterreise*, he was also prescient: the second half of the statement has borne out. Although his friends and other early listeners were initially dismayed by the gloominess and magnitude of the cycle (one early reviewer grumbled, "It might have become one good song had it not become twenty-four of them"),[3] before long, their bewilderment turned to enthusiasm. The composer's circle came to venerate the work – "More beautiful German songs probably do not exist," his friend Joseph von Spaun later wrote – as, over time, did the wider public. Fulfilling Schubert's confident prediction, *Winterreise*, his second song cycle with poetic texts by Wilhelm Müller (1794–1827), has become one of the most esteemed works of his compositional oeuvre.

Given *Winterreise*'s virtually unrelieved mood of despondency, minimal plot, limited melodiousness, and great length, such high regard was hardly guaranteed. Schubert's first Müller cycle, *Die schöne Müllerin*, composed several years earlier, offered listeners a less formidable portrayal of love's rejection. The traditional story of a miller lad who falls for a miller maid who falls for a hunter develops with a clear narrative arc, and the musical settings, fusing qualities of folk-song with compositional artistry, have a natural appeal. Unsurprisingly, during much of the nineteenth century, the "Müllerlieder," as the first cycle was widely known on account of both its protagonist and its poet, enjoyed greater popularity than the second cycle (although neither was performed publicly in its entirety until mid-century). Both cycles are large-scale works with the emotional intensity and dramatic immediacy of opera. But with *Winterreise*, Schubert had made an extraordinary leap, re-envisioning what a song cycle could express and how it could do so, creating challenges for both performers and listeners. His claim "you will come to like [these songs] as well" – recalling Beethoven's terse comment about listeners' difficulty appreciating one of his late string quartets: "Some day it will suit them"[4] – betrays no hint of impatience, but rather recognition that widespread appreciation of groundbreaking works takes time. As it turned out, this was more time than Schubert was given.

Winterreise shortly preceded the composer's death. Schubert wrote the cycle between late 1826 or early 1827 and October 1827, fully aware that syphilis, the disease he had contracted five years earlier, would result in his early demise. The only uncertainties were when this would occur and, relatedly, whether he would survive long enough to enter the final stage of the disease, which could bring about insanity and the loss of his creative faculties. The *Winterreise* protagonist's longing for death and the possibility that he joins the *Leiermann* (hurdy-gurdy player) in madness at the end of the cycle thus resonate painfully with Schubert's personal story. That Schubert in fact died before suffering a ravaged mind may be due, ironically, to his composition of the cycle. Spaun, in his 1858 reminiscences, wrote, "There is no doubt in my mind that the excitement in which he composed his most beautiful songs, and especially his *Winterreise*, contributed to his early death."[5]

To what extent did Schubert, who corrected the proofs to Part II of the cycle on his deathbed, project himself onto the work? How closely did he identify with the wanderer's journey into the unknown? Spaun notes that Schubert had been depressed for some time before working on *Winterreise*. Johann Mayrhofer, another member of the composer's circle, drew a fairly direct connection to the winter wanderer: "[Schubert] had been long and seriously ill, had gone through disheartening experiences, and life for him had shed its rosy colour; winter had come for him."[6] Beyond his own illness, he was profoundly saddened by Beethoven's death on March 26, 1827. Presumably Schubert gravitated to Müller's poetic cycle *Die Winterreise* in part because he felt a kinship with the despondent wanderer. In his final days, perhaps he also felt a bond with Mozart, a composer he greatly admired ("O Mozart, immortal Mozart, how many, oh how endlessly many such comforting perceptions of a brighter and better life hast thou brought to our souls!" he once wrote in his diary),[7] and whose compositional career was also tragically cut short by illness. It is fitting that a performance of the Mozart Requiem – a work that shortly preceded its composer's death, that had preoccupied him on his deathbed,[8] and that Schubert revered – took place in the latter's honor shortly after his own untimely death on November 19, 1828.

Schubert died at the age of thirty-one, but nearly two hundred years later, *Winterreise* lives on. With its symphonic proportions, complexity, and seriousness, it has become a mainstay of the Western canon, as reflected in an unending stream of performances and recordings, important compositional progeny, an array of musical transcriptions and artistic reworkings, and a vast scholarly literature. The work is regularly taught in music history, theory, performance, and German literature and culture courses. Interest in *Winterreise*, which grew significantly during the late nineteenth century and even more so during the twentieth, shows no signs of abating. While the cycle may be rooted in early nineteenth-century aesthetics and intimately connected with Schubert's personal plight, its themes of isolation, alienation, and suffering are broadly relevant today, and its musical renderings of poetic imagery, emotions, and ideas still leave listeners in awe.

The cycle is the central focus of several recent books, most notably Susan Youens' *Retracing a Winter's Journey: Schubert's* Winterreise (1991), Lauri Suurpää's *Death in* Winterreise: *Musico-Poetic Associations in Schubert's Song Cycle* (2014), and Ian Bostridge's *Schubert's Winter Journey: Anatomy of an Obsession* (2015). Youens – to whom the contributors to this volume and other Schubert enthusiasts are deeply indebted for her extraordinary contributions to Schubert scholarship – provides detailed information about the cycle's cultural milieu, genesis, and sources, and closely examines the poetry and music of each of the twenty-four songs. Suurpää draws on Greimassian semiotics and Schenkerian analysis to elucidate the musico-poetic expression of longing for death in songs 14–24. Bostridge, a renowned Lied interpreter, as well as historian, who has performed *Winterreise* hundreds of times, offers a performer's insights into the cycle while also illuminating the cycle's dense web of historical, literary, philosophical, and scientific associations. Richard Kramer's illuminating *Distant Cycles: Schubert and the Conceiving of Song* (1994) and Arnold Feil's *Franz Schubert:* Die schöne Müllerin, Winterreise (1975, Eng. trans. 1988) provide a wealth of information and analytical/interpretive insights about the cycle, as do two comprehensive studies of Schubert's songs, John Reed's *The Schubert Song Companion* (1985) and Graham Johnson's magisterial, three-volume *Franz Schubert: The Complete Songs* (2014). (Johnson's substantial entry on *Winterreise* is a virtual monograph within the larger encyclopedic study.) The Further Reading section at the end of this volume lists many other valuable resources.

Rather than offer a detailed, song-by-song analysis of *Winterreise*, as do many of the studies cited above, this *Companion*, aimed at students though hopefully also of interest to scholars and general music lovers, is intended to illuminate a wide range of topics pertaining to the cycle. While the aforementioned books deal with some of the topics addressed here, they mostly do so within discussions of individual songs. By contrast, the essays in the present volume, authored by scholars in multiple disciplines, are organized in five parts focusing on different aspects of the cycle, its background and contexts, and its continuing impact on music and other art forms across nearly two centuries.

Our goal is to provide two types of information: background knowledge to help readers understand what *Winterreise* meant in its own time, and direct commentary on the work itself as it has been interpreted and understood more recently. In the first category, we address topics such as the place of this cycle in the biographies of its two creators, the genre of the song cycle in the 1820s, the relation of the work to historical events, the contemporary understanding of psychological topics in the period, and the contemporary view of science that would influence readers' and listeners' understanding of winter weather phenomena and other scientific topics touched on in the cycle. In the second category, we consider the cycle of poetry and song in itself, addressing topics such as how poetic images and musical motives are passed among poems and songs in the cycle, what types of musical material (such as harmony, rhythm, and the relation between piano and voice) are used to create meaning, and how the cycle has been interpreted as an existential expression of loneliness and a journey through time and space that transcends the specifics of its plot.

Part I of the book offers an introduction to the political, cultural, and musical environments in which Schubert's *Winterreise* was created. Andrea Lindmayr-Brandl describes early nineteenth-century Vienna, the "City of Music." With an eye for intriguing detail, she surveys the broad range of performing venues, musical institutions, concert series, and home music-making, including "Schubertiades" hosted by the composer's friends, and discusses the rise of the freelance musician, of which Schubert is a prime early example. Marjorie Hirsch illuminates Schubert's ties to tradition and his groundbreaking transformation of the Lied by examining his two settings of Goethe's "An den Mond" – a thematic precursor to *Winterreise* – in conjunction with settings of the poem by earlier composers. Lisa Feurzeig explores the topics of winter and wandering in poetry and song, tracing an evolution away from the pious perspective of the eighteenth century to a more open-ended, questioning presentation of those topics in Schubert's songs and the poetry he selected. She also outlines the development of the song cycle and its predecessor, the *Liederspiel*, before *Winterreise*.

Part II addresses Wilhelm Müller and his poetic cycle *Die Winterreise*. Kristina Muxfeldt describes Müller's formative experiences, from his exposure to controversial thinkers at the University of Berlin to his military travails in the Wars of Liberation to his friendships, love interests, and travels. Muxfeldt argues that the poems of *Die Winterreise* are related not only to other *Wanderlieder* but also to prose writing projects by Müller, including a biography of the poet Lord Byron and a book on the transmission of Homeric myth. Rufus Hallmark, after recounting the three-stage publication history of the *Winterreise* poems and Schubert's two-stage discovery of them, discusses the significance of Schubert's alterations to Müller's cycle, from the order of songs to changes in wording. Hallmark also casts a spotlight on unusual and largely overlooked metrical/rhythmic aspects of Schubert's settings, inviting new ways of understanding the cycle's stylistic heritage.

Part III illuminates *Winterreise* by looking beyond music and poetry to the realms of psychology, science, sociology, and political history. The two-part chapter by David Romand and Lisa Feurzeig considers the cycle's relation to psychology. Romand outlines the important developments in that nascent field of study at the time, emphasizing German writers and their concerns, and concludes that Müller's writing is rather distant from that approach. Feurzeig seeks closer relationships to the cycle in literature: popular novels, semi-fictional narratives, and poetry; she also describes the strange world of amateur animal magnetism, a type of psychological treatment at the time, and Schubert's direct encounter with that practice. Blake Howe draws parallels between the solitary wanderer in *Winterreise* and early nineteenth-century scientists who undertook similar journeys through the vast unknown of the natural world, recording their observations of landscapes, plants, animals, weather conditions, and atmospheric phenomena, including mysterious lights such as mock suns and will-o'-the-wisps. As Howe explains, the external world of nature and the internal subjectivity of the wanderer are dynamically connected. George S. Williamson associates the *Winterreise* protagonist with the legions of "wandering people" in early nineteenth-century Europe – those who took to the road, as outcasts, beggars, pilgrims, robbers, student nationalists, military deserters, minstrels, grifters, Jews, Gypsies, and travelers on the mail coaches. Williamson also examines political undercurrents in *Die Winterreise* against the backdrop of political developments from the French Revolution to the Restoration.

Part IV focuses more directly on the song cycle. James William Sobaskie compares *Winterreise* to *Die schöne Müllerin* with regard to the narratological concept of "identification." In examining song forms, textural elements, and contextual processes within the two cycles, he illuminates listeners' closer identification with, and empathy for, the *Winterreise* protagonist. Susan Wollenberg discusses overarching elements, or "connecting threads," in the words and music of *Winterreise*. In addition to investigating text–music relationships, she deepens understanding of ties between the cycle and the broader corpus of Schubert's music by identifying numerous "fingerprints" of his compositional style. Xavier Hascher scrutinizes the cycle's loose sense of coherence – the impression of uniformity, with shades of difference among the songs, created from resonances across the cycle rather than motifs or a harmonic scheme. In doing so, he analyzes the tonal journey through four harmonic quadrants linked to the poetic content, and identifies "associative relations" among the songs involving texture, timbre, register, and articulation, among other elements. Deborah Stein argues that the cycle is characterized primarily by a sense of discontinuity in both the poetry and the music. She supports this view with a close analysis of poetic themes (many associated with German Romanticism), the overall tonal design, and various temporal aspects of the cycle.

Finally, Part V concentrates on *Winterreise* in the nearly two centuries since its completion in the fall of 1827. Benjamin Binder traces the performance and reception history of the cycle, describing its rise in popularity as the sentimental nineteenth century yielded to the neurotic twentieth, the impact of recordings, and two common, contrasting approaches to interpretation – dramatic enactment vs. lyrical narration – that vocalists have adopted from Schubert's time to our own. As a fitting conclusion to the volume, Laura Tunbridge addresses the canonical status and vast cultural legacy of *Winterreise*. Her far-ranging discussion covers musical arrangements, reworkings, and homages, as well as references and transformations in film, literature, and the visual arts – a rich demonstration of changing attitudes towards Lieder generally and *Winterreise* in particular, and a testament to the cycle's endless allure.

The musical score to *Winterreise* is readily available; readers are encouraged to keep a copy of it close at hand. For their convenience, we have included an English translation of Müller's *Die Winterreise* cycle in an appendix. We are grateful to Celia Sgroi for kindly allowing us to reproduce her translation.[9]

Notes

1. As quoted by Joseph von Spaun in his 1858 reminiscences of Schubert. Translation by Susan Youens, *RWJ*, 27. See also *SMF*, 138 and *SEF*, 160–61.

2. The autograph manuscript of *Winterreise* is housed in the Morgan Library in New York City, NY. The manuscript for Part I (songs 1–12) comprises working versions for most of the songs as well as fair copies for two whole songs and parts of three others. The manuscript for Part II (songs 13–24) consists entirely of fair copies. For more on the manuscript, see Susan Youens, Introduction to *Franz Schubert: Winterreise: The Autograph Score* (New York: The Pierpont Morgan Library and Dover Publications, 1989), vii–xvii.
3. *SR*, 786.
4. Reminiscence of Gerhard von Breuning, as cited in O. G. Sonneck (ed.), *Beethoven: Impressions By His Contemporaries* (New York: Dover, 1926; 3rd ed.1967), 206.
5. *SMF*, 139.
6. *SMF*, 15.
7. Schubert wrote this encomium to Mozart in his diary on June 14, 1816 after attending a performance of a Mozart string quintet. *SR*, 60. As Susan Wollenberg discusses in Chapter 10 of this volume, Mozart's influence can be detected in *Winterreise*. For a more extensive discussion of Mozart's influence on Schubert, see *SF*, 133–59.
8. Mozart worked on the Requiem during the fall of 1791, but died in December before finishing it; in his final hours, he reportedly sang through the work with several friends gathered around his bedside.
9. Sgroi's texts and translations (1998), which may be found at gopera.com/winterreise/songs/cycle. mv, differ in a few details from Schubert's song texts. For the poetic originals and a song-by-song itemization of Schubert's textual changes, see Maximilian and Lily Schochow, *Franz Schubert: Die Texte seiner einstimmig und mehrstimmig komponierten Lieder und ihre Dichter*, 2 vols. (Hildesheim: Georg Olms, 1997), vol. 2, 395–410.

PART I

Schubert's *Winterreise* and Its Musical Heritage

1 Music and Culture in Schubert's Vienna

ANDREA LINDMAYR-BRANDL

In Schubert's time, musical and cultural life developed in an exciting way, shifting from the private to the public sphere. Simultaneously, a new type of musician emerged who was no longer sustained by the aristocracy or the court, but was a socially independent, freelance artist who made his living solely by giving concerts, getting commissions, and selling his published music. Franz Schubert was one of the first composers who lived such a life. He was successful in doing this and made a career in a place that is still known as the "City of Music."

That Schubert could make such a career still needs some explaining, however. Contemporary reports that portray Vienna as a liberal and open-minded place in which artists could easily thrive must be examined for what they are worth. The following example of such a report by Johann Friedrich Reichardt, a North German composer and writer, appears too good to be true:

> For anyone who is able to fully appreciate life's pleasures, Vienna is surely the happiest, richest, and most agreeable dwelling place in Europe. This pertains especially to artists, and perhaps particularly to musicians. Vienna has everything that marks a great residential city, and this to a very splendid great extent. It has a great, rich, educated, art-loving, hospitable, and civilized fine aristocracy; it has a rich, social, and hospitable middle class, which also does not lack educated and well-informed men and amiable families; and it has a well-off, good-humored, and merry population. All social classes love enjoyment and good living, and life is arranged so that everyone can find any amusement that is known and loved in the modern world in high-quality events, and can enjoy them safely and with full convenience.[1]

As Reichardt was a privileged person who took part in high society, the social circumstances of ordinary people were beyond his awareness. His description of the lower class of society was particularly far from reality.[2] The conditions of everyday life in Schubert's native city were not joyful, but difficult. Prices for food, rent, and clothing were steadily rising, sanitary and medical arrangements insufficient, the drinking water was contaminated, winter damp, and summer dusty. As a result, the average life expectancy was quite low. About 250,000 people lived in

Vienna, including 984 clergy; 4,342 peers, officials, and notables; and 9,201 wealthy middle-class citizens, tradesmen, and artists. There were also 31,552 peasants, about 40,000 house servants, and 6,000 footmen – as well as 5,196 horses, 113 oxen, and 1,233 cows.[3] These numbers summarize the population of the inner city of Vienna (today the first district) and the thirty-three suburbs that are spread out in a circle and confined by a brick wall and the river Danube in the north (see Figure 1.1). The inner city, where the court, most of the clergy, and the aristocrats lived with their servants, was characterized by narrow but paved roads and heavy traffic. Its marvelous buildings, such as the Hofburg, which housed the imperial family and many government offices, along with several great churches and many palaces, still shape the appearance of the city today. It was the center of cultural life. In the suburbs, the lifestyle was quite rural, with country houses that were less densely built and often had spacious gardens. Schubert, the son of a schoolteacher, was born in one of those suburbs and moved to the inner city at age eleven to get his professional musical education. He stayed there for the rest of his life, but enjoyed excursions to the countryside of the suburbs and further off in his leisure time.[4]

The Political Context

The period when Reichardt visited Vienna – from the end of November 1808 to the beginning of April 1809 – was politically turbulent and unstable. Austria was in the throes of the Napoleonic wars, with volatile fortunes. It had already lost territories in the south and west of its vast empire, and in 1804, as the Holy Roman Empire crumbled, Franz I was declared Emperor of Austria, anticipating his loss in 1806 of the title of Holy Roman Emperor. After Napoleon crowned himself King of Italy, his army reached Vienna on November 13, 1805. Many people fled, but the city was not damaged, and Beethoven's opera *Fidelio* was premiered soon afterwards with an audience of mostly French soldiers. The foreign troops stayed only two months, but threatened the city again three years later. In the last days of his visit, Reichardt attended a public festival in the large courtly *Redoutensaal*, where the national enthusiasm of the people was encouraged through music, leading to an enormous euphoria and glorification of war. Reichardt could anticipate where this would lead, and departed soon after this impressive event.[6]

The purpose of the propaganda was the building of a militia army – but it retreated, and Napoleon re-entered Vienna on May 13, 1809, mere weeks after Reichardt's departure. This time the city suffered severely: the artillery

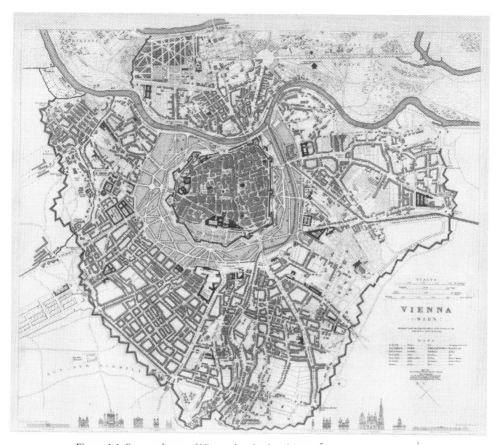

Figure 1.1 Engraved map of Vienna, hand colored (1833)[5]

bombardment destroyed structures and killed many people. Everybody who could flee left the city. Joseph Haydn died two weeks later, and Schubert's school, the Stadtkonvikt, was hit by a shell. In the next months, Vienna's population suffered from mass starvation, and daily life was very hard. According to the terms of the Treaty of Schönbrunn, signed in October, Napoleon was again expelled, but Austria paid a high price: Emperor Franz gave his daughter Marie-Louise to the French emperor as a bride and forfeited lands with a population of 3.5 million. Moreover, the high war debts resulted in state bankruptcy in 1811, with an 80 percent deflation of Austrian currency. In the next years, Napoleon was defeated, first at the Battle of Leipzig (1813) and finally at the Battle of Waterloo (1815). The young Schubert reacted to these historical events with two songs – "Auf den Sieg der Deutschen" (The Victory of the Germans, D81) and "Die Befreier Europas in Paris" (Europe's Liberators in Paris, D104) – and the canon "Verschwunden sind die Schmerzen" (The Pains Have Disappeared, D88).

At the Congress of Vienna (1814–15), the borders of Europe were newly drawn and a balance of power established, intended to prevent future wars. For Austria a time of peace began, with the motto of "tranquility and order" on its flags. This promising restart, however, was marred by a strong police and a system of spies intended to nip any revolutionary ideas in the bud. The state chancellor, Prince Clemens von Metternich (1773–1859), came to personify these oppressive policies that restricted civil society in order to prevent conspiracies. No work could be published without approval from the Office of Censorship.[7] Schubert suffered from these regulations when the libretto of his opera *Der Graf von Gleichen* (D918) was rejected in 1826, and the opera was never finished.

Turning back again to Reichardt's report of Vienna's cultural life, it was not all wrong and has its merits despite its restricted perspective. As a musician and man of the theater, Reichardt attended an astonishingly large number of musical events that the city offered even in these difficult times. He attended twenty-one opera performances, sixteen major public concerts, nine dance events, and almost sixty semi-public or private gatherings with music, often mounted at palaces and combined with tea or dinner. Sometimes he even attended three performances in a day: a lunch concert, a chamber concert in the afternoon, and a theater production in the evening. The rich offerings of cultural life are reflected in a survey of musical art in Vienna that was published by a local newspaper a few months before Reichardt arrived. It emphasizes that "nowhere else is music played by so many people, so deeply loved, and so intensely practiced as here."[8]

Performance Venues, Musical Institutions, and Types of Events[9]

In Schubert's lifetime, Vienna had five theaters: two court theaters in the inner city and three playhouses in the suburbs. At the Burgtheater, one could enjoy the performance of classical German dramas on the highest level, performed by an internationally acclaimed company. Schubert appreciated this theater, although its facilities were shabby and uncomfortable. It was built for about one thousand spectators and had good acoustics but bad ventilation. The Theater am Kärntnerthor specialized in opera and ballet. Its furniture was elegant, but the house was cramped, stuffy, and hot. It had its own orchestra and a resident dance company. From 1810 onwards, the theater presented operas and musical comedies by Mozart, Weigl, Spontini, and Méhul, all in the German language. Light operas were often combined with a ballet. Schubert contributed his one-act Singspiel *Die Zwillingsbrüder* (D647) to the repertoire and was engaged for a short time as a vocal coach. Meanwhile, the audience lost its interest in German operas, preferring the Italian repertoire. In 1821, the Kärntnerthor-Theater was given into the hands of the Italian impresario Domenico Barbaja, who attracted famous opera singers trained in the Italian style and offered Rossini a place to present his most recent works. Rossini's opera *Il barbiere di Seviglia* was staged there in 1819, and many other works by the Italian followed, also admired by Schubert. Rossini's light-hearted operas, with their melodious arias and effervescent plots, were extremely popular with Viennese audiences.

Among the theaters in the suburbs, the Theater an der Wien had the largest and most beautiful building. With its modern set design, it exceeded even the court theaters. More than 2,000 seats were offered, and a broad variety of repertoire was presented. Its program included dramas, folk and magic plays, light operas, ballets, and melodramas. Schubert's music for the magic play *Die Zauberharfe* (D644) was premiered there. The level of the orchestra was high and comparable to the court orchestra. Tickets were cheaper than for the theaters in the inner city, but significantly higher than for the two other suburban houses. In the Theater in der Josefstadt, the great Austrian actor and playwright Ferdinand Raimund (1790–1836) achieved his initial successes. In 1817, he took over the company of the Theater in der Leopoldstadt and led the Viennese folk comedy to a climax. Schubert was quite interested in this popular genre, which often featured catchy, memorable music. In 1822, he may have attended a performance of a magic play by Adolph Bäuerle: *Alina oder Wien in einem anderen Erdteil* (*Alina or Vienna on Another Continent*), its music by the highly successful theater composer Wenzel Müller (1767–1835).

The theaters served other purposes as well. Due to the small number of performance venues for orchestras, they were also used for public concerts on religious or state holidays, when theater performances were forbidden and the stages were available. To keep the costs for lighting and heating in the winter as low as possible, the noon hour was preferred for such extra events. The earliest concert organization was the *Tonkünstler-Sozietät*, founded in 1771. Four times a year, this society produced a benefit concert in the Burgtheater for widows and orphans of professional musicians – but its frequent performances of Haydn's oratorios *Die Schöpfung* (The Creation) and *Die Jahreszeiten* (The Seasons) attracted more and more criticism. In the first decades of the nineteenth century, this society faded in importance.

The idea of these benefit performances was taken over by other social groups. Concerts to support needy personnel of both court theaters were organized, and events to promote the public hospital were launched. Such benefit academies were an essential element of Vienna's concert life in the early nineteenth century. Though they were not always on the highest artistic level, their diverse repertoire and entertaining quality made them something special. Italian arias from current operas and virtuoso solo pieces were as popular as the interspersed recitations of poems and panto-mimed depictions of tableaus.

There were also many concerts featuring excellent local musicians or traveling virtuosos performing for their own financial benefit. Every reputable Viennese musician, including Beethoven and Schubert, pre-sented "Privat-Concerte" with his students, friends, and family mem-bers in the audience. These performances also had mixed programs. Vocal and instrumental pieces, overtures, and individual movements from multi-movement works were presented in random order.

For the new genre of the public concert, venues other than the theaters were available. The *Redoutensaal* in the Hofburg was particularly favored by external virtuosos who could expect a more numerous audience. The even larger hall of the same place was used less often. It could be filled only by larger organizations or when a star such as Niccolò Paganini was in town. Benefit concerts, larger productions by local musicians, and events with full orchestra were performed in the university hall and in the hall of Lower Austria's statehouse (*Landständischer Saal*). The latter had two sweeping exterior staircases and convenient acoustics, but unfortunately no heating.

More comfortable venues were rooms in inns, which could be rented for smaller events. They bore typical names such as *Zum römischen Kaiser* (The Roman Emperor), *Zur Mehlgrube* (The Flour Pit), or *Zum roten Igel* (The Red Hedgehog). During the carnival season before Lent, the same rooms were used for dancing. Dance music was very popular, and dance orchestras emerged in various sizes according to the dimensions of the location. In inns, small ensembles were sufficient; the *Redoutensaal* needed ten to fifteen musicians; and in the *Apollosaal* the orchestra comprised as many as sixty members. The latter was a very spacious, newly built establishment catering to both the bourgeoisie and the aristocracy; it was in the suburb Schottenfeld (today known as Neubau, Vienna's seventh district). A dance event started with a promenade, followed by a slow march or a polonaise, and then a series of quadrilles and quick dances, such as the galop. The typical Viennese waltz was not established until about 1820.

Members of the middle class, such as Schubert, and of lower social classes – those who did not travel with closed carriages within the city – attended outdoor musical events. There were many of these in public gardens, markets, fairs, squares, streets, and backyards. The musicians who were active in these public spaces in Vienna around 1800 included itinerant harp players, folk-singers, ballad-sellers, and organ-grinders. Many of them were blind, ill, or disabled people who made their livings from donations. Thus the Viennese populace supported some of the poorest members of society.[10]

Finally, music was performed in church services. The most prestigious venue was the imperial court chapel, where a full mass was performed every Sunday at 11 a.m. Performances of high quality could also be heard in the Augustiner church. Other churches in the inner city and the thirty parishes in the suburbs made great efforts and performed church music at a high level. The parish church in the suburb of Lichtental was Schubert's native church, where he took music lessons from the organist in his early days. Schubert was also friendly with Salomon Sulzer, a famous Jewish cantor with an extraordinary voice who was active in Vienna from 1820 onwards. For Sulzer, Schubert composed his *Psalm 92* (D953), a song for the Sabbath set for choir and baritone solo.

Private or semi-private musical events traditionally occurred in the palaces of the aristocracy, where Reichardt was invited so often. Depending on their financial capabilities, these noble families main-tained a string quartet, a wind band, or even a small house orchestra. This was the social world of Beethoven, but not of Schubert, who was closely affiliated with Vienna's bourgeoisie. After the fortunes of most of the aristocratic families were dramatically reduced as a result of major contributions to armament during the war years, this social class grad-ually had to withdraw from its leading role in Viennese musical life. At the same time, private circles emerged around distinguished individuals such as court officials, wealthy artists, and members of the upper classes. The privy councilor Raphael Kiesewetter, court secretary Ignaz Mosel, brewery owner Vincenz Neuling, and the writer Karoline Pichler, who hosted a highly esteemed salon, belonged to this group. One needed a written invitation to attend, but visitors came from different social groups and did not always know each other. While courtly etiquette was imitated in such circles, the enjoyment of art rather than social interaction stood at the center of interest.

Making music together as evening entertainment was also appreciated by ordinary citizens. People met privately with their friends or in the immediate family circle, enjoying domestic music in its proper sense. Schubert, for instance, gained his first musical experience in his family string quartet. The so-called Schubertiades, a phenomenon of his later years, are discussed below. Minor genres that were rarely on the program of public concerts were particularly fostered: vocal ensembles, songs, instrumental works in smaller scorings, string quartets, and piano music. Piano dances were the favorite genre. The atmosphere of such meetings was friendly and informal, with invitations often made only by word of mouth. In some cases, small orchestras developed out of such circles that were able to perform entire symphonies in private homes. When the famous Viennese music critic Eduard Hanslick described the years from 1810 to 1820 as the pinnacle of musical dilettantism, he did not mean it in a negative sense.[11] In this time, "dilettante" meant a person who made music privately rather than as a profession, but on a level often comparable with that of professional musicians.

Concert Series and Professionalization

It was also a bourgeois initiative that led to the foundation of the *Gesellschaft der Musikfreunde* (Society of Friends of Music) in 1812. During the nineteenth century, this society became the most prominent musical institution in Vienna, and it is still active today. The founding members were responding to the often one-sided and shallow programs of public concerts, which also promoted "classical" works by composers such as Haydn or Mozart. According to the by-laws of 1814, the chief aim of the *Gesellschaft* was the development of all branches of music. Leading personalities of this organization were its first president, the aforementioned Ignaz Mosel, and Josef Sonnleithner, who belonged to a respected music-loving family of lawyers. The *Gesellschaft der Musikfreunde* was open only to dilettantes and soon counted a thousand members. It organized an annual music festival with significant works on the program. In 1815, Händel's *Messiah* was scheduled. Performances could be attended by anyone who paid an entrance fee.

An important issue within the society was the equal status of all its members. Seats were assigned by lottery, and in the early years, soloists, conductors, and instrumentalists were only chosen from among the members in alternation. A special pride lay in the fact that musicians of all social classes played together, united by the society in their shared love for music. In the orchestra, counts sat next to clerks, head officials next to secretaries, professors next to students, while aristocratic ladies sat beside girls from the bourgeoisie in the choir. The German poet Ludwig Rellstab, who visited Vienna in 1825, was enthusiastic about the quality of the performances and commented: "It would be great if we could achieve a similar level in Berlin."[12]

Each season had four society concerts and about sixteen smaller evening concerts. They were mainly for members, who formed either the audience or the orchestra. Symphonies and overtures by renowned Viennese composers, as well as solo music with orchestral accompaniment and major choral works, were on the program of the society concerts. Because of their great success, these events soon had to move from the smaller to the larger *Redoutensaal*. In late fall 1817, the concert series known as *Abend-Unterhaltungen* (Evening Entertainments) began. These performances, regularly scheduled on Thursdays between 7 and 9 p.m., were more like events in Viennese salons than public concerts. They actually started in private houses and later moved to the official location of the society, the *Roter Igel*. Leopold Sonnleithner, Joseph's nephew, made himself a name by managing the *Abend-Unterhaltungen*, where chamber music for string ensembles, pieces for solo instruments, songs with piano accompaniment, vocal quartets, arias, and duets were played. From 1825 on, Schubert was the composer played most often after Rossini; in earlier years, Mozart and Beethoven were slightly ahead of him.[13]

In the same year, 1817, the society established a singing school, which soon developed into a conservatory offering instruction on all orchestral instruments. The musical education of young people was already laid down in the by-laws and was one of the society's central concerns. Initially nobody expected that through these regular lessons, instrumentalists would be trained at such a high technical level that they were competitive with professional orchestra musicians. These trained performers also gradually displaced the dilettantes from active concert life. Thus the original function of the society was finally undermined by its own conservatory, and the musical scene in Vienna became more and more professional.[14]

A second bourgeois concert series called *Concerts spirituels* was started by the choir director of the Augustiner church, Franz Xaver Gebauer. At first, the musicians met every two weeks in the inn *Zur Mehlgrube* to cultivate serious music, and later they moved to the *Landständischer Saal*. Their first public concert took place on October 1, 1819, followed by seventeen concerts each season. The ambitious program, played by a choir and an orchestra totalling about one hundred musicians, proved quite popular at the beginning. In this concert series, Schubert heard Mozart's Symphony No. 41 ("Jupiter") and presumably also the first movement of Beethoven's Ninth Symphony. Only in later years did critics lament the low quality of the performances due to the small number of rehearsals. In some cases, the orchestra had to play symphonies and oratorios at sight.

A new type of event was subscription concerts: series of concerts for which people could buy a cheap season ticket. The first such concert series was founded in 1804 by Ignaz Schuppanzigh, the first violinist of the famous so-called Rasumovsky Quartet that had close ties to Beethoven. This professional ensemble premiered several string quartets at the highest level, including Schubert's A Minor Quartet (D804). Vienna was the first European city where one could hear quartets performed in public concerts on a regular basis. However, in all other areas of institutional music life, it lagged behind cities like Paris and London.[15]

Lied, Biedermeier, and Musical Public

In the first half of the nineteenth century, the Lied genre did not play an important role in public musical life, but it was central to the culture of sociability. In almost every bourgeois household in Vienna, a piano was available, and music lessons were provided for the children of such families, including girls. Private and semi-private gatherings were the domain for the performance of songs, with the Schubertiade as a paramount example. The first known event of this type took place in January 1821 when Franz von Schober, one of Schubert's best friends, invited fourteen of his acquaintances to his home. Although the word "Schubertiade" was not mentioned, this seems to have been the starting point for an irregular series of such gatherings.

Schubert's friends gave detailed reports in their letters and diaries about what usually happened at these events. According to their notes, it was always a great entertainment with drinking, eating, dancing, and music-making until late at night. Schubert was often sitting at the piano, playing his four-hand pieces with a friend or accompanying his songs performed by the opera singer Johann Michael Vogl, his favorite interpreter. For the composer, it was a great opportunity to present his new works in a semi-public sphere. The audience of about twenty people consisted of intellectuals and artists from Viennese society: writers, painters, musicians, actors, and officials, who were all on friendly terms and gathered mainly for social reasons. Women, usually those associated with the invited male guests, also attended.[16] The last Schubertiade took place at the end of January 1828, the year Schubert died. The pieces performed that time included some four-hand piano variations and one of his piano trios.

Domestic music-making has been interpreted as a retreat from the policed public life and the suppressing policy of the government. It is seen as an epitome of Biedermeier culture, which fostered a private, non-political civic life. The term "Biedermeier" was applied to this time period later, referring to a literary figure called Gottlieb Biedermeier, who was the protagonist in a series of satirical articles in the journal *Fliegende Blätter* (1855–57). He was a schoolmaster who represented a confident, philistine, and complacent man from the middle class. Since it appears to lack any element of social protest and represents an ideal, family-centered world, Biedermeier art is often suspected of being naïve or even trivial.[17]

Schubert's songs, though, and specifically his *Winterreise*, hardly meet this description. They were also not completely excluded from public musical life. The first Schubert song heard in public was "Schäfers Klagelied" (D121; Shepherd's Lament) which was performed at the end of February 1819. The concert at the inn *Zum römischen Kaiser* was organized by Eduard Jäll, a member of the orchestra at the Theater an der Wien and principal of the Hatwig private orchestra, in which Schubert played the viola. The song was integrated into a typical mixed program, squeezed between a polonaise for solo violin and a recitation of a poem. The singer, Franz Jäger, was a colleague of Jäll's in the same theater, and the pianist's name is not mentioned. "Schäfers Klagelied" was repeated a month later at a benefit concert for impoverished theater performers, and another month later in the *Landständischer Saal*.

Another important occasion for song performances was the *Abend-Unterhaltungen* of the *Gesellschaft der Musikfreunde*. At the beginning of this concert series, vocal ensembles by Schubert were more popular; songs with piano only gradually became part of the program. On January 25, 1821, the famous "Erlkönig" (D328) was the first Schubert song that could be heard there; this was the first public performance of that song. The *Abend-Unterhaltungen* were also the venue for the premiere of *Winterreise*, at least in part. Only the first number of the cycle, "Gute Nacht," was performed on January 10, 1828, shortly after its publication. This was the only public performance of a song from *Winterreise* during Schubert's lifetime.[18] Concerts presenting exclusively or mostly songs developed only in the second half of the nineteenth century, and the practice of performing song cycles in full became normal even later.[19]

Musical life in Schubert's time had two sides. On the one hand, Biedermeier house music cultivated a musical experience for a broad segment of the population within a private, intimate ambiance. On the other hand, public music and commercial concert life developed and made important advances, despite the governmental fear of revolutionary activism within such societies. Police approval was required for all public concerts, and the programs and texts had to pass the censor. That music events could indeed be an opportunity for political discussions is documented in a report from 1828 by another visitor to Vienna: the well-traveled and colorful, though somewhat unreliable writer Charles Sealsfield (pen name of Carl Anton Postl). Like Reichardt, Sealsfield had access to the aristocratic salons, which were by then a declining institution and only a sideshow of the rich public musical life. He wrote:

> It is in the circles of the nobility, and the wealthier class of bankers, that you will find a certain degree of political freedom and liberty of speech, newspapers, and as they are called, "Verbotene Bücher," (prohibited books) in every tongue. There are no political saloons of liberals, as there are in Paris, except [in] the very highest families of the nobility; where, however, none but the most intimate and confidential friends are admitted: but during a dancing, a dining, or whist party, some couples of gentlemen will loose themselves from the tables, and step just occasionally into the next room; or a letter received from Paris or London – of course not through the post – will glide from hand to hand, in that imperceptible way which Metternich has taught them. That is the way to concert in Austria, measures, plans, and even something more – in the midst of pleasure and gaiety. They are forced into this; as the Emperor though far from being a Caesar, acts fully on this principle with respect to his subjects, – and thinks himself and his family secure as long as his subjects are dancing and singing.[20]

The mounting social, economic, and political tensions that seethed below the surface of society culminated in the Revolutions of 1848. They brought the Biedermeier period to an abrupt end. In Austria, people protested against the long-standing conservatism of the government, fighting for liberal and democratic changes. These strong movements did not destroy, but did shake the Habsburg Empire. The revolt was finally suppressed, the weak emperor Ferdinand I replaced by his nephew Franz Joseph, and a new phase of neo-absolutism was entered. By the time these political turbulences happened, Sealsfield was in Switzerland in a safe haven, and Schubert had already been dead for twenty years.

Notes

1. Gustav Gugitz (ed.), *Johann Friedrich Reichardt. Vertraute Briefe, geschrieben auf einer Reise nach Wien und den Österreichischen Staaten zu Ende des Jahres 1808 und zu Anfang 1809* (Munich: Georg Müller, 1915), vol. 2, 145.
2. Gugitz, *Johann Friedrich Reichardt*, Introduction, xv–xx. Andrea Lindmayr-Brandl, "Es ist doch eine wahrhaft große, herrliche Stadt! Vertraute Briefe von Johann Friedrich Reichardt aus Wien," *Schubert-Jahrbuch 2006–2009* (2009), 27–37.
3. *Vaterländische Blätter für den österreichischen Kaiserstaat*, 15 July 1808, 171–72, available online through www.anno.onb.ac.at.
4. Waltraud Heindl, "People, Class Structure, and Society," in Raymond Erickson (ed.), *Schubert's Vienna* (New Haven and London: Yale University Press, 1997), 36–54.
5. Vienna. Published by the Society for the Diffusion of Useful Knowledge. Drawn by W. B. Clarke, architect. Engraved & printed by J. Henshall. Published by Baldwin & Cradock, 47 Paternoster Row, 1833. London: Chapman & Hall, 1844. David Rumsey Map Collection. www.davidrumsey.com/luna/servlet/detail/RUMSEY~8~1~21041~540018:Vienna–Wien-.
6. Gugitz, *Johann Friedrich Reichardt*, vol. 2, 104–6.
7. Raymond Erickson, "Vienna in Its European Context," in *Schubert's Vienna*, 3–35.
8. *Vaterländische Blätter*, 27 May 1808, "Übersicht des gegenwärtigen Zustandes der Tonkunst in Wien," 39.

9. Alice M. Hanson, *Musical Life in Biedermeier Vienna* (Cambridge: Cambridge University Press, 1985). Alice M. Hanson, "Vienna, City of Music," in *Schubert's Vienna*, 98–118. Raymond Erickson, "Music in Biedermeier Vienna," in Robert Pichl, Clifford A. Bernd, and Margarete Wagner (eds.), *The Other Vienna. The Culture of Biedermeier Austria* (Vienna: Lehner, 2002), 227–41.

10. Gertraud Schaller-Pressler, "Volksmusik und Volkslied in Wien," in Elisabeth Theresia Fritz and Helmut Kretschmer (eds.), *Wien. Musikgeschichte. Teil 1: Volksmusik und Wienerlied* (Vienna: Lit Verlag, 2006), 3–147.

11. Eduard Hanslick, *Geschichte des Concertwesens in Wien* (Vienna: Braumüller, 1869), vol. 1, 139.

12. Cited after Hanslick, *Geschichte des Concertwesens*, vol. 1, 155.

13. Otto Biba, "Schubert's Position in Viennese Musical Life," *19th-Century Music* 3 (1979): 106–13.

14. Ingrid Fuchs (ed.), *Musikfreunde. Träger der Musikkultur in der ersten Hälfte des 19. Jahrhunderts* (Kassel: Bärenreiter, 2017).

15. Hans-Joachim Hinrichsen, "Musikalische Geselligkeit und Selbstorganisation des Bürgertums. Musikvereine des 19. Jahrhunderts im europäischen Vergleich," in Fuchs (ed.), *Musikfreunde. Träger der Musikkultur in der ersten Hälfte des 19. Jahrhunderts*, 207–17.

16. Reinhold Brinkmann, "*Fragmente einer Sozial- und Aufführungsgeschichte des Liedes im 19. Jahrhundert,*"in H. Danuser (ed.), *Musikalische Lyrik* (Handbuch der musikalischen Gattungen 8) (Laaber: Laaber, 2004), vol. 2, 86–124. Otto Biba, "Public and Semi-Public Concerts: Outlines of a Typical 'Biedermeier' Phenomenon in Viennese Music History," in *The Other Vienna*, 257–70.

17. Erickson, "Music in Biedermeier Vienna," 227–41. Carl Dahlhaus, "Romantik und Biedermeier. Zur musikgeschichtlichen Charakteristik der Restaurationszeit," *Archiv für Musikwissenschaft* 31 (1974): 22–41.

18. Otto Biba, "Franz Schubert in den musikalischen Abendunterhaltungen der Gesellschaft der Musikfreunde," in Franz Grasberger and Othmar Wessely (eds.), *Schubert-Studien* (Vienna: Österreichische Akademie der Wissenschaften, 1978), 7–31.

19. Hanslick, *Geschichte des Concertwesens*, vol. 2, 214.

20. Primus-Heinz Kucher (ed.), *Charles Sealsfield – Karl Postl. AUSTRIA AS IT IS: or Sketches of Continental Courts, by an Eye-Witness. London 1828* (Vienna: Böhlau, 1994), 92.

2 Tradition and Innovation in Schubert's Lieder

MARJORIE W. HIRSCH

On August 19, 1815, a dozen years before undertaking *Winterreise*, Franz Schubert composed a song that treads similar poetic ground. Like the winter wanderer of Wilhelm Müller's cycle, the protagonist of Johann Wolfgang von Goethe's "An den Mond" (D259; To the Moon) roams through a natural landscape evoking inner terrain; the moonlit wood and valley conjure the recesses of his (or her) mind, intimating a journey of self-discovery. The protagonist's present solitude, recollection of joyful and troubled times, glancing reference to faithless love, direct address to a river, allusion to the harshness of winter, mention of his own song, and mysterious closing reference to wandering by night through the labyrinth of the heart all anticipate ways that Müller, in a darker mode, conveys existential isolation and suffering in *Winterreise*.

"An den Mond" was one of five Goethe poems Schubert set that day, reflecting both the outpouring of Lieder during 1815, his celebrated "year of song," and the importance that Goethe already held for him. (He composed 142 solo songs in 1815, up from just twenty-four the previous year, and fewer still before that. D259 is the twenty-sixth of his seventy-five Goethe solo settings.)[1] Schubert made a fair copy of the song and included it in the second volume of his Goethe settings, which he intended to send to the revered poet.[2] Since the volume was never delivered, one can only guess whether Goethe would have liked the tuneful Lied in E♭ major. But Schubert himself may not have been satisfied, for he later set "An den Mond" again, probably in 1820,[3] and this second setting (D296) has a vastly different effect. From the opening notes, the music sounds far more emotional, evocative, and intricate. Indeed, the second setting is not a variation of the first but rather a complete reinterpretation of Goethe's poem; a compositional gulf separates the two songs. With its strophic form, simple rhythms, and subordinate accompaniment, the first setting largely harkens back to eighteenth-century Lied conventions. The second, by contrast, while maintaining some ties to tradition, displays the expressive intensity and complex artistry characterizing many nineteenth-century Lieder. Its aesthetics are thus much more closely allied with those of *Winterreise*, a massive cycle of twenty-four such songs.

Schubert's reconceptualization of "An den Mond" serves as a useful point of entry for exploring his seminal role in the development of the Lied. As is widely known, between 1810 and 1828 Schubert composed over 600 Lieder, inspiring several generations of composers – Robert Schumann, Felix Mendelssohn, Fanny Hensel, Robert Franz, Franz Liszt, Johannes Brahms, Hugo Wolf, Gustav Mahler, Richard Strauss, and countless others – to follow in his footsteps. Authors often claim that Schubert's "Gretchen am Spinnrade" (D118), composed on October 19, 1814, marks the "birth" of the nineteenth-century Romantic Lied. "Gretchen" certainly represents an extraordinary achievement: Schubert crafted music that conveys not only the outward scene in which Goethe's heroine sits singing and spinning at her wheel, but also her inner whirl of emotions as she remembers encounters with her lover Faust and fantasizes about future intimacy. A comparable success is Schubert's setting of Goethe's suspenseful ballad "Erlkönig" (D328; October 1815), in which the musical evocation of a galloping horse bearing a father and his seemingly delusional son homeward on a stormy night converges with the expression of mounting terror. But the outsize prestige and popularity of these and a handful of other early Schubert songs have obscured the gradual emergence of the Lied as a quintessential Romantic genre. The Romantic Lied did not spring into being during a single day or year, and its history does not follow a straight line of development from simple to complex settings. In fact, its history does not even begin with Schubert, as evidenced, for example, by his early enthusiasm for the songs and ballads of Johann Rudolph Zumsteeg (1760–1802), and his desire, according to his friend Joseph von Spaun, to "modernize Zumsteeg's song form."[4] Individually and collectively, Schubert's Lieder are tied to the past yet also forward-looking, often astonishingly so. His settings of "An den Mond" exemplify this duality.

This chapter focuses on both Schubert's ties to tradition and his innovations in song composition, providing readers unfamiliar with the emergence of the nineteenth-century Romantic Lied with a foundation for the study of *Winterreise*. Several excellent recent essays offer insight into Schubert's transformation of the Lied by discussing myriad innovations in songs dating from throughout his life.[5] The present chapter takes a different approach, illuminating his groundbreaking accomplishments as a song composer through close consideration of his two versions of "An den Mond" in conjunction with settings of the poem by previous composers. Examining the treatment of musical elements such as harmony and texture, the role of expressivity and symbolism, the nature and interrelationships of the voice and piano parts, and the technical demands placed on the performers deepens understanding of how Schubert transformed the Lied into an artistic medium superbly suited to projecting the range and complexity of human experience.

Goethe's "An den Mond"

Goethe's poem "An den Mond" ("Füllest wieder Busch und Tal") has an intriguingly convoluted history linked to two sorrowful episodes in his life. On the frigid night of January 16, 1778, Christel von Lassberg, the daughter of a Weimar court official, drowned in the River Ilm near the poet's garden house while he ice-skated unaware on a nearby pond. A copy of Goethe's wildly popular epistolary novel *The Sorrows of Young Werther* (1774), whose protagonist kills himself over unrequited love, and which had inspired a number of copycat suicides, was reportedly found in her pocket. Not long afterwards, in a letter to his platonic lover Charlotte von Stein describing the effect upon him of Lassberg's tragic death, Goethe enclosed a six-stanza poem he had written (possibly years earlier) entitled "An den Mond," set to the music of a pre-existing song composed by his friend, the Zurich composer Philipp Christoph Kayser (1755–1823). A decade later, after Goethe had secretly decamped to Italy, forsaking Charlotte, she wrote and sent him an altered version of the poem, expressing grief over her abandonment and the dissolution of their relationship. Goethe then revised his poem, expanding it to nine stanzas and incorporating some of Charlotte's changes. He published this final version in 1789, and Schubert used it as the text for both of his song settings (see Figure 2.1).

The external structure of Goethe's poem derives from the Kayser song whose original text – a poem also titled "An den Mond," written by Heinrich Leopold Wagner (1747–1779) – Goethe had replaced with his own verse. Like Wagner's poem, Goethe's comprises a series of quatrains with alternating 4- and 3-stress lines in trochaic meter. Each quatrain features an alternating line rhyme scheme (abab cdcd ...) in which every line ends with a stressed syllable. These structural features convey folk-like simplicity, yet artful complexity and depth of thought and feeling are also evident throughout. Tellingly, the nine stanzas do not all form self-contained units but rather fall into an irregular pattern, with syntactically and semantically linked stanzas on either end: 1–2, 3, 4, 5, 6–7, 8–9. Because of this structure and the sequence and interconnections of imagery, ideas, and emotions, Goethe's "An den Mond" projects a sense of both linear progression and return.

The first five stanzas evince increasing tension. In stanzas 1–2, the protagonist addresses the moon, with each stanza shifting focus from (and thereby linking) the moon to the self, exposing the poem's deeply

1.	Füllest wieder Busch und Tal Still mit Nebelglanz, Lösest endlich auch einmal Meine Seele ganz;	Once more you silently fill wood and vale With your hazy gleam, And at last Set my soul quite free.
2	Breitest über mein Gefild Lindernd deinen Blick, Wie des Freundes Auge mild Über mein Geschick.	You cast your soothing gaze Over my fields; With a friend's gentle eye You watch over my fate.
3	Jeden Nachklang fühlt mein Herz Froh- und trüber Zeit, Wandle zwischen Freud' und Schmerz In der Einsamkeit.	My heart feels every echo Of times both glad and gloomy. I hover between joy and sorrow In my solitude.
4	Fliesse, fliesse, lieber Fluss, Nimmer werd ich froh, So verrauschte Scherz und Kuss, Und die Treue so.	Flow on, beloved river! I shall never be happy; Thus have laughter and kisses rippled away. And with them constancy.
5	Ich besass es doch einmal, Was so köstlich ist! Dass man doch zu einer Qual Nimmer es vergisst.	Yet once I possessed A thing so precious! What torment Never to be able to forget it!
6	Rausche, Fluss, das Tal entlang, Ohne Rast und Ruh, Rausche, flüstre meinem Sang Melodien zu,	Murmur on, river, through the valley, Without cease, Murmur on, whispering melodies, To my song,
7	Wenn du in der Winternacht Wütend überschwillst, Oder um die Frühlingspracht Junger Knospen quillst.	When on winter nights You angrily overflow, Or when you bathe the springtime splendour Of the young buds.
8	Selig, wer sich vor der Welt Ohne Hass verschliesst, Einen Freund am Busen halt Und mit dem geniesst,	Happy he who, without hatred, Shuts himself off from the world, Holds one friend to his heart, And with him enjoys
9	Was, von Menschen nicht gewusst Oder nicht bedacht, Durch das Labyrinth der Brust Wandelt in der Nacht.	That which, unknown to And undreamt of by men, Wanders by night Through the labyrinth of the heart.

Figure 2.1 Goethe, "An den Mond" (To the Moon), final version[6]

subjective nature. As the moon casts its gaze over the earthly domain of the protagonist, a peaceful, contemplative mood prevails. Although stanzas 1–2 are in present tense, the temporal horizons seem to expand at the simile in stanza 2 comparing the moon to a friend observing the protagonist's "fate" (*Geschick*). Stanza 3 mentions memories of happy as well as troubled times, the mood darkening as the protagonist's thoughts turn to the past. In stanza 4, the protagonist shifts attention from the flowing moonlight to a flowing river – symbol of life, passing time, and lost happiness. Sorrow and a strain of bitterness emerge in the veiled reference to faithless love. Stanza 5 brings the mounting tension to a climax: the protagonist mentions the "torment" (*Qual*) he experiences over memories of the precious love now lost, and the knowledge that his anguish will never cease.

During the remaining four stanzas, however, the tension gradually subsides. In stanzas 6–7, nature and art merge in the protagonist's call for the river's rushing waters to whisper countermelodies to his own "song" (*Sang*). The mention of artistic expression suggests a degree of separation from raw anguish. Emotional recovery is further implied as the poetic evocation of a river angrily flooding its banks on winter nights cedes to a gentle, consoling image of the river helping buds to bloom amidst the splendor of spring. The last two stanzas move beyond the protagonist's immediate experience into a more abstract realm. As if adopting the omniscient perspective of the moon alluded to in stanzas 1–2, the protagonist makes a final mystical pronouncement about the blissfulness of seclusion from worldly affairs, of close companionship, and of wandering at night through the hidden pathways of the heart. Reflecting the protagonist's nostalgia, the poem recalls its initial peacefulness and linking of moon and self even as it reaches its abstruse conclusion.

Early Settings of "An den Mond" and Eighteenth-Century Lied Conventions

Schubert's first setting of "An den Mond" (D259) consists of a lightly accompanied, sixteen-measure vocal melody and four-measure piano postlude. The concluding repeat sign signals strophic form – the conventional eighteenth-century Lied form – but a thorny problem immediately surfaces: the impossibility of performing the entirety of Goethe's text. Because the musical strophe encompasses two poetic stanzas, all nine cannot be accommodated. Performers today typically omit the fifth stanza, whose reference to torment marks the emotional peak of the poem, although doing so undermines the poem's integrity.

A number of composers before Schubert wrote strophic settings of "An den Mond," nearly all of them avoiding this structural problem by composing short musical strophes that encompass only one stanza; the single strophe could be performed nine times. Table 2.1 provides an overview of six settings from 1778 to 1815(?), with music by Siegmund Freiherr von Seckendorff (1744–1785),[7] Andreas Romberg (1767–1821), Johann Friedrich Reichardt (1752–1814), Friedrich Heinrich Himmel (1765–1814), Carl Friedrich Zelter (1758–1832), and Václav Jan Tomášek (1774–1850), along with Schubert's two settings. As indicated, Tomášek

Table 2.1 *Early song settings of Goethe's "An den Mond"*

Composer, Identifying number	Date	Meter	Tempo	Key	Length	Form	Vocal range	Description
Seckendorff (Kayser)	1778 (1775–76)	2/4	—	E minor	8 mm.	strophic (1 stanza per strophe)	d♯' – e" (m9th)	- setting of Goethe's first version of "An den Mond" (6 stanzas long) - no introduction or postlude - piano RH doubles vocal line
Romberg	1793	2/2	Langsam. Sanft	B♭ major	8 mm.	strophic (1 stanza per strophe)	d' – d" (P8ve)	- no introduction or postlude - piano RH mostly doubles vocal line - rocking 8th-note chordal accompaniment - two accented syncopated chords
Reichardt	1794 pub	2/4	Sanft	E♭ major	14 mm.	strophic (1 stanza per strophe)	d' – f" (m10th)	- no introduction or postlude - top line of chordal piano RH doubles vocal line - rocking 8th notes throughout piano LH - different conclusion for last 2 stanzas
Himmel (Op. 21/1)	1806	4/4	Melancho-lisch	C major	16 mm.	strophic (1 stanza per strophe)	b – e" (P11th)	- 3-mm. introduction and 4-mm. postlude - piano RH partly doubles vocal line - mostly chordal accompaniment - expressive changes in dynamics and articulation - occasional chromaticism - rhythmic variety
Zelter	1812 pub	4/4	Ruhig	E♭ major	10 mm.	strophic (1 stanza per strophe)	b♭ – e♭" (P11th)	- no introduction, 2-mm. postlude - no piano doubling of vocal line - broken-chord accompaniment - pervasive triplet rhythms in vocal line and piano RH

Table 2.1 (cont.)

Composer, Identifying number	Date	Meter	Tempo	Key	Length	Form	Vocal range	Description
Tomášek (Op. 56/4)	1815?	4/8	Andantino	A♭ major	34 mm.	strophic (3 stanzas per strophe)	f′ – f″ (P8ve)	- 4-mm. introduction and 6-mm. postlude - no piano doubling of vocal line - broken-chord accompaniment - word-painting in postlude - internal ABA′ form
Schubert (D259)	Aug. 19, 1815	2/2	Ziemlich langsam	E♭ major	20 mm.	strophic (2 stanzas per strophe, requiring omission of 1 stanza)	e♭′ – g″ (M10th)	- no introduction, 4-mm. postlude - minimal piano doubling of vocal line - word-painting
Schubert (D296)	after Mar. 1820?	3/4	Langsam	A♭ major	60 mm.	modified strophic (ABABAB′CA′B″)	a♭ – g♭″ (m14th)	- 5-mm. introduction, 1-m. postlude - multiple doublings - expressive 7th harmonies - delayed resolution of dissonance - expressive changes in dynamics - modulations to remote keys - word-painting

Example 2.1 J. F. Reichardt, "An den Mond," mm. 1–14[8]

sidesteps the structural issue by writing a long strophe encompassing three stanzas intended to be performed three times. Neither this approach nor that of the other composers, however, accords with the irregular syntactical structure of Goethe's poem.

The early settings of "An den Mond" by Schubert and his predecessors exemplify a number of eighteenth-century Lied conventions besides strophic form. In the settings by Seckendorff, Romberg, and Reichardt, for instance, there is no piano introduction or postlude, and the piano right hand doubles the vocal line, both aspects underscoring the primacy of the vocal melody. In fact, in all six of the pre-Schubert settings, the keyboard accompaniment mainly provides harmonic and rhythmic support for the voice and could be omitted with minimal loss. Even in settings without doubling, the piano remains a subordinate partner, avoiding counter-melodies or other attention-grabbing elements. The harmonies are almost entirely diatonic and remain close to the tonic key, which, in every setting except Seckendorff's, is in major mode. None of the settings include melismas, rhythmic complexities, or leaps larger than a sixth.

Reichardt's "An den Mond" exemplifies the compositional simplicity characterizing all six pre-Schubert settings (see Example 2.1; the two different endings that Reichardt wrote for the last two stanzas are not shown). Written on two staves, this song in 2/4 time features a chordal right hand, the top notes of which form the vocal line, over rocking eighth notes in the left hand – an easy arrangement for one person to both play and sing. Reichardt sets the verse in alternating four- and three-measure phrases ending with half notes, aligning the music with the length and metrical stresses of the poetic lines. The music shifts to the dominant key in the middle of each stanza (mm. 5–11), creating slight intensification, but then returns to the tonic, E♭ major. Marked *Sanft* (gentle), Reichardt's setting projects a peaceful atmosphere matching the contemplative poetic tone of the opening stanzas, but does not illustrate the meaning of individual words or phrases, or reflect the heightening and diminishment of tension over the nine stanzas. The setting has a uniform and simple design, avoiding any surprises.

Schubert's first setting of "An den Mond" shares some of these traits (see Example 2.2). The strophic form imparts a largely uniform expression to the song as a whole, and the homophonic texture highlights the voice, with the piano mainly providing harmonic and rhythmic support. The straight quarter-note rhythms in mm. 1, 5, 9, and 11 of the vocal line project naturalness and simplicity, an impression furthered by the song's initial four-measure phrases and diatonic harmonies.

Schubert's setting nevertheless displays greater compositional sophistication than those of his predecessors, reflecting a more nuanced poetic interpretation. Rather than hew to four-measure phrases, Schubert adopts an accelerating phrase structure (4 + 4 + 2 + 2 + 1 + 1 + 2) that presses toward, and thus emphasizes, the last line of the strophe. He also finds ways to convey poetic meaning. In m. 1, the parade of quarter-note rhythms in both voice and piano evokes the protagonist's footsteps as he wanders through wood and valley. Recurrences of the quarter-note pattern within the strophe, compounded by each strophic repetition, are a continual reminder of this walking motion. The folk-like simplicity of the vocal rhythms also hints that the protagonist has an uncomplicated nature and may be of a lower social class (cf. Leporello's opening music in *Don Giovanni*). Rocking eighth notes introduced in the piano part at m. 9 conjure the motion and sounds of a rippling stream, suggested in stanza 4 by the phrase "Fliesse, fliesse, lieber Fluss!" ("Flow on, beloved river!"). Schubert also emphasizes individual words. Through an ascending vocal leap of a sixth, rhythmic syncopation, and an accented dissonant sonority in m. 6, he underscores the meaning and significance of "Schmerz" ("sorrow") in stanza 3. The melodic outline of a diminished fifth and supporting diminished seventh harmony in m. 14 impart tension to the crucial word "Kuss" ("kiss" rendered as "kisses" in the translation) in stanza 4. Schubert's first setting of "An den Mond," one could say, conjures a literal woodland journey undertaken by a humble protagonist whose memories of lost love spark momentary emotional pangs, but without undermining his essential cheerfulness.

Despite their simplicity, the early settings of "An den Mond" by Schubert and his predecessors do anticipate some features of nineteenth-century Romantic Lieder. Seckendorff, Reichardt, Himmel, Zelter, and

Example 2.2 Schubert, "An den Mond," 1st version (D259), mm. 1–20

Schubert all have vocal melodies exceeding the range of an octave. The settings of Himmel and Tomášek include both an introduction and a postlude, signaling a more prominent role for the piano. Tomášek's piano postlude features a twisting, descending, chromatic pattern that suggests the image of wandering through a labyrinth in stanza 9. The larger proportions of Tomášek's strophe and the heightened expressivity of Himmel's setting – achieved through contrasting dynamics (*pp* to *f*), varied articulation (staccato, legato, and sforzando), syncopations, vocal leaps, chromatic lines, and harmonic instability – also point to future developments in the genre. Schubert's first setting does so as well, and with greater effectiveness.

Schubert's Second Setting of "An den Mond" and the Romantic Lied

Schubert's second setting of "An den Mond" (D296), a more expansive song of sixty measures, displays significantly greater artistry and emotional intensity than any of the earlier settings; it is in every sense a "Romantic Lied." Here, the challenge posed by the uneven number of stanzas is surmounted by dispensing with purely strophic repetitions. Schubert employs a modified strophic form (ABABAB'CA'B'') whose loose ternary organization projects the poem's dual sense of linear progression and return. After the piano introduction, the first musical strophe (mm. 6–22) encompasses stanzas 1–2 (AB), supporting their syntactical and semantic connection (see Example 2.3). The same strophe, which begins and ends in A♭ major, is repeated for stanzas 3–4. While stanza 5 begins with yet another iteration of the strophe (A), the song veers unexpectedly into the parallel minor at stanza 6 (B'), as the protagonist addresses the river. The second half of stanza 6 and all of stanza 7 (C) present new thematic material in the remote keys of C♭ major (m. 34) and D♭ minor (m. 39), suggesting further progression into unfamiliar terrain (physical and emotional). Stanzas 8 and 9 are then set to a varied version of the original strophe (A'B'') in the tonic key, implying some sort of return.

This modified strophic form, though more responsive to the text than the pure strophic form of Schubert's first setting, has still met with some criticism. Writers have claimed that it does not exactly align with the protagonist's developing thoughts. As John Reed writes,

> The music for the placid opening and the existential questioning of the last verses is the same. The link between verses 4 and 5, which are both concerned with the sense of lost innocence, is destroyed; and the musical climax, in verses 6 and 7, comes in a sense in the wrong place, since the poem is not about the river but about one man's complex state of mind as he stands watching it in the moonlight.[9]

One might respond that the restatement of the opening music at the end highlights the parallel, seemingly omniscient perspectives of the moon

Example 2.3 Schubert, "An den Mond," 2nd version (D296), mm. 1–22

and the protagonist (and it is a *varied* restatement). Moreover, stanza 5 is linked to stanza 3 as much as to stanza 4 in juxtaposing positive and negative elements (st. 5: precious thing/torment; st. 3: joy/sorrow). Schubert's placement of the musical climax during stanzas 6 and 7 can be understood as suggesting a particular way of interpreting the poetic text: the rhythmically active music of these stanzas evokes not only the river's motion but also its sound – natural "melodies" that join in song with the protagonist. The dramatic arc of Schubert's setting thus insinuates the consoling power of art.

Reed himself acknowledges that the seeming misalignment of musical structure and poetic imagery is ultimately unimportant because Schubert "has matched the *Innigkeit* [inwardness] of the poem with music of a comparable grandeur and depth," making the voice "a kind of vehicle for the soul."[10] Indeed, one senses that this second setting portrays a metaphorical journey more than a literal one. Significantly, the song includes no rhythmic evocations of footsteps, and the triple meter counters any impression of walking. Filled with yearning, the protagonist turns inward on a quest for self-understanding.

The piano introduction ushers in a mood of quiet meditation with its slow tempo, pianissimo dynamics, and stepwise melody, while the non-tonic opening, harmonic suspensions, and delayed resolution of dissonance project longing. Perpetuating the mood, the vocal strophe introduces another hushed, poignant dissonance: a half-diminished seventh "color" chord (mm. 6 and 9) placed prominently on the downbeat. Diminished seventh sonorities are indeed the signature element of the song; with their tension and variable resolutions, they are particularly well-suited for the protagonist's nostalgic ruminations. In the first half of the strophe (mm. 6–11), harmonic instability combines with a balanced phrase structure (3 + 3). The piano interlude (mm. 12–13), however, increases tension with music drawn from the introduction, and the second half of the strophe (mm. 14–22), with its thicker texture, irregular phrase structure (2 + 1 +2 + 2), and prominent diminished seventh sonorities, further undermines the peacefulness. In stanzas 6–7, modulations to distant keys, dynamic swells, and faster rhythmic activity suggest further mental wandering and emotional disturbance. During the last two stanzas, however, the varied return of the opening music insinuates the restoration of inward calm achieved through the adoption of a new perspective.

Along with form and harmony, musical texture is one of Schubert's most powerful means of conveying meaning. As noted, the shift from chordal harmonies to swirling sixteenth-note arpeggios in the piano right hand at m. 34 evokes both the flowing motion of the river and its sound, or "melody." Also striking is the piano's multiple doubling of the

Example 2.4 Schubert, "An den Mond," 2nd version (D296), mm. 49–60

vocal line. While in several pre-Schubert settings the piano right hand doubles the voice, it does so as an aid to amateur singers. In Schubert's second setting, however, melodic doubling has powerful symbolic value. The piano right hand, doubling the voice first with two lines (mm. 6ff) and later three (mm. 45ff), floats above the singer's melody, conjuring the moon, a celestial *Doppelgänger*.[11]

Toward the end of the song, Schubert uses texture as an interpretive tool in another way. Beginning in m. 50, at the protagonist's mystical reference to that which is unknown to men, the vocal line unexpectedly pulls away from the melodic doubling (see Example 2.4). While the piano right hand continues with the melody (doubled in the left hand), the voice

drops to e'♭. For two measures, it doubles the bass line, its pitches largely
obscured by the full piano chords above. The voice then shifts slightly
upwards to double the piano's tenor line, and then shifts up again to double
the piano's alto line, followed by another brief doubling of the bass. From the
third beat of m. 55 to the end, the voice proceeds on its own, suggesting the
protagonist's solitude. In having the vocal line weave its way through
the layers of the piano texture, Schubert ingeniously conveys "That which,
unknown to / and undreamt of by men, / Wanders by night / Through the
labyrinth of the heart." With the triple pianissimo repetition of the voice's
final phrase in the high register, one senses the protagonist emerging from
his wandering ruminations, having achieved a degree of serenity.

While Schubert's second setting of "An den Mond" remains tied to
tradition in certain respects, most notably the partial strophic repetitions,
it is far more intricate and distinctive than the earlier settings. Through
innovative treatment of musical structure, melody, harmonic language,
texture, rhythm, register, vocal range, and dynamics, Schubert conveys his
reinterpretation of Goethe's poem. Dynamics, dissonance, texture, and
register are particularly crucial expressive elements. The vocal line, spanning almost two octaves (a♭ – g♭″) and including an enormous ascending
leap of a twelfth (m. 57), places considerable demands on the singer. The
piano does not merely provide harmonic and rhythmic support for the
singer but shares responsibility with the vocal line in conveying Schubert's
interpretation. Moreover, the relationship between voice and piano conveys meaning as much as either part alone.

Why did Schubert return to Goethe's "An den Mond" well after he had
first set it? Beyond perhaps wanting to rectify the structural problem in his
initial setting, he may have felt a need to engage more deeply with
the complex organization, meaning, and expressivity of the poetic text –
compositional challenges comparable to those in "Gretchen am Spinnrade"
and "Erlkönig." Schubert's productivity as a Lied composer during the mid
and later 1810s – years filled with experimentation – had made him better
equipped to do so.

Schubert's Transformation of the Lied: Early Critical Reactions

In 1802, music theorist Heinrich Christoph Koch (1749–1816) echoed a
host of eighteenth-century writers, including Johann Christoph Gottsched
(1700–1766), Johann Adolph Scheibe (1708–1776), Christian Gottfried
Krause (1719–1770), and Johann Abraham Peter Schulz (1747–1800),
when he defined the Lied as an unpretentious genre intended for amateurs:

Lied. With this name one generally designates any lyrical poem of many strophes that is intended for song and associated with a melody repeated for each strophe, and that is capable of being performed by anyone who has healthy and not entirely inflexible vocal chords, without need of artistic instruction. It thus follows that a Lied melody should have neither so wide a range nor such vocal mannerisms and extended syllables as characterize the artful and cultivated aria; rather it should express the sentiment in the text through simple but hence all the more efficient means.[12]

Just two decades later, the first extended reviews of Schubert's Lieder appeared, with authors expressing awe, bewilderment, and sometimes dismay at the striking changes he had introduced. Many reviewers emphasized his elevation of the hitherto humble art form. "The young composer Schuberth [sic] has set to music several songs by the best poets (mostly Goethe), which testify to the profoundest studies combined with genius worthy of admiration, and attract the eyes of the cultivated musical world," wrote a critic in the Dresden *Abendzeitung* in January 1821.[13] "Not often has a composer had so large a share of the gift for making the poet's fancy so profoundly impressive for the receptive listener's heart," gushed a writer for the Vienna *Allgemeine musikalische Zeitung* in January 1822.[14] "Schubert's songs raise themselves by ever undeniable excellences to the rank of masterpieces of genius," asserted Friedrich von Hentl in the *Wiener Zeitschrift für Kunst* a few months later.[15]

If Schubert had elevated the Lied, he had also stretched it, and his sometimes startling departures from standard practice elicited both admiration and consternation. Such mixed reactions emerge in a detailed review appearing in the Leipzig *Allgemeine musikalische Zeitung* on June 24, 1824.

Herr F. S. does not write songs, properly speaking, and has no wish to do so (though those which come more or less near to it are No. 3 in Op. 21, No. 2 in Op. 22, Nos. 1–3 in Op. 23 and No. 2 in Op. 24) but free vocal pieces, some so free that they might possibly be called caprices or fantasies. In view of this intention the poems, most of them new but greatly varying in quality, are favourably chosen and the translation of them into music is praiseworthy in general, for the author succeeds almost throughout in laying out the whole and each detail according to the poet's idea; but not nearly so well in execution, which seeks to make up for the want of inner unity, order and regularity by eccentricities which are hardly or not at all justified and by often rather wild goings-on. But without these qualities, indeed, no artist's work can become a fine work of art, for their lack quite decidedly produces only bizarre and grotesque things. The voice-part, usually declamatory, is sometimes too little singable and not seldom unnecessarily difficult, and it has the peculiarity that the composer often writes even a soprano part in octaves with the instrumental bass . . . [M]odulation is free, very free, and sometimes rather more than that. This reviewer at any rate knows no composition of this kind, indeed perhaps no composition of any sort, which goes, he will not say farther, but even as far.[16]

The previously mentioned reviewer Hentl also alludes to tradition-bending aspects of Schubert's songs, but comes to his defense:

> Whoever is inclined to doubt whether Schubert can write pure melody and to reproach him with relying for the effect of many of his songs on harmony and characteristic expression alone by means of excessive accompaniments, as for instance in "Margaret," has only to hear his lovely and extremely simple "Hedge-Rose," to take up "Shepherd's Complaint" or the tender "Cradle Song," to consider the melodic passages in "Erl King," "The Wanderer," &c.[17]

If Schubert's Lieder at times exhibit originality bordering on eccentricity, Hentl suggests, it is for good reason, and in any event, the composer has not forsaken melody – the traditional mainstay of the genre.

Concluding Thoughts

Schubert did not invent the Romantic Lied. It was founded upon a well-established tradition, and developments within that tradition, reflecting the influence of early Romantic poetry (especially verse from the 1770s and 80s, or "age of sensibility"), preceded his efforts. That said, he instituted substantial changes that effectively revolutionized the genre. His sensitivity and attraction to poetry of all kinds inspired songs of extraordinary diversity, from folk-like strophic settings to modified strophic Lieder to single-strophe Romantic miniatures to through-composed dramatic scenes and ballads.

Among the most revolutionary aspects of Schubert's song composition are his marshalling of all musical elements in service of his expressive ideas, and his elevation of music in relation to the text. While composers such as C. P. E. Bach, Mozart, Reichardt, Zelter, Zumsteeg, and Tomášek at times produced songs that deviate from convention for expressive or narrative purposes, these works are atypical. Usually Schubert's predecessors heeded tradition, relying on a few musical elements (e.g., tempo, mode, and rhythm) to convey the central mood of the poem while making little effort to illustrate textual details. Schubert, by contrast, drew on every possible resource – form, melody, harmony, mode, rhythm, meter, tempo, texture, dynamics, timbre, register, and articulation, as well as the relationship between voice and piano – to project his poetic interpretation. Some of his most striking departures from convention occur in the realms of harmony, piano-writing, form, and voice–piano relationships, as discussed by Kristina Muxfeldt, Susan Youens, and Marie-Agnes Dittrich, among others.[18] A striking juxtaposition of unrelated chords, a modulation to a distant key, the incorporation of operatic elements, the obsessive repetition of a distinctive rhythmic figure, an unusual hybrid form, the voice's doubling of the bass line – Schubert had endless ideas for how music can engage with the meaning and structure of a poem. His second setting of "An den Mond" exemplifies many such innovations.

Through his enormous expansion of music's expressive capabilities, Schubert fundamentally altered the relationship between music and poetic text in the Lied. Eighteenth-century Lied theorists and composers had suggested that the main function of music in a song is essentially that of adornment: music should "clothe" the poem, enhancing it yet always remaining subservient to the poetic body (or soul) within.[19] With the great majority of Schubert Lieder, the metaphor does not fit. Schubert's music is not subordinate to the poem but as important: the two media interact, creating a powerfully expressive artistic fusion. Significantly, the controlling artistic vision is the composer's. The composer appropriates the text, incorporating it into a conception that may diverge significantly from the poet's. This new musico-poetic entity often places considerable demands on the singer and pianist as both individuals and collaborators; because of their technical and interpretive challenges, Schubert's mature Lieder are beyond the reach of untrained musicians. Although in various ways his songs evoke the aesthetic ideals of naturalness and simplicity that guided Lied composition throughout the eighteenth century, Schubert's text-setting exemplifies originality and artfulness of the highest order, and nowhere is his achievement more evident than in the twenty-four masterful songs of *Winterreise*.

Notes

1. *FSCS*, vol. 1, 141; vol. 3, 813–25.
2. A fair copy of D259 is in the Conservatoire collection, Bibliothèque Nationale, Paris.
3. Scholars have suggested various composition dates between fall 1815 and 1820. According to Walther Dürr, D296 was written at the earliest in March 1820. Dürr (ed.), *Franz Schubert. Neue Ausgabe sämtlicher Werke*, Series IV: Lieder, vol. 9 (Kassel: Bärenreiter, 2011), XXIII. The autograph manuscript (Berlin, Staatsbibliothek Preussischer Kulturbesitz) and copies in the Witteczek-Spaun collection (Vienna, Gesellschaft der Musikfreunde) are undated. D296 was first published in 1868.
4. *SMF*, 127.
5. See, e.g., Kristina Muxfeldt, "Schubert's Songs: The Transformation of a Genre," in Christopher H. Gibbs (ed.), *The Cambridge Companion to Schubert* (Cambridge: Cambridge University Press, 1997), 121–37; Susan Youens, "Franz Schubert: The Lied Transformed," in Rufus Hallmark (ed.), *German Lieder in the Nineteenth Century*, 2nd ed. (New York and London: Routledge, 2010), 35–91; Marie-Agnes Dittrich, "The Lieder of Schubert," in James Parsons (ed.), *The Cambridge Companion to the Lied* (Cambridge: Cambridge University Press, 2004), 85–100.
6. Translation by Richard Wigmore. Graham Johnson, *Franz Schubert: The Complete Songs*, 3 vols. (New Haven and London: Yale University Press, 2014), vol. 1, 143-44. Use of this English translation is kindly permitted by Richard Wigmore and Yale University Press.
7. Max Friedlaender lists the first setting of Goethe's "An den Mond" as a 1778 Lied by "Seckendorff oder (wahrscheinlich) Ph. Chr. Kayser." Friedlaender, *Das deutsche Lied im 18.*

Jahrhundert: Quellen und Studien (Hildesheim: Georg Olms, 1962), vol. 2, 180. The Seckendorff setting has the same melody that Kayser composed, likely between 1775–76, for Wagner's "An den Mond." See Helmut Arntzen's entry on "An den Mond" in Regine Otto and Bernd Witte (eds.), *Goethe Handbuch, vol. 1: Gedichte* (Stuttgart and Weimar: J. B. Metzler, 1996), 180–81. In the following discussion, I will identify the composer of the first setting of Goethe's "An den Mond" as Seckendorff.

8. The original score, appearing in *Das Erbe deutscher Musik*, vol. 58 (Munich: G. Henle Verlag, 1964), 43, has been reset with kind permission from Henle.
9. *SSC*, 27.
10. Ibid.
11. *FSCS*, vol. 1, 145.
12. Heinrich Christoph Koch, *Musikalisches Lexikon* (Frankfurt am Main and Offenbach, 1802; reprint, 1964; abridged 1807 as *Kurzgefasstes Handwörterbuch*), 901–4. On eighteenth-century conceptions of the Lied, see James Parsons, "The Eighteenth-Century Lied," in Parsons (ed.), *The Cambridge Companion to the Lied*, 35–62, and J. W. Smeed, *German Song and Its Poetry 1740–1900* (London: Croom Helm, 1987).
13. *SR*, 155.
14. Ibid., 206.
15. Ibid., 214.
16. Ibid., 353–54.
17. Ibid., 218.
18. See note 5.
19. Smeed, *German Song and Its Poetry*, 79.

3 Precursors to *Winterreise*: Songs of Winter and Wandering, the Early Song Cycle

LISA FEURZEIG

Müller's poetic cycle *Die Winterreise* and Schubert's song cycle *Winterreise* bring together two themes – the winter season and the experience of travel – that both appear in earlier literature and song. This chapter explores European and especially German precursors to *Winterreise*, focusing on the eighteenth and early nineteenth centuries.

Poetry and Music About the Seasons (Winter In Particular)

Why do poets use the seasons, or a season, as subject matter? We can find one set of answers in a set of children's songs published in Vienna in 1791, the *Liedersammlung für Kinder und Kinderfreunde am Clavier*. Four volumes were originally planned, but only those for spring and winter have survived.[1] The poems used as song texts date from 1766 to 1791; some were pre-existing and others likely written for the collection. All are clearly aimed at an audience of children. In the winter collection of thirty songs, several focus on children's activities and pleasures during the winter – for example, "Die Schlittenfahrt" (The Sleigh Ride) and "Fritzchens Freude über das Schneien" (Little Fritz's Joy When It Snows) – but there are also songs that emphasize pleasant indoor activities of the winter, such as dancing and storytelling. Other texts emphasize the empathy children feel for creatures who are victims of the cold – for example, "Amaliens Empfindung beim Anblicke eines erstarrten Würmchens" (Amalie's Feelings on Seeing a Frozen Little Worm). A few remind the presumably well-off children whose families can afford the song-book that others are less fortunate in winter: "Das Schneegestöber, worin ein armer Mann umkommt" (The Snowdrift in which a Poor Man Perishes).

These song-books, linked with an Enlightenment educational reform movement known as philanthropinism, present typical if idealized childhood experiences, while using the seasons as a vehicle for teaching moral principles. Poetry for adults in the eighteenth century often had similar purposes. Writing about literature of the Baroque era and the Enlightenment that followed, Jane Muenzer Mehl focuses her attention on those poets who "emphasized the dignity of creation and the goodness of the temporal, sensual world" and for whom "nature had assumed major significance in its own right as a manifestation of divine wisdom, power and reason." She observes that during the Enlightenment "ever-increasing attention was paid to the evolutionary process in nature ... [T]he polar states of physical life and life after death ... were grasped within the framework of a gradual, continuous process occurring in time."[2] Mehl cites many poems that use either times of day or seasons of the year as metaphors for the stages of a human life, with winter or evening representing old age and the approach of death. These poems, she observes, ultimately take a positive view, based on our knowledge that night is always followed by day and winter by spring. Thus the seasons in this type of poetry become a symbol of religious faith and the goodness of God.

Haydn's oratorio *Die Jahreszeiten* (The Seasons), composed at the turn of the nineteenth century, reflects similar Enlightenment ideas. The text for the oratorio is drawn from *The Seasons*, by Scottish poet James Thomson (1700–1748), translated into German and adapted by Gottfried van Swieten (1733–1803). Van Swieten, whose father had been Empress Maria Theresia's personal physician and scientific advisor, was a diplomat and court official; both father and son took a deep interest in music. The oratorio recounts the seasons of the year, ending with winter. Set in a village, it depicts typical scenes, activities, and weather in the countryside at various times of year. In spring, the fields are plowed; in summer, the shepherd takes the flocks to pasture and a spectacular thunderstorm occurs; fall features the grape harvest and the hunt. The winter section begins by describing cold foggy weather and frozen bodies of water. A wanderer arrives in the village, desperate and alone – and unlike Müller's wanderer some twenty years later, he is welcomed by the villagers. Similar to the children's songs discussed earlier, the text now describes the villagers' sociable winter activities: the women spin as the young men mend nets, accompanied by storytelling and song. The work ends with an aria that explicitly compares the seasons to the stages of a human life, followed by an ensemble in which soloists and chorus praise the "great morning" and "eternal spring" that await all good people. Though a secular work, the oratorio reflects the pious outlook of the eighteenth century.

Among Schubert's settings of poetry about the seasons, we can find similar material in a set of early partsongs on texts by Ludwig Hölty (1748–1776). One representative example is "Trinklied im Winter" (Drinking Song in Winter) (D242). Written for two tenors and a bass, it is marked *Feurig* (fiery) to indicate the spirited mood in which it should be sung. In keeping with the German tradition of men's singing clubs, this is a strophic unaccompanied song with six stanzas. The text exhorts the men to appreciate how wine counters the cold of winter: "Der edle Most / Verscheucht den Frost, / Und zaubert Frühling hernieder" (The noble grape juice / Scares off frost / And magically attracts springtime). Eventually the remaining element of "wine, women and song" makes an appearance, as the men scold proud women and bawdily suggest that they remove their ermine shawls. Schubert's setting is jolly despite its F♯ minor key, combining arpeggios and scalar passages in the short repeated verse. In many ways, this song resembles some of the children's seasonal songs discussed above: it comments on winter weather while emphasizing pleasant indoor activities.

Winterreise is Schubert's most extensive work focusing on a season. Several songs in the cycle can be linked to music from the 1826 play *Der Bauer als Millionär* (The Peasant as Millionaire) by Ferdinand Raimund, at that time the most prominent actor and playwright in the Vienna popular theater, or *Volkstheater*. The music by Joseph Drechsler quickly entered the Viennese consciousness. Two songs in particular, "Brüderlein fein" (Dear Little Brother) and the "Aschenlied" (Ashes Song) – their melodies likely by Raimund himself – captured a sense of despondency that was widely shared.

The play's title character, Fortunatus Wurzel, is a peasant who unwittingly becomes a tool of magical beings. At this juncture of the play, he has become fabulously wealthy and moved to the city, but he is punished for his arrogance by receiving two successive visits from Youth and Old Age personified. After Youth visits him to say goodbye in the duet "Brüderlein fein," Old Age comes to call, and Wurzel instantly grows old – specifically, his hair suddenly turns white. He loses his wealth and becomes an ash collector, the equivalent to someone now who wanders from house to house to collect and sell recyclables. Humbled by this experience, he starts to appreciate the true virtues that should be valued.

Three *Winterreise* songs have melodic ties to these two songs, as I have detailed elsewhere. The strongest link to the idea of winter is found in the textual similarity between Müller's poem "Der greise Kopf" and the scene described above. In Müller's text, the wanderer observes that his hair has become white with frost and likens this to suddenly growing old. Since he wishes to die, he laments the melting away of that frost. In the final stanza, he comments that "From the sunset to the dawn / Many a head turns white." As this is precisely what happens to Fortunatus Wurzel, it is not surprising that Schubert designed a melody whose contour and emphasis of a tritone are reminiscent of the "Aschenlied."[3]

In his later years, as *Winterreise* exemplifies, Schubert's poetic choices shifted away from eighteenth-century poets such as Hölty and toward more contemporary writers. This poetry focused more on personal

Example 3.1 "Der Winterabend," mm. 1–5[6]

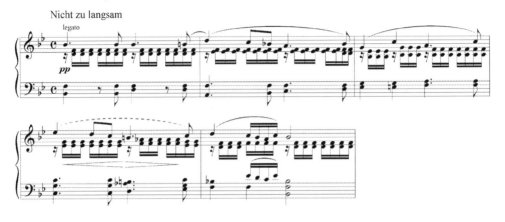

emotional states than on abstract religious optimism. Two seasonal songs from the last year of his life show this development: "Der Winterabend" (D938), composed in January 1828, and "Herbst" (D945), composed in April 1828. As a pair, these songs represent wholly different responses to the late seasons of the year and the late stages of a human life. "Der Winterabend," on a poem by Karl Gottfried von Leitner (1800–1890) – who was only in his twenties when he wrote it – represents the emotions of an old man, sitting by the fire on a snowy evening. In his moonlit room, he meditates on the past, remembering his long-lost love.[4] Schubert's music, in B♭ major, portrays the warmth and comfort of the little room. Steady pulsing sixteenth notes support soaring melodies, while the overall soothing harmonies are enriched by some dissonance. These features can be observed in the piano introduction, shown in Example 3.1.[5]

"Herbst," on a text by Ludwig Rellstab (1799–1860), tells a different story. Each stanza begins by describing the outside world of Nature in fall – cold winds blowing, leaves falling – and concludes with a comparison to human experience. For example, the first stanza ends with the lines "So welken die Blüthen / Des Lebens dahin" (So wither the blossoms / Of life away). There is a veiled pun in the poem's title, as the noun *Herbst* contains the adjective *herb*, which means "bitter." Rellstab's poetic persona feels a personal bitterness that is mirrored by the cold and infertile season. Schubert's setting opens with tremolo third patterns in the right hand over a rising and falling bass line, suggesting images of trembling leaves and the sharp gusts of wind that threaten them. This creates a musical tension that continues throughout the song, as seen in Example 3.2, the next-to-last phrase in the voice part.

Example 3.2 "Herbst," mm. 13–16

These two songs were composed the year after Schubert completed *Winterreise*, with its grim and existential portrayal of the cold season. While one is nostalgic and the other bitter, neither takes the position that Nature's seasonal cycles reflect a divine promise of new life; there is no reference to the coming of spring. The optimistic religious outlook of the previous century has been displaced by a new humanistic perspective in which individual experiences and emotions prevail over abstract faith.

Wandering and Wanderers

Wandering as a literary theme goes back to ancient times, with Homer's Odysseus being perhaps the most famous example of a wanderer. The importance of this theme and this type of character took on special depth and intensity during the Romantic period. Who were the wanderers depicted in Romantic literature and paintings – and did they correspond with real people in nineteenth-century society? Why did Romantics identify so strongly with such wanderers?

Das Wandern, the German term for the act of wandering, was used to describe everything from leisurely walks through the outdoors to extended trips across the European landscape. Both in literature and in reality, some wanderers did this by choice and others because of circumstances beyond their control; some traveled for positive reasons and others out of desperation.

A love of nature and curiosity about other lands and cultures was one motivation for wandering for Romantic artists across Europe. In 1798, members of the Berlin and Jena circles of Romantics traveled together to Dresden to visit the great collection of Renaissance art that was on display there, and they collectively wrote a response to those paintings, representing their varied outlooks. The Nazarenes, a group of religiously inspired painters from Austria and Germany, relocated in 1810 to Rome, where they lived communally, often traveling throughout Italy to paint their Renaissance-inspired works. In the late 1830s, the French Romantics developed an interest in walking tours, and novelist George Sand wrote about one outlook over a frightening drop that "[a]ll of this seemed horrible and delicious at the same time ... [A] fear of vertigo was not without its charm."[7]

Sand's remark brings out an important element in the Romantic love of wandering: the new appeal of danger and fear, as opposed to the view of the countryside as picturesque, pastoral, and sentimental that had mostly characterized eighteenth-century culture. Edmund Burke had explored this topic in his essay *A Philosophical Enquiry into the Origin of Our Ideas of the Sublime and Beautiful,* defining the sublime as "productive of the strongest emotion which the mind is capable of feeling," and explaining that "[w]hen danger or pain press too nearly, they are incapable of giving any delight, and are simply terrible; but at certain distances, and with certain modifications, they may be, and they are delightful, as we every day experience."[8] Burke was ahead of the curve by discussing this in 1757; it was only a few decades later that the thrill and desirability of sublime experiences claimed the attention of Romantic writers, artists, and musicians.

The paintings of north German artist Caspar David Friedrich (1774–1840) are tremendously important in conveying a sense of how the Romantics perceived Nature. Friedrich often portrayed formidable landscapes: vast overlooks on the sea, mountains that seem unconquerable, bare jagged winter trees. He also frequently placed one or a few people in the foreground, often seen from behind to indicate that they, like viewers of the painting, are contemplating the immensity of Nature. These paintings capture the type of sublime experience that Romantics frequently sought.

Some travel was for the purpose of pilgrimage: a religious journey to an important site, such as a shrine to a saint or a place where important events had taken place. Just as the Romantic movement began to conceive of art and music as religious experiences, the concept of pilgrimage was also understood in a more metaphorical way. Rather than aiming for a specific religious site, this kind of pilgrim might wander without a predetermined destination, using the experience of travel to seek a new understanding of his role in the world or a new place where he felt at home. Any lonely, unsatisfied person with the means to do so and without a clear place in society might choose to wander through the world in this way, observing landscapes, artistic creations, and people in an attempt to reach happiness and fulfillment. In the 1830s, Franz Liszt took this role when he traveled to Switzerland and then Italy with his mistress, the Countess Marie d'Agoult, writing a collection of piano works that he titled *Années de pèlerinage* (Years of Pilgrimage). Most of these pieces were named for particular places they visited or for famous legends linked to those places. Like Liszt, many fictional wanderers were artists. One cliché of the genre was the minstrel whose music, while growing out of sorrow, inspired joy in its listeners. This theme is found in texts set by Schubert, notably August Wilhelm Schlegel's "Die gefangenen Sänger," set in 1821 as D712, in which caged nightingales serve as a metaphor for suffering artists.

While some Romantic travelers were inspired purely by the desire to explore or to seek deeper truths, there were also economic reasons for travel. Traders and merchants traveled to obtain and transport goods. For young men learning the traditional trades governed by the guild system, the second stage of training was the journeyman phase. During this time, each young craftsman had to leave his original master, seeking employment elsewhere in order to hone his skills by learning from different masters. Therefore, a significant number of young men in their late teens or early twenties could be found on the road, seeking new positions and seeing the world on the way. There were also various groups of people from outside normal society who wandered. Gypsies were a source of fascination in the nineteenth century because their way of life did not conform to the norms of Christian culture; they were constantly on the move, and often viewed with fear and suspicion. While most Jews in nineteenth-century Europe were settled, the myth of the "wandering Jew" who could not find a home lingered. Finally, known criminals and political exiles might be forced to leave their homes and wander in order to remain safe from prosecution. (See Chapter 8 for more details on various types of wanderers.)

While the typical wanderer in Romantic literature is male, there are occasional female characters in a similar position. One famous example from Goethe's novel *Wilhelm Meister's Apprenticeship* (1795–96) is Mignon, a girl in her mid-teens who belongs to a traveling troupe of actors. From a young age, she has been journeying, far from a home she longs for but only vaguely remembers. Only later in the novel is it made clear why and from where she has wandered. This sorrowful figure is marked by a history she does not know – she is the product of incest – and dies young as a result of that past. Another character in the novel, the Harper, is a more typical wanderer: an artist who travels to perform but is largely misunderstood by his audiences. These two unhappy individuals eventually discover that they are father and daughter. Through Mignon's longing for her childhood home, Goethe presents an idealized view of Italy, where he himself had traveled. These two characters drew Schubert's attention across the years: he wrote multiple settings of their poetic texts. For example, he set the poem "Nur wer die Sehnsucht kennt" (Only he who knows longing) five times from 1815 through 1826: four times as a solo for Mignon and once as a duet between her and the Harper.

Ingrid Horrocks discusses wandering women in British literature, focusing on poetry and novels from the late eighteenth and early nineteenth centuries by Charlotte Smith, Ann Radcliffe, Mary Wollstonecraft, and Frances Burney.[9] Horrocks labels the characters portrayed by these authors as "reluctant wanderers": they may travel to overcome poverty, to escape from forced marriages, or even because they have been kidnapped. While some male wanderers had positive reasons for wandering and embarked on their journeys with optimism and excitement, the social position of women made it unlikely that they could travel voluntarily for the purposes of growth and exploration.

Susan Youens explores another female-wanderer scenario in her discussion of poet Eduard Mörike's relationship with Maria Meyer. This young woman, likely mentally ill, came from a destitute background. Fascinated by religious mysticism and political rebellion, she was both manipulated and manipulative. Between affairs with various members of the intellectual elite, she was frequently on the roads in Germany and Switzerland, finding whatever jobs were available to tide herself over. This troubled woman inspired the character Peregrina in Mörike's poetry.[10]

Schubert's Wandering Songs

Although there was little travel in Schubert's own life – he traveled twice to Hungary, but otherwise remained in Austria and mostly in or near Vienna – he was drawn to poems about wanderers, of which there were many to choose from. Both his song cycles (which are compared in Chapter 9) focus on wanderers: in *Die schöne Müllerin* (D795), the protagonist is a journeyman whose first song is about the pleasure of wandering, and the narrator of *Winterreise* is an unhappy wanderer who leaves a town where he had hoped to stay in the aftermath of a failed love relationship. Schubert also selected and set to music many individual poems about wanderers. We will examine three of these: "Der Wanderer" (D489) on a text by Georg Philipp Schmidt von Lübeck, "Der Pilgrim" (D794) on a text by Friedrich Schiller, and "Der Wanderer" (D649) on a text by Friedrich Schlegel.[11] A comparison of these three, along with "Das Wandern," the first song of *Die schöne Müllerin*, reveals four contrasting characters whose stories about their journeys inspired a range of compositional responses from Schubert. Schubert's settings of two poems by Goethe, each titled "Wandrers Nachtlied" (D224 and D768), are equally interesting, but space prevents discussion of those examples.

The poem by Schmidt von Lübeck (1766–1849) features a melancholy wanderer who seeks an ideal land but never finds it. Here are three key lines from the text as set by Schubert that capture the wanderer's mood:

"Und immer fragt der Seufzer, wo?" (And my sigh always asks: where?)
"Ich bin ein Fremdling überall." (I am a stranger everywhere.)
"Da, wo du nicht bist, blüht das Glück." (There, where you are not, blooms happiness.)

Example 3.3 "Der Wanderer," mm. 19–22

Schubert's setting is in C♯ minor with excursions to the relative E major. The song opens with a piano introduction that establishes a dark moodiness through right-hand tremolo triplets over shifting arpeggiated chords in a low register. From that point on, Schubert matches the changeability of the poem through frequent shifts in theme, dynamics, and meter. Oddly, he ends the song with a cadence in E major, as if to represent the happiness that eludes the singer. Schubert reused the third theme of the song, which sets the text "Die Sonne dünkt mich hier so kalt" (The sun here seems so cold to me), as the theme of the second movement of his Fantasy (D760) for piano, which is therefore often called the "Wanderer" Fantasy. Example 3.3 shows the questioning phrase quoted above; here Schubert brings out the idea of fruitless searching with the Italian sixth accompanying the words "Seufzer" and "immer."

Schiller's poem "Der Pilgrim" also presents a disillusioned wanderer, but unlike Schmidt's character, Schiller's pilgrim begins his journey in an optimistic frame of mind, seeming confident that he will find what he seeks. Early in the text, he declares, "Denn mich trieb ein mächtig Hoffen / Und ein dunkles Glaubenswort, / 'Wandle,' rief's, 'der Weg ist offen,' / Immer nach dem Aufgang fort." (For I was driven by a powerful hope / And a dark word of faith, / "Wander," it called, "the path is open," / Move onward toward the rising.)

The wanderer encounters huge barriers to his travel – mountains, rivers, abysses – and labors heroically to overcome them. Finally, he throws himself into a wide river and lets it carry him out to sea, only to find that the vast expanse of water cannot be crossed. He laments that "[n]äher bin ich nicht dem Ziel" (I am no closer to the goal). By the end of the poem, his hope for a satisfying arrival or revelation has vanished, and he mourns that "das dort ist niemals hier" (the there is never here).

Schubert represents the protagonist's naïve optimism in 4/4 time at a moderate tempo. He would later frequently use this combination in *Winterreise* to illustrate the steady pace of his traveler. Both piano and voice take part in this theme in a confident D major (though Walther Dürr notes that the autograph is in E major, a key he associates with rapture, reflecting the poem's religious element and taking it beyond a simple *Wanderlied*).[12] As time passes without success, the song modulates – first to F major and then into a chromatic sound world. This passage, describing the natural barriers on the journey, teems with accidentals as it moves upward through minor keys a half step apart. (See Example 3.4.)

Sadly, the traveler's constant efforts bring no tangible result: the music quickly returns to the opening theme, now in the key of F. Soon after this, the meter shifts to 3/4 time in a gloomy slow tempo (*Sehr langsam*), and in dirge-like tones the pilgrim pronounces his conclusion that his original hope is unattainable. Though John Reed views this song as mostly uninspired,[13] its foursquare arpeggiated opening theme effectively represents the naïvely hopeful young pilgrim, while the intense chromaticism that accomplishes nothing substantial captures the ironic pessimism of this poem.

Unlike the wanderers described in the previous two songs, Friedrich Schlegel's wandering character is contemplative rather than desperate. He believes that he is called to wander by the moon, who advises him as follows: "Folge nicht dem alten Gleise, / Wähle keine Heimat nicht." (Do not follow the old path, / Do not choose a homeland.) He wanders neither to flee nor to seek a specific goal, but rather as an onlooker, appreciating

Example 3.4 "Der Pilgrim," mm. 57–65. Translation: "Mountains lay in my path, / Streams constrained my steps. / Over abysses I built walkways, / Bridges through the wild river."

the view of the world illuminated by moonlight. As James Parsons writes, "Schlegel's poem is given over to an arresting inversion of a topos long-favored by eighteenth-century literature: the trek of a lone wanderer toward a clearly defined yet distant destination. The journey, while arduous, is carried out by and large with optimism, given that it takes ignorance and darkness as its starting-point and moves toward self-understanding and light."[14] Schubert writes in a chorale-like style, featuring block chords and plagal cadences, to represent this wanderer's calm observation of the world's beauty in the moonlight.

"Das Wandern" from *Die schöne Müllerin* is often viewed as a perfect example of the expressive potential in a strophic song. The young miller is a journeyman, not a wanderer by choice, but he embraces and praises wandering in the short term, as he is optimistically seeking employment. He explains that millers love to wander, and they have learned this from the tools of their trade: water, mill wheels, and millstones, which all move in the process of making the mill grind flour. The first half of Schubert's folk-like melody consists mostly of leaps that energetically illustrate motion, and the second half is more stepwise. Meanwhile, the piano plays a sturdy regular rhythm, and its part is so designed that an artful pianist can alter dynamics and articulation in each stanza so as to suggest the varying subject matter – more fluidity for water, heaviness for stones, and so on.

The Song Cycle Before *Winterreise*

During the nineteenth century, beginning in German-speaking countries, it became increasingly popular to publish songs in groups, often intended as a connected set. Various German terms such as *Liederkreis* (song circle), *Liederkranz* (song garland), and *Liederzyklus* (song cycle) were used. Susan Youens gives a broad definition: "a group of individually complete songs designed as a unit for solo or ensemble voices with or without instrumental accompaniment," while noting that "song cycles may be difficult to distinguish from song collections, which were frequently presented in a planned design."[15] Some of the early song cycles, including Beethoven's *An die ferne Geliebte* (To the Distant Beloved, 1815–16) and Schubert's two cycles, *Die schöne Müllerin* and *Winterreise*, are settings by one composer of texts by a single poet that were intended as a connected set telling a story. The singer in each of these works represents the central character of the story, and the lyric poetry traces his emotional trajectory as he experiences the loss of a love relationship. Later song composers, including Robert Schumann and Hugo Wolf, often selected and organized poems independent of the poets. For example, Schumann's *Eichendorff-Liederkreis*, Op. 39, is a compilation of poems from different works by poet Joseph von Eichendorff. It presents an emotional trajectory without a clear narrative, and the texts seem to represent the experiences of more than one person. Wolf's collections of Spanish and Italian folk-songs translated into German (the *Spanisches Liederbuch* and *Italienisches Liederbuch*) are even more assorted, linked mostly by national origin and associations, but not by a narrative or protagonist. It can be debated whether these works should be classified as cycles or collections of songs.

The forerunner of the song cycle in German culture was known as the *Liederspiel* (song play). A *Liederspiel* was designed for a group of performers who acted out a story. It explicitly included songs for various characters. Luise Eitel Peake explores this genre in her dissertation,[16] suggesting that behind their clear narratives, some *Liederspiele* also contain hidden numerological messages. As we shall see, the *Liederspiel* genre plays a role in some of Schubert's work.

Beethoven is widely acknowledged as the initiator of nineteenth-century song cycles with *An die ferne Geliebte* on poetry by Alois Jeitteles. The narrator is a man whose beloved has departed and is now far away. He sits outdoors, observing and personifying Nature (the mountains, clouds, swallows, and so on) and singing of his longing for her. At the end, he offers his songs to his beloved. He imagines her singing them after he himself has sung them and is comforted by the idea that these songs and the act of singing them will bridge the physical distance between them. Unlike most later song cycles, this one has a continuous piano accompaniment. The six songs are clearly separated in their themes and keys, but there are no pauses; Beethoven uses the piano to create musical transitions between songs.

Morten Solvik presents convincing evidence that Schubert's twenty settings of poetry by Ludwig Gotthard Kosegarten were intended as a *Liederspiel* – its plot designed by Schubert, not the poet – even though the songs were not published as a set.[17] They tell a tale of Wilhelm, a young man of wandering affections, and various young women with whom he has relationships. The songs are divided among Wilhelm and two of these women, Ida and Luisa.

Conversely, the poetry of Schubert's first song cycle grew out of a *Liederspiel*. The young Wilhelm Müller belonged to a circle of friends in Berlin who, in 1816–17, put together and acted out a story of a miller's daughter and her various suitors.[18] Several of these people went on to make their mark in various art forms: Wilhelm Hensel as a painter (who married Fanny Mendelssohn); Ludwig Rellstab, Clemens Brentano, Luise Hensel, and Müller as poets; and Ludwig Berger as a composer. The romantic intrigues around the miller maid were mirrored within this group of friends, as several of the young men were enamored of Luise. Both Berger and Müller (whose name means "miller" and who played that role) later published revised materials from the *Liederspiel*; see Chapter 4 for more on this. The whole series of events offers an opportunity, as Susan Youens writes, "to peer into the long-distant chambers from which a major genre of European music was emerging and into the lives and hearts of those who were among its early creators."[19]

It was Müller's published collection that Schubert set as his song cycle *Die schöne Müllerin* in 1823, removing five poems, including the two framing ones spoken by a narrator. For most of the work, the singer represents the protagonist and the piano the brook that becomes his confidant. At the end, though, the middle verse of the penultimate song, "Der Müller und der Bach" (The Miller and the Brook), is assigned to the brook, so the singer switches roles. The final lullaby is also sung by the brook, as the miller has drowned himself in its water. Outside of this small deviation, though, this work shows the progression away from a multi-character *Liederspiel* towards the focused individual subjectivity often found in song cycles.

Finally, we turn to two song collections composed by Conradin Kreutzer (1786–1849) setting poetry by Ludwig Uhland (1787–1862).[20] These two works make a good close to this chapter, as one is about a season and the other about wandering. Kreutzer's *Frühlingslieder* (Spring Songs, Op. 33) and *Wanderlieder* (Wandering Songs, Op. 34) were composed before 1818, and Luise Eitel Peake believes they were likely intended to be paired. They could easily have been performed together, as the first has only five songs and the second nine. It is also of interest that Kreutzer suggests that the *Frühlingslieder* could involve various singers; the final song can be sung either as a solo or a trio – so that set was conceived as a *Liederspiel*. The *Wanderlieder*, by contrast, are all sung by one protagonist, so that set fits the narrower model of a song cycle.[21] (See Chapter 4 for another perspective on the *Wanderlieder*, including Müller's response to Uhland's poetry.)

Joseph von Spaun reported that Schubert played these songs for his friends and praised them.[22] The one Uhland poem set by Schubert, "Frühlingsglaube" (Faith in Spring) (D686), also appears in Kreutzer's *Frühlingslieder*, and Schubert likely encountered the poem there. The story implied by the *Wanderlieder* bears some interesting resemblances to *Winterreise*. It begins as two lovers part and the male protagonist leaves town. The fifth poem, "Nachtreise" (Night Journey), includes the line "Mein Lieb zu Grab getragen" (my love carried to the grave), which Peake interprets as referring to the funeral of the beloved. That line can be read metaphorically as describing the wanderer's renunciation of an impossible love, rather than the death of the woman herself, which makes the final song "Heimkehr" (Return Home) more logical. Song 7, "Abreise" (Departure), foreshadows the alienation from society felt by Müller's wanderer: the protagonist observes that the townspeople were not aggressive – "Man hat mir nicht den Rock zerrissen / ... Noch in die Wange mich gebissen" (They did not tear my coat / ... Or bite me on the cheek) – but then ironically comments that nobody lost any sleep over his departure. The set ends in ambiguity, as song 8 describes our protagonist's rest under a friendly apple tree and song 9 his nervous and eager return to his beloved. Perhaps months have passed since song 6, "Winterreise" (Winter Journey), and in some way the return of spring has undone whatever obstacles to their love made it necessary for him to leave her in the first place.

This chapter has briefly surveyed German-language poetic and musical works about the seasons and the act of wandering. While the inevitable progression of time from spring to winter was accepted by Baroque and Enlightenment culture as part of the natural and divine order, some Romantic writers came to understand winter as a bitter, lonely emblem of alienation. Similarly, wandering could be an active choice – a way to explore and grow up – or it could be forced upon unhappy people who were outcasts from the social order. Many early song cycles examined love relationships and the experience of loss, with nature often serving to contrast or reflect human emotions.

Though its existential despair is more extreme than that of many other works, *Winterreise* continued this tradition of depicting a lover's journey through natural landscapes as he mourns the loss of his beloved.

Notes

1. David J. Buch (ed.), *Liedersammlung für Kinder und Kinderfreunde am Clavier (1791): Frühlingslieder and* Winterlieder. Recent Researches in the Music of the Classical Era 95 (Middleton, WI: A-R Editions, 2014). See the foreword for a detailed discussion of the poets, composers, and background of the song collection.
2. Jane Muenzer Mehl, "The Imagery of Time and Season in the German Baroque and Romantic Poetry" (Ph.D. diss., State University of New York at Binghamton, 1973), 193–94.
3. See Lisa Feurzeig, "The Queen of Golconda, the Ashman, and the Shepherd on a Rock: Schubert and the Vienna Volkstheater," in Christopher H. Gibbs and Morten Solvik (eds.), *Franz Schubert and His World* (Princeton: Princeton University Press, 2014), 166–73.
4. See Diether de la Motte, "Die Aufhebung der Zeit in Schuberts endlosen Liedern," in Erich Wolfgang Partsch (ed.), *Schubert: der Fortschrittliche? Analysen – Perspektiven – Fakten* (Tutzing: H. Schneider, 1989), and Michael Spitzer, "Axial Lyric Space in Two Late Songs: Im Freien and Der Winterabend," in *RS*, 253–74.
5. Susan Youens includes a chapter on Leitner and Schubert's Leitner settings in *Schubert's Late Lieder: Beyond the Song Cycles* (Cambridge: Cambridge University Press, 2002), 202–300.
6. The original scores of the examples in this chapter, appearing in the *Neue Schubert-Ausgabe*, Series IV: *Lieder*, have been reset with kind permission from Bärenreiter.
7. "Tout cela m'a paru horrible et délicieux en même temps. J'avais peur, une peur inouïe et sans cause, une peur de vertige qui n'était pas sans charme." "Histoire de ma vie," in Georges Lubin (ed.), *Oeuvres autobiographiques*, 2 vols. (Paris: Bibliothèque de la Pléiade, 1970–71), vol. 2, 60. For the broad picture, see C. W. Thompson, *Walking and the French Romantics: Rousseau to Sand and Hugo*. French Studies of the Eighteenth and Nineteenth Centuries 13 (Bern: Peter Lang, 2003).
8. Edmund Burke, *A Philosophical Enquiry into the Origin of Our Ideas of the Sublime and Beautiful* (London: R. and J. Dodsley, 1757), 13–14.
9. Ingrid Horrocks, *Women Wanderers and the Writing of Mobility, 1784–1814*. Cambridge Studies in Romanticism 115 (Cambridge: Cambridge University Press, 2017).
10. See Susan Youens, *Hugo Wolf and His Mörike Songs* (Cambridge: Cambridge University Press, 2000), 18–37.
11. See David Gramit, "Schubert's Wanderers and the Autonomous Lied," *Journal of Musicological Research* 14 (1995): 147–68.
12. See "Vermittelnde Ästhetik? Friedrich Schillers Gedicht *Der Pilgrim* in Vertonungen von Reichardt und Schubert," *Schubert: Perspektiven* 9 (2009): 119–35 (126).
13. See *SSC*, 121.
14. "'My song the midnight raven has outwing'd': Schubert's 'Der Wanderer,' D. 649," in Siobhán Donovan and Robin Elliott (eds.), *Music and Literature in German Romanticism* (Studies in German Literature, Linguistics, and Culture) (Rochester, NY: Camden House, 2004), 165–82 (166).
15. Youens, "Song Cycle." *Grove Music Online* (2001). Retrieved Mar. 16, 2019. www.oxfordmusionline.com.ezproxy.gvsu.edu/grovemusic/view/10.1093/gmo/9781561592630.001.0001/omo-9781561592630-e-0000026208.
16. Luise Eitel Peake, "The Song Cycle: A Preliminary Inquiry Into the Beginnings of the Romantic Song Cycle and the Nature of an Art Form" (Ph.D. diss., Columbia University, 1968).
17. "Schubert's Kosegarten Settings of 1815: A Forgotten *Liederspiel*," in Christopher H. Gibbs and Morten Solvik (eds.), *Franz Schubert and His World* (Princeton: Princeton University Press, 2014), 115–56.
18. Susan Youens, "Behind the Scenes: *Die schöne Müllerin* Before Schubert," *19th-Century Music* 15/1 (1991): 3–22.
19. Ibid., 4.

20. Barbara Turchin discusses various settings of *Wanderlieder* by Uhland and other poets in relation to *An die ferne Geliebte* and *Winterreise*; see "The Nineteenth-Century *Wanderlieder* Cycle," *Journal of Musicology* 5/4 (1987): 498–525.

21. See Luise Eitel Peake, Introduction to *Conradin Kreutzer's* Frühlingslieder *and* Wanderlieder: *A Facsimile Edition with New Translations* (Stuyvesant, NY: Pendragon Press, 1989), ix–xiii.

22. Peake, Introduction, xvi, quoting *SMF*, 135.

PART II

Die Winterreise: Poetic Cycle

4 Wilhelm Müller's Odyssey

KRISTINA MUXFELDT

Born to a master tailor and his wife in the provincial town of Dessau, Johann Ludwig Wilhelm Müller (1794–1827) was the sole one of their seven children to survive infancy. The family occasionally received small financial assistance from Leopold Franz III, the Prince of Anhalt-Dessau, elevated in 1807 to its Duke. The Anglophile peace-loving regent created one of the most progressive and prosperous of the smaller German states. He cultivated educational and social reforms, supported architectural and landscape design and scientific inquiry, and encouraged religious tolerance in a state that was home to congregants of several Christian denominations and a growing Jewish community. The first German-language Jewish newspaper was founded in Dessau in 1806.[1] Müller attended the local Gymnasium, excelling in the study of languages. Following a period of university studies, military service, and scholarly *Wanderjahre*, he eventually settled down as a teacher in the city of his birth.

In the spring of 1812, Müller left his hometown to matriculate at the University of Berlin, a two-year-old Prussian institution founded by the philosopher and linguist Wilhelm von Humboldt (1767–1835). Among the inaugural faculty were renowned – and controversial – thinkers such as theologian Friedrich Schleiermacher (1768–1834), philosopher Johann Gottlieb Fichte (1762–1814), historian Karl Savigny (1779–1861), and philologists August Böckh (1785–1867) and Friedrich August Wolf (1759–1824). Müller applied himself in ancient philology, history, and modern English literature until the "Wars of Liberation" interrupted his studies.[2] When Prussia's king in February 1813 called for volunteers to confront Napoleon's forces on their retreat from Russia, nearly half the university's six hundred students joined up to free their homeland from French occupation.[3] Müller fought, apparently unharmed, in the battles of Lützen, Bautzen, Haynau, and Kulm, was stationed as a lieutenant in Prague during Leipzig's bloody "Battle of the Nations" (the decisive battle that forced Napoleon's army to retreat to France), and ended his military service in a garrison in Brussels. His enthusiasm waned as the months wore on, especially after the death in battle in May 1813 of his close friend

Ludwig Bornemann. He left his regiment on November 18, 1814 –
apparently a deserter.

The messy details surrounding Müller's departure from military service
and his return to his studies in Berlin remain obscure. Later personal
papers and literary writings speak of almost unbearable anguish and
a forbidden affair with an unknown woman (possibly named Therese).
The so-called "Brussels sonnets" preserved in a manuscript dated August 8,
1814 (published only in 1902, after both Müller's children had died) depict
this harrowing time. Recent scholars view these poems as source material
for *Winterreise*.[4] In one sonnet, Müller rails against narrow-minded religi-
osity. I paraphrase: "The old, white-bearded god, as you drew him in my
children's lesson book, who according to your bible, saved but one
people . . . to whom you pay sacrifice in heaven and whom you banish
from his own earth . . . I deny him . . . So strike me from your lists, as anti-
Christ and atheist!" Another describes a man who flees his doubts: "Just as
the furies in wild assembly, / Once robbed Orestes of his peace, / Thus must
I flee from my doubts."[5] So closes the only sonnet with a title, *Orestes*,
which opens with the cry: "My belief dead! Cast out and abandoned, /
I must carry my life across this earth, / Can complain of my grief to no
one's ear, / Even in death must hold my silence." The sonnet's central lines
(5–8) call up but do not make explicit the deed for which the speaker is
decried: "I have committed no misdeed, / I only acted from conviction, /
Yet now it's seen as criminal / And they've laid an eternal curse upon me."
The poem's "lyric-I" seems here to speak as one with Orestes. Those
despondent middle lines are partitioned by a period from the alarming
confession: "A mother I have slain. / O do not ask me her sweet name, / Let
me alone, alone continue onwards!" Orestes, acting in the belief that filial
duty demanded Clytemnestra's murder, was pursued by guilt and doubt.
Did Müller's fate align somehow with Orestes'? Or is this but a student's
exercise in mythic hyperbole? Even this early in his poetic career Müller
understood how to capture a reader's attention with an arresting blend of
autobiographical suggestion and shielding myth. His early wartime experiences and the long journeys from military post to post no doubt stayed
with him.

Upon resuming his studies in Berlin, Müller joined a "Society for
German Language." Its membership cultivated German literary heritage
from the Middle Ages to the present, continuing a long-standing debate in
German letters about national linguistic norms. Among the personalities
he encountered there were the charismatic nationalist Friedrich Ludwig
Jahn (1778–1852), advocate for a free German "fatherland," and the
xenophobic – anti-French and anti-Jewish – Christian Friedrich Rühs
(1781–1820), whose lectures on medieval history he also attended. (Rühs'

monograph *Über die Ansprüche der Juden an das deutsche Bürgerrecht* [Berlin, 1815] touched off heated debates regarding Prussia's official policy of Jewish emancipation. Rühs advocated the gradual elimination of Judaism through conversion and assimilation of the Jewish population into Christendom.) Proponents of ethnic or lingual purism and cosmopolites in German universities at this time frequently argued over their visions for a future German nation, even as wartime patriotism united them. The society brought Müller into frequent contact with such established poets as Clemens Brentano (1778–1842) and Baron de la Motte Fouqué (1777–1843).

He also gathered with war veterans his own age, notably the visual artist and poet Wilhelm Hensel (1794–1861), son of a Lutheran pastor, with whom he had served on the front. Hensel later married Fanny Mendelssohn, a grandchild of the Dessau philosopher Moses Mendelssohn. Hensel's sister Luise (1798–1876), a devout religious poet, captured Müller's heart. To his disappointment, she desired solely his friendship, not a romance. The friends gathered often in Berlin's fashionable literary salons, and nearly weekly in the home of Friedrich August von Stägemann (1763–1840), privy councilor to King Friedrich Wilhelm III. Others in this circle worshipped Luise Hensel too – Brentano and the composer Ludwig Berger (1777–1839) vied for her hand – yet she stayed true to her religious calling and eventually took a vow of celibacy; through Brentano she learned about Catholicism, to which confession she quietly converted in 1818. (So, too, did numerous old guard Romantics in a time when Martin Luther's protest against church authority came to symbolize the rebellious nationhood movement.) The poetic cycle *Die schöne Müllerin*, based on a traditional tale about a miller maid's many suitors, had its origin in this social setting.[6]

In 1817, a request to the university to provide a scholarly travel companion for Royal Chamberlain Baron Albert von Sack (1757–1824) ended Müller's student career. On the enthusiastic recommendation of his philology professor Friedrich August Wolf, he was invited to accompany the baron to Greece and Egypt on a mission to decipher and catalogue ancient inscriptions. This extraordinary opportunity put his erudition to practical use and quickly broadened his perspective on the world. During an initial two-month stay in Vienna, Müller met leaders of the Philikí Etairía, a group supporting Greek emancipation from the Ottoman Empire, whose cause he would later champion in celebrated volumes of *Griechenlieder*, published between 1821 and 1824. The War of Independence (1821–30) from which Greece emerged a sovereign nation became a model for aspiring nationhood movements across Europe. Together with the baron and the artist Julius Schnorr von Carolsfeld

(1794–1872), who joined them in Vienna, Müller traveled to Italy. Carolsfeld went only as far as Florence; Müller and Sack continued on, spending several months in Rome, where Müller gathered impressions for a popular travelogue, *Rom, Römer und Römerinnen*. He parted company with the baron prematurely (for reasons not entirely clear) before they ever reached Greece and, after visiting the ruins of Pompeii, Naples, and Paestum on his own, returned to his native land in December 1818. His homecoming was not easy: the travels abroad had made him painfully conscious of the provincial moralism in the country of his birth.

The following year Müller was appointed teacher of classics in the Gelehrtenschule at Dessau and soon after also head of the ducal library, the first public library in Germany. In 1821, he married Adelheid von Basedow (1800–1883), an accomplished singer and the granddaughter of a prominent educational reformer (whose school in Dessau, the Philanthropinum, educated together children of the wealthy and the poor and renounced corporal punishment).[7] Müller's work duties left him plenty of time to write, edit, and travel, often to the relatively close cultural centers of Berlin, Leipzig, or Dresden where he met publishers and spent time with friends. Notable artist companions during the 1820s included the poet Ludwig Tieck (1773–1853) and the composer Carl Maria von Weber (1794–1826), godfather to Müller's son Max (1823–1900) and the "master of German *Gesang*" to whom Müller dedicated the book of poems containing *Die Winterreise*. He remained in these posts in Dessau for the rest of his short life, dying of a heart attack at the end of September 1827, just before his thirty-third birthday.

Genesis of the Song Cycles

Before examining *Die Winterreise* in relation to other projects on the poet's desk, let us recall the contrasting genesis of Müller's earlier *Die schöne Müllerin* poems. Many of these were first crafted for a *Liederspiel* (a play with interpolated songs), which Müller and his friends performed in the Stägemann salon in winter 1816. The players each contributed lines for his or her character, and Ludwig Berger set their poems to music. Unsurprisingly, Müller took the role of the journeyman miller lad. Luise Hensel played a gardener; the Stägemanns' daughter Hedwig the milleress. In 1818, ten (revised) songs by Berger were published as *Gesänge aus einem gesellschaftlichen Liederspiele "Die schöne Müllerin,"* Op. 11.

The theme continued to occupy Müller as his Berlin student days faded into memory. Several of the poems appeared in literary journals between 1817 and 1818.[8] Over the following years he gradually distilled and expanded the miller's part into a "monodrama" of twenty-three poems, framed by a wry prologue and epilogue in which the figure of The Poet bids "lovely ladies and clever gentlemen" into a performance hall for a "brand new play in the latest sparkling new style." The poet-marketeer of the prologue proclaims that his tale will transport us from a wintry present to springtime and into the freedom of the outdoors (hinting at a political undercurrent). As he paints the scenery – a green floral carpet, moon and star lanterns – he draws attention to the artifice in the "artless" tale and highlights the division between "miller" and "poet." The Poet stands apart, like the narrator in a ballad. And yet: the lyric play has been funneled into a one-man show, a poetry reading requiring a single skilled orator to perform the whole.

In August 1820, Müller read aloud his cycle of poems to Ludwig Tieck, who expressed serious reservations about the tragic ending (the miller's suicide) but evidently encouraged Müller to publish the work.[9] Tieck's concern probably stemmed only partly from the eponym. Happy endings had long been the norm on opera stages, and the modern fashion for tragic endings even in spoken theater was still a novelty, a break from strict convention. *Die schöne Müllerin* appeared at the head of the 1821 solo-authored publication *Sieben und siebzig Gedichte aus den hinterlassenen Papieren eines reisenden Waldhornisten* (Seventy-seven poems from the posthumous papers of a traveling horn player).[10] Franz Schubert discovered the tale there and, in the spring of 1823, set the poems to music; his cycle was issued serially in 1824 in five song-booklets ("Liederhefte"), the standard format at that time for song publications. Schubert omitted Müller's prologue, epilogue, and three internal poems, but retained the remaining sequence of Müller's poems.

The temporality of *Die Winterreise* is far less linear than that of the miller's tale. Portrayed in a series of psychological "landscapes" is the journey, emotional and physical, of a wanderer taking flight from a bitter affair. Müller's propensity to revise poems post-publication and later to gather them into larger works obtained for this collection too. In January 1822, he sent the prestigious firm F. A. Brockhaus in Leipzig twelve poems for publication in the poetic yearbook *Urania. Taschenbuch auf das Jahr 1823.*[11] There the cycle appeared as twelve "wandering songs" under the heading *Wanderlieder von Wilhelm Müller. Die Winterreise. In 12 Liedern.* By all indications, this was a complete work. At its conclusion stood "Einsamkeit," a little poem that elaborates a simile: the wanderer is like an affectless cloud moving through bright skies on a day when the fir tree's crown barely stirs. It pains him that the air should be so still: "When the storms still raged, / I was not so miserable." An oblique meaning emerges if Müller's simile is understood to index political weather: the fir tree was a symbol of the nationhood cause, which had stagnated after the war. (The first student association for German nationhood formed in 1815 at the *Grüne Tanne* [Green Fir], an inn in Jena.)

Ten further poems soon appeared in the Breslau literary daily *Deutsche Blätter für Poesie, Litteratur, Kunst und Theater*, five each in the March 13 and 14, 1823 issues. A footnote indicated that this cluster of poems headed *Die Winterreise. Von Wilhelm Müller* belonged to the same cycle ("Cyklus") as the twelve recently printed in *Urania ... 1823*. The following year the ten new poems appeared, together with the original twelve and two further ones not previously published, as *Die Winterreise*, a cycle of twenty-four poems, in *Gedichte aus den hinterlassenen Papieren eines reisenden Waldhornisten II*. (Schubert omits the article "Die" from the title, shifting attention away from the narrator.) Not only was the sequence of the poems changed when twelve new poems were interspersed, but Müller kept refining details. The two late additions, "Die Post" and "Täuschung," both address forms of self-deception. In "Die Post," the wanderer questions his heart, conscious that embers of hope still glow. In "Täuschung," he embraces the comfort of a long-accustomed self-deception.

Only the barest hints in the opening poem, "Gute Nacht," suggest a motivation for the wanderer's departure from the town in which he arrived a stranger and leaves again as one. There was a girl, who spoke of love, her mother even of marriage. "Let stray dogs howl / In front of their master's house." The relationship between past, present, or even imagined future blurs in the poem's rumination on the moment of leave-taking. Müller's poem is in four eight-line stanzas. At the ends of stanzas 1 ("Now the world is so gloomy") and 2, present tense indicates a journey already underway: in the shadow of the moon, the wanderer seeks the footprints of wild game in the snow. Stanzas 3 and 4 flash back to the moment he tiptoed out the door and past the gate (by the house where he lodged or perhaps the city's gate) onto which he writes "Good night" – "So that you may see / That I thought of you."[12] "Why should I linger here until I am driven out?" begins stanza 3, alluding to the inevitability of this rupture. The situation fits well that of a soldier or a student quartered in a foreign town: *Fremd*, the cycle's first word, may mean either "strange" or "foreign." In song 2, we learn that the daughter of the house is now a wealthy bride. The scenes between this and the last song's desolate portrait of the old hurdy-gurdy player whose small plate stays ever empty only occasionally coalesce into a temporally ordered sequence. At the end of the cycle stands a sober question, addressed to the old man: "Will you play your organ / To my songs?"

Poetic Models and Tropes

A striking precursor to Müller's *Die Winterreise* is a collection of nine *Wanderlieder*, by the Swabian poet Ludwig Uhland (1787–1862), published in the journal *Deutscher Dichterwald* in 1813 and set to music by the composer Conradin Kreutzer (1780–1849).[13] Müller expressed admiration for these folk-like poems in an 1827 essay, noting that they had left a long trail of imitations. One can hardly open a poetic journal anymore without finding "Wanderlieder," he remarked.[14] Uhland's nine poems trace a narrative arc from farewell ("Lebewohl") to homecoming ("Heimkehr"), telling the story of a man who tries to part from the lover he may have impregnated, only to come rushing back home at the end. In the sixth poem, "Winterreise," the protagonist laments that his passion has been extinguished, his feelings gone cold. In the seventh, "Abreise," he leaves the town. In the penultimate poem, "Einkehr," he finds sweet nourishment and rest under the protective shade of an apple tree, an inn, whose "Schild" (signage) is a golden apple hanging from a long branch. The story of "Einkehr" is relayed in past-tense narration ("Recently I was the guest of a wondrously gentle innkeeper"). When he asks what he owes his host, the apple tree shakes his verdant crown. Golden apples presumably rain down, like Zeus's shower of gold (a symbol of fertility). Uhland relates only the wanderer's profuse thanks. Next, in "Heimkehr," a breathless speaker nearly trips over his poetic feet:

> Oh break not, bridge, / you seem to shake / Don't threaten, ridge, / and, earth, don't quake! / World, do not end now, /Sky do not fall in / before I'm with my love again!
> (O brich nicht, Steg, / du zitterst sehr! / O stürz' nicht Fels, / du dräuest schwer! / Welt, geh' nicht unter, / Himmel, fall' nicht ein, / Eh' ich mag bei der Liebsten seyn.)[15]

Müller singled out this tiny bolt of energy: "The little poem 'Homecoming' has always seemed to me the greatest among the *Wanderlieder*. It is so full of love and longing that it wants to shatter. Every spark of such a rocket could lend warmth to the long-winded efforts of our most beloved rhyme-makers."[16] Earlier, he remarks on the affinity between "wandering songs" and ballads, in which a narrator impersonates several characters, and how easily one converts into the other. The shift in narrative voice from "Einkehr" to "Heimkehr" prepares its exuberant happy end (one tinged with fright for the wanderer's safety). Uhland's wanderer is no social outcast. He leaves to sow his wild oats only to find he wants desperately to return home.

Students of *Die Winterreise* have long noted small correspondences between Müller's poems and the images or poetic meter in Uhland's

Wanderlieder.[17] Indirect evidence of Müller's meditation on the narrative arc of this collection exists in a group of six *Wanderlieder* published in *Waldhornisten II.* The mini-ballad "Der Apfelbaum" reads like a trope on Uhland's tale, now given a bitter end.[18] The structure of Müller's poem encourages readers to try out the verses set in quotation marks from various perspectives. A wanderer departing before dawn through the city gate makes it safely across the bridge, and past the lake. When the tree's branches make a rustling ("rauschen") sound, he becomes strangely woeful ("so wunderweh"). "Who shakes the branches? There is no wind," someone asks. A heavy splash comes from the water. "My dearest, it must be from the tree that I planted in your garden. / The lovely apples, so red, so round, / now they lie down upon the cold ground." (What grisly thing has just happened? It all depends on what you take the apples to mean.)

The years separating the publication of the two volumes of *Waldhornisten* poems were some of the most productive in Müller's career. In addition to composing many collections of poems, he reviewed the works of contemporary poets, edited three volumes of seventeenth-century German poetry, and wrote critical essays, translations, and prose works on a remarkable range of subjects. Two significant prose projects that overlapped with his work on *Die Winterreise* subtly illuminate the song cycle's themes. The first involves an intensive engagement with the life and semi-autobiographical poetry of the English Romantic poet George Gordon Byron (1788–1824); the second is Müller's monograph on the transmission of Homeric myth.

Müller's Byron

Lord Byron was for Müller one of the most important poets of the modern age and a kindred spirit for his support of the Greek War of Independence. He first introduced Byron to a German literary public in an essay printed in *Urania. Taschenbuch auf das Jahr 1822.* The same issue of this yearbook contained three small collections of Müller's own poems (including a cluster of four *Wanderlieder*). His Byron article in *Urania* was largely an abridged translation of an essay by an anonymous English critic in the January 1821 issue of the *London Magazine*, which to Müller's dismay the publisher failed to acknowledge. Müller had left standing the critic's reproaches against Byron's personal life and character: he painstakingly distanced himself in his later writings from the moral judgement. Political references in the essay – depicting Napoleon as a friend of freedom, not its enemy – led to a ban of *Urania ... 1822* within the Austrian Empire, and required over a year of negotiations before the prohibition was lifted.[19] Translations of Byron's poetry and shorter critical essays followed, and, in 1825, the year after the poet's death (from a fever) in Missolonghi, Müller completed the fullest biography of Byron in any language, titled simply *Lord Byron*. Parallels with his own oeuvre leap out from many pages of this engaging and personal study.

A persistent strand in Müller's Byron biography is the relationship between life and work. He delights in finding elements of Byron's picaresque life mirrored in the four cantos of *Childe Harold's Pilgrimage* (1812–18) and notes traces of Byron's youthful love for Mary Chaworth in the poem "The Dream" (1816). Byron's passionate relationships with both men and women, and then an affair with his half-sister Augusta, sparked such public furor in England that he feared for his life. He fled into exile in Italy and Greece. Müller alludes to these matters as common knowledge, drawing on his rhetorical skill to weld life and work into myth: "The ordinary poet is distinguished only by following in the footsteps of the ruling favorite of the day. The true poet tries exactly the opposite. He plunges into the tide of public opinion, even when its current weighs most strongly against him." That oceanic metaphor surges into a simile: Byron is like the heroic Julius Caesar.[20] Müller felt that Byron's personality was too large to suppress and that his characters were often masks: "His Manfred is like Childe Harold, like the Corsair, like Lara, and like almost all his heroes, a mysterious creature in whose deep soul a tremendous abomination, a horrible act, a terrible fate lies buried."[21] About Byron's arrival in Greece, he rhapsodizes: "Thereupon the lord crisscrossed many provinces of the old Hellas, probably not yet suspecting that he would one day die for the freedom of this land . . . [H]ow his heart must have leapt even then at the great idea of freedom for the motherland of all freedom***."[22] Perhaps worried that his characterization of Byron's sentiment might ring untrue, Müller inserted asterisks to direct us to Canto 2, verse 15, in *Childe Harold*, where Byron's impressions seem to speak through his character:

> Cold is the heart, fair Greece, that looks on thee,
> Nor feels as lovers o'er the dust they loved;
> Dull is the eye that will not weep to see
> Thy walls defaced, thy mouldering shrines removed
> By British hands, which it had best behoved
> To guard those relics ne'er to be restored.
> Curst be the hour when from their isle they roved,
> And once again thy hapless bosom gored,
> And snatched thy shrinking gods to northern climes abhorred!

A few pages later comes an impassioned account of the English poet's rejection of "pseudo-patriotism," the uncritical embrace of everything originating from one's own country. Byron is of greater mind and more just towards the world, driven by a conception of what his native land could and should be, and for this reason the sharpest critic of the homeland he loved.[23] This meditation elaborates a clumsy footnote that Müller had inserted into the *Urania ... 1822* article on the very page that caught the censor's eye. Müller's Byron became a mirror for his own evolving ideas about love of country, national chauvinism, and the claims of a wider world. (The socio-political spectrum itself comes under scrutiny in Müller's novella *Debora* [1826], in which a medical student, who keeps *Childe Harold* at his bedside, travels through Italy with an old aristocrat. Irreconcilable worldviews drive them apart.)

We may sense something yet more personal in Müller's account of a feud between Lord Byron and the poet Robert Southey (1774–1843), who equated Byron's work with that of the "atheists" he accused of inciting the French Revolution. Byron defended the French philosophers from this charge and then described the revolution as a necessary consequence of the rulers' actions. During his Italian exile, Byron's frequent companion was the poet Percy Bysshe Shelley (1792–1822), "a man decried in his fatherland for political and religious free-thinking." That reputation had pursued Shelley ever since the publication of his pamphlet *The Necessity of Atheism* while he was a student at Oxford.[24] Müller was plainly moved by Byron's devotion to a fellow poet who had "made his entire life unsettled and unpleasant" by airing in public the "errant eccentricities" of his youth. Talk of atheism made Müller uneasy not because Shelley's mind had strayed from commonly accepted beliefs but because he had endured such harsh consequences for expressing his views.[25]

A poet's work in large measure is his life. Things encountered on the written page blend with lived experience. *Die Winterreise*'s wanderer, like Byron and Shelley, like Childe Harold in Italy, like Orestes, is an outcast and a stranger. Müller was attracted often to this narrative archetype. In one electrifying moment in the cycle, the fourth wall threatens to shatter. Pummeled by winter weather and under cover of "madness," the wanderer bellows out an uncensored blasphemy: "If there's no God upon the earth, / Then we ourselves are Gods!" (Will kein Gott auf Erden sein, / Sind wir selber Götter!) For the first time in the cycle, a plural is invoked. Who is this "we"? The wanderer's eruption in "Mut!" (Courage) comes out of nowhere. In Schubert's unforgettable setting, unhinged cadences magnify Müller's provocative rhyming of "Wetter" and "Götter" (weather and gods). Echoed in the unexpected poetic pairing, upon reflection, is the whistling weathervane from song 2, a swiveling cross that sits atop the beloved's house: "And I thought in my delusion, / That it [she] mocked the poor fugitive [Sie pfiff' den armen Flüchtling aus]. // He should have noticed sooner / The symbol displayed on the house [Des Hauses aufgesteckes Schild], so he wouldn't ever have expected / To find a faithful woman within."

Müller's Homer

In 1824, the same year in which *Die Winterreise* appeared, Müller completed a study that he judged to be his greatest critical achievement yet. Widely admired by his contemporaries, his *Homerische Vorschule*[26] offers tantalizing glimpses into his scholarly engagement with creative process. The book is not included in the bicentennial edition of Müller's oeuvre (Gatza, 1994), presumably because it was deemed too derivative to belong among his independent literary products. He did indeed borrow liberally from his teacher Friedrich August Wolf's foundational work on the transmission of Homeric myth.

"Classical scholars have written few classics, but F. A. Wolf's *Prolegomena to Homer* is certainly one of them," begins an invitingly readable commentary and English translation of Wolf's 1795 (Latin) book. The editors continue: "Its literary impiety enraged traditionalists. Its vision of a primitive Homer captivated poets. Its elegant, fine-spun arguments convinced everyone that grammatical technicalities could be interesting. It thrust classical studies to the center of the German intellectual stage."[27] Wolf's work on the *Iliad* and *Odyssey* overturned ingrained beliefs about Homer as "author" of the famed epics, and inspired later scholars to examine the transmitted texts for signs of the shift from oral performance to written literary culture. He understood that the epics were first written down centuries after they were composed.

Müller, who had attended Wolf's German-language lectures while a student in Berlin, felt that his teacher's stimulating ideas deserved a wider audience. He now taught Homer regularly in secondary schools in Dessau. Combining his university lecture notes and aural recollection with a free retelling in German of Wolf's *Prolegomena*, Müller created his own pre-study to reading Homer. While the scholarly foundation of the *Homerische Vorschule* is mainly his teacher's, his speculations and explanations grow from his own interests, illustrated by passages he has either discovered himself or carefully retraced. Wolf, indeed, encouraged students to make ideas their own in this way. We do not know what he thought of his former pupil's work; he passed away in Rome weeks after the book appeared in print.

Müller believed that ancient oral rhapsodies cohered even before acts of writing by editors (*diaskeuasts* is his word) imposed an order on them. In the *Odyssey* more than in the *Iliad*, he noted, certain episodes form self-contained wholes – "The Travels of Telemachus" or "The Return of Odysseus," for example.[28] He saw in the profusion of epithets that recur unvaried, "not wishing in the least to become interesting through change," telltale signs of extemporary practice. Many descriptions of battles, evening meals, the rising and setting of the sun, and so on, are nearly interchangeable. Müller speculated that this allowed later rhapsodes and diaskeuasts to weave together nearly seamless episodes from genuine Homeric material.[29]

Müller was keen to distinguish forms of poetic coherence that are "made" (gemacht) from those gradually "accrued" (entstanden). The "made" features reminded him of Spanish medieval epics such as the *Cantar del Mio Cid*. Yet whereas the "very small lieder" of the medieval romances were composed from the start in linear trajectory, with marked beginnings and ends, the so-called "cyclic poets" who wrote down and ordered the Homeric narratives had first to dismantle the outlines of an inherited corpus and rearrange its poems to create a linear narrative.[30] The significance of one (quite detailed) discussion of this process for a study of Müller's own poetic oeuvre will not be lost on students of *Winterreise*. The passage begins: "A no less eye-catching trace of a later uniting of two *Gesänge*, each of which had originally formed a self-contained whole, and as such had its own beginning and end, emerges from a comparison of the first one hundred lines of part one of the *Odyssey* with the beginning of part five."[31]

Müller's *Homerische Vorschule* refracts Wolf's ideas through the eyeglasses of a modern poet. Both writers were interested in the creative processes that produced these great epic poems. The poet, however, lingers over problems that occupy him in his day-to-day work. How have the verses comprising an epic been ordered and arranged? Does the story have a clear beginning and end or does it start some place in the middle? What is its timescale? Can poetic segments be unconnected or reconnected to make cohesive new tales? Does an epic poem tell of a single person or event or of several? What was conceived for oral performance, what for the written page? How does individual authorship interact with tradition?

Müller's scholarly meditations invite analogous questions about *Die Winterreise*. Why were select poems interwoven with Müller's original twelve, and other "wandering songs" using the same images not? What makes these poems belong to one "Cyklus"? Do the *Müllerin* songs constitute another episode in the same life's odyssey? Questions such as these and further forays into the poet's wider oeuvre will clear new paths to understanding how nineteenth-century authors distilled and memorialized lived experience in poetry.

Notes

1. *Sulamith, eine Zeitschrift zur Beförderung der Kultur und Humanität unter der jüdischen Nation* (Dessau and Leipzig, 1806).
2. Erika von Borries, *Wilhelm Müller, der Dichter der "Winterreise": Eine Biographie* (Munich: C. H. Beck, 2007), 33.
3. Cecilia C. Baumann, *Wilhelm Müller, the Poet of the Schubert Song Cycles: His Life and Works* (University Park: Pennsylvania State University Press, 1981), 3.
4. The nine Brussels sonnets are printed in Wilhelm Müller, *Werke, Tagebücher, Briefe*, ed. Maria-Verena Leistner (Berlin: Gatza, 1994), vol. 2, 271–75. See also Borries, *Wilhelm Müller*, 37–44.
5. Orestes: "Mein Glaube tot! Verstoßen und verlassen, / Muß ich mein Leben durch die Erde tragen, / Kann meine Schmerzen keinem Ohre klagen, / Im Tode selbst muß stumm ich einst verblassen. / Ich habe keine Missetat begangen, / Mit Überzeugung nur hab ich gehandelt, / Und zum Verbrechen hat man's umgewandelt / Und hat mit ew'gem Fluche mich behangen. / Ich habe eine Mutter hingemordet, / O fragt mich nicht nach ihrem süßen Namen, / Laßt mich nur einsam, einsam weiter ziehen! / Wie einst die Furien sich wild gehordet, / Und dem Orestes seinen Frieden nahmen, / So muß auch ich vor meinen Zweifeln fliehen."
6. On the Stägemann gatherings, see Susan Youens, "Behind the Scenes: *Die Schöne Müllerin* Before Schubert," *19th-Century Music* 15/2 (1991): 3–22.
7. On philanthropinism, see Chapter 3 of this volume.
8. For details, see Müller, *Werke, Tagebücher, Briefe*, vol. 1, 287.
9. Baumann, *Wilhelm Müller, the Poet of the Schubert Song Cycles*, 63.
10. Müller may have taken the fiction of the "posthumous papers" from a collection of *Studentenlieder* subtitled "Aus den hinterlassenen Papieren eines unglücklichen Philosophen Florido genannt, gesammelt und verbessert von C. W. K. [Christian Wilhelm Kindleben]," first published in 1781. Müller, *Werke, Tagebücher, Briefe*, vol. 1, 282.
11. For more on the poems' publication history, see Chapter 5 of this volume.
12. For a probing study of timescale in *Winterreise*, see the chapter "Mountains and Song Cycles" in Charles Rosen, *The Romantic Generation* (Cambridge, MA: Harvard University Press, 1995), 116–236.
13. Conradin Kreutzer and Ludwig Uhland, *Conradin Kreutzer's* Frühlingslieder *and* Wanderlieder, trans. Luise Eitel Peake, facsim. ed. (Stuyvesant, NY: Pendragon Press, 1989). Kreutzer's *Neun Wanderlieder von Uhland*, Op. 34 was first published in 1818.
14. "Ueber die neueste lyrische Poesie der Deutschen. Ludwig Uhland und Justinus Kerner," *Hermes, oder Kritisches Jahrbuch der Literatur*, 28 (1827): 94–129. Müller's essay is included in Rudolf Brandmeyer's digital edition of historical texts in poetic theory. www.uni-due.de/lyriktheorie/texte/1827_mueller.html#edition.
15. I quote Luise Eitel Peake's metric translation. *Conradin Kreutzer's* Frühlingslieder *and* Wanderlieder, xxvi.
16. "Ueber die neueste lyrische Poesie der Deutschen." Note 14 gives a digital link.
17. On Wanderlieder, see Chapter 3 of this volume, and Barbara Turchin, "The Nineteenth-Century *Wanderlieder* Cycle," *Journal of Musicology* 5/4 (1987): 498–525. See also *RWJ* for comparisons of Schubert's and Conradin Kreutzer's musical settings.
18. Wilhelm Müller, *Gedichte aus den hinterlassenen Papieren eines reisenden Waldhornisten*, vol. 2 (Christian Georg Ackermann: Dessau, 1824), 144.
19. A reference to Marie Louise of Austria, daughter of Emperor Franz II and wife of Napoleon, may have prompted the ban of the volume, but that phrase in Müller's English source ("Proud Austria's mournful flower") is absent in the copy of *Urania . . . 1822* held in the Bayerische Staatsbibliothek's digital archive: Compare *Urania . . . 1822*, 236 with "Living Authors – Lord Byron" in *London Magazine* 3 (January 1821), 59. The quoted words are from Byron's 1814 poetic cycle "Ode to Napoleon Buonaparte." Müller's letter of October 1, 1821 to Brockhaus leaves unclear whether he knew this. Müller, *Werke, Tagebücher, Briefe*, vol. 5, 190–91.
20. Müller, *Werke, Tagebücher, Briefe*, vol. 4, 162–288 (194).
21. Ibid., 215.
22. Ibid., 185.
23. Ibid., 189.
24. Ibid., 239ff; 214.
25. Ibid., 247.

26. Wilhelm Müller, *Homerische Vorschule: Eine Einleitung in das Studium der Ilias und Odyssee* (Leipzig: F. A. Brockhaus, 1824).

27. Friedrich August Wolf, *Prolegomena to Homer*, trans. and ed. Anthony Grafton, Glenn W. Most, and James E. G. Zetzel (Princeton: Princeton University Press, 1985), ix. For a lucid early nineteenth-century American review article of Wolf's *Prolegomena*, see "Origin of the Homeric Poems," *American Quarterly Review* 4 (Philadelphia: Corey Lea & Corey, 1827), 307–37.

28. Müller, *Homerische Vorschule*, 117–18. Anyone who has heard Richard Dyer-Bennet perform these episodes from the *Iliad* and *Odyssey* will know what Müller means. This twentieth-century bard's working method is documented in a thirty-minute film. Richard Dyer-Bennet, Susan Fanshel, Jill Godmilow, Jeri Sopanen, and Homer, *The Odyssey Tapes* ([New York]: Museum of Modern Art, 1980). Fascination with oral epics endures, as evident in the many editions of Albert B. Lord's *The Singer of Tales* (Cambridge, MA: Harvard University Press, 1960).

29. Müller, *Homerische Vorschule*, 109–10.

30. Ibid., 110–11.

31. Ibid., 108.

5 Schubert's Treatment of Müller's Poems: Some Issues

RUFUS HALLMARK

DEDICATED TO CHARLES BURKHART[1]

Concocting the Cycle

If one reads the poem titles of Wilhelm Müller's earlier cycle *Die schöne Müllerin* from its original edition and the titles of the songs in Schubert's published score, one quickly notes that while Schubert omitted the long Prologue and Epilogue and three other poems, he retained all the rest of the *Müllerin* poems and kept them in the same order as the poet's.[2] Schubert did a bit of judicious cutting, but left the poetic cycle largely intact.

But a comparison of the titles from the first publication of the twenty-four poems of Müller's cycle *Die Winterreise* (Table 5.1, Column D) with the titles in Schubert's published cycle (Column E) leads to a very different conclusion. All the poems are present in both, but one immediately notices multiple discrepancies in their ordering, mainly in the second half, some quite radical. How did Schubert arrive at this sequence?

The ordering of the poems in Schubert's cycle was arguably the result of unforeseen events. Müller published his poems in three waves. The first two were installments in periodicals: the first twelve poems in 1823 in *Urania* (Column A), ten more later the same year in *Deutsche Blätter für Poesie, Litteratur, Kunst und Theater* (Column C). The third publication (in 1824), of these twenty-two poems plus two more (Column D), was his complete cycle of twenty-four poems, in a volume of his poetry with the whimsical title *Sieben und siebzig Gedichte aus den hinterlassenen Papieren eines reisenden Waldhornisten* (Seventy-seven Poems from the Surviving Papers of an Itinerant Horn Player). Schubert encountered the poems in this piecemeal manner, coming first upon the publication in the periodical *Urania*. One can presume that he was so taken with these twelve poems that he set them to music straightaway, unaware of the possibility that the poet might have a larger design. This presumption is based on internal evidence other than the selection and order of the poems. First, Schubert's texts in four instances correspond to the readings in the *Urania* poems, but differ from those in *Waldhornisten*. (To cite one example, in "Erstarrung," both *Urania* and

Table 5.1 Müller's and Schubert's orderings compared

A Müller *Urania* (1823)	B [Schubert *Winterreise* (1826? early '27)]	C Müller *Deutsche Blätter* (1823)	D Müller *Waldhornisten* (1824)	E Schubert *Winterreise* (1827)
				Gute Nacht
				Die Wetterfahne
				Gefror'ne Tränen
				Erstarrung
				Der Lindenbaum
			Gute Nacht	Wasserflut
			Die Wetterfahne	Auf dem Flusse
			Gefror'ne Tränen	Rückblick
			Erstarrung	Irrlicht
			Der Lindenbaum	Rast
			<u>Die Post</u>	Frühlingstraum
		Der greise Kopf	Wasserflut	Einsamkeit
		Letzte Hoffnung	Auf dem Flusse	<u>Die Post</u>
		Die Krähe	Rückblick	**Der greise Kopf**
		Im Dorfe	**Der greise Kopf**	**Die Krähe**
		Der stürmische Morgen	**Die Krähe**	**Letzte Hoffnung**
		Die Nebensonnen	**Letzte Hoffnung**	Im Dorfe
		Der Wegweiser	**Im Dorfe**	**Der stürmische Morgen**
		Das Wirtshaus	**Der stürmische Morgen**	Täuschung
		Mut!	<u>Täuschung</u>	**Der Wegweiser**
		Der Leiermann	**Der Wegweiser**	**Das Wirtshaus**
Gute Nacht	Gute Nacht		**Das Wirtshaus**	**Mut**
Die Wetterfahne	Die Wetterfahne		Das Irrlicht	**Die Nebensonnen**
Gefror'ne Tränen	Gefror'ne Tränen		Rast	**Der Leiermann**
Erstarrung	Erstarrung		**Die Nebensonnen**	
Der Lindenbaum	Der Lindenbaum		Frühlingstraum	
Wasserflut	Wasserflut		Einsamkeit	
Auf dem Flusse	Auf dem Flusse		**Mut!**	
Rückblick	Rückblick		**Der Leiermann**	
Das Irrlicht	Irrlicht			
Rast	Rast			
Frühlingstraum	Frühlingstraum			
Einsamkeit	Einsamkeit]			

NOTE: The information in this table is based on https://de.wikisource.org/wiki/Die_Winterreise, and on Maximilian and Lily Schochow, *Franz Schubert: Die Texte …* (see Bibliography). **Column A.** "Wanderlieder von Wilhelm Müller. Die Winterreise. In 12 Liedern" (regular typeface) in *Urania für das Jahr 1823.* 5. *Jahrgang,* 207–22. Leipzig. **B.** Hypothetical initial composition, inferred from exact correspondence of these 12 songs in Schubert's finished cycle with Müller's 12-song cycle in *Urania* and Schubert's use of the wording of the *Urania* texts rather than the revised readings in *Waldhornisten* version. **C.** *Deutsche Blätter für Poesie, Litteratur, Kunst und Theater* (1823), No. 41, 161–62, and No. 42, 165–66 (**boldface**). **D.** *Sieben und siebzig Gedichte aus den hinterlassenen Papieren eines reisenden Waldhornisten,* Bd. 2, 75–108, Dessau, 1824 (added poems underlined). **E.** Autograph manuscript, Morgan Library, Mary Flagler Carey Collection, No. 215 (Record I.D. ID 115668). Viewed at www.themorgan.org. First edition, published in two parts by Tobias Haslinger, Vienna, in 1828, I, 1–12 (February), II, 13–24 (October).

Schubert's setting read "Wo sie an meinem Arme / Durchstrich die grüne Flur," whereas *Waldhornisten* has "Hier, wo wir oft gewandelt / Selbander durch die Flur.")[3] Second, inspection of Schubert's autograph manuscript strongly suggests that the first twelve songs constitute a distinct compositional stage because they have many more corrections than the second half of the cycle, which appears to be the clean manuscript of the latter twelve songs.[4]

Schubert may have been unaware of the publication of Müller's second set of ten more poems in *Deutsche Blätter*, but when he discovered the complete set of twenty-four poems in *Waldhornisten*, he was motivated to add the twelve remaining poems to his song cycle. Initially, however, there was what must have appeared to Schubert a nearly insurmountable problem: In adding the ten poems from *Deutsche Blätter* (shown in boldface in Table 5.1) plus two new ones (underlined) to the original set to create the complete *Waldhornisten* cycle (Column D), Müller integrated some of these into his earlier twelve and appended others. The poet thus fractured the sequence Schubert had already composed (Column B). The composer faced a difficult choice: Either he could do a full-scale revision and augmentation of his original song cycle, adhering to Müller's new sequence, or he could just make the best of the situation and compose the remaining twelve poems as a second part. He of course decided on the latter course, setting these twelve poems in the order in which they occur in *Waldhornisten*, except for the reversal of "Mut!" and "Die Nebensonnen" (compare Columns D and E).

Since *Die Winterreise*, unlike the *Müllerin* cycle, is not a linear narrative, one seeks to understand the significance of the poet's orderings. Apparently, Müller himself did not regard the sequence of the first twelve poems as sacrosanct, for in the final version he inserted some of the newer poems into that first group. So neither, perhaps, might Schubert have felt he would damage Müller's cycle with his own, different ordering. But if there is not a story, what holds the poems together? Context, to be sure – season and landscape and state of mind – but is there more? We can agree that "Gute Nacht" must stand at the beginning since it provides essential exposition of the situation that sends the protagonist on his winter journey, and "Die Wetterfahne" must probably come next for the same reason. "Der Leiermann" is the best candidate for closing the cycle, given its single meeting with another human character, its open-endedness, and its absolutely flat affect. But beyond these, what?

Should we regard Müller's own order as preferable, or might we so regard Schubert's? Does the order of the poems, outside the first two and the last, matter? Does Schubert's music provide its own ordering principles? Nowhere in the literature on *Winterreise* are these questions definitively answered, though Susan Youens, Richard Kramer, and others have speculated on them at length, including finding common motivic and harmonic features in several songs. Far be it from me to attempt even a summary of this imponderable issue here. Perhaps one must fall back on this formulation by Kramer: "[*Winterreise* is] a complex grouping of songs that bear on one another in ways that everyone acknowledges to be significant, even as the specific nature of their relatedness has proved to be elusive in the extreme."[5] It should be acknowledged that Kramer's statement stands at the beginning of his own ambitious attempt to pin down that relatedness.

Altering Müller's Texts

Schubert made only a few changes to Müller's poems. Most of these appear to be relatively minor, worthy of a textual note at best, since they do not significantly affect the sound or sense of the verse. A handful of alterations, however, reward close study, for they are interesting in themselves and reveal Schubert's attention to detail. (Here I look only at word changes, and do not consider word and line repetition or violation of line and strophe integrity.)

In the fourth and final eight-line stanza of the first poem, "Gute Nacht," the young man says that as he leaves the house at night, he closes the door quietly so as not to disturb his beloved's sleep, and writes on the gate, "Ich hab' an dich gedacht" (I thought of you). In his song, Schubert altered Müller's text to "An dich hab' ich gedacht." This changes neither the words themselves nor their meaning, but it rearranges their order, with expressive results:

```
             .  /   .  /   .  /
Müller:    Ich hab an dich gedacht
              .  /   .  /   .  /
Schubert: An dich hab ich gedacht
```

Schubert's altered line creates an internal rhyme – "dich" and "ich" – and aligns both of their -*ch* sounds with that of the closing accented syllable ("ge-dacht"), bringing out the assonance. The "dich" and "ich" rhymes also both occur on a descending fourth motive (f#″–c#″, d″–a′; mm. 85–87). This all passes by quickly, but it creates a pleasing aural effect. It is worth adding that if Schubert had used the earlier, corresponding phrase ending (mm. 49–51, 53–55, or 81–83), the transposed melody would have carried the singer to a high a″ within the *pianissimo* dynamic!

In song 4, "Erstarrung" (stanza 5, line 1), Müller wrote "Mein Herz ist wie erfroren" (My heart is as if frozen), but Schubert changed "erfroren" to "erstorben" (dead). This raises the emotional temperature of the utterance considerably, but it vitiates the poet's metaphor. The poem goes on to say, "Her image frozen cold within; / If my heart ever thaws again, / Her image will melt away, too!" The metaphor depends on the image of his heart as ice. Apparently, the image of a dead rather than merely frozen heart was so potent that Schubert was willing to sacrifice Müller's tidy metaphor.

In song 6, "Wasserflut" (stanza 3, line 2), Schubert actually changed Müller's wording:

```
              /   .   . /   /   .     /
Müller:    Sag mir, wo-hin geht dein Lauf?
              /   .  /   .   /   .    /
Schubert: Sag, wo-hin doch geht dein Lauf?
```

The meaning is not affected by Schubert's change, but Müller's reversed second foot, an iamb within the trochaic line, would have created a problem. In this compound strophic setting, Schubert used the same music for stanzas 3 and 4 that he composed for 1 and 2. One can see in the autograph manuscript that he first inserted Müller's line unchanged into his score where the notes had originally served the straight trochaic line, "Ist gefallen in den Schnee." He quickly realized that his dotted rhythm and bouncing melodic line would not serve the reversed foot (or better, that Müller's words would not fit his melody), and he altered the text then and there, crossing out "mir, wohin" and substituting "wohin doch."

At the beginning of song 14, "Der greise Kopf," Schubert ignored a subtlety of verb tense sequence. Müller's first couplet is in the past perfect tense – "Der Reif hatt' einen weissen Schein / Mir über's Haar gestreuet" (The frost *had* spread a white sheen all over my hair). The second is in the simple past tense – "Da meint' ich schon ein Greis zu sein" (I thought myself already an old man) (my translations). *Waldhornisten* reads "meint'" in line 2, but Schubert changed this to "glaubt'." In line 1 "hatt'" is short for "hatte," the auxiliary verb which creates the past perfect with the participle "ges-treuet," but this is apparent only if one is looking at the poem on the printed page. In spoken or sung language, there is no distinction between "hat" and "hatt'," so I would argue that Schubert disregarded the tense sequence and simply wrote "hat." The meaning is clear despite the sacrifice of Müller's subtlety. (The *Neue Schubert-Ausgabe* restores Müller's reading.)

In song 17, "Im Dorfe," Schubert removed the syntactical variation in Müller's opening lines and also softened a condescending depiction of the "snoring" villagers. Müller's first two images present the predicate before the subject – "Es bellen die Hunde, es rasseln die Ketten" (There bellow the hounds, there rattle the chains) – while for variety and emphasis in the second line he reverts to normal word order – "Die Menschen schnarchen in ihren Betten" (People snore in their beds) (my translations). Perhaps Müller meant thereby to emphasize his unflattering comparison of the snoring villagers to the bellowing hounds. Schubert changed "schnarchen" to "schlafen" and preserved the inverted word order ("Es schlafen die Menschen"). His villagers are sleeping quietly. But if Schubert removed this mildly derogatory auditory image, he did not soften the implication of the emptiness of their lives in Müller's subsequent lines. (Graham Johnson fears that if Schubert had left Müller's text intact, many singers would be tempted to mimic a snoring sound on the word "schnarchen";[6] this would indeed be easy to do with a rolled *r* and guttural *ch*.)

In song 20, "Der Wegweiser," Schubert changed a rhyme word, perhaps unawares. Müller's quatrains have an alternating rhyme scheme, and the third stanza rhymes Strassen/zu/Massen/Ruh. But Schubert changed "Strassen" to "Wegen." The meaning of the line is not hindered, but the rhyme scheme is. Here is an instance in which one is sorely tempted to restore the poet's reading, despite the editorial principle of being faithful to the composer's last written intention, even if the text alteration might have been unintentional. It is possible that Schubert altered the word to impart fourfold alliteration to this quatrain (Weiser, Wegen, Weisen, wandre); notice that the poem's first stanza also contains considerable alliteration (Was, Wege, Wo, Wandrer; versteckte, verschneite). But this would be the sole instance in *Winterreise* of Schubert corrupting a rhyme. (Johnson believes that Schubert substituted "Wegen" because "Strassen" is "unsuitably banal," but he doesn't explain this opinion.[7])

Setting the Poems: Unusual Uses of Triple Meter

In this section, my focus narrows from the whole cycle to a group of eight songs, all of which are in triple meter:

Song 5	"Der Lindenbaum"
Song 6	"Wasserflut"
Song 8	"Rückblick"
Song 9	"Irrlicht"
Song 14	"Der greise Kopf"
Song 16	"Letzte Hoffnung"
Song 23	"Die Nebensonnen"
Song 24	"Der Leiermann"

In general, triple meter is used infrequently in Lieder. A "quick and dirty" survey of the 446 songs in the seven-volume Peters Edition of Schubert songs (about 75 percent of his total output) reveals only 101 songs in triple meter, and twenty-four of these use triple meter only within internal sections. Thus only seventy-seven of 446 songs start in and are wholly or largely in triple meter; this is 17 percent, or fewer than one song in five. Of the twenty *Die schöne Müllerin* songs, only four are in triple meter, or 20 percent of the total. By contrast, in *Winterreise*, eight of the twenty-four songs are in triple meter, a full 33.3 percent. (*Schwanengesang* has an even larger proportion: six of fourteen, or 43 percent.)

One of the primary decisions a song composer makes is how the text will be declaimed in *time* – the choice of meter, the note durations used, their placement within each measure. This is not the place to delve into the intricacies of poetic and musical meter and rhythm, but the reader must be aware of these kinds of things during the following discussion.[8] Duple meters like 4/4, 2/4, and the compound meter 6/8 all accommodate the trimeter and tetrameter lines of the era's lyric poetry straightforwardly and "naturally." "Gute Nacht" provides a good example of three-foot lines, in which the last foot of each line is extended or followed by a rest. "Die Krähe" provides a straightforward instance of four- and three-foot lines in alternation.

The conventional procedure in *triple* meter is to set the feet to an alternation of long and short notes. "Der Lindenbaum" is the first song in triple time in *Winterreise*. The first and third feet of the trimeter line fall on downbeats and are extended through the second beat; the second foot falls on the third beat of the measure:

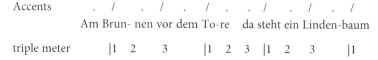

Accents   .   /   .   /   .   /   .   .   /   .   /   .   /

           Am Brun- nen vor dem To-re   da steht ein Linden-baum

triple meter |1   2   3 |1   2   3 |1   2   3 |1

This song flows so pleasantly with its undeniably charming major-key melody (except for the turbulent middle section, of course) that it has easily become the signature song of the cycle for many listeners. No other triple-meter song in *Winterreise* follows its conventional rhythmic setting. In contrast, all but one of the triple-meter songs in *Die schöne Müllerin* do follow this customary pattern. Besides its more common rhythmic setting, the overall major tonality of "Lindenbaum" contrasts with the minor keys of other triple-meter songs; a major key does not open and predominate with such clarity in a triple-meter song until "Die Nebensonnen." Though "Letzte Hoffnung" has an E♭ major signature, it acts as though it is in the parallel minor much of the time. ("Rückblick" is the negative image of "Lindenbaum": pounding rhythms in G minor open in the present time, while the placid central section of past memories is in G major.)

In stark contrast to this conventional use of triple meter, the rhythmic settings in songs 6, 9, 14, 16, and 23 stand out. (The remaining triple-meter songs – "Rückblick" and "Der Leiermann" – draw on another rarely used text-setting manner, discussed below.) In these five triple-meter songs, the vocal lines open with two measures of a short–long pattern, the first poetic foot aligned with the *first* metric unit and the second occupying the rest of the measure, reversing the customary triple-meter declamation. This same pattern is anticipated in the piano introductions of four of these songs (but not in song 16). The short–long pattern recurs to varying degrees throughout each of the triple-meter songs. There is a second component to the patterning in most of them: the two measures of the short–long pattern constitute the first half of the musical phrase, and they are followed by two measures that progress without a break to a cadence in the fourth measure, the whole pattern represented as 1 m. + 1 m. + 2 m. Here are the opening texts of these songs (6, 9, and 16) shown schematically:

	1 meas.	+	1 meas.	+	2 meas.
beat	1 2 3		1 2 3		1 2 3 1
stress	/ . / .		/ . / .		/ . / . / . /
3/4	Manche Trän' aus		| meinen Au- gen |		ist ge- fallen in den | Schnee
3/8	In die tief - - sten		| Felsen- grün - - de |		lockte mich ein Irrlicht | hin
3/4	Hie und da ist		| an den Bäu - - men|		manches bun-te Blatt zu | sehn

It is possible that we have simply failed to notice the special, individual qualities of this group of triple-meter songs because the cycle is so familiar. One hopes this fresh look will prompt further study.

Notice that "Wasserflut," "Irrlicht," and "Letzte Hoffnung" are all in trochaic meter and have four stresses in each line; hence the pattern fits them like a glove. "Der greise Kopf" (song 14) alternates four-stress lines with three-stress lines, which fit this declamation pattern less easily. There are too few syllables in the even-numbered lines to place a foot on each quarter note of the third measure of the phrase and have a foot left for the final measure; Schubert, however, convincingly keeps the melodic motion going with untexted notes into the cadential fourth measure, as shown in (a). "Die Nebensonnen" is entirely in tetrameter with enough syllables in line 2 to fill out the third measure of the phrase, but Schubert, responding to the primary stress on the first syllable of "angesehn," saves the whole word for the next measure, as shown in (b). He sticks to this declamation throughout, and, in fact, it suits the other affected lines well; see mm. 12–13, 22–23, 28–29. Thus in both of these songs, the overall phrase pattern (1 + 1 + 2) is still distinguishable.

a)

| 1 meas. | + | 1 meas. | + | 2 meas. |

```
                  1    2   3    1    2   3    1    2     3     1   2
                   .  /  . /   .  /  . /    .  /         .  /   . /    .
```

3/4   Der | Reif hat ei - - - nen | weissen Schein   mir | ü - - - - - - - -bers Haar ge | streuet

b)

| 1 meas. | + | 1 meas. |

```
        .   /   . /  .  . /    . /    .   /   . /     .   /  . /
```

3/4   Drei | Sonnen sah ich am | Himmel stehn   hab' | lang und fest   sie | angesehn

                    INSTEAD OF   +   2 meas.

```
                            /    .   /   . / . | /
```

                    | lang und fest sie   ange - | sehn

Schubert's use of this patterning seems, however, not always to be related to the relative stresses in the lines, at least not unambiguously. For example, in the first of these songs, "Wasserflut," it is clear that line 1 has stressed substantives (Trän', Augen) on the second and fourth feet of the line, with weaker-stressed adjectives on the first and third (manche, meinen). Youens and Johnson note these relative stresses, and both observe that Schubert accorded an extended duration and high pitch to "Trän'" to compensate for their placement on the relatively weak second beat of the triple meter.[9] But why does Schubert set himself this hurdle to leap? Why not follow an easier path? He might have placed his rising arpeggiation figure on the upbeat and then have continued with this same pattern, aligning it as follows:

```
     .          /        .        /        .       /          .      /
    3     | 1   2    3   | 1   2    3   | 1    2    3   | 1
Manche| Trän' aus meinen | Au - gen ist ge-  | fal—— len in den | Schnee
Seine  | kal - - ten Flocken | sau - gen durstig | ein      das heisse | Weh.
```

This would be a more commonplace metric declamation of this line in triple meter. It is a perfectly usable solution, adhering to the more common convention. It might even seem a more "natural" or straightforward metric setting of the lines, putting the more heavily accented or significant words/syllables on the downbeats, rather than on the second, weaker beat of a triple measure, and having to compensate for that position through higher pitch and/or dynamics.

But looking ahead, perhaps, Schubert saw and heard that in the second and fourth lines of the stanza, he would want to place the noun "Flocken" (flakes) on a strong beat, that the anthropomorphically important adjective "durstig" (thirsty) was ill-suited to an upbeat, and that the adverb "ein" (complementing "saugen") would sound odd on the downbeat. Thus the "unnatural" placement of the syllables turns out to work very well for parts of this poem. Moreover, and perhaps more significantly, this short–long setting presents an arresting declamation pattern.

The short–long pattern and phrase structure permeates each of these five songs to varying degrees. In "Wasserflut," though the poem's second and fourth stanzas are set to different melody and harmony, they preserve the short–long pattern and 1 + 1 + 2 phrase structure (mm. 19–28). The form is thus ABAB. In "Irrlicht" the short–long pattern is missing in the second couplet's first line (m. 9), but the phrase pattern is present, and the second stanza is a slight variation of the first (mm. 17–26). The last stanza is free, making the song's form AA′B. In "Der greise Kopf," the first stanza's patterning and phrase structure return in stanza 3 (mm. 29–42), though they are absent in the middle of the song, creating an ABA form. In "Letzte Hoffnung," the piano prelude does not anticipate the short–long pattern (as in songs 6, 9, 14, and 23), and the vocal line, though adhering to the short–long pattern in the first couplet, loosens its hold in the second. The second stanza is wholly free of the pattern, but in the third stanza, the pattern and phrase structure return for the first three lines (elongated with piano echoes and interludes); the final line breaks free of the pattern and, by repetition, stretches the conclusion of the song to nine measures (mm. 35–43). Finally, "Nebensonnen" adheres to the short–long gesture and four-measure phrase except for two lines of quasi-recitative in the middle. (The pattern is slightly modified in songs 14 and 23, as noted earlier.)

Arnold Feil says this pattern in "Wasserflut" "drags so slowly that it conveys the impression of exhaustion, even apathy,"[10] but he does not call attention to Schubert's use of it in other triple-meter songs. Youens points to "the second-beat durational emphases [of earlier songs] as premonitory of the hurdy-gurdy tune in the final song,"[11] but it seems to me there is more to this pattern than a foreshadowing of the last song. Yonatan Malin notes most of these distinct triple-meter patternings in *Winterreise*, commenting that "Schubert seems to have liked this schema."[12] The object of Malin's book is to provide a systematic categorization of the schemata by which poetic lines of varying lengths align with musical meter and rhythm in German Lieder in general, but he does not set out to study the expressive role of any particular schema in the literature.

The two remaining triple-meter songs, "Rückblick" and "Leiermann," share a *different* distinctive patterning, that of declaiming *two* lines of the poem in even metric units with no break at line endings – a kind of "run-on" declamation. The result is so different in these two cases that one can miss the fact that they share this trait. "Rückblick" has four-foot lines, so the eight feet of two lines continue for two and two-thirds measures of 3/4 meter without stopping. The pairs of three-foot lines of "Leiermann" completely fill up two measures. The long and syllable-saturated phrasing in "Rückblick," abetted by the pounding piano accompaniment with its syncopated echoes, lends a driven quality to this song. The similar unbroken declamation of "Leiermann," with a melody that curls around itself and its bare accompaniment, creates a wholly different effect, one of lassitude and stasis rather than energy. Youens notes the driven quality of "Rückblick" and attributes it to the saturated declamation,[13] but does not note that the same declamation principle – albeit with shorter lines and quite different effect – occurs in "Leiermann."

While the vocal melody of neither of these songs has anything to do with the short–long pattern, the *piano* music of "Leiermann" most certainly does echo that pattern. The vocal melody by itself, on the other hand, is ambiguous; one could easily hear its meter as duple (2/4).[14] I believe this ambiguity continues into the third stanza and is emphasized by the new declamation at "Wunderlicher Alter" (mm. 53–55) where, for the first time, two lines are not run together and the second line, "Soll ich mit dir geh'n?," begins on the second beat of the second measure. It is as if the triple meter in the piano is sounded against duple meter in the voice; thus the metrical disjunction between voice and piano continues. The last two lines in the voice (mm. 56–57) finally conform unambiguously with the 3/4 meter of the piano because of the use of the same melody for both lines. The wanderer thereby answers his own question – "soll ich mit dir geh'n?" (shall I go with you?) – by agreeing in the end with the hurdy-gurdy's meter: he and the Leiermann are finally singing and playing together.

Some Conclusions

Arnold Feil describes "Nebensonnen" as a "carefully measured walking dance, serious and slow," resembling a sarabande.[15] This slow, stately Baroque dance in triple meter stresses the first beat, but emphasizes the second beat by lengthening it. As we have seen, five of the triple-meter songs in *Winterreise* have these characteristics. Furthermore, sarabande phrase structure often consists of two segments of the short–long pattern followed by a flowing cadential segment twice as long. For example, J. S. Bach's sarabandes in his French Suites 1, 4 and 6 clearly manifest this structure. This is by no means to claim that Schubert consciously modeled these songs on Bach or any other particular eighteenth-century pieces, but rather that the older sarabande may have cast its shadow over these songs.

I have no explanation for Schubert's fondness for the sarabande-like patterning of these songs. Nor do I insist on this Baroque dance name, which I use only as an identifier of these musical characteristics. What I do insist on is that this pattern is unmistakably present in five of the triple-meter songs of *Winterreise* and that it bestows a distinct expressive quality on these songs and therefore on the cycle.

Here are some concluding observations. Schubert, in his encounter with the first twelve of Müller's poems, composed *four* songs in triple meter: "Lindenbaum," a "model" 3/4 setting; "Wasserflut," one of the sarabande-like songs; "Rückblick," one of the run-on-line settings; and "Irrlicht," another sarabande. Then, when he set the twelve remaining poems, he seemingly balanced this earlier group with four more distinctive triple-meter songs: "Der greise Kopf," "Letzte Hoffnung," and "Nebensonnen" are all three sarabandes, and "Leiermann" is a second run-on setting. We don't know how much time elapsed between Schubert's work on the two parts of this cycle, but there is unanimous scholarly agreement on the proposition that these parts were composed with a time gap between them, despite the fact that there is no single airtight bit of evidence.[16] However long or short that gap was, Schubert retained a predisposition for triple-meter songs and likely sought to find appropriate texts for such treatment in Part II.

* * * * *

One marvels at the austere beauty of *Winterreise.* Despite Schubert's unavoidable rearrangement of Müller's poems and his alteration of many textual details, the haunting spirit of Müller's cycle is not only retained, but enhanced. While the poet transmutes the protagonist's bitter, sad, and despairing experience into winter imagery, Schubert's music sublimates that unrelenting verse into transcendent music. The idiosyncratic triple-meter settings of Müller's poems make a telling contribution to the musical spell that this cycle casts, and their distinctive character is lessened neither by one's inability to account for why Schubert employed them nor by their effect's stubborn resistance to explanation.

Notes

1. Charles Burkhart, distinguished music theorist, sensitive pianist-musician, and my erstwhile colleague at Queens College, CUNY, invited me to learn and perform *Winterreise* with him in

the Schubert year 1997. This collaboration turned into one of the richest musical experiences of my life and led eventually to my scholarly work on the cycle.

2. I wish to thank Anne Hallmark, Fred Lerdahl, Marjorie Hirsch, and Lisa Feurzeig for carefully reading and constructively commenting on drafts of this chapter; and James Webster for critiquing some of my early ideas about the triple-meter songs.

3. These correspondences can be easily seen in the table of text variants ("Lesarten") in the *Die Winterreise* entry on Wikisource, cited in Table 5.1.

4. *RWJ*, 29–30, 34–44; *DC*, 152–53.

5. *DC*, 159.

6. *FSCS*, vol. 3, 697.

7. Ibid., 707.

8. For a concise discussion of accommodating poetic meter and rhythm to music, see Yonatan Malin, "From Poetic Rhythm to Musical Rhythm," in *Songs in Motion: Rhythm and Meter in the German Lied* (Oxford: Oxford University Press, 2010), 13–19.

9. *RWJ*, 175; *FSCS*, vol. 3, 653.

10. *FSSMW*, 98.

11. *RWJ*, 292–93.

12. Malin, *Songs in Motion*, 20–21.

13. *RWJ*, 192–93.

14. Both Feil (*FSSMW*, 127–28) and Youens (*RWJ*, 301–2) discuss the ambiguity of the vocal meter in this song; they come to conclusions different from mine.

15. *FSSMW*, 123.

16. See *RWJ*, 24–28 for a close discussion of the chronology.

PART III

Cultural and Historical Contexts

6 Two Perspectives on Psychology in *Winterreise*

Section 1: The Emerging Discipline of Psychology

DAVID ROMAND

Section 2: Explorations of Human Behavior Outside the Academic Sphere

LISA FEURZEIG

This chapter explores the psychological significance of *Die Winterreise* from two directions. Examining the birth of psychology as an academic field, particularly in Germany, David Romand finds only limited connection to *Die Winterreise*, while Lisa Feurzeig finds many links to Müller's cycle in more popular, less academic pursuits of the time.

In seventeenth- and eighteenth-century philosophy, continental Rationalists asked what is true, while British Empiricists addressed the question of how human thought is related to the physical world. Despite their differences, both forms of philosophy assumed that people are rational beings and used rationality as the basic model for understanding human actions. By contrast, all the trends discussed in this chapter – early psychological research, fiction, poetry, and popular animal magnetism – recognized that people frequently act in non-rational ways, making it necessary to seek different models of human behavior. Thus, the two sections of this chapter are linked, even though their views of *Die Winterreise* are different.

SECTION 1: THE EMERGING DISCIPLINE OF PSYCHOLOGY

In 1824, the same year Wilhelm Müller's *Die Winterreise* was published, Johann Friedrich Herbart published the first volume of his *Psychologie als Wissenschaft* (Psychology as a Science),[1] which proved highly influential and was soon regarded as a milestone in the history of psychology. In Germany, the beginning of the nineteenth century was a period of considerable innovation for psychology that led to dramatic and irreversible changes in how the mind was contemplated and its study conceived. As Herbart's title suggests, this period was *par excellence* that of the making of "scientific" psychology, German psychologists striving to define the specific object and methods of their field of investigation and to establish it as an autonomous discipline. Paradoxically, while being characterized by a quest for scientificity, early nineteenth-century Germany was also the favorite playground of Romanticism, an aesthetic, artistic, and intellectual movement known for its appetite for irrationality and brash speculation. The two kindred currents of Romantic philosophy and *Naturphilosophie* had a strong impact on contemporary German scientific thought, and psychology itself was far from immune to this influence. Here I aim to give an overview of how psychological research was carried out in Germany during the first decades of the nineteenth century by exploring the epistemological issues at stake, the originality of the theoretical contributions, and how this scientific/philosophical context may be reflected in contemporary literature. After briefly reviewing the debates about the scientificity of psychology at the turn of the nineteenth century, analyzing the emergence of the new German psychological science, and discussing the concept of Romantic psychology, I address the question of the place of psychological issues in literary Romanticism in general and Müller's *Die Winterreise* in particular.

How Scientific Was Psychology in the Late Eighteenth and Early Nineteenth Centuries?

From One Century to Another: Continuity and Renewal of Psychological Thought

In *The Sciences of the Soul: The Early Modern Origins of Psychology*,[2] Fernando Vidal maintains that psychology as it developed during the eighteenth century already had most of the characteristics of a scientific discipline. At this time, scholars definitively abandoned the Aristotelian conception of the soul by restricting the concept to its "intellective" dimension and treating it as an entity to be investigated *per se*, independently from the body. In the wake of this epistemological turn, the word "psychology" acquired its modern meaning – the study of mental processes as opposed to material processes – and came to refer, at least in Germany, to a specific domain of knowledge producing its own specialized literature.

Without undermining the value of Vidal's developments and the innovativeness of the eighteenth-century authors, it seems important neither to overemphasize the "modernity" of the eighteenth-century psychological tradition nor to ascribe to it more scientific value than it could have within the intellectual context of the time. As a rule, theorists of the mind during that period did not clearly distinguish between psychological issues, strictly speaking, and epistemological concerns, nor did they satisfactorily identify the relationship between psychology and philosophy on the one hand and natural sciences on the other. Moreover, one is forced to admit that eighteenth-century authors did not adequately define the subject matter of psychology – the nature of the mental phenomena that it is supposed to deal with – and that they failed to specify what makes the psychological approach different from other disciplines.[3] The great merit of the German psychologists of the early nineteenth century is their decisive contribution to the clarification of these ontological, taxonomic, and methodological issues, paving the way to an authentically scientific reassessment of psychological concerns.

A Contested Science: Kant's Criticisms of Psychology's Pretense to Scientificity

The fact is that, at the turn of the nineteenth century, the question of the disciplinary and scientific status of psychology was far from uncontroversial. The staunchest opponent to the idea that the study of the mind could be founded on the model of the natural sciences was Immanuel Kant (1724–1804), who famously addressed the problem in the preface to his *Metaphysical Foundations of Natural Science*, first issued in 1786.[4]

In line with most of his contemporaries, Kant regarded psychology (*Seelenlehre, Psychologie*) as specifically relating to the inner sense (*der innere Sinn*), "the thinking nature" that constitutes one of the two chief domains of experience, as opposed to "the extended nature" of the outer sense (*der äussere Sinn*), which is investigated by the physical sciences. Insofar as it deals with the objects of the inner sense, he explains, psychology has no chance of becoming an authentic natural science, or, to put it in his own words, a "rational natural doctrine," along the lines of physics. Instead of a science of the mind (*Seelenwissenschaft*), one can hope to elaborate, at best, a "historical natural doctrine of the inner sense" (*historische Naturlehre des inneren Sinnes*), a purely descriptive and classificatory discipline "that contains nothing but systematically ordered facts of natural things."[5]

In Kant's view, there are two main reasons why psychology can make only a limited claim to scientificity. The first lies in the fact that, time being *par excellence* the form of the inner sense, psychological phenomena have only one dimension, the law of continuity, so that mathematics cannot be applied to them. The second has to do with the problem of self-observation: since the subject is the only possible observer of phenomena of the inner sense, the psychological object is inexorably altered while being observed, so that inner observations can never be established precisely.

Founding the Science of the Mind: Herbart and the Idea of Scientific Psychology

Some decades after the publication of *Metaphysical Foundations of Natural Science,* Kant's skeptical views about the scientificity of psychology were

challenged by Johann Friedrich Herbart (1776–1841),[6] the German philosopher and psychologist who is rightly viewed as instrumental in the rise
of scientific psychology and the making of the new nineteenth-century
German psychological paradigm.[7]

Although Herbart did not propose any systematic refutation of Kant's
ideas, the conception of psychology that he advocated from the mid-1810s
onwards stands in striking contrast to the Kantian approach of psychological knowledge as a descriptive, classificatory, and non-mathematizable
field of investigation. Psychology, Herbart emphasized, is likely to become
an authentic science based on the model of physics, which obeys laws and
to which mathematics can be applied. As we see in the next section, he
regarded the mind (*Seele*) as a dynamic system of single representations
(*Vorstellungen*), elementary contents of consciousness that, in addition to
each having a definite quality, always manifest themselves with a given
magnitude or intensity. In Herbart's view, representations are basically
mental forces that, by interacting with each other in consciousness, result
in a great variety of quantitative relationships. According to this view,
mental life, far from being boiled down to its mere temporal dimension,
can be quantified in many different ways, which, in Herbart's view, paves
the way to the mathematization of the mind.[8] As Herbart highlighted, the
mind is characterized at all times by countless "states" and "activities,"
whose laws should be established on the basis of what he called the "statics"
and "mechanics of the spirit."[9]

Beyond the question of the mathematization of mental life, Herbart's
approach to psychology significantly departs from Kant's by calling into
question the dictate that mental life consists of undefined and vanishing
processes and cannot be satisfyingly subjected to observation. Herbart
innovatively maintains that psychological phenomena, although by nature
subjective, can be "objectivized": singled out from the rest of consciousness
and characterized on the basis of specific features, just like objects of the
physical world.[10] According to him, the psychologist's task is to reduce the
complexity and apparent indeterminacy of the manifestations of mental
life by referring them to definite kinds of representations and to their way
of interacting with each other.

It is important that for Herbart, psychological investigation is not about
the inner sense – the private self secluded from the manifestations of
perceptual experience – but rather about what he called "inner experience"
or "perception" (*die innere Erfahrung/Wahrnehmung*), which includes all
that we can immediately experience in ourselves. Herbart thus extended
the realm of psychology by aggregating to it experiential dimensions that
Kant regarded as specifically belonging to the outer sense. In Herbart's
view, psychology has to do with the totality of the facts of consciousness

considered in their immediate relation to the subject, that is, in their strictly phenomenological aspect.

Toward a New German Psychological Science

As a reformer of psychology, Herbart did not simply affirm the possibility of exploring the mind scientifically; he also laid the foundations of an authentic psychological research program. Together with physiologist Johannes Müller, he epitomized the deep renewal of psychological thought in the 1810s through the 1830s and the emergence of a radically new way of investigating psychological phenomena. Herbart's formalization of the concept of mental state and Müller's theory of specific sense energies can be regarded as the formative stages of a scientific paradigm that reached maturity in the 1860s and 1870s and that, *mutatis mutandis*, remained that of German psychology until the early twentieth century.[11]

Herbart and the Formalization of the Concept of Mental State

Before addressing Herbart's ideas about the ontology of psychical processes, it is worth saying a word about the basic tenets of his representation-based psychology. Representations (*Vorstellungen*) are, in his view, the ultimate constituents of the mind, the entities that ensure what he calls its "self-conservation."[12] They can be simple – in which case they are also called "sensations" (*Empfindungen*) – or complex, as soon as they combine with each other in the form of definite "series." Every single representation, Herbart emphasizes, is characterized by a specific quality (*Qualität*): an elementary and irreducible phenomenological property. According to this view, representations are qualitatively determined but quantitatively variable mental entities: at all times, they occur in consciousness with a given magnitude (*Stärke*) or intensity (*Intensität*). In other words, a single representation always has a given degree of consciousness, which can vary from null to some maximal value, depending on how it interacts with other representations. For Herbart, indeed, the activity of representations originates in their capacity to conflict with each other, that is, to strive to stay in consciousness and to expel the others from it, as a result of which they are more or less obscured or repressed. As he explains, when they are being totally repressed, representations are said to fall below the threshold of consciousness and to be converted into a latent state.

Beyond his speculations regarding the conflict of representations and the mathematization of conscious life, Herbart's psychology makes a crucial contribution to the question of the nature and ontological status of physical phenomena. The central issue of his above-mentioned ideas is that the constitutive elements of the mind are autonomous entities that can be identified with small consciousness *sui generis*.[13] More specifically, what Herbart called "representation" consists of two basic properties, namely, the act (*Act, Actus*), the fact of occurring at a given moment in consciousness, and the content (*Inhalt*), a particular qualitative determination. In other words, Herbart established a clear distinction between "the fact of representing" (*das Vorstellen*) – representation as it effectively exists – and "what is represented" (*das Vorgestellte*) – representation as it expresses a definite experiential reality. Although conceptually distinct, representational act and representational content are inextricably linked in consciousness: they are two complementary sides of one unique psychical entity. This "act/content dialectics" is what characterizes psychical processes and how they differ from the physical phenomena given in outer perception. In this respect, Herbart deserves credit for having formalized the concept of *mental state*, a notion that is crucial in cognitive psychology and the philosophy of mind.

The mind is, in Herbart's eyes, only a provisory arrangement of representations that compete at a given time for consciousness, these being for him the only entities of a mental nature that really exist.[14] Indeed, Herbart became famous for his devastating criticism of the psychology of faculties (*Vermögenspsychologie*): the view, still largely hegemonic in the early nineteenth century,[15] that the manifestations of mental life should be ascribed to broad categories of mental powers. For him, the so-called faculties are not substantial divisions of the mind, but simply collective terms under which a great variety of representational processes can be subsumed. According to the explanatory model he proposed, all psychological functions can be analyzed on the basis of the nature and interrelations of the elementary components that underline their appearance.

Relationships between Mental and Physical Revisited: Johannes Müller's Theory of Specific Sense Energies

In the 1820s and 1830s, while Herbart was discussing the foundations of psychology and formalizing the concept of mental state, Johannes Peter Müller (1801–1858) decisively contributed to reassessing the nature of the relationships among sensations, stimuli, and the nerves by expounding his so-called theory of the *specific sense energies*.[16]

Based on his own experimental studies and those of other contemporary physiologists, Müller advocated the view that the same kind of sensation (*Empfindung*) can be aroused by a variety of stimuli (*Reize*) and, conversely, that the same kind of stimulus can arouse very different sensations.[17] Thus, he emphasized, one must admit that there is no necessary connection between a definite stimulus and a given sensation, but only a possible relation of functional dependence between them. Stimuli are just external factors that indirectly arouse the appearance of sensations in consciousness by acting on definite nerve endings.[18] In Müller's view, sensory nerves make sensory data possible. By virtue of their constitutive "nervous principle," they determine both the mode of a sensation – its belonging to a broad category such as sight, sound, or taste – and its specific quality, such as being red, warm, or sour. Müller used the term "specific sense energy" (*specifische/eigenthümliche Sinnesenergie*) for the physical property of sensory nerves and their extensions that underlies both the effective appearance of sensations and their qualitative determination.[19]

In the wake of Herbart's seminal ideas, Müller's theory of specific sense energies represents a decisive step in the evolution of psychological ideas by shedding new light on the nature of the relationship between the mental and the physical. By maintaining that sensations, while caused by external stimuli, are ultimately determined by the activity of certain parts of the nervous system, Müller paved the way to a radical reformulation of the mind–body problem.

Psychology in the Context of Romanticism and *Naturphilosophie*

Romantic Philosophy and *Naturphilosophie*

Far more clearly than its more or less contemporary counterparts in Britain and France, German Romanticism was, from the beginning, a highly intellectualized movement that developed in close relation to academic life and was characterized by a marked inclination towards theorization and speculation.[20] In the German Romantics' eyes, metaphysical, ethical, religious, and anthropological concerns proved as important as literary, artistic, or aesthetic concerns. In this respect, it is customary to speak of Romantic philosophy (*romantische Philosophie*) when discussing the complex but relatively easily identifiable worldview of Nature, God, the soul, etc., endorsed by German-speaking Romantic authors and their followers.

A key stakeholder of Romantic philosophy, Friedrich Wilhelm Schelling (1775–1854) is also known for having fostered a cognate school of thought, *Naturphilosophie*, which would become very influential in Germany in the first half of the nineteenth century. Taking its name from Schelling's writings, *Naturphilosophie* is a speculative system of thought that advocates a pantheistic, panpsychical, and hylozoistic approach to Nature, based on the search for analogies and the interactions

between microcosm and macrocosm.[21] As Michael Heidelberger emphasizes, "instead of a 'soulless mechanism,' *Naturphilosophie* posits an
'ensouled organism' and tries to grasp and to explain the phenomena of
life and consciousness in their development and in their relation to the
inorganic world."[22] The basic tenets of *Naturphilosophie*, as well as its chief
representatives, are not essentially different from those of Romantic philosophy. The question of how much the two domains can be separated is
still a matter of debate.[23] For Robert J. Richards, "*Naturphilosophie* specifically focuses on the organic core of nature, its archetypal structure, and its
relationship to mind, while Romanticism added aesthetic and moral features to this conception of nature."[24]

Is There a Romantic Psychology?

Some scholars speak of "Romantic psychology" (*romantische
Psychologie*) to refer to psychological research as it developed within
the context of German Romanticism, which they view as an important
psychological current of the first half of the nineteenth century. Kurt
Röttgers, for example, tries to delineate the outlines of Romantic psychological thought and to show how it was elaborated as a definite field
of investigation at the crossing point of various disciplines.[25] Klaus
Sachs-Hombach identifies "romantic psychology," alongside "mechanical psychology," the approach launched by Herbart, as one of two
leading paradigms of early nineteenth-century German psychological
thought.[26] The place of psychological ideas and motifs in the German
Romantic literary tradition has been demonstrated, in particular by
Matthew Bell.[27]

In my view, the role played by the Romantics in the history of
psychology should not be overemphasized, and there are good reasons
to challenge the claim that there is a clearly recognizable Romantic
psychological paradigm. Romantic authors rarely addressed psychological issues systematically. Moreover, when considering the psychological concepts at stake in the Romantic tradition, it is sometimes hard
to see what might be specifically "Romantic" in them. Finally, the question of what the so-called Romantic psychology owes to non-Romantic
psychological traditions has not been satisfyingly clarified. It is true,
however, that a few representatives of German Romanticism published
writings specifically devoted to psychological issues. Röttgers identifies
three major theorists of so-called Romantic psychology: Friedrich
Schlegel, Carl August von Eschenmayer, and Gotthilf Heinrich von
Schubert.[28] Compared with contemporary "professional" aestheticians
such as Herbart or Friedrich Eduard Beneke, though, none of those
scholars made any decisive contribution to the understanding of mental

processes or the shaping of psychology into a discipline; their writings are of secondary importance in the history of psychology. By comparison, it is worth mentioning another author: Carl Gustav Carus, who was indisputably the most important theorist of psychology within the context of *Naturphilosophie* and, by extension, of Romanticism,[29] although his contribution to psychological thought cannot be reduced to this specific context.

Carl Gustav Carus and the Psychology of the Unconscious
Carl Gustav Carus (1789–1869) was one of the most complete polymaths of the nineteenth century. He made remarkable contributions to philosophy, psychology, anatomy, physiology, medicine, and geology, and was also a renowned painter and art theorist. While his artistic and aesthetic oeuvre clearly belongs to Romanticism, his philosophical and scientific writings have more directly to do with *Naturphilosophie*. Between 1831 and 1866, he published a number of psychological writings[30] that are closely related not only to *Naturphilosophie*, but also to anatomical and physiological concerns. As a psychologist, Carus established himself as the most famous theorist of the unconscious of his time.[31]

For Carus, psychology basically consists of the study of vital processes: how the organism emerges, develops, and remains stable through the manifestation of an abstract idea (*Idee*). By identifying the soul (*Seele*) with life (*Leben*), Carus appears to be a typical representative of *Naturphilosophie*: he advocated a vitalistic, pantheistic, and hylozoistic worldview, according to which the "idea," as it manifests itself at the individual organic level, is an emanation of God and thereby is in correspondence with the rest of the world, which is itself something alive and animated. He referred to the unconscious (*das Unbewusste*) as the "vital force" (*Lebenskraft*) or the "formative impulse" (*Bildungstrieb*) that the soul partakes of, so that in his view, the whole organism should be regarded as the expression of an unconscious psyche. As defined by Carus, the unconscious is a basic organic activity that underpins the appearance not only of psychical phenomena strictly speaking, but also of instinctive behaviors and vegetative life. In this respect, he distinguished between an "absolute unconscious" that ensures the implementation of physiological functions and a "relative unconscious" that pertains to mental life and interacts with consciousness. Moreover, Carus emphasized, the unconscious can be either "Promethean" (*prometheisch*) or "Epimethean" (*epimetheisch*), depending whether it is endowed with an anticipative or a retentive power. In his model, consciousness is a secondary mental phenomenon that results from the making and the storage of representations (*Vorstellungen*) correlatively with the importance of the nervous system and the development of memory. Carus identified three conscious stages: consciouslessness (*Bewusstlosigkeit*), world-consciousness (*Weltbewusstsein*), and self-consciousness (*Selbstbewusstsein*), which are also found in the scale of beings. What Carus called the relative unconscious corresponds to all representations that are stored at a given moment in a latent state and constitute, in this respect, a condition of the possibility of consciousness.

Psychological Issues in German Romantic Literature: An Overview in Context

Psychological topics and motifs of German literary Romanticism do not tend to reflect the new German "scientific" psychology that emerged in the 1810s–1830s. Only in the second half of the nineteenth century did the new psychology begin to make a significant impact on other disciplines, including aesthetics.[32] It is Romantic psychology, because of its close intellectual and institutional relation to the literary milieu, that may have inspired contemporary writers.[33] Leaving aside the question of how concepts circulated between psychological science and literature in the early nineteenth century, I would like to highlight the commonalities that existed between the two domains by identifying the chief psychological topics at stake in the literary works of that period and showing how they echo contemporary psychological research.

Affectivity

"Affectivity" is a convenient word to refer to emotion-like conscious phenomena, which are also said to be "affective states" or "processes." Here we are dealing with a notion that was famously at the core of Romantic literature and, more generally speaking, art and aesthetics. The centrality of affectivity in Romanticism is too well-known to deserve further comment.[34] The fact is that, in the late eighteenth and early nineteenth centuries, affectivity became a major subject of interest in Germany at the crossing point of psychology, art, aesthetics, philosophy, and theology.[35]

From Kant to Herbart, affective processes were gradually characterized from the psychological point of view and identified as a definite category of mental states.[36] During that period, German psychologists fixed the specific terminology related to the broad categories of affective life and formalized the corresponding psychological concepts – an affective typology that is found, *mutatis mutandis*, in contemporary literary texts. Let us briefly review the German language of affectivity as it established itself at the turn of the nineteenth century. *Fühlen* (affectivity) referred to the affective function in general.[37] It was usually taken as a synonym of the common and hardly translatable word *Gemüt*, which Eisler, in his *Dictionary of Philosophical Concepts*, defines as "the unit of the affective dispositions, the ability to be aroused in an affective way[,] the feeling mind in contrast to intelligence, to the thinking consciousness."[38] The most widespread and central term of the then emerging German affective psychology is *Gefühl* (feeling), which refers to the constitutive element of affective life.[39] From the early nineteenth century onwards, German psychologists carefully distinguished *Gefühle* from: (1) *Empfindungen* (sensations), the sensory data that take part in the making of representations (*Vorstellungen*) and that have, *per se*, nothing to do with affectivity;[40] and (2) *Affekte*, a term best translated as "emotions"[41] which referred to the strong and sudden manifestation of *Gefühle* in consciousness along with the manifestation of organic sensations and specific expressive movements.[42] Finally, it is worth mentioning *Stimmung*, a word usually translated as "mood" that referred to the kind of experience in which feelings manifest themselves "atmospherically," as something vague and diffuse.[43]

An important idea related to affectivity that emerged at the time of Romanticism was *Einfühlung* (empathy): the subject's capacity to project him- or herself onto the perceived objects of the external world and to "live" in them.[44] As Andrea Pinotti demonstrates,[45] the expressions *hineinfühlen* and *sich hineinfühlen* – literally, "feeling into" and "feeling oneself into," in other words, empathizing – were coined in the late eighteenth century by proto-Romantic and Romantic authors such as Herder, Novalis, and Wackenroder to refer to the ego's affective participation in Nature and the understanding of others. The topic of empathic experience is a well-known aspect of the Romantic *Weltanschauung*, found in literary motifs such as the ensoulment and animation of Nature[46] and the *Doppelgänger*.[47]

The Dream

The place of the dream (*Traum*) in German Romantic literature was famously studied by Albert Béguin in his pioneering essay "L'Âme romantique et le rêve" [The Romantic Soul and the Dream],[48] first published in 1937. Béguin reviews the topic of dreams in the chief representatives of literary Romanticism by insisting on the centrality of the concept in literary theory and practice, while proposing interesting developments in the role played for some authors by the analysis of one's own dreams. It is commonly accepted that, regarding the psychology of dreams, Romantic writers' main source of inspiration was the *Naturphilosoph* Gotthilf

Heinrich (von) Schubert, who published his best-selling *Die Symbolik des Traumes* (The Symbolism of the Dream)[49] in 1814. Schubert regarded dreams as the activity of the mind carrying universally understandable symbols, as the expression of a poetic language that is likely to put human beings in relation to the cosmos. Dreams were an important topic in Romantic psychology, as exemplified by Carus, who referred to them as "the imprisonment of consciousness in the unconscious."[50]

Dreams were also investigated within the framework of the new German "scientific" psychology. In the second volume of his *Psychology as a Science*,[51] Herbart devotes a number of pages to this topic, which he strives to explain on the basis of his "mechanics of the spirit." In 1826, Johannes Müller published a booklet entitled *Über die phantastischen Gesichterscheinungen* (On Fantastical Visual Phenomena), in which he deals with "subjective visual phenomena": images that occur in consciousness without any external stimulation.[52] Among other types, Müller discusses oneiric images (*Traumbilder*), which he strives to describe from his own experiences and to explain in light of his theory of specific sense energies.

The Unconscious

The unconscious (*das Unbewusste*), which is closely related to the topics of the dream and insanity that are at issue here, is a psychological notion that directly echoes Romantic writers' taste for irrationality, the power of imagination, and human beings' relationship with Nature and the cosmos.[53] The unconscious is regarded, rightly, as a core concern of *Naturphilosophie*, from which it is often wrongly thought to originate.[54] Carus was the chief theorist of the unconscious within the context of Romantic psychology. Despite his fame, his influence on Romantic writers may have been limited, because his first psychological publications date back only to 1831.[55]

In any case, it would be mistaken to believe that the unconscious was the privilege of Romantic psychologists, as it turns out that it was also an important topic for the emerging paradigm of the "new" German psychology.[56] Herbart's seminal ideas on the threshold of consciousness, the degree of consciousness, the darkening and repression of representations, etc., should be regarded as the starting point of the scientific-psychological research program regarding the unconscious that developed in German-speaking countries until the early twentieth century.[57]

Insanity

Another central aspect of German Romantic literature and aesthetics that is directly linked to psychology is insanity. The literary fascination with insanity is epitomized by E. T. A. Hoffmann, who masterfully took up the then widespread psychopathological topics of hallucination, possession, split personality, etc., in some of his most famous tales, such as *The Sandman* and *The Golden Pot*.[58] But he was far from the only author preoccupied with psychological-literary motifs.[59]

It is common knowledge that, at the turn of the eighteenth century, psychiatry established itself as an autonomous discipline and practice, with new social and institutional recognition, in close relation to anatomy, physiology, and psychology.[60]

Historians have insisted on the centrality of Johann Christian Reil (1759– 1813) as a link between the emerging field of psychiatry and the Romantic cultural milieu.[61] Reil was an acclaimed scholar who, in addition to having been a pioneer of psychiatry and psychotherapy, was a distinguished physiologist and anatomist. In 1803, he published his highly influential *Rhapsodien über die Anwendung der psychischen Curmethode auf Geisteszerrüttungen* (Rhapsodies on Applying the Psychological Method of Treatment to Mental Breakdowns),[62] in which he interprets psychiatric disorders in psychological terms as a disturbance of the balance between mental forces in their interactions with the nervous system, while proposing innovative curative methods for the insane. Not only was Reil avidly read by Romantic writers, but he also became an active member of the Romantic community,[63] thus greatly contributing to implanting psychiatric ideas in German literary Romanticism.

Psychological Motifs in Müller's *Die Winterreise*: An Attempt at an Interpretation

By way of conclusion, I will briefly comment on the place of psychology in Wilhelm Müller's *Die Winterreise*. Here my intention is not to systematically interpret the text in light of the four above-discussed psychological topics, but simply to identify recurrent psychological or psychological-like motifs and, when possible, to show how they may make sense when placed within their scientific context. This is clearly not an easy task, because Müller's poetic language in *Die Winterreise* appears to be much less imbued with explicit psychological concerns than the verse of most German Romantic poets. His references to psychology are most often conventional and general, and thus hardly conducive to contextual interpretations.

Die Winterreise paradoxically tells us relatively little about affectivity-related issues. The affective nouns and adjectives Müller uses, such as *Liebe* (love), *Leid* (pain), *Hoffnung* (hope), *Verlangen* (craving), *trüb* (gloomy), *heiter* (serene), *matt* (dull), and *still* (quiet), belong to the traditional lyrical/elegiac register. Neither the psychological vocabulary nor the way in which Müller uses it is appreciably original. Though the verb *fühlen* (to feel) appears four times, the noun *Gefühl* (feeling), which is emblematic of the German Romantic poetic lexicon, is not mentioned once in the whole cycle. Beyond these terminological concerns, it is worth noting the emotional atmosphere that runs through the work and that fluctuates between melancholy and despair – but, here too, the psychological hints are so meager that there is not much to say regarding its contextual significance.

As a recurrent psychological motif of *Die Winterreise*, the dream is expressed most explicitly. In the cycle, the nouns *Traum* and *Träumer* are encountered five times and once respectively, while the verb *träumen* appears five times. The dream is, as the name indicates, the main topic of "Frühlingstraum" and is an important issue in at least three other poems ("Gute Nacht," "Der Lindenbaum," and "Im Dorfe"). It is taken either as a positive psychological experience, associated with reverie, or as a negative one, related to disillusionment and loneliness. Nevertheless, this topic is only superficially characterized from the psychological point of view and hardly reflects the scientific context of the time.

Insanity is the third major psychological motif present in *Die Winterreise* and the only one more or less suitable for a context-based analysis. This notion is at the heart of "Täuschung," "Das Irrlicht," "Die Nebensonnen," "Mut!," and "Der Leiermann," and more or less explicitly surfaces in "Der greise Kopf," "Die Krähe," "Im Dorfe," "Der Wegweiser," and "Frühlingstraum." Müller explicitly refers to insanity through expressions such as *"Welch ein törichtes Verlangen"* (what a foolish craving) and *"Klagen ist für Toren"* (complaining is for fools). More specifically, as developed through the cycle, the motif of insanity has to do with persecution, estrangement, seclusion, and, first and foremost, personality split and hallucination – two psychological issues that, especially in "Täuschung" and "Die Nebensonnen," are closely related. While keeping in mind that Müller's poetic choices have to do with rhetoric and Romantic topoi, especially that of the *Doppelgänger*, awareness of the contemporary psychological investigations discussed above helps put them into context.

SECTION 2: EXPLORATIONS OF HUMAN BEHAVIOR OUTSIDE THE ACADEMIC SPHERE

Popular Fiction and Poetry

In the eighteenth and nineteenth centuries, the novel became a central literary genre. By emphasizing characters' actions and motivations, novels highlight individual subjectivity and decision-making. Many authors used that emphasis to explore the lives of people very different from the idealized rational being imagined by moral philosophers whose decisions are governed by logic. Fictional and semi-fictional genres often featured characters such as criminals, pirates, the poor, and the uneducated, showing a keen interest in how various types of people behave and the mix of emotional impulses, rules, and beliefs that influence their choices. A few examples will illustrate these factors.

Daniel Defoe's novels about criminals, such as *Moll Flanders* (1722), came shortly before John Gay's libretto for *The Beggar's Opera* (1728), whose tale of corruption in the London slums skewered Italian operatic conventions. Pirate narratives – often presented as memoirs so as to seem as authentic as possible – combined sensationalism and horror with critiques of respectable society, often exposed as cruel and unjust by comparison with pirate customs.

Another strand of emotional exploration took place in French and English sentimental novels. Antoine-François Prévost's *Manon Lescaut* (1731) traces the experiences of a young man whose entanglement with a beautiful courtesan shatters his life. This novella inspired operas by Massenet and Puccini. Samuel Richardson's *Pamela; or, Virtue Rewarded* (1740) is a quintessential example of sentimentality. In letters to her parents, the housemaid Pamela breathlessly recounts her master's ongoing campaign to seduce her. Her naïve resistance eventually pays off when he proposes marriage. A related book presenting a woman's experiences through letters was *The History of Lady Sophia Sternheim* (1771) by German author Sophie von LaRoche, whose title character, though of a higher social class than Pamela, endures similar trials. Both women learn that their expectation that most people strive to be good does not match the petty selfish reality that surrounds them.

Three extremely popular authors in eighteenth-century Germany were Benedikte Naubert, Carl Gottlob Cramer, and Christian Heinrich Spiess. Naubert, a pioneer of historical novels that often featured women, such as *The Story of Countess Thekla von Thurn* (1788), made evident the importance of education for women as well as men. Cramer criticized German court life in *The Life and Opinions of Erasmus Schleicher* (1789 and 1791). Spiess was noted for horror stories set in medieval times, but particularly relevant here are his *Biographies of Suicides* (1785) and *Biographies of the Insane* (1796), collections of stories he claimed were based on real cases. In a typical biography, he describes the central character's early life and then explains what led him or her to commit suicide or go crazy. He usually emphasizes the injustice and extremity of circumstances: factors such as economic hardship, injustice, and social discrimination against illegitimate children are usually more to blame than a subject's innate character. Love relationships opposed by parents frequently play a role, prefiguring *Die Winterreise*. As in pirate narratives, drama and sensation are used to point out the inequity of established institutions such as the Church and the class system. Most of Spiess's characters are basically good people whose unusual behavior is shown to result from their extreme situations. Müller's protagonist could be viewed in this light, with his descent into isolation and possible madness a natural result of cruel circumstances.

Some decades later, English sensation novels – such as *The Woman in White* by Wilkie Collins (1860), Ellen Wood's *East Lynne* (1861), and Mary Braddon's *Lady Audley's Secret* (1862) – returned to the intensity and melodrama of these eighteenth-century stories. Some of these novels addressed mental illness, both real and pretended, as it was a common plot device for characters to suppress inconvenient family members by sending them to insane asylums.

Romantic lyric poetry explores subjectivity differently from prose. Instead of decision-making, poetic texts emphasize emotional response, frequently using metaphor to describe it. Descriptive language about nature can accentuate a character's inner state, as in Joseph von Eichendorff's poem "In der Fremde," which Schumann set as the first song in his *Liederkreis* Op. 39. The poem begins: "Aus der Heimat hinter den Blitzen rot / Da kommen die Wolken her, / Aber Vater und Mutter sind lange tot, / Es kennt mich dort keiner mehr."[64] (From my homeland behind the red lightning flashes / The clouds are approaching. / But Father and Mother are long dead, / No one there knows me now.) While this passage might seem mostly descriptive, it can be read psychologically. Threatening weather coming from the place where one grew up symbolizes loneliness and alienation from the past. Like weather, our emotions and the irrational parts of our consciousness are beyond our control.

Heinrich Heine was another master of metaphor who implies a great deal in few words, as in these last three stanzas of his introductory poem (1839) to the reprint of his *Buch der Lieder*, from which both Schubert and Schumann selected poetry. In the earlier stanzas, the poet enters a *Märchenwald* (fairy-tale wood) where the nightingale sings. He encounters a sphinx and kisses her human face; she returns his kiss, while tearing him with her lioness claws.

Entzückende Marter und wonniges Weh!	Rapturous martyrdom and wondrous woe!
Der Schmerz wie die Lust unermesslich!	The pain, like the pleasure, immeasurable!

Derweilen des Mundes Kuss mich beglückt,	Even as the mouth's kiss delights me,
Verwunden die Tatzen mich grässlich.	The claws wound me horribly.
Die Nachtigall sang: "O schöne Sphinx!	The nightingale sang: "O beautiful sphinx!
O Liebe! Was soll es bedeuten,	O love! What can it mean
Dass du vermischest mit Todesqual	That you mix with deathly torment
All deine Seligkeiten?	All your blissfulness?
O schöne Sphinx! O löse mir	O beautiful sphinx! O solve for me
Das Rätsel, das wunderbare!	This riddle so mysterious!
Ich hab darüber nachgedacht	I have meditated on it already
Schon manche tausend Jahre."	For many thousand years."

The sphinx's duality symbolizes the idea, traceable to Petrarch in the fourteenth century, that love generates diametrically opposed experiences. Heine leaves it to the nightingale to reflect on love's mysteries. He then remarks that "I could have said all of this very well in good prose,"[65] but his ironic comment only accentuates how differently prose and poetry explored the irrational aspects of human experience.

Animal Magnetism for Amateurs

Dr. Franz Anton Mesmer (1734–1815) began his work in Vienna in the 1760s and achieved fame when he moved to Paris in 1778. He argued that there was a "magnetic" fluid permeating all things, and that illness arose from imbalance in this fluid. Healers could direct the fluid in their patients' bodies, using magnets or hand motions to provoke violent healing "crises." Mesmer's ideas were challenged by the scientists of his time, but also attained some respectability, with a professor specializing in animal magnetism appointed at the University of Berlin in 1817.[66] Matthew Bell in particular convincingly analyzes the importance of animal magnetism in the writings of Hoffmann and Heinrich von Kleist.[67]

Mesmer's approach to healing is now viewed by historians of science as a forerunner of psychiatry. The ailments that he and his followers cured – cramps, convulsions, paralysis of limbs, and so on – were usually more psychological than physiological. Patients developed strong bonds with their magnetizers, whose touch and gaze were part of the therapy.

Mesmer's students and followers (usually not medically trained) moved animal magnetism in a new direction. The Marquis de Puységur developed the technique so that it could lead patients into a trance state. Known as "clairvoyants," these patients showed remarkable abilities and were able to prescribe treatment for themselves and others while in "magnetic sleep."[68] Most magnetizers were male and worked mostly with female patients, adding a suppressed erotic element to the therapy that was not fully recognized.

Animal magnetism was forbidden in Austria, but amateur magnetizers from elite society practiced nonetheless. One such person was Friedrich Schlegel (1772–1829), formerly a central figure of the early German Romantic movement in the 1790s. By 1820, he had become a religious mystic and embraced conservative politics, moving to Vienna to work for Metternich's government. Schlegel's most prominent patient, the Polish countess Franziska Lesniowska, had a vision while in magnetic sleep and sent Schlegel to find a new magnetic therapist: the painter Ludwig Schnorr von Carolsfeld (1789–1853). Recruited through the countess's dream, Schnorr discovered that he indeed had a great ability to put patients into a trance. He began an extensive magnetic practice, working closely with Schlegel for the next several years.

As Schnorr was a peripheral member of the Schubert circle, Schubert had various connections to magnetic treatment. Marie Schmith, a young woman in her late teens whom Schnorr treated in 1822 and 1823, was a younger cousin of his friends the Spauns. Her deep psychological problems led her to desire Schnorr sexually, and she punished herself by prescribing the treatment of being burned with hot coals. Schubert probably heard about this case, which Joseph von Spaun briefly described in his family's chronicle, saying that she "caused a great sensation" in Vienna.[69]

Two members of the Esterházy family, likely the same branch of the family whose daughters Schubert taught piano, consulted with Marie Schiessel, one of Schnorr's clairvoyant patients, in 1824.[70] On March 24, 1825, Schnorr invited Schubert to attend a treatment session for Louise Mora, playing his music to help her go into a trance. Schubert then instructed her not to awake while Schnorr took notes on how different types of music affected her, mentioning that some sounds "caused the most marvelous motions and contortions of her body."[71]

While a specific connection to *Winterreise* is not obvious here, Schubert's direct encounter with this type of psychological therapy and mysterious connections between music, emotions, and physicality informed his understanding of human experience. His experience with

Louise Mora may have influenced his later settings of songs about passionate women, including "Die junge Nonne" (D828), "Delphine" (D857
No. 2), and "Heimliches Lieben" (D922).[72]

The Transparent Chest

Spiess's biographies have a broad relevance to our topic, as evidence of the
growing interest in abnormal behavior and psychology. Beyond that, one
of them has a particular link to *Winterreise*. "Der gläserne Ökonom" (The
Glazed/Transparent Estate Manager) tells the tale of a young man who is
managing his family property and falls in love with the housekeeper,
a young woman considered a totally inappropriate match for him. He
confides his love only to one close friend, so he cannot comprehend how it
can be that several people at a family wedding the next day warn him
sternly against such a misalliance. He abruptly leaves the party after
drinking too much, and in the bitter winter landscape he has a vision of
his mother's ghost, who tells him that his chest is now transparent. He flees
society and hides miles away. When found a few days later under
a haystack, he refuses to remove his hands from his chest. "At Cousin
Michael's wedding, my chest became a lantern! . . . It is horrible when
everyone can look into my heart and instantly discover my most secret
thoughts."[73] Although eventually able to function effectively in his previous managerial role, he is never fully cured of this delusion.

Alexander Košenina traces the image of the *gläserne Brust* (glazed
chest) as far back as a story by Cervantes, and he discusses the Spiess
version in some detail,[74] but the link to Müller's *Die Winterreise* has not
been recognized before. Müller may well have encountered this image in
Spiess's story, as his generation was captivated by that type of popular
literature, though it is not impossible that he read Cervantes' novella *The
Lawyer of Glass* (*El Licenciado Vidriera*). Details in Spiess that correspond to Müller's presentation of the story include the reference to
a wedding, the winter season, and the fact that Spiess's protagonist
believes that the "glass" that reveals his heart is soft at first, then hardens
and freezes. The *Winterreise* character, who leaves his beloved prior to
her marriage to another man, frequently reflects on the transformations
of ice to water and vice versa. His tears, the river, and even his heart
freeze, but he imagines how they will melt when spring comes. In
"Erstarrung," Müller writes: "Mein Herz ist wie erfroren, / Kalt starrt
ihr Bild darin; / Schmilzt je das Herz mir wieder, / Fliesst auch ihr Bild
dahin!" (My heart is as if frozen, / Her image frozen cold within; / If my
heart ever thaws again, / Her image will melt away, too!) (Schubert

changed the word "erfroren" to "erstorben" [dead].) Without explicitly stating it, Müller's language strongly suggests that the wanderer's chest is transparent, making it possible to see his heart and the image of his beloved.

Psychological Elements in *Die Winterreise*

As David Romand points out, Müller does not use the academic psychological terms of his time period. Despite this, his poetic cycle *Die Winterreise*, particularly in Schubert's setting, has inspired a great deal of commentary and interpretation grounded in the idea that it engages with psychological issues. For example, many scholars and performers have grappled with the question of whether the protagonist's decision to join forces with the hurdy-gurdy man is a sign that he is crossing over to insanity. Many other chapters in this volume provide further examples of psychological interpretations of the cycle.

One way to understand this discrepancy is to assume that Müller, while not conversant with the work of Herbart, Carus, and others of that ilk, had encountered the popular-culture materials described in the last few sections. He likely knew the writings of Naubert, Cramer, and Spiess, and perhaps also English novels by Richardson and his contemporaries. (In Chapter 4, Kristina Muxfeldt discusses Müller's interest in Byron, confirming his awareness of English literature.) He also likely knew something of the contemporary practice of animal magnetism, even if he did not have Schubert's bizarre direct encounter with it.

As Müller imagined the wanderer's experiences and crafted poetry describing his character's thoughts and emotions, he often employed figures of speech and metaphors rather than direct descriptions. We can trace some of these in poems 1 and 2. In stanza 6 of "Gute Nacht," the wanderer observes that "Love loves to wander – / God made it that way." By personifying Love, he somewhat neutralizes the anger and blame that he likely feels toward his beloved. In poem 2, as he leaves her home, he looks up at the weathervane on the house, comparing her fickleness with the way it moves and changes direction in the wind. This simple everyday object takes on deeper meaning. Eichendorff's thunderclouds symbolize a character's alienation and separation from home, Heine's sphinx the entanglement of pleasure and pain in intense love. Similarly, Müller's weathervane represents infidelity, and his frozen river becomes a symbol of repressed emotions. The traveler imagines a graveyard to be an inn without a room for him; this reflects his wish for death. In these and similar examples, Müller engages with psychological topics through symbolic language.

As a handbook, this volume offers an overview of many aspects of *Winterreise* and its context. The context includes both the newly developing academic perspective on psychology exemplified by thinkers such as Herbart, Johannes Müller, and Carus, and the popular perspective reflected in literature and the odd subculture of amateur animal magnetism. Any intellectual in that time period might have encountered any or all of this material – but given his background and profession, Wilhelm Müller was more likely to know of the literary approach exemplified by pirate narratives, letter novels, and similar writings. In particular, the work of Spiess exploring how and why certain people were driven by circumstance to insanity or suicide seems to provide a direct precursor to Müller's two poetic cycles set by Schubert – suicide in *Die schöne Müllerin* and possible insanity in *Die Winterreise*. Müller's reuse of the "gläserne Brust" metaphor found in Spiess's *Biographies of the Insane* strengthens this presumption.

Notes

1. Johann Friedrich Herbart, *Psychologie als Wissenschaft, neu gegründet auf Erfahrung, Metaphysik und Mathematik*, 2 vols. (Königsberg: Unzer, 1824–25).
2. Fernando Vidal, *The Sciences of the Soul: The Early Modern Origins of Psychology*, trans. Saskia Brown (Chicago: University of Chicago Press, 2012).
3. David Romand, "La théorie herbartienne de la représentation *(Vorstellung)*: une dialectique de l'acte et du contenu," *Studia Philosophica* 75 (2016): 175–88.
4. Immanuel Kant, "Metaphysische Anfangsgründe der Naturwissenschaft," *Kants Werke, Akademie Textausgabe* (Berlin: De Gruyter, 1968), 467–71.
5. Ibid., 468.
6. Johann Friedrich Herbart, *Über die Möglichkeit und die Nothwendigkeit, die Mathematik auf die Psychologie aufzuwenden* (Königsberg: Bornträger, 1822).
7. Romand, "La théorie herbartienne."
8. Herbart, *Über die Möglichkeit.*
9. Herbart, *Psychologie als Wissenschaft*, vol. 1, 327–514.
10. Romand, "La théorie herbartienne."
11. David Romand, "Johannes Müller (1801–1858) et la théorie des énergies sensorielles spécifiques," in Céline Cherici and Jean-Claude Dupont (eds.), *Les Querelles du cerveau. Comment furent inventées les neurosciences* (Paris: Vuibert, 2008), 255–69; Romand, "La théorie herbartienne."
12. Romand, "La théorie herbartienne."
13. Ibid.
14. Ibid.
15. Klaus Sachs-Hombach, *Philosophische Psychologie im 19. Jahrhundert: Entstehung und Problemgeschichte* (Freiburg and Munich: Alber, 1993), 78–80.
16. Johannes Peter Müller, *Handbuch der Physiologie des Menschen für Vorlesungen*, 2 vols. (Coblenz: Hölscher, 1834). See also Romand, "Johannes Müller (1801–1858)."
17. Ibid.
18. Ibid.
19. Ibid.
20. Georges Gusdorf, *Le Savoir romantique de la nature* (Paris: Payot, 1985); Robert J. Richards, *The Romantic Conception of Life: Science and Philosophy in the Age of Goethe* (Chicago and London: University of Chicago Press, 2002).

21. Ibid.
22. Michael Heidelberger, *Die innere Seite der Natur. Gustav Theodor Fechners wissenschaftlich-philosophische Weltauffasung* (Frankfurt am Main: Klostermann, 1993), 34.
23. Richards, *The Romantic Conception of Life*, 1–14.
24. Ibid., 516.
25. Kurt Röttgers, "Romantische Psychologie," *Psychologie und Geschichte* 3 (1991): 24–64.
26. Sachs-Hombach, *Philosophische Psychologie.*
27. Matthew Bell, *The German Tradition of Psychology in Literature and Thought, 1700–1840* (Cambridge: Cambridge University Press, 2005).
28. Röttgers, "Romantische Psychologie."
29. Sachs-Hombach, *Philosophische Psychologie.*
30. Carl Gustav Carus, *Vorlesungen über Psychologie, gehalten im Winter 1829/30 zu Dresden* (Leipzig: Fleischer, 1831); Carl Gustav Carus, *Psyche. Zur Entwicklungsgeschichte der Seele* (Leipzig: Kröner, 1846).
31. Albert Béguin, *L'Âme romantique et le rêve. Essai sur le romantisme allemand et la poésie française* (Paris: José Corti, 1960), 123–44; Bell, *The German Tradition*, 212–21.
32. David Romand, "Nahlowsky's Psychological Aesthetics," *British Journal of Aesthetics* 58/1 (2018): 17–36.
33. Gusdorf, *Le Savoir romantique*; Richards, *The Romantic Conception of Life*, 17–203; Bell, *The German Tradition*, 54–207.
34. Georges Gusdorf, *L'Homme romantique* (Paris: Payot, 1984), 88–126; Joel Faflak and Richard C. Sha (eds.), *Romanticism and the Emotions* (Cambridge: Cambridge University Press, 2016).
35. David Romand, "Külpe's Affective Psychology (1887–1910). The Making of a Science of Feeling," *Ricerche Filosofiche* 27/2 (2017): 177–204.
36. Ibid.
37. Ibid.
38. Rudolf Eisler, "Gemüt," in Rudolf Eisler (ed.), *Wörterbuch der philosophischen Begriffe, historisch-quellenmässig bearbeitet*, vol. 1, A–K (Berlin: Mittler, 1910), 414.
39. Romand, "Külpe's Affective Psychology."
40. Ibid.
41. Ibid.
42. Ibid.
43. Rudolf Eisler, "Stimmung," in Eisler (ed.), *Wörterbuch*, vol. 3, SCI–Z, 1429–30.
44. Andrea Pinotti, *Empatia, Storia di un'idea da Platone al postumano* (Rome and Bari: Laterza, 2011).
45. Ibid., 34–35.
46. Keren Gorodeisky, "Nineteenth Century Romantic Aesthetics," in Edward N. Zalta (ed.), *The Stanford Encyclopedia of Philosophy* (Fall 2016 edition).
47. Andrew J. Webber, *The Doppelgänger: Double Visions in German Literature* (Oxford and New York: Clarendon, 1996).
48. Béguin, *L'Âme romantique et le rêve.*
49. Gotthilf Heinrich Schubert, *Die Symbolik des Traumes* (Bamberg: Kunz, 1814).
50. Carus, *Psyche*, 238.
51. Herbart, *Psychologie als Wissenschaft*, vol. 2, 488–514.
52. Johannes Peter Müller, *Über die phantastischen Gesichterscheinungen, Eine physiologische Untersuchung mit einer physiologischen Urkunde des Aristoteles über den Traum, den Philosophen und Aerzten gewidmet* (Coblenz: Hölscher, 1826).
53. Bell, *The German Tradition*, 167–207; Jürgen Barkhoff, "Romantic Science and Psychology," in Nicholas Saul (ed.), *The Cambridge Companion to German Romanticism* (Cambridge: Cambridge University Press, 2009), 209–26.
54. David Romand, "Fechner as a Pioneering Theorist of Unconscious Cognition," *Consciousness and Cognition* 21/1 (March 2012): 562–72.
55. Carus, *Vorlesungen.*
56. Romand, "Fechner as a Pioneering Theorist."
57. Ibid.
58. Bell, *The German Tradition*, 193–207.

59. Kathrin Geltinger, *Der Sinn im Wahn: "Ver-rücktheit" in Romantik und Naturalismus* (Marburg: Tectum Verlag, 2008), 37–69.
60. Edward Shorter, *A History of Psychiatry: From the Era of the Asylum to the Age of Prozac* (New York: Wiley, 1997).
61. Richards, *The Romantic Conception of Life*, 252–88.
62. Johann Christian Reil, *Rhapsodieen über die Anwendung der psychischen Curmethode auf Geisteszerrüttungen* (Halle: Curtschen Buchhandlung, 1803).
63. Richards, *The Romantic Conception of Life,* 273–78.
64. Joseph von Eichendorff, *Werke*, ed. Wolfdietrich Rasch (Munich: Carl Hanser Verlag, [1959]), 233.
65. Heinrich Heine, *Werke*, vol. 1 (Cologne and Berlin: Kiepenheuer & Witsch, [1962]), 9–10.
66. Bell, *The German Tradition*, 176.
67. Ibid., 180–207. See also Barkhoff, "Romantic Science and Psychology," 216–18.
68. On Puységur and others who continued magnetism in France and Germany, see Henri F. Ellenberger, *The Discovery of the Unconscious: The History and Evolution of Dynamic Psychiatry* (New York: Basic Books, 1970), 70–83, and Hans Peter Treichler, *Die magnetische Zeit: Alltag und Lebensgefühl im frühen 19. Jahrhundert* (Zurich: Schweizer Verlagshaus, 1988).
69. Otto Erich Deutsch, "Dr. Med. Anton Schmith – ein vergessener Freund Mozarts," *Mozart Jahrbuch* 11 (1960/61): 22–28.
70. Lisa Feurzeig, "Heroines in Perversity: Marie Schmith, Animal Magnetism, and the Schubert Circle," *19th-Century Music* 21/2 (Autumn 1997): 230–31.
71. Harry Goldschmidt, "Schubert und kein Ende," *Beiträge zur Musikwissenschaft* 25 (1983): 291–92.
72. Feurzeig, "Heroines in Perversity," 241–43.
73. Christian Heinrich Spieß, "Der gläserne Ökonom," in Wolfgang Promies (ed.), *Biographien der Wahnsinnigen* (Neuwied: Luchterhand, 1966), 52.
74. Alexander Košenina, "Gläserne Brust, lesbares Herz: ein psychopathographischer Topos im Zeichen physiognomischer Tyrannei bei C. H. Spiess und Anderen," *German Life and Letters* 52/2 (April 1999), 151–65.

7 Nature and Science in *Winterreise*

BLAKE HOWE

A solitary wanderer journeys through a strange, desolate landscape, bracing himself against the harsh weather. He repeatedly interrupts his travels to observe and reflect upon the natural world around him: striking landscapes, flora and fauna, and mysterious, seemingly magical atmospheric phenomena. This wanderer, of course, is the unnamed speaker in Wilhelm Müller and Franz Schubert's *Winterreise* – but his fictional travels mirror in interesting ways the real-life adventures of some early nineteenth-century scientific explorers and naturalists.

In 1799, the brilliant and daring German scientist Alexander von Humboldt (1769–1859) embarked on a multiyear journey through the Americas, where he crossed dangerous mountainsides, endured swarms of mosquitos, and observed stunning meteor showers. The impetus for such a precarious journey was Humboldt's insatiable curiosity. He collected thousands of plant specimens, recorded detailed meteorological data, and maintained a personal diary that formed the basis of a wildly popular travelogue: *Voyage aux régions équinoxiales du nouveau continent* (1814–25). (A German edition first began to appear in 1815 – the same year a young Wilhelm Müller noted in his diary that "the cosmopolitan Alex. v. Humbold" was a topic of conversation in Berlin.)[1] Around this time, the geologist Christian Leopold von Buch (1774–1853) traveled throughout Silesia, Italy, and Scandinavia, sometimes on foot, in order to collect minerals and rocks, study volcanic formations, and record his observations. He would later publish several influential books about his travels, including *Geognostische Beobachtungen auf Reisen durch Deutschland und Italien* (1802–9) and *Reise durch Norwegen und Lappland* (1810). This was also the era of John James Audubon (1785–1851), who spent most his twenties as a kind of vagrant, slipping in and out of bankruptcy, wandering alone from town to town – all while observing the extraordinary wilderness of America and hunting birds that he would eventually paint in *The Birds of America* (1827–38).[2]

To be sure, these adventurers were not impelled by the melancholic alienation and lovesickness that haunt Müller and Schubert's wanderer. And yet their fictional wanderer often adopts the observational posture of a scientist. He examines the cause-and-effect relationship between wind and weathervane ("Die Wetterfahne"), between subzero temperatures and his own hot tears ("Gefror'ne Tränen," "Wasserflut"). He offers reflections upon frozen rivers ("Auf dem Flusse"), mountain chasms ("Irrlicht"), extreme weather ("Der stürmische Morgen"), plants ("Der Lindenbaum," "Einsamkeit"), and animals ("Die Krähe"). And he is entranced by the otherworldly shining of mysterious lights ("Täuschung"), like the *Irrlicht* and *Nebensonnen*. He journeys, he stops, he observes something strange, he tries to make sense of it, and he journeys on. His *Heimweh* (longing for home) is but a Janus-faced expression of the explorer's *Fernweh* (longing for the unknown, for some place far away).

The wanderer's reactions to the natural world are more poetical than scientific, more subjective than objective. But, as Humboldt himself would have argued, imagination, creativity, and the arts were essential to scientific exploration. The frontispiece for Humboldt's *Ideen zu einer Geographie der Pflanzen* (1807) features a naked Apollo, one hand holding his lyre, the other lifting the veil from a statue of Artemis of Ephesus, symbolizing nature.[3] The allegory is clear: through art, we may come to understand the natural world. Humboldt had dedicated that book to another great polymath, his friend Johann Wolfgang von Goethe, who is famous not just for his novels, plays, and poems, but also for his scientific investigations into morphology, botany, light, and color. Thus the disciplinary lines that today separate the arts from the sciences were not always so strictly drawn. Instead, Romantic art and Romantic science were often coupled: both ventured beyond the mundane to seek the vast and mysterious unknown. It was the "Age of Wonder," as Richard Holmes's book on Romantic science declares.[4] And it is this expansive sense of wonderment – encompassing curiosity, awe, mystery, and terror – that abounds in *Winterreise*.

Theories of Interconnectedness

The natural world of *Winterreise* is interconnected, each of its elements conspiring against the wanderer in his quest for peace. Where there is cold weather, there are frozen rivers, and where there are frozen rivers, there are barren trees, and where there are barren trees, there are squawking crows and snarling dogs. They oppose the wanderer with a united front, one that externalizes his own despair, his own self-pity. For hope, he counterbalances the present by retreating into his imagination, pairing the cruelty before him with soothing memories: warm weather not cold weather, flowing rivers not frozen rivers, nightingales not ravens. This is a dynamic landscape. Whether organic or inorganic, whether observed or remembered, its diverse elements interact with each other, steering the wanderer further down his dark path.

Müller's vision of nature has a long poetic tradition, but it also reflects contemporaneous scientific attitudes and philosophies. Consider the case of Humboldt, the aforementioned geologist and explorer. Before embarking on his American journey, he wrote that he hoped "to find out how nature's forces act upon one another, and in what manner the geographic environment exerts its influence on animals and plants. In short, I must find out about the harmony of nature."[5] In subsequent treatises and travelogues, he wrote about "the interconnectedness of natural forces."[6] and the "great chain of causes and effects, [in which] no single fact can be considered in isolation."[7] In previous centuries, scientists had sought mechanistic explanations of the natural world, segmenting the complex biologies of living things into discrete classifications, structures, and systems. Rejecting this approach, Humboldt instead studied diverse elements – geology, geography, climate, animals, plants, human civilizations – and sought to discover how "all forces of nature are interlaced and interwoven."[8] Traces of this dynamic conception of nature may be found throughout *Winterreise* – for example, in "Wasserflut," in which vegetation (grass), weather (wind), and geography (melting snow forming a brook) symbiotically form a unified landscape.

The core dialectic in Humboldt's vision of nature – unity vs. diversity, *Einheit* vs. *Vielfältigkeit* – informed many branches of Romantic science. For example, in his writings on morphology, Goethe posited a generative "germ" that unifies an organism's various parts. In plants, this unifying element is the leaf: "All is leaf," Goethe writes, "and through this simplicity the greatest multiplicity is possible."[9] A plant's roots, trunk, branches, and flowers are all morphological extensions of this unifying leaf: it is what binds the organism together into a single entity. Goethe extended this conception of organic unity and applied it broadly to the similarities shared by different organisms. He posited an *Urpflanze* (archetypal plant) – a kind of model or template that encompasses the shared qualities of different plant species. It is by the *Urpflanze* that we might understand grasses, shrubs, and trees to be related in some fundamental, primordial way. Although he wrote about these ideas in scientific treatises, he also summarized them in a poem, "Die Metamorphose der Pflanzen" (1798), set in a garden of flowers: "Like unto each the form, yet none alike; and so the choir hints a secret law, a sacred mystery." (The "mystery," of course, is the *Urpflanze*, which Goethe sought but never actually found.) Something unites the different plants to each other, and something unites the different parts of a plant into a single, self-contained organism: "Asleep within the seed the power lies, foreshadowed pattern, folded in the shell, root, leaf, and germ."[10]

Throughout the nineteenth century, musical works were evaluated on the basis of their "organicism," on how they (like Goethe's plants) achieved unity from diversity.[11] Most famously, E. T. A. Hoffmann praised Beethoven's Fifth Symphony for the ways in which "everything contributes to a single end ... It is the intimate interrelationship among the themes that engenders that unity which alone has the power to hold the listener firmly in a single mood."[12] But the very genre of the song cycle also embodies this dialectic. A single song in *Winterreise* is but a small part of a larger, unified whole; it can be appreciated in isolation, yes, but at the expense of the connections it might have with other songs. For example, the barking dogs in "Im Dorfe" are reminiscent of those in "Gute Nacht" (the first song) and prophetic of those that will appear in "Der Leiermann" (the last). "The whole," as Goethe would argue in his poem, is "reflected in each separate part."

Both Humboldt and Goethe were admirers of Friedrich Wilhelm Joseph von Schelling (1775–1854), a philosopher whose audacious *Naturphilosophie* (nature philosophy) provided some Romantic scientists with an intellectual, spiritual, and aesthetic framework for their explorations and discoveries. Across several treatises, Schelling developed a monistic vision of nature, its elements (organic and inorganic, physical and metaphysical) continuously seeking balance in a kind of invisible, magnetic interaction of oppositional forces. "All nature is one vast organism, one living whole, which is undergoing constant growth and development," Frederick Beiser writes in a study of Schelling's philosophy.[13] Rocks, plants, animals, and, ultimately, humans are dynamically related – just as they are in *Winterreise*, which presents a similarly monistic vision of nature, relentlessly cold and relentlessly bleak. The wanderer perseveres in part by envisioning the opposite of everything that seeks to devastate him. In "Frühlingstraum," he dreams of "many-colored flowers, the way they bloom in May," "green meadows," and "merry bird calls" – inversions of the icy weather, the barren monochromatic landscape, and the sinister ravens and crows. This, too, reflects Schelling's *Naturphilosophie*. According to Schelling, nature is not static but active, and its productivity results from an eternal struggle between two oppositional forces – one generative, the other restrictive. As Beiser writes, "We cannot conceive of one force without the other, Schelling contends, anymore than we can conceive of something positive without something negative, and conversely."[14] The "omnipresence of polarity throughout nature" is central to *Winterreise*'s thematics: for every object in the bleak, cold present, there is its opposite, remembered from the warm, distant past.

Among the most important consequences of Schelling's *Naturphilosophie* was its conflation of the external natural world with the internal subjectivity of the person who studies it. Schelling's monistic conception of nature encompassed both realms, and they were governed by the same oppositional forces. "As long as I myself am identical with nature," Schelling writes, "I understand what living nature is as well as I understand myself."[15] To know nature is to know the self, and to know the self is to know nature. Nineteenth-century poets were certainly attracted to this notion, hence the many Romantic settings (haunted forests, expansive seas, starlit nights, babbling brooks) that externalize some internal feeling or sentiment. This attitude also affected some Romantic scientists, who were not as inclined as scientists today to segment their observations from their imaginations. For example, in his evocative writings on nature, Humboldt describes how the emotions of the soul compensate for what objective measurements fail to record: "On the banks of a lake, in a vast forest, at the foot of summits covered with eternal snows, it is not the simple magnitude of the objects, that penetrates us with secret admiration. What speaks to the soul, what causes such profound and various emotions, escapes our measurements, as it does the forms of language."[16] The wanderer in *Winterreise*, constantly inflecting descriptions of nature with his own emotional responses, would surely agree.

In an essay titled "Über die Vegetation" (1808), the philosopher-physicist Henrik Steffens (1773–1845) parrots Schelling: "Do you want to investigate nature? Then cast a glance inwards and in the stages of spiritual formation it may be granted to you to see the stages of natural development. Do you want to know yourself? Investigate nature and your actions are those of the Spirit there."[17] In *Winterreise*, the wanderer also embarks on these dual investigations, one internal (through the mind) and the other external (through the landscape). The landscape is always colored by his impressions of it; his mood, likewise, seems to reveal itself in the natural world before him. In "Erstarrung," he says "I want to kiss the ground, / Penetrate ice and snow / With my hot tears." In "Auf dem Flusse," he asks "My heart, in this stream / Do you now recognize your image?" In "Letzte Hoffnung," he says "I watch a particular leaf / And pin my hopes on it; / If the wind plays with my leaf / I tremble from head to foot." This rich, dynamic interconnectedness – of nature to itself, of mind to the matter it beholds – is fundamental to the worldview that Müller expresses in *Winterreise*.

Winter in *Winterreise*

Weather, of course, is the primary way that Müller fuses external and internal realms in *Winterreise*. Throughout the cycle, the bitter cold of the natural world serves as both a projection and a reflection of the wanderer's alienation. In "Der stürmische Morgen," the wanderer even envisions himself in the storm clouds: "My heart sees in the heavens / Its own image painted – / It's nothing but the winter, / Winter cold and wild!" And in "Der greise Kopf," a sheen of frost grays the wanderer's hair in a manner that convinces him he has aged prematurely. Wanderer and snow are one and the same. Indeed, there is hardly a song in *Winterreise* that does not foreground coldness in some way, as either snow, ice, wind, or storm. It is the unifying concept around which the cycle revolves.

Listening to *Winterreise* can be a bone-chilling experience, even if the climate of Müller and Schubert's Europe is mostly lost to us today. Due to human-induced climate change, average global temperatures have risen approximately two degrees (Fahrenheit) since the nineteenth century. This period of intense warming comes after several hundred years of global cooling – a period colloquially known as the "Little Ice Age" (*c.* 1500–1850), when temperatures fell about one degree below historical averages. The sizes of glaciers in the Alps reached their most recent maximum during this time and have declined at alarmingly fast rates ever since.[18] The Swiss scientist and engineer Ignaz Venetz (1788–1859) devoted much of his career to the study of these massive glaciers, and in 1821 he proposed that a vast sheet of ice had once covered parts of Europe. This was an early foray into ice age theory, which would become more widely studied and accepted several decades later.

An especially cold year was 1816. This was the infamous "Year without a Summer," when global temperatures dropped by approximately one degree. The sudden cold was caused by the volcanic eruption of Mount Tambora (in present-day Indonesia), one of the largest explosions in recorded history. Ash and sulfuric gases spread across the Earth's atmosphere and stratosphere, partially reflecting incoming sunlight. A yearlong period of cooler, wetter weather devastated parts of Europe; Vienna was "extraordinarily cold and dark."[19] Luke Howard (1772–1864), a pioneering meteorologist best known for his study of cloud types, traveled the continent that year and recorded his impressions:

> The excessive rains of this summer … took place over a great part of the continent of Europe. From the sources of the Rhine among the Alps, to its embouchure in the German ocean, and through a space twice or thrice as broad from east to west, the whole season presented a series of storms and inundations. Not meadows and villages alone, but portions of cities and large towns, lay long under water: dikes were broken, bridges blown up, the crops spoiled or carried off by torrents, and the vintage ruined by the want of sun to bring out and ripen the fruit.[20]

Harvests failed, and food was scarce, leading to what climate historian John Post called "the last great subsistence crisis in the Western world."[21] Other catastrophes ensued. In the western Alps, newly accumulated glacier ice formed a dam that resulted in an enormous mountain lake; it burst in 1818, destroying towns and killing residents below in an avalanche of snowy, rocky sludge.[22]

The strange weather of 1816 coincided with several innovations in the burgeoning field of meteorology. That year, the German physicist Heinrich Wilhelm Brandes (1777–1834) proposed the creation of the very first synoptic weather maps, partially as an attempt to explain the recent frequency of storms. Also around this time, Humboldt embarked on an effort to explain how different places might share similar climates. In 1817, he introduced his concept of isotherms, visualized as wavy horizontal stripes spread across a world map, connecting regions of similar latitude and elevation together, despite the oceans and continents that might separate them. In a manner resembling the ideology of Schelling's *Naturphilosophie*, the burgeoning field of meteorology sought to understand weather as another kind of dynamic, interconnected system, in which atmospheric pressure somewhere causes storms somewhere else, or a volcanic explosion on one side of the globe produces floods and famine on the other. Thus, in a poem like "Einsamkeit," weather is an essential part of Müller's monistic vision of nature: a "dreary cloud moves through the sky," just as a "faint breeze blows" through the tops of trees, just as the wanderer travels onward "with sluggish feet." It is weather that shapes much of the landscape of *Winterreise*, and it is weather that determines much of the wanderer's fate.

Phenomena and Illusions

On three different occasions in *Winterreise*, the wanderer sees strange, mysterious lights, each one blurring an increasingly fragile distinction between reality and fantasy. In "Täuschung," a flickering light seems to have a life of its own. It "does a friendly dance before me," then lures the wanderer ahead: "I like to follow it and watch," he says. Perhaps the light is a reflection of some unseen shiny object, its radiance intensified by the intense glare of the sun on the white landscape. Or maybe it's a flake of snow, suspended in air, adrift in wind, and gliding in and out of light and shadow. But when the light leads the wanderer to a "bright, warm house" with "a loving soul within," the riddle is solved. It was all an illusion, the wanderer believes – and "only illusion lets me win!"

Light, then and now, is mysterious. It is at once real and intangible: one can see it, find it, locate it, trace it, examine it, yet never clasp it or hold it – hence the proverbial "pot of gold" under a rainbow. It is raw energy, and its motions (like those of a dancing flame) are often anthropomorphized; yet it is also wholly inorganic, even as its fires consume the remnants of living things. It is humanity's connection with the gods (from whom Prometheus first stole fire): our world is illuminated by the otherworldly light of celestial orbs that, like Fortune's wheel, constantly encircle us overhead. Light plays tricks on its viewers, as in the extraordinarily popular phantasmagoria of the early nineteenth century; there, attendees could view frightening displays of ghosts and skeletons, produced by magic lanterns, concave mirrors, and other optical devices.[23] Real and illusory, natural and supernatural, visible and invisible – these are the contradictions of light.

For these reasons, light (from candles, stars, fires, and the sun) was an exemplary symbol for Romantic poets. But Romantic scientists, too, were fascinated by light's peculiar nature, and many devoted their careers to discovering its underlying properties. William Herschel (1738–1822), an astronomer (and part-time composer), used his telescopes to study the solar system. He discovered a planet (Uranus), mapped the Milky Way Galaxy, and studied the effects of sunspots on the Earth's climate. His observations led him to argue for the existence of extraterrestrial life – on other planets, on the Earth's moon, and even deep within our own Sun. Joseph von Fraunhofer (1787–1826), an expert glassmaker, built spectroscopes with diffraction gratings to break different sources of light into their constituent parts, as in a prism. When trained at the sun, his instruments were advanced enough to reveal hundreds of black lines – Fraunhofer lines – within an otherwise continuous spectrum, indicating wavelengths that are absorbed by the light source itself. As mentioned earlier, Goethe focused his scientific studies on the properties of light and color and their physiological effects on observers. For example, he wrote about the discolored "afterimage" (*Blendungsbild*) that lingers in the eye after a bright object vanishes. This strange, uncanny effect is brimming with paradox: it is at once visible and invisible, real and illusory, there and not there.

False Suns
"I saw three suns in the sky," says the wanderer, in the astonishing opening line of "Die Nebensonnen." Three suns! Surely these are delusions from the wanderer's tortured imagination, and yet the suns linger in front of him, "so stubbornly / That it seemed they didn't want to leave me." (Unadvisedly, he "stared at [the suns] hard for a long time." Never do this.) Internalizing the external, he interprets the extra two suns as eyes – his beloved's eyes – and barks, "Go, look into someone else's face!" He yearns for their setting, and presumably for his own death: "I will feel better in the dark."

Figure 7.1 "Two Mock Suns" (engraved by Hay, from a drawing by Craig)[24]

The two extra suns described in *Winterreise* are not imaginary, but nor are they real. They are an extraordinary atmospheric illusion known as "parhelia" (sundogs, mock suns) (Figure 7.1).

Observed since antiquity, parhelia were often interpreted ominously as a divine omen, until a flurry of scientists in the seventeenth century (including René Descartes, Christiaan Huygens, and Giovanni Domenico Cassini) and eighteenth century (including Isaac Newton, Joseph Priestley, and Pieter van Musschenbroek) sought a natural cause. Fraunhofer, the aforementioned physicist and glassmaker, gave the topic extensive coverage in his treatise on atmospheric phenomena, *Theorie der Höfe, Nebensonnen und verwandter Phänomene* (1825). He begins his study by listing some notable modern accounts of parhelia, with appearances ranging from areas around Rome (1629) to Gdańsk (1660), London (1796), and Dillingen (1815), a town outside of Augsburg. The latter example came from Joseph Weber (1753–1831), a priest, philosopher, and professor of physics, who was lucky to witness an elaborate and colorful intersection of sun halos:

> At 11:30, a rainbow-colored circle [halo] formed around the sun at a radius of about 45°; red was on the inside, closest to the sun, and blue was on the outside. A second, northerly circle joined itself around it, such that it intersected the first circle at two points and went straight through the sun. The circles had the same brightness as the sun, and the two points of intersection were brighter than and the same size as the sun, so that two parhelia [*Nebensonnen*] appeared . . .

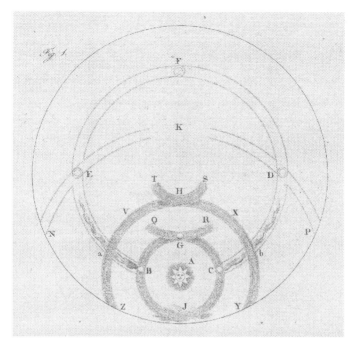

Figure 7.2 Joseph von Fraunhofer's diagram of sun halos and parhelia[26]

> A larger, brighter, more colorful stripe appeared along the south (60° away from the sun), which was redder close to the sun and bluer further from the sun; and it revealed a piece of an even larger circle. The air was quiet, hot, and dry, with medium atmospheric pressure; the sky was lined with partially translucent clouds ... The meteor [atmospheric phenomenon] was very active at midday, then faded and began to disappear at about 1:00.[25]

In his diagram of the phenomenon (Figure 7.2), Fraunhofer shows how halos and arcs of various sizes can radiate around the sun (labeled A); where the largest complete circle and smallest circle intersect (B and C), two parhelia form, with fiery, colorful stripes extending outward like inverted rainbows (a and b). Although modern diagrams differ in the number, arrangement, and shape of these halos, Fraunhofer's visualization captures their extraordinary magnitude and geometric complexity – like giant, cosmic eyes, staring down on lowly mortals below.

Scientists generally agreed that these strange solar shapes were caused by the reflection and refraction of sunlight through some unseen atmospheric filter. But they differed in the details, including the nature of the filter itself (moisture? clouds? ice crystals?), its larger formation (vertical columns? horizontal lines? a thin or thick mass?), and the shape of its individual particles (round? cylindrical? hexagonal?). The correct explanation – verified in laboratory simulations with prisms and crystals – postdates *Winterreise.*

A thin, wispy cirrus cloud full of minuscule ice crystals acts as a translucent filter. Most rays of sunlight shine straight through it, unimpeded; these present themselves to the viewer as the real sun. But because ice crystals are hexagonally shaped, some rays of light are refracted, changing their direction; these refracted light rays create illusory lights. When ice crystals point in different directions, they scatter the sunlight randomly (up, down, left, right), creating the circular shape of a halo. But when wind and atmospheric conditions cause thin, flat ice crystals to float in the same orientation (parallel to the ground), the refracted light is concentrated in two spots – two *Nebensonnen*. Depending on the purity, density, and variety of ice crystals, more complex patterns are possible, including the spectacular arrangement of halos, arcs, and stripes diagrammed by scientists like Fraunhofer.

The effect is uncanny, combining what is real and illusory in one magnificent, surreal display. The sun in the center is real, yes, but the other encircling lights are simultaneously there and not there; they shine, but as illusions, as phantoms. These *Nebensonnen* externalize the wanderer's alienation, his fantasies, his delusions. Their unreality likewise brings into question everything else – wait, which sun was the real one, again?

Irrlicht

In "Irrlicht," the wanderer is confronted with another light, which lures him off his path into "the deepest mountain chasms." He acknowledges that he might become trapped, but that doesn't concern him: "How to find a way out / Doesn't worry me much. // I'm used to going astray." From the interior of the chasm, he reaches "the mountain stream's dry channel," which he uses to descend – following the parallel paths of a river to its outlet in the ocean and (again fusing external and internal realms) "every sorrow to its grave."

What is an *Irrlicht*? The German word consists of two parts: as an adjective, "irre" primarily meant "false" or "astray"; "Licht" is "light." Put together, the word is a rough translation of the Latin term *ignis fatuus*, "fire of fools," with additional connotations suggesting illusion ("false light") or deception ("light that leads one astray"). But despite what these translations might suggest, the *Irrlicht* and *ignis fatuus* were not products of delusion. They were observed but unexplained phenomena, usually described as a flickering of light above a bog or marsh (Figure 7.3). (English terms for this florescent phenomenon – "will-o'-the-wisp," "jack-o'-lantern" – have a different etymological lineage, deriving from folklore.)

Sightings were (and still are) rare. One remarkably detailed account (first published in 1729, and frequently reprinted and paraphrased

Figure 7.3 "An Ignis Fatuus, or Will-o'-the-Wisp, as seen in Lincolnshire & taken upon the spot in 1811" (engraved by T. W. Cook, from a drawing by Pether)[27]

throughout the eighteenth and early nineteenth centuries) reports on the appearance of an *ignis fatuus* in Italy:

> Travelling sometime in *March* last, between eight and nine in the Evening, in a mountainous Road . . ., as he approached a certain River, called *Rioverde*, [a traveler] perceived a Light, which shone very strongly upon some Stones that lay upon the Banks. It seemed to be about two Foot above the Stones, and not far from the Water of the River: In Figure and Largeness it had the Appearance of a *Parallelopiped*, somewhat above a *Bolognese* Foot in Length [0.38 meters or 1.2 US feet], and about half a Foot high, its longest Side lying parallel to the Horizon: Its Light was very strong, insomuch that he could very plainly distinguish by it Part of a neighbouring Hedge, and the Water in the River; only in the East Corner of it the Light was pretty faint, and the square Figure less perfect, as if cut off, or darkened by the Segment of a Circle.

Notably, the *Irrlicht* in *Winterreise* seems to taunt the wanderer, perhaps by changing or moving, leading him deeper and deeper into the rocky mountains. This, too, is part of the Italian report:

> The Gentleman's Curiosity tempted him to examine it a little nearer; in order to which, he advanced gently towards the Place, but was surprized to find, that insensibly it changed from a bright Red to a yellowish, and then to a pale Colour, in Proportion as he drew nearer, and that when he came to the Place it self, it was quite vanished. Upon this he stepp'd back, and not only saw it again, but found that the farther he went from it, the stronger and brighter it grew; nor could he upon narrowly viewing the Place where this fiery Appearance was, perceive the least Blackness, or Smell, or any Mark of an actual Fire.[28]

The *ignis fatuus* appears and disappears, brightens and dims, and changes color. It is alluring but also inconstant and fickle – and thus another unsuccessful diversion in the wanderer's quest for comfort, security, and peace.

Attempts to explain the *ignis fatuus* varied widely. Because few writers had actually seen the phenomenon and most relied instead on the testimony of others, speculation was rampant. Some rooted their hypotheses in bioluminescence; it was, they proposed, nothing more than a swarm of fireflies or a mass of glowworms. Others attributed the phenomenon to vapors – whether as gases spewing from rotten, putrefying food and carcasses, or as a kind of earthly phosphorescent flatulence, released from deep within the soil and discharged into the air. Alessandro Volta (1745–1827) – the celebrated scientist whose pioneering studies in electricity we continue to honor today with the term "volt" – suggested that an inflammable gas emanating from marshes might be ignited by some naturally occurring electrical spark, like lightning. In the absence of persuasive explanation, and in the scarcity of conclusive testimony, supernatural associations flourished: "the superstitious ascribe [the *Irrlicht*] to evil spirits, which lure travelers to madness,"[29] begins an entry on the topic from an early nineteenth-century German encyclopedia. In two popular Viennese *Singspiele* – *Der Irrwisch* (1779) and *Das Irrlicht* (1783) – a cursed prince metamorphizes into an *Irrlicht* every night, and only the love of a woman can break the spell. The shenanigans in Goethe's short story *Das Märchen* (1795) are caused by two laughing, dancing, shapeshifting *Irrlichter*, who shed pieces of gold onto the mortals they encounter.

Spirit or fire, myth or reality, magic or science – here, at the flickering of the *Irrlicht*, the natural world seems to join the supernatural world. This is the *Irrlicht* of *Winterreise*. But in 1832, well after Müller's poems and Schubert's cycle were published, a more detailed, more credible account of the phenomenon appeared in print, one that correlates with some later experiments of the underlying chemistry. Much in the mold of the explorer-scientist described above, Louis Blesson (1790–1861) traipsed through marshes and forests in the middle of the night seeking appearances of the *ignis fatuus*. He found several – in a marshy area outside of Dresden (date unrecorded), in the forests of Upper Silesia (1811), in the mountainous regions between Silesia and Bohemia (1812), in the hills of Lower Saxony (1812), and in Porta Westfalica (1814). After so many vague second- and third-hand accounts, Blesson's testimony is refreshing. He approached the dancing light so closely that he could ignite a piece of paper with its flames. Like the Italians quoted above, Blesson also noted the movement of light, but was able to attribute it to swirling air caused by his own movements. Writing two decades later, he concludes, "[The lights] are of a chemical nature, and become inflamed on coming in contact with the atmosphere, owing to the nature of their constitution."[30] This is also the conclusion of a few twentieth- and twenty-first-century scientific studies. In peat bogs and marshes, a stew of decaying organic material can release gases (methane and phosphine). In the right amounts, the gases spontaneously combust with oxygen. The combustion produces a green flame.[31]

Like learning a magician's trick, reading modern scientific studies of the *ignis fatuus* might produce a brief sense of epiphany (eureka!) followed by a perfunctory sigh (was that all?). But this mystery is far from solved. Why did eighteenth- and nineteenth-century reports describe differently colored flames – blue, red, and yellow, but not green? Further, phosphine and methane produce an intensely bright, smoky fire, quite different from the pale, odorless light of earlier accounts. Unfortunately, the phenomenon has become all but extinct, possibly because many European marshes were drained in the late nineteenth and twentieth centuries for farmland and suburban development. Today, scientists must recreate the fire in their laboratories, albeit in an atmosphere very different from a stewy, sludgy bog. In such an artificial environment, in the midst of a scattered, contradictory historical record, and in the scarcity of the phenomenon today, one wonders whether a convincing answer will ever arrive – and, if one does, how we will ever determine that it is correct.

And so the unknown continues to lure us – as it did the Romantic scientist, and as it does *Winterreise*'s wanderer. We follow him, and he follows a mysterious light, deeper and deeper and deeper into the mountainous abyss.

Notes

1. *Diary and Letters of Wilhelm Müller*, ed. Philip Schuyler Allen and James Taft Hatfield (Chicago: University of Chicago Press, 1903), 58.
2. For more examples of scientific explorers and travelers, consult A. S. Troelstra, *Bibliography of Natural History Travel Narratives* (Utrecht: KNNV Publishing, 2016).
3. Frederika Tevebring, "Unveiling the Goddess: Artemis of Ephesus as a Symbol of Nature at the Turn of the Nineteenth Century," *Lychnos* (2012): 153–66.
4. Richard Holmes, *The Age of Wonder: How the Romantic Generation Discovered the Beauty and Terror of Science* (New York: Pantheon, 2008).
5. Alexander von Humboldt, Letter to Karl Freiesleben (June 1799), excerpted and translated in Donald Worster, *Nature's Economy: A History of Ecological Ideas*, 2nd ed. (Cambridge: Cambridge University Press, 1994), 133.
6. Alexander von Humboldt, *Views of Nature*, ed. Stephen T. Jackson and Laura Dassow Walls, trans. Mark W. Person (Chicago and London: University of Chicago Press, 2014), 25.
7. Alexander von Humboldt and Aimé Bonpland, *Essay on the Geography of Plants*, ed. Stephen T. Jackson, trans. Sylvie Romanowski (Chicago and London: University of Chicago Press, 2009), 79.
8. Alexander von Humboldt, Letter to David Friedländer (April 11, 1799), excerpted and translated in Andrea Wulf, *The Invention of Nature: Alexander von Humboldt's New World* (New York: Vintage Books, 2016), 51.

9. Robert J. Richards, *The Romantic Conception of Life: Science and Philosophy in the Age of Goethe* (Chicago and London: University of Chicago Press, 2002), 396.

10. Johann Wolfgang von Goethe, *The Metamorphosis of Plants*, trans. Douglas Miller (Cambridge, MA, and London: MIT Press, 2009), 1–4. A few years later, in 1802, Friedrich Schlegel would also use the metaphor of a chorus to probe the dialectic of unity and diversity: in the final lines of his poem "Abendröte" (later set by Schubert), he describes "everything [das All] as a single choir, many songs from One voice." For more, see Lisa Feurzeig, *Schubert's Lieder and the Philosophy of Early German Romanticism* (Abingdon and New York: Routledge, 2016), 63–128.

11. Ruth Solie, "The Living Work: Organicism and Musical Analysis," *19th-Century Music* 4/2 (1980): 147–56. See also Xavier Hascher's discussion of organicism in Chapter 11 of this volume.

12. E. T. A. Hoffmann, "Beethovens Instrumental-Musik" (1813), trans. Oliver Strunk, in Ruth A. Solie (ed.), "The Nineteenth Century," in *Strunk's Source Readings in Music History* (revised edition), ed. Leo Treitler (New York and London: W. W. Norton, 1998), 1193–98 (1196).

13. Frederick C. Beiser, *German Idealism: The Struggle against Subjectivism, 1781–1801* (Cambridge, MA, and London: Harvard University Press, 2002), 517.

14. Beiser, *German Idealism*, 532.

15. Richards, *The Romantic Conception of Life*, 134.

16. Alexander von Humboldt and Aimé Bonpland, *Personal Narrative of Travels to the Equinoctial Regions of the New Continent*, trans. Helen Maria Williams, 2nd ed. (London: Longman, Hurst, et al., 1825), vol. 4, 134.

17. Jürgen Barkhoff, "Romantic Science and Psychology," in Nicholas Saul (ed.), *The Cambridge Companion to German Romanticism* (Cambridge: Cambridge University Press, 2009), 209–25 (211).

18. Julia Schilly, "The Shrinking Glaciers of Austria," *The Guardian* (September 1, 2015). www.theguardian.com/environment/2015/sep/01/the-shrinking-glaciers-of-austria. See also SWJ, 169–84.

19. Elizabeth McKay, "Schubert and 'The Year without Summer,'" *Schubert durch die Brille* 27 (2001): 65–78 (73).

20. Luke Howard, *The Climate of London Deduced from Meteorological Observations*, vol. 1 (London: W. Phillips, et al., 1818), unpaginated notes for Table 122.

21. John D. Post, *The Last Great Subsistence Crisis in the Western World* (Baltimore, MD, and London: John Hopkins University Press, 1977). See also William K. Klingaman and Nicholas P. Klingaman, *The Year Without Summer: 1816 and the Volcano that Darkened the World and Changed History* (New York: St. Martin's Press, 2013), 194–218.

22. Gillen D'Arcy Wood, *Tambora: The Eruption that Changed the World* (Princeton, NJ, and Oxford: Princeton University Press, 2014), 159–69.

23. C. J. Wright, "The 'Spectre' of Science: The Study of Optical Phenomena and the Romantic Imagination," *Journal of the Warburg and Courtauld Institutes* 43 (1980): 186–200; and Terry Castle, "Phantasmagoria: Spectral Technology and the Metaphorics of Modern Reverie," *Critical Inquiry* 15 (1988): 26–61.

24. In Edward Polehampton, *The Gallery of Nature and Art* (London: R. Wilks, 1815), vol. 4, 520. Science, Industry & Business Library, The New York Public Library.

25. Joseph von Fraunhofer, *Theorie der Höfe, Nebensonnen und verwandter Phänomene* ([Munich, 1825]), 12–13. For more information, see SWJ, 445–60.

26. In Fraunhofer, *Theorie der Höfe, Nebensonnen und verwandter Phänomene*. Science, Industry & Business Library, The New York Public Library.

27. In Polehampton, *The Gallery of Nature and Art*, vol. 4, 494. Science, Industry & Business Library, The New York Public Library.

28. William Derham, "Of the Meteor called the *Ignis fatuus* . . .," *Philosophical Transactions* 36 (1729–30), 204–14 (212–13).

29. "Irrlicht," in *Conversations-Lexicon* (Amsterdam: Kunst- und Industrie-Comptoir, 1809), vol. 2, 243.

30. Louis Blesson, "Observations on the Ignis Fatuus, or Will-with-the-Wisp, Falling Stars, and Thunder Storms," *The Edinburgh New Philosophical Journal* (October 1832–April 1833): 90–94 (92). See also SWJ, 193–206.

31. A. A. Mills, "Will-o'-the-Wisp Revisited," *Weather* 55 (2001): 239–41.

8 On the Move: Outcasts, Wanderers, and the Political Landscape of *Die Winterreise*

GEORGE S. WILLIAMSON

The protagonist of *Winterreise* wanders through a landscape that is both real and imagined. Banished from one home but unable to conceive another, he follows a path that circles back on itself repeatedly, leading only to exhaustion and defeat. Yet while the singer of *Winterreise* appears to inhabit a lonely landscape, Wilhelm Müller's verses and their musical setting by Franz Schubert would also have evoked a concrete social world for their audiences, that of the road (*Landstrasse*). The road, by its very nature, was filled with people on the move, some of them (journeymen, pilgrims) heading purposefully from one place to another, but others with no particular destination, whose poverty, criminality, or "dishonorable" status banished them from their towns and villages. These last types, the "wandering people" (*fahrendes Volk*), had become well established as an object of public fascination and state scrutiny by the eighteenth century.

The French Revolutionary and Napoleonic wars of 1792–1815 added new numbers to the "wandering people," as armies crisscrossed the German lands, leaving a trail of destruction and forcing thousands of civilians to abandon their homes. The defeat of Napoleon would lead to a partial restoration of the European monarchical order, but not an end to the political forces that had arisen to challenge it. Over the next years, student nationalists and radical activists took to the road to assemble, discuss, and disseminate their ideas. After a crackdown on such activity in 1819, many fled the German lands into exile.

This social and political context lies largely below the surface of *Winterreise*, though at times it breaks through to become visible. But whether implicit or explicit, it formed part of the interpretive horizon in which this song cycle was conceived and received in early nineteenth-century Germany. With the theme of "outcasts and wanderers" as its guiding thread, this chapter explores the social world of the road in the German lands of the late eighteenth and early nineteenth centuries, while considering how the Napoleonic wars and their aftermath influenced the way Müller and his contemporaries came to see the road and its inhabitants.

The "Wandering People"

Who exactly were the "wandering people"? One can gain a good sense from a decree issued in 1747 by the margrave of the small German territory of Baden-Durlach. The decree called for the roundup and arrest of

> vagrants and beggars, tramps and deserters, bagpipers and similar strolling minstrels, traveling students, unlicensed peddlers and hucksters of cheap wares, singers, bearers of grab bags and curios, gamers, magicians, tricksters, animal trainers, mountebanks, Jewish beggars, persons collecting alms for fires and the like without authorization, con artists, brush makers and tinkers of pans, pots, and baskets who are unknown and foreign to the land, also those . . . who lay about, beg, or falsely give themselves out to be journeymen.[1]

This ordinance was by no means unique: authorities issued hundreds of similar decrees from the seventeenth through the early nineteenth centuries, to varying degrees of effect.[2] What makes the Baden-Durlach decree interesting in the present context is the range of people and occupations it sought to ban, from begging to bagpiping.

Any visitor to a town or large village in the Holy Roman Empire would have been confronted with people asking for alms. During the Middle Ages, alms-giving was viewed as a Christian duty, and the poor were seen as the responsibility of their local community. Beginning around 1700, however, attitudes toward the poor hardened, as towns and territories adopted measures to expel beggars and the homeless from their borders. Once on the road, beggars often found it useful to spin stories to win the sympathies of potential alms-givers. Some claimed they were collecting funds to build a church or rebuild a village destroyed by fire, even producing "official" letters (often forgeries) attesting to the worthiness of their cause.[3] Others presented themselves as aristocrats who had lost everything through some stroke of bad fortune. So-called "strong beggars," however, used more forceful means to get what they wanted. Traveling in large groups, they might show up at a rural home and demand lodging, food, or money, threatening the inhabitants with arson if these were not forthcoming.[4]

As the 1747 decree indicates, authorities were also deeply suspicious of peddlers and others involved in the "itinerant trades." Because such peddlers operated outside the framework of the guilds, which regulated trade in the towns, they were often viewed with hostility by authorities determined to protect local sellers. There were also questions about their wares, which were seen as shabby and potentially harmful. Such was the case with sellers of printed matter, whose offerings included horoscopes, ghost stories, tales of murder, or, after 1800, "political" diaries, the latter often attached to the folk calendars routinely purchased by all classes of people.[5]

The "itinerants" also included minstrels and musicians, who arrived in towns from time to time, ready to sing a bawdy ballad or play a tune on the hurdy-gurdy. On church festivals or market days, they might be joined by magicians, jugglers, and animal handlers, or purveyors of attractions like peep boxes, puppet shows, and games of chance. These "players" were often viewed with hostility, not only by the authorities but also by the educated public, who saw their entertainments as "base arts that . . . hamper the progress of good taste and morality."[6] But the players, like the peddlers, came under suspicion also because their itinerant ways brought them into close contact with the *Gauner*.

The German word *Gauner* is perhaps best translated as "grifter." In the eighteenth and early nineteenth centuries, it was used to denote transients who engaged in various types of criminality. These might include "false begging," "false gaming," medical quackery, and counterfeiting, as well as pickpocketing, crop theft, and low-level burglary.[7] Insight into the lives and careers of these individuals can be gleaned from the *Gaunerliste*, published lists of wanted criminals that included names, aliases, known associates, physical descriptions, and criminal history. A significant percentage of the individuals mentioned in these lists were women, whose fraud and theft often formed part of a family division of labor, with the men perpetrating more violent crimes.[8]

The *Gauner* of the eighteenth and early-nineteenth centuries inhabited a distinct subculture, the world of the *Kochemer* (derived from the Hebrew word for "clever" or "initiated"), as opposed to the world of the *Wittische* (the "dumb" or "honorable").[9] The *Kochemer* possessed their own dialect, *Rotwelsch*, which borrowed heavily from Hebrew, and a system of written signs and symbols known as *Zinken*. An encyclopedia article from 1815 reported that "as soon as someone is accepted among the *Gauner* he receives, alongside his surname, a group- or nick-name, for example, Lips Tullian, Cheese-Beer, Bavarian Sepp . . ."[10] The same article described the *Gauners'* favored abodes as forested areas near mountains and ravines, with isolated houses that could serve as hideouts.[11]

The close affinity of *Rotwelsch* to Hebrew is testimony to the role of Jews in the *Kochemer* world. Beginning in the 1300s, Jews had been expelled from most of the territories and towns of the Holy Roman Empire, and those Jews who remained tended to live in villages protected by a local knight. Other Jews turned to the ambulant occupations prevalent among the "wandering people," including peddling and cattle trading. Most of the "begging Jews" originated from Poland or Bohemia, where they had been driven out by pogroms and other forms of persecution. During the seventeenth and eighteenth centuries, local and territorial authorities repeatedly issued decrees banning "begging Jews" from their lands. Such bans were justified less on the basis of the Jews' begging (which mostly affected their fellow Jews) than the fear that they were carrying plague or some other disease.[12] In addition, Christians tended to associate Jews with fraud and deceit and assumed they were hiding money they had acquired dishonestly, a prejudice at the basis of the Grimms' fairy tale "The Jew in the Thorn Bush."

On the furthest margins of the *Gauner* world were the "Gypsies" (*Zigeuner*), a pejorative word for the itinerant Romani peoples who had lived on the margins of European society since the early modern era. Although the Romani were of South Asian origin, it was widely believed (including among some Romani) that they were from Egypt. Indeed, many Christians believed that they were condemned to wander after their ancestors had denied the holy family refuge on their flight to Egypt.[13] Like others among the "wandering people," the Romani engaged in itinerant, semi-reputable occupations like horse trading and small crafts, although their knowledge of fortune telling and medicine was valued among rural peasants.[14] But state authorities and most of the population viewed them as a menace more alien and threatening than even Jews. A 1783 treatise by Heinrich Grellmann described "Gypsies" as "useless for farming, useless for any type of industry. On the contrary, they make themselves irksome with their begging, cause harm with their hundredfold deceptions and, what is more, as thieves and robbers they bring insecurity into the state."[15]

The rise of absolutism in the seventeenth and eighteenth centuries contributed to a concerted attempt to criminalize the "stray riffraff" (*herrenloses Gesindel*).[16] Legal decrees, like the 1747 mandate quoted above, were part of a broader effort to expel unwanted populations from individual towns and territories. These decrees were backed up with threats of public whippings, forced baptisms (in the case of the Romani), even the death penalty. To keep foreign beggars and vagrants away, officials set up warning signs on the outskirts of towns or at highway crossings. These "Gypsy Posts" described, in graphic terms, the punishments to be meted out against those caught in a town or territory. Officials also organized "hunts" to capture and expel unwanted persons, with cash rewards for a good bounty.[17] By the beginning of the nineteenth century, however, most states had moved away from expulsion and toward confining vagrants in workhouses or conscripting them into the army. At the same time, officials took measures to make unauthorized travel more difficult, requiring all travelers to carry passports with information about the starting point, destination, and purpose of their journey.[18]

The Robbers

If Romani, beggars, and Jews made up the lowest ranks of the *Kochemer* world, then its aristocracy were the bandits who operated in the western parts of Germany and who attained a peak of notoriety in the period 1785–1814. In literature, bandits were often shown robbing the coaches of the rich and powerful, but in fact their methods varied considerably, from burglary to home invasion to murder, as did their targets, which included both wealthy merchants and impoverished peasants. This can be seen in the case of Johannes Bückler, nicknamed Schinderhannes (1779– 1803), perhaps the most notorious robber of his era. The son of a flayer (*Schinder*), Bückler began work in his father's "dishonorable" occupation, but after being convicted of stealing cowhides he escaped prison and began a life on the run. Between 1797 and 1802, he was involved in some fifty-two crimes, including burglary, robbery, and murder. Many of these crimes were carried out along the border between the French-occupied Rhineland and the western territories of the Holy Roman Empire, as Schinderhannes appealed to the anti-French sentiments of the German population to win sympathy for his cause. In reality, he tended to target moderately wealthy farmers and especially Jews, whose Christian neighbors often reacted to their plight with indifference or even *Schadenfreude*.[19] On his arrest in 1802, Schinderhannes presented himself as deeply remorseful and yet also as a victim of circumstances, an essentially good man who had fallen in with the wrong crowd. One newspaper described him as "a powerful soul" who, under other circumstances, "would have won renown in the struggle for the fatherland."[20]

This image of Schinderhannes as an "honorable robber" built on tropes in a burgeoning literature on robbers. A classic in this genre was Friedrich Schiller's play *The Robbers* (1782), which portrayed a band of robbers as rebels against princely authority. The leader of the bandits, Karl Moor, is the wayward son of a count but a fundamentally moral person. His unjust expulsion from his father's patrimony leads him to reject the authority of the state and embrace the freedom of the bandit's life. "I am supposed to lace my body in a corset, and straight-jacket my will with laws," he complains early in the play. "The law never yet made a great man, but freedom will breed a giant, a colossus."[21] Under this banner of "freedom," the robbers carry out a series of atrocities that Moor eventually comes to regret, and at the end of the play he gives himself over to justice. But while *The Robbers* ultimately affirmed the legal-judicial order, it demonstrated a sympathy for its protagonist that would be typical of the robber plays and novels that appeared from 1785 to 1815, when the campaign against brigandage was at its height.[22]

The world of the road, including not just robbers but the wider "travel-ing people," left its mark on another classic of German literature, Johann Wolfgang von Goethe's novel *Wilhelm Meister's Apprenticeship* (1795). Goethe's Wilhelm is a young man of means who abandons a career as a merchant and takes up with a loose band of actors (another itinerant and semi-reputable occupation). On his travels, Wilhelm befriends a thirteen-year-old tightrope walker and an aged harpist and invites them to join his troupe. After an unsuccessful performance at the castle of a nobleman, the troupe stops for a picnic alongside the road, and for a moment Wilhelm imagines himself the leader of a "wandering colony." Suddenly the troupe is attacked by robbers. In the ensuing gunfight, Wilhelm is shot, but he is nursed back to health and is able to carry on. In the end, Goethe's book fits into the genre of the "novel of education," which typically featured a young man on a journey of self-discovery. In *Wilhelm Meister*, the acting troupe and, more broadly, life on the road, are evoked as alternatives to the responsible life that Wilhelm initially abandons but eventually reclaims, albeit at a more enlightened level. Thus where Schiller's *Robbers* high-lighted the tragic opposition between freedom and social order, Goethe's novel imagined their successful synthesis.

The Post

For men and women of means, to take to the road usually meant to aim at a particular destination, with the goal of arriving there as quickly and comfortably as possible. In early nineteenth-century Germany, the most efficient way to travel long distances over land was by mail coach, which carried letters and paying travelers according to a set schedule.[23] The arrival of the mail coach was announced by the blowing of the coach driver's horn. (In Schubert's setting of "Die Post," the arpeggiated triplet-like eighth notes of the piano introduction imitate the postal horn's arrival call.) Those who wished to travel on the mail coach bought a ticket at a post station and then traveled to the next post station, where the coach would stop to change horses, a process that could take hours. Despite its slow pace, however, the mail coach became the basis for an emerging bourgeois culture of travel. As Klaus Beyrer notes, travel to faraway places came to be seen as a voluntary escape from quotidian existence, an opportunity to cultivate certain sentiments (awe, nostalgia), and a means of "freeing the bourgeois self from its shadow existence in the old aristocratic world."[24]

Yet if travel could be seen as an act of individual emancipation, to hop into a mail coach was also to deliver oneself to various forms of depend-ency and unfreedom. Whatever their rank or station in civil society, once travelers departed the post station they (and their baggage) were very much at the mercy of the coach personnel and their individual whims. In his popular treatise *On Conversing with People* (1788), Adolph Freiherr von Knigge (1752–1796) offered advice on how to carry oneself while traveling. On the one hand, one should not be too extravagant with one's money, particularly in front of others, since this might make one a target. On the other hand, one should tip the coach personnel generously, since this would incline them to be helpful rather than unscrupulous toward the traveler.[25] Indeed, a traveler on the mail coach could be subject to all manner of scams, such as overcharges for wagon repairs or being forced to exchange currency unnecessarily (an issue at Germany's many internal borders). One could complain to the authorities, but that would only delay the journey, a fact scammers took into account.[26] There was also the chance that the coach might be robbed by bandits, though this danger loomed larger in literature than it did in reality. But this threat, too, showed that even the well-to-do could not completely avoid the world of the grifters and robbers when they ventured onto the road.

Revolution, War, Nationalism

The outbreak of the French Revolution in 1789 generated considerable attention, even enthusiasm, in Germany. Yet only a few observers believed these events had a bearing on the German lands since, so the thinking went, their rulers had long embraced the cause of enlightened reform while the French monarchy had descended into bankruptcy and corruption. This attitude changed in 1792 as revolutionary France launched war against Austria and Prussia. After nearly suffering calamity in its opening campaigns, the French army found its footing and soon took the battle to the Low Countries and the western lands of the Holy Roman Empire. By 1795, Prussia had taken itself out of the war, leaving the Austrians to hold off the French on their own, which they managed to do only temporarily. By 1797, both Prussia and Austria had recognized France's annexation of the formerly German lands of the Rhineland. Here the French imposed revolutionary reforms, including religious toleration and the abolition of feudal rents. At the same time, they engaged in plunder and spoilage that turned the local populations against them. It was precisely in this region that robbers like Schinderhannes operated most successfully, moving back and forth between "French" and German territories and playing on the patriotism of the locals to avoid capture.

In 1799, Napoleon joined a coup d'état against the revolutionary regime in Paris and emerged as "First Consul" of France. Five years later, he crowned himself emperor, challenging Europe's ancient dynasties with his own claims to imperial power. As First Consul and then as Emperor, Napoleon moved aggressively to redraw the map of Germany, overseeing the absorption of dozens of smaller territories by larger principalities like Baden, Bavaria, and Württemberg, which in turn entered into alliances with France. This reorientation of German loyalties, along with Napoleon's stunning defeat of the Austrians at Austerlitz in 1805, paved the way for the formal dissolution of the Holy Roman Empire in August 1806, as Franz II of Austria, bowing to pressure from Napoleon, gave up the old imperial crown. Prussia had sat out these conflicts, but in October 1806 a series of provocations led King Friedrich Wilhelm III to declare war on Napoleon. The French forces proceeded to destroy the overmatched Prussian army at the battles of Jena and Auerstedt, before riding triumphantly into Berlin. In the ensuing peace treaty, Prussia lost nearly half of its territory and entered into an exploitative "alliance" with France. Napoleon's dominance in Europe seemed secured.

The French Revolutionary and Napoleonic wars left their mark everywhere in Germany, including the road. Soldiers had always been a major presence on highways, but now they moved in unprecedented numbers, with both sides fielding armies of well over one hundred thousand men. Whether friend or foe, the appearance of soldiers was never a welcome sight, and the arrivals of these enlarged armies often had the effect of a natural disaster, as they plundered food stores, requisitioned cattle, and impressed locals into service.[27] Once fighting began, destruction took place on a scale not seen since the Thirty Years War. Traveling to Mannheim in 1796, the philosopher Friedrich Schelling bore witness to the devastation caused by France's unsuccessful siege of the city a year earlier. "The whole way one sees dead horses to the right and the left, as well as tossed up and half destroyed embankments, ruined fields, and so forth. [...] As one comes into the city through the Heidelberg Gate, the traveler is confronted everywhere with scenes of devastation, particularly in the neighborhood of the gunpowder magazine that blew up."[28]

As French armies advanced toward German towns, their populations took to the road, fleeing for safety. Goethe's epic poem *Hermann and Dorothea* (1797) turns on the love between Dorothea, a destitute refugee from the western side of the Rhine, and Hermann, the respectable son of a Mainz innkeeper. At the outset of the poem, Goethe describes the thoughts of one Mainz resident as his neighbors rush out to witness the arrival of refugees:

> What curiosity won't do! Here everyone is running
> To look at the sad procession of pitiful exiles . . .

But I would not stir from my play to witness the suffering
Of good, fugitive people, who now, with their rescued possessions,
Driven, alas! from beyond the Rhine, their beautiful country,
Over to us are coming . . .[29]

Hermann and Dorothea culminates in a happy marriage, but the fate of most refugees was less certain. In Württemberg, the latter stages of the war coincided with a temperature drop that ruined crops and led to widespread hunger. A ban on emigration kept the population from leaving, but after the war, some 17,000 Württembergers departed for Russia, where they were welcomed by Tsar Alexander I.[30]

Most Germans viewed their sufferings through traditional frameworks of interpretation, e.g., as God's punishment for human sin or as a foreboding of the Last Judgement. However, an important segment of the educated public viewed the conflict through the lens of nationalism, arguing that the defeat and humiliation of Germany, and especially Prussia, signaled the need for a political reordering of the German lands along national lines. In a series of lectures in Berlin, Johann Gottlieb Fichte (1762–1814) called for a rejection of French political and cultural hegemony and argued for the superiority of the German language, which, he alleged, had never been corrupted by interminglings with Latin. It was also in Berlin that Friedrich Ludwig Jahn (1778–1852) initiated the gymnastics movement (*Turnbewegung*), in which young men strengthened their bodies through a regime of exercise and training while being indoctrinated in anti-French nationalism. Such open Francophobia could not be endorsed by the Prussian monarchy, which remained officially allied with Napoleon. Nonetheless, Friedrich Wilhelm III and his ministers embarked on a series of reforms that were designed to strengthen Prussia economically and militarily, with a view to an eventual war against France.

In 1812, Napoleon launched an invasion of Russia, with the French Grande Armée supported by some 150,000 troops from Prussia, Austria, and other German allies. After some early victories, the invasion bogged down due to poor supply lines and the onset of winter. By December 1812, the commander of the Prussian contingent had concluded that Napoleon had no prospects of victory. After secret talks with his Russian counterpart, he declared the Prussian forces neutral, an act of insubordination that would come to be celebrated as a heroic act of resistance. Three months later, Prussia declared war on Napoleon. Friedrich Wilhelm III called on his subjects to make sacrifices on behalf of Prussia, suggesting he would introduce further reforms (including a parliament and a constitution) once the enemy had been defeated. A large army was quickly raised, while men of non-military age rushed to join the militia and the home guard. In addition, patriotic women's associations were founded to raise money for the war effort and to support families of soldiers killed or disabled in the fighting.[31] It was in this moment of patriotic enthusiasm that Wilhelm Müller, then a university student in Berlin, volunteered for the Prussian army. He would see combat at the battles of Lützen, Bautzen, Haynau, and Kulm.[32]

The decisive battle of what would become known as the "Wars of Liberation" took place outside Leipzig in October 1813, as the combined forces of Prussia, Russia, and Austria (an ally since June) defeated Napoleon's army and forced him into retreat. By April 1814, Napoleon had surrendered and gone into exile, the Allies had marched into Paris, and the "legitimate" Bourbon king had been restored to the throne. Napoleon would return once more in March 1815, deposing the French king and raising an army before being defeated for good at Waterloo.

Restoration and Opposition

Since September 1814, representatives of Europe's great and small powers had been meeting in Vienna to decide on the contours of a post-Napoleonic order. The presiding spirit of the Congress of Vienna was the Austrian foreign minister Clemens von Metternich, who was deeply suspicious of the new political forces unleashed by the French Revolution. It would be wrong to describe Metternich simply as a reactionary – he supported religious toleration and the abolition of the slave trade, and he was willing to countenance constitutional government to a degree. But he was also determined that the monarchical order be re-established within Europe. For Germany, this did not entail a revival of the Holy Roman Empire and its hundreds of vanished territories. Instead, the surviving thirty-nine German states were organized into a "German Confederation" with no capital, no emperor, and a spare "constitutional act" holding them together. Although some German states implemented constitutions and parliaments, Austria and, most disappointingly, Prussia did not, this despite Friedrich Wilhelm III's repeated promises to do so, including, most explicitly, in an ordinance of May 22, 1815 that was issued while Napoleon was still on the loose.

For the student-veterans of the Napoleonic wars (including Müller), this was a most unhappy state of affairs. On their return to university, many of them joined nationalist fraternities, or *Burschenschaften*, pledging themselves to the virtues of "Germanness, militancy, chastity, and honor." In October 1817, on the fourth anniversary of the Battle of Leipzig and the 300th anniversary of the Protestant Reformation, some 450 mostly

Protestant *Burschenschaft* members gathered for a days-long festival at Wartburg castle near Eisenach. While speakers called for the unification of Germany as a constitutional monarchy, several of Jahn's followers held a symbolic "book-burning" that featured writers deemed reactionary or anti-German. Among the books burned in effigy was a *History of the German Empire* (1814) by the playwright August von Kotzebue (1761– 1819). This initiated a war of words between Kotzebue and oppositionists (both students and faculty) at the University of Jena that would grow increasingly bitter over the next two years.

Although Müller never joined the *Burschenschaft* movement (it did not reach Berlin until 1818), he developed close contacts with some of its guiding figures. After resuming his studies in 1815, he joined the Berlin Society for the German Language, which promoted the purification of the German language from French and other influences.[33] There he encountered Jahn, the nationalist firebrand August Zeune, and the Romantic-nationalist poets Clemens Brentano and Friedrich de la Motte Fouqué, whose celebrations of German folk-song and the *Nibelungenlied* left their mark on Müller. Although a student of classical philology, he began to focus on medieval German literature, which brought him close to the Berlin historian Friedrich Rühs (who in 1816 publicly opposed citizenship rights for Jews). In general, Müller's views were typical of early German liberalism at this historical juncture: opposed to the current order, insistent on constitutional reform, but also firmly nationalist and (for the moment) anti-French.

The growth of nationalist agitation and student radicalism was deeply troubling to Metternich and many other conservatives, who viewed the nationalist movement as a new form of Jacobinism. Those fears seemed to be realized on March 23, 1819, when Carl Sand, a Jena student and a fanatical nationalist, assassinated Kotzebue in his Mannheim apartment.[34] After attempting unsuccessfully to kill himself, Sand was arrested and eventually tried, found guilty, and executed. In the meantime, police authorities in Prussia issued arrest warrants for a number of leading nationalists, including Jahn. At Metternich's urging, in September 1819 the German Confederation approved the Carlsbad Decrees, a series of four laws that required the disbanding of the *Burschenschaften*, tight supervision over universities, stricter press censorship, and a federal investigation into the dangers posed by "revolutionary machinations" in Germany. Several outspoken university professors lost their jobs, and a number of student radicals were thrown in prisons. Some, such as Sand's mentor Karl Follen, fled Germany altogether.

At the time of Sand's assassination of Kotzebue, Müller had just returned to Berlin from a year-long trip to Italy, so while some of his acquaintances received unwanted attention from police investigators, he did not. Nonetheless, the events of 1819 left an impression on him. In a January 1820 dedication to a travel book, Müller described his mood as sober and "serious," because "the great Lenten season of the European world, looking forward to Holy Week and awaiting redemption, does not permit an indifferent shrug of the shoulders or capricious arrangements or excuses. Whoever cannot act in this era can at least remain quiet and mourn."[35]

Müller's sullen mood did not last, however. In March 1821, Greek nationalists launched a revolution against their Ottoman rulers, a development that thrilled Müller, who had been a supporter of Greek independence for years. The Philhellenist cause won support from a wide range of European figures, notably Lord Byron, but it held special appeal for German liberals, since supporting the Greeks was a way to challenge the conservative politics of Metternich and like-minded officials in Prussia. In the weeks after the outbreak of the Greek revolution, Müller wrote a series of "Greek Songs" (*Griechenlieder*), whose undisguised political content drew the ire of censors.

Müller appears to have written the poems that would comprise *Die Winterreise* just after the imposition of the Carlsbad Decrees, a moment when Germany seemed to have slipped headlong into political reaction. Where the Philhellenist poems are openly political, the *Winterreise* poems seem apolitical, with most of them consisting of dialogue between a spurned lover and a cold and inhospitable nature. Yet there are indications that the narrator's sense of betrayal is rooted in more than just a failed romance; indeed, at least one scholar has pointed to the influence on Müller of Schopenhauerian *Weltschmerz*.[36] But between the individualistic and the cosmic levels of signification, it is possible to interpose an additional reading of *Die Winterreise*, which treats its central narratives of betrayal and exile as a kind of political allegory.[37] This dimension of the poems would likely have been readily apparent to those who shared Müller's political convictions (including the Austrian Franz Schubert, himself an opponent of Metternich), but not so obvious as to draw the attention of the censors.[38] Moreover, this political message is given an additional social depth through the many allusions in *Die Winterreise* to the world of the road.

Thus we learn in the first song ("Gute Nacht") that the narrator has not only been expelled from his lover's house but is now an outcast from the entire town, condemned to wander the road, making him what he was before: a stranger (*fremd*). Müller's word choice brings to mind the stories of those who, through some misstep or misfortune, have been banished from their hometowns, as well as of those who have never had a home and are condemned to wander, whether because of an ancient curse or religious hatred. Yet there are clues, too, that Müller understands *fremd* in the more modern political sense of being alien to a particular state. "The girl spoke of love, / Her mother even of marriage" denotes familial misfortune, but it also evokes Friedrich Wilhelm III's promise that victory over Napoleon would lead to the introduction of a parliament and a constitution in Prussia.[39] As James Brophy has shown, the theme of unkept promises figured heavily in the political songs of the immediate post-Napoleonic years, as lyricists urged Germany's rulers, especially Friedrich Wilhelm III, to carry through on their prior commitments.[40] But by the time Müller began writing the *Winterreise* poems, it had become clear that the Prussian king should never have been trusted. "Censorship and political inquisition . . . These are the trophies of the German Battle of Nations at Leipzig," he wrote in December 1819.[41] In "Die Wetterfahne," the narrator realizes too late that the weathervane atop the house of his "beloved" was a signal that when the wind shifted she would change her mind and her lover would become a "refugee" (*Flüchtling*), a word that could refer to those escaping war or those fleeing a persecuting state.

The narrator's expulsion from a home he thought he had gained (but never really had) elicits a variety of reactions. He cycles through nostalgia, false hope, bitterness, delusion, and rage, all while making his way through a bitter cold (indeed, the years 1816–1817 had been among the coldest on record). The narrator even suggests that it is this icy cold that binds him to the image of his lover; should the rushing currents of spring ever return, they would wipe away her memory forever. But if this last image suggests the possibility of revolution, such hopes are faint and grow still fainter as the cycle continues. Instead, we see the narrator gradually accepting the role of an outcast or outlaw. Even though he has committed no crime, he avoids the highways and travels along "hidden pathways" and through "snowy mountain tops," ever further from human community, or at least from those villagers content to see their needs fulfilled in dreams, but not in reality. By the end of the cycle, the narrator has acquiesced to his fate: to sing his songs alongside the hurdy-gurdy man, begging for coins, despised by all, always on the move.

Notes

1. Wolfgang Seidenspinner, "Bettler, Landstreicher und Räuber. Das 18. Jahrhundert und die Bandenkriminalität," in Harald Siebenmorgen (ed.), *Schurke oder Held? Historische Räuber und Räuberbanden* (Sigmaringen: Jan Thorbecke, 1995), 27–38 (27).
2. See Ernst Schubert, *Arme Leute: Bettler und Gauner im Franken des 18. Jahrhunderts* (Neustadt: Degener, 1983), 331–40.
3. Ibid., 223–33.

4. Ibid., 182–85; Uwe Danker, *Die Geschichte der Räuber und Gauner* (Düsseldorf: Artemis & Winkler, 2001), 67.
5. Schubert, *Arme Leute*, 234; James Brophy, *Popular Culture and the Public Sphere in the Rhineland, 1800–1850* (Cambridge: Cambridge University Press, 2007), 18–53.
6. Schubert, *Arme Leute*, 238.
7. See the entry "Gauner" from the 1815 *Brockhaus-Conversations-Lexikon*, excerpted in Michael Krausnick, *Von Räubern und Gendarmen: Berichte und Geschichten aus der Zeit der großen Räuberbanden* (Würzburg: Arena, 1978), 85–92.
8. Danker, *Geschichte*, 66.
9. Seidenspinner, "Bettler," 29–30.
10. "Gauner," in Krausnick, *Von Räubern*, 89.
11. Ibid., 90.
12. Schubert, *Arme Leute*, 172–73.
13. Martin Lange, *Räuber und Gauner ganz privat: Räuberbanden und die Justiz im 18. und frühen 19. Jahrhundert* (Marburg: Tectum Verlag, 2007), 77.
14. Danker, *Geschichte*, 57–58.
15. Heinrich Grellmann, *Historischer Versuch über die Zigeuner*, 2nd ed. (1787), excerpted in Beate Althammer and Christina Gerstenmayer (eds.), *Bettler und Vaganten in der Neuzeit (1500–1933): Eine kommentierte Quellenedition* (Essen: Klartext, 2013), 238.
16. On this point, Seidenspinner, "Bettler," 30–31.
17. Danker, *Geschichte*, 264; Seidenspinner, "Bettler," 31.
18. Danker, *Geschichte*, 263–65.
19. Ibid., 18–21.
20. Ibid., 28.
21. Friedrich Schiller, *The Robbers/Wallenstein*, trans. F. J. Lamport (London: Penguin, 1979), 36.
22. On this, see Danker, *Geschichte*, 275–97.
23. On the post coach, see Klaus Beyrer, *Die Postkutschenreise* (Tübingen: Vereinigung für Volkskunde, 1985); Klaus Beyrer (ed.), *Zeit der Postkutschen: Drei Jahrhunderte Reisen 1600–1900* (Karlsruhe: Braun, 1992); Bruno Preisendörfer, *Als Deutschland noch nicht Deutschland war: Reise in die Goethezeit* (Cologne: Kiepenheuer & Witsch, 2015), 57–74.
24. Klaus Beyrer, "Aufbruch in die Welt der Moderne: Bürgerliches Reisen nach 1800," in Beyrer (ed.), *Zeit der Postkutschen*, 226.
25. Adolph Freiherr von Knigge, *Über den Umgang mit Menschen* (Frankfurt am Main: Insel Verlag, 1977), 269.
26. Knigge, *Umgang*, 272.
27. On this, see esp. Ute Planert, *Der Mythos vom Befreiungskrieg: Frankreichs Kriege und der deutsche Süden: Alltag – Wahrnehmung – Deutung, 1792–1841* (Paderborn: Schöningh, 2007).
28. Friedrich Schelling to his parents (Apr 3, 1796), in G. L. Plitt (ed.), *Aus Schellings Leben in Briefen* (Leipzig: Hirzel, 1869), vol. 1, 101–2.
29. Johann Wolfgang von Goethe, *Hermann and Dorothea*, trans. Ellen Frothingham (Boston: Roberts, 1879), 1–2 (translation modified by author).
30. Planert, *Befreiungskrieg*, 361–63.
31. On the Prussian mobilization, see esp. Karen Hagemann, *"Männlicher Muth und Teutsche Ehre": Nation, Militär und Geschlecht zur Zeit der Antinapoleonischen Kriege Preussens* (Paderborn: Schöningh, 2002).
32. Erika von Borries, *Wilhelm Müller, der Dichter der* Winterreise: *Eine Biographie* (Munich: Beck, 2007), 34.
33. Friedrich Max Müller, "Wilhelm Müller," *Allgemeine Deutsche Biographie (ADB)*. www.deutsche-biographie.de/
34. See George S. Williamson, "What Killed August von Kotzebue? The Temptations of Virtue and the Political Theology of German Nationalism, 1789–1819," *Journal of Modern History* 72 (2000): 890–943.
35. Wilhelm Müller, *Rom, Römer, Römerinnen* (1820), as cited in "Wilhelm Müller," *ADB*.
36. See, e.g., Jürgen Hillesheim, *Die Wanderung ins "nunc stans": Wilhelm Müllers und Franz Schuberts* Die Winterreise (Freiburg: Rombach, 2017).
37. Borries, *Wilhelm Müller*, 150–52, also argues for the political significance of this cycle.

38. On Schubert's politics and their influence on his musical setting of *Die Winterreise*, see Reinhold Brinkmann, "Musikalische Lyrik, politische Allegorie und die 'heil'ge Kunst': Zur Landschaft von Schuberts *Winterreise*," *Archiv für Musikwissenschaft* 62/2 (2005): 75–97.

39. In this context, it is useful to compare Novalis's "Faith and Love, or the King and the Queen" (1798), which presented the royal marriage as a symbol of the Prussian monarchy.

40. Brophy, *Popular Culture,* 67, quotes Ludwig Uhland's "Am 18. October 1816": "Did you forget the day of battle, / . . . When the people rid you of your disgrace, / When you tested their loyalty / Now it's up to you, not to console with words, / But to honor what you promised."

41. Wilhelm Müller to Per Daniel Amadeus Atterbom (Dec. 12, 1819), in Maria-Verena Leistner (ed.), *Wilhelm Müller: Werke, Tagebücher, Briefe*, 5 vols. (Berlin: Gatza, 1994), vol. 5, 147–48.

PART IV

Winterreise: Song Cycle

9 Identification in *Die schöne Müllerin* and *Winterreise*

JAMES WILLIAM SOBASKIE

Introduction

The devastating impact of Franz Schubert's *Winterreise* arises from our identification with its primary persona. We walk with the wanderer, privy to his thoughts, and imagine ourselves in his shoes, psychologically associating ourselves with the authorial creation. Schubert's *Die schöne Müllerin* also inspires identification, but our rapport with its central character gradually grows tenuous. We witness the journeyman's[1] enthusiasm, but become troubled by his choices and perceptions, wondering why common sense or rationality do not intervene. Both cycles set Wilhelm Müller's poetry, feature rejected unfortunates, and address mortality. Yet we regard and respond to their focal figures differently. *Die schöne Müllerin* solicits sympathy for its greenhorn, encouraging us to understand his feelings and regret his unhappiness. Nevertheless, as *Die schöne Müllerin* unfolds, we gradually retreat, distancing ourselves from the journeyman. In contrast, *Winterreise* elicits empathy for its outcast, inducing us to share his emotions and experience similar distress. Consequently, *Winterreise* evokes our own existential fears as we are drawn near to the wanderer.

Our identification with the protagonists of *Die schöne Müllerin* and *Winterreise* depends on Müller's portrayals. But Schubert's music reifies Müller's characters and reveals their interiority. Studied side by side, the cycles mutually inform and illuminate.

To begin, narrative summaries of *Die schöne Müllerin* and *Winterreise* will establish the cycles' dramatic foundations for identification and enable comparison.[2] Next, three factors that influence identification will be explored: form, texture, and contextual processes. Surveys of the cycles' song forms suggest that formal diversity and structural complexity, rather than simplicity, may enhance identification by demanding and gaining more involved interpretation. Similarly, textural change and complexity appear to promote identification through heightened engagement. Finally, characteristic contextual processes manipulate expectation and enhance dramatic climaxes in certain songs, intensifying identification. Given the richness of *Die schöne Müllerin* and *Winterreise*, comprehensive analysis is impossible. And superiority won't be decided. But the framework and observations provided here should prompt further inquiry into identification as well as new investigations of narrative, form, texture, and contextual processes within these monuments. Let's start with their stories.

The Narratives of Schubert's *Die schöne Müllerin* and *Winterreise*

In *Die schöne Müllerin*, a miller's helper with wanderlust leaves his master and encounters a babbling brook that leads him to another mill. The journeyman finds work there, plus a maiden who infatuates him. Grateful but curious, he wonders if the maiden or the brook had drawn him. At the mill, his tiring labor dispirits him because it doesn't gain the maiden's attention. So he asks the brook if she loves him, since he's sure she should have seen his interest. No answer arises. One morning when the eager admirer greets the maiden at her window, she turns away. Undeterred, he plants forget-me-nots below her window as a gentle gesture. Perhaps it works, for one evening, the two sit beside the brook, observing the moon and the stars mirrored in its flow. But the simple swain, who watches her eyes move from the water to him within its reflections while she waits for a word, is too shy to speak and becomes spellbound by the brook's babbling. When rain falls, all blurs, she says goodbye, then ups and leaves. Daylight finds him not disheartened but ecstatic, wishing to silence the stream, millwheels, and birds to proclaim that the maiden is his. His heart bursting with joy, the young man can't sing, fearing self-revelation, so he ties a green ribbon around his lute and hangs it on a wall to avoid temptation. When the maiden admires the ribbon (green is her favorite color), the fellow sends it to her, hoping she ties it in her hair. Unfortunately, a passing hunter attracts the maiden, vexing the journeyman. Perceiving rejection, hating the color green, and fixated on hunting, he becomes preoccupied with death, wishing for a verdant grave. Morose, the unfortunate consoles himself with the thought that if he were buried with the maiden's flowers, her remorseful tears would raise new blooms over his grassy mound in spring. Conversing with the brook, the sad soul ventures that when a lovesick heart dies, everything mourns. But the brook differs, asserting such death provides release from sorrow and brings new life. Persuaded of the brook's good will, while wondering how it knows love, the fellow perceives its flow's relief. So, he bids it to continue. Ultimately, only the brook remains, having welcomed the journeyman to watery rest with a lullaby.

In *Winterreise*, an ardent suitor, mortified by his beloved's marriage to a rich man, slips away from the scene of his rejection, leaving "good night" traced in snow on her gate. With the wind-whipped weathervane mockingly creaking atop her house, he realizes it'd earlier signaled her fickleness and her family's indifference. Frozen tears fall from the outcast's cheeks, surprising him, for he's unaware of his weeping and his waning sensitivity. Curiously, he imagines, the freezing weather has dulled his pain yet preserved the woman's image within his now-numb heart as a souvenir. Should his heart thaw, he muses, her image would drain away. Passing a familiar linden tree, which seems to bid him to stay and rest, the fugitive closes his eyes and resists consolation, shunning the tree's warm memories and sheltering comfort for a cold road. Yet its rustle continues calling after he leaves. While the glacial chill freezes his burning tears as they fall into the snow, he is sure that their fervent glow will return when they melt and run into the brook by his beloved's house. Like the nearby river, now ice-encrusted, the exile suspects that his now hardened heart also might hide a torrent, and wonders if it, too, sees its reflection in the river's frozen flow. Anxious to leave town and escape its memories, yet sorely tempted to glance backward toward his ex-sweetheart's house, he doesn't succumb. Instead, the fugitive follows a flickering "will-o'-the-wisp" into rocky chasms below the town, wending his way in the dark along a dry stream bed into wilderness. Later, an abandoned hut provides refuge though no respite, for his body aches and his heart stings. Nevertheless, he sleeps, dreaming of spring and his beloved, only to wake up cold and alone, ever more wretched in the morning stillness. A distant posthorn makes his heart pound, reminding of the town and prompting him to seek news, but he doesn't respond. Three omens – including frost that greyed the young man's black hair, a crow that trailed him as if he were prey, and a leaf that clung to a tree branch and fluttered like his hope – all forewarn but don't daunt him. Barking dogs in a nearby village, the poor fellow figures, might disturb its residents' dreams, but he has no more dreams nor any need for further delay. So he ventures into the now-stormy morning, led on by another illusory light. Following disused paths and ignoring city signposts, the outcast relentlessly pursues solitude, reaching a graveyard where he might rest for a while, yet the cemetery holds none for him. Without sleep, and without any particular goal, he pushes forward against wind and storm, driven by faithless and fatalistic courage. Phantom suns at the morning horizon transfix him, prompting the figment that since his beloved's bright eyes are gone from his life, his last source of light might as well follow. Outside another village, the wanderer sees a barefoot and benumbed hurdy-gurdy player grinding alone, ignored except by snarling dogs. Perceiving their similar situations and parallel prospects, the wanderer asks: "Shall I go with you? Will you play your organ to my songs?"

The Journeyman, the Wanderer, and Us

Today, some aspects of these stories seem senseless. Who abandons family, friends, community, connections, and job for utter uncertainty? Who chats with a brook or naps in a boneyard? Even assuming dysfunction, certain parts of these narratives remain foreign, incomprehensible, or indeterminate. Each protagonist transforms from *naif* to reject to wretch, a progression few of us know. Which conclusion is more tragic – a suicide or a shattering – is debatable. So is whether either story offers catharsis. Yet somehow these tales prompt us to suspend disbelief and identify with their characters, albeit in different ways and to varying degrees.

In *Die schöne Müllerin*, portrayal of a detailed past, unexpected immaturity, extreme behavior, and a supernatural context suppresses identification in favor of observation. *Winterreise* also presents extreme behavior, but its narrative's absorbing events and compelling interiority prompt self-projection. With fewer historical specifics and no supernatural presence, *Winterreise*'s evocative context elicits imaginative compensation that augments engagement. *Die schöne Müllerin* features a more traditional plot, variations on common characters, familiar situational elements, foreshadowing, decisive action, plus an epilogue, all of which would induce and reinforce an observational mindset. But it would seem that the focus on thoughts, feelings, and reactions in *Winterreise* hits home hard by eliciting deep-seated resonances within unguarded and receptive listeners. In any event, certain traits and choices of the central characters induce identification within us. The more we share with a character, the more we identify with and self-project upon him or her. The more that is alien to our nature and experience, the more we disassociate.

All of us can recall being anxious and curious about the future like the journeyman of *Die schöne Müllerin*. We also can remember being excited by our attraction to another while being uncertain about reciprocation and impatient to be noticed. So it's easy to accept the fellow's initial anthropomorphizing of the brook as idle reverie. And it's easy to recall feeling ignored or rebuffed by a heartthrob, hoping that a small kindness might help, as well as being too shy to respond at an opportune moment. Our resonance corresponds to identification. However, the young man's misinterpretation of the maiden's abrupt departure during their rendezvous represents an unsettling and alienating development. And while we may understand the journeyman's jealousy of the hunter and perceive his depression about the maiden's new fascination, his death wish and delusion regarding the young woman's remorse are too much to bear. His final conversation with the brook elicits rue, as does his irrevocable choice, though both distance us. Serious questions arise. Was that last exchange between the journeyman and the brook imaginary . . . or was it real? Even more disconcerting is the sneaking suspicion that an apparently benign yet possibly malevolent being may have been present all along. Was the brook stalking him from the start? As engaged auditors of Schubert's *Die schöne Müllerin*, we gradually distance ourselves in self-defense, pitying the fellow more than identifying with him. When the brook provides the song cycle's epilogue in "Des Baches Wiegenlied," with the journeyman nowhere near, we are left with a character we neither know nor trust – the brook – and feel pulled back into the scene while the longest song of the cycle unfolds. Although the narrative's primary persona is no longer there, our identification with him continues, causing us to feel uneasy in the brook's presence.

While few of us have suffered the humiliation endured by the wanderer in *Winterreise*, many have felt the need to escape after rejection or betrayal, recognizing signals of imminent rupture only in retrospect. In such situations, one is overwhelmed by emotions of differing intensities – unaware of some because others obscured, unsure what each was, uncertain how to respond, unclear what to do next – and one spurns solace to sublimate pain by whatever works. Of course, seeking seclusion in a nocturnal forest isn't something most would do, nor is staying overnight in a derelict dwelling. However, we can accept these conceits for the sake of the story, the flow of the music, and our own curiosity. Surely sleep's relief is a familiar experience, as is the shock of reality's return at dawn. So is the inability to anticipate welling memories, along with the need for sidestepping situations that summon them. What *Winterreise* does so well in its second half is portray the wanderer's gradual, inexorable descent into a much darker place, one that all of us have glimpsed or can imagine: a depressive and disoriented state in which perceptions and judgement should become suspect, but do not, wherein one steels oneself to press ahead, yet without a clear goal, and through which wellbeing is not a priority, though it should be. While the wanderer doesn't determinedly pursue oblivion, one senses that if Death, Fate, Nature, or some other claimant came for him, he wouldn't resist. The "will-o'-the-wisps," ominous indications, and phantom suns – all readily-explainable sights – seem more immediate and serious than they really are. But to the despondent outcast who's not slept for twenty-four-plus hours, they're plausible parts of his mental landscape. Happening upon an apparently similar soul at the end of

Winterreise, he senses kinship and directly addresses another human for the first time. But serious questions arise here too. Is the hurdy-gurdy player real? What happens next? Unlike with *Die schöne Müllerin*, we do not feel drawn back into the final scene of *Winterreise* because we never really left. Instead, our identification becomes ever more intense, for we, from our vantage point, cannot fully fathom what's going on in the winter wanderer's mind or grasp what his future holds, only guess.

It's not imperative that Müller and Schubert answer any open questions regarding *Winterreise* or *Die schöne Müllerin*. Posing them was the point. By providing a shared aesthetic experience to audiences, the artists increase affiliation, initiate conversation, and perhaps inspire kindness. Clear conclusions constrain cordial conversation! So, how does Schubert enhance our identification with Müller's characters? Form, texture, and contextual processes assist.

Song Forms and Identification in Schubert's Song Cycles

Formal diversity and structural complexity influence identification in Schubert's *Die schöne Müllerin* and *Winterreise*. How they do so may surprise. Let's examine the song forms.

Within Schubert's *Die schöne Müllerin*, eight Lieder exhibit simple strophic form, a design primarily founded on the principle of repetition. Each features a repeat-sign-bound span supportive of two to five sections, symbolizable as ‖:A(+A′,[etc.]):‖.[3] These include "Das Wandern," "Ungeduld," "Morgengruss," "Des Müllers Blumen," "Mit dem grünen Lautenbande," "Der Jäger," "Die liebe Farbe," and "Des Baches Wiegenlied." Additionally, "Tränenregen" is semi-strophic. It begins with three sections involving repeated music but concludes with an abbreviated variation of that material that serves as a coda, representable as ‖:A(+A′,A″):‖A‴.

Four Lieder in *Die schöne Müllerin* employ the principles of contrast, return, and variation to produce ternary forms representable as **ABA′**. These include "Am Feierabend," "Mein!," "Pause," and "Der Müller und der Bach." "Der Neugierige," portrayable as **ABB′**, just stresses the principles of contrast and variation, while "Trockne Blumen," expressible as **AB**, only features contrast. Finally, five may be considered through-composed, including "Wohin?," "Halt!," "Danksagung an den Bach," "Eifersucht und Stolz," and "Die böse Farbe." While these through-composed Lieder certainly draw upon the principles of contrast, return, and variation, plus that of development, all impress more as unique designs rather than instances of a common pattern.

Schubert's *Winterreise* includes only one simple strophic song, "Wasserflut," representable as $\|{:}A(+A'){:}\|$. Another, "Gute Nacht," features modified strophic form expressible as $\|{:}A(+A'){:}\|A''A'''$. Its opening sections present the same accompanimental music, the third incorporates significant variation, while the last bears even more substantial developmental changes. "Der Lindenbaum" lacks repeat signs and stresses variation, presenting a structure symbolizable as $AA'A''$ that mixes strophic, ternary, and variational characteristics. Its second section presents a change of mode as well as reinterpreted material with a substantial extension, while the third features further reinterpretation, a brief extension, plus a postlude.

Even more diverse designs that draw upon the principles of contrast, return, variation, and development appear within *Winterreise*, including these thirteen:

ABA′B′	"Die Post"
ABA′B′coda	"Erstarrung"
ABA′	"Rückblick," "Der greise Kopf," "Die Krähe," "Im Dorfe," "Täuschung," "Die Nebensonnen"
AA′	"Rast"
ABCA′B′C′	"Frühlingstraum"
AA′B	"Der Wegweiser," "Mut!," "Der Leiermann"

The remaining eight, including "Die Wetterfahne," "Gefror'ne Tränen," "Auf dem Flusse," "Irrlicht," "Einsamkeit," "Letzte Hoffnung," "Der stürmische Morgen," and "Das Wirtshaus," present even more unique designs and may be best understood as through-composed.

The preceding summary highlights two factors involving formal diversity and structural complexity in Schubert's *Die schöne Müllerin* and *Winterreise*. One pertains to strophic form, the other to structural design distribution.

Strophic form, characteristic of folk-songs and ballads, bears a bardic impression and elicits a corresponding listening posture. We settle in for an intriguing tale or moralistic story with repeated music and predictable breaks in the action that permit brief relaxation. One might assume that predictable, familiar music, plus time for reflection, would assure automatic and deep immersion in the narrative, but that's not always nor necessarily true. Strophic form's archaic aura distances us, diminishing identification by regular reminding that its recitation relates to a character from the past. Strophic form is interruptive – our concentration recedes, then ramps – and this cannot help but affect our focus, and in turn, the intensity of our identification with the protagonist. And of course, some stories in strophic forms chafe at their repeated musical vehicles, with later verses not fitting as well as earlier.

Sectional and through-composed songs are less predictable in nature, and their unfolding structures often are more extended in length, more internally complex, and more responsive to their texts. One might assume because they require more continuous attention and sustained interpretation, even over divisions and pauses, that we become overwhelmed. However, their increased interpretive demands actually appear to intensify identification by immersing us in detail, encouraging recognition and association, both consciously and subliminally. Of course, Schubert's engaging musical style contributes too!

Eight of the twenty Lieder in *Die schöne Müllerin* express simple strophic form, while just one of twenty-four in *Winterreise* does. With limited emphasis on that familiar form – which distracts by drawing attention to itself – and a great diversity of forms whose structural complexity requires a consistently high level of focus and interpretation, *Winterreise* seems to promote a correspondingly high level of identification with its primary persona. Engrossing us, *Winterreise* prompts perception of personal connection with its central character.

To sense how this is so, we may begin by comparing and contrasting increasingly complex Lieder from the two cycles, starting with two songs from *Die schöne Müllerin*. "Ungeduld" – a strophic song representable as ||:A(+A′,A″,A‴):|| – and "Tränenregen"– a semi-strophic song representable as ||:A(+A′,A″):||A‴. Both begin in A major and present outdoor vignettes sketched by the journeyman miller. In "Ungeduld," the young man's exuberant expression of love is infectious and unyielding, a portrait of bottled impatience. In "Tränenregen," which recounts the rendezvous by the brook, his ardor remains, though more subdued as it is sustained through the first three spans. However, "Tränenregen" takes a surprising turn within its final section, where initially familiar material briefly tonicizes C major (m. 28), quickly returns to A major (m. 32), and closes in A minor (m. 36) to underscore the young man's shattered reverie and his beloved's abrupt departure. Its narrative and musical shifts demand more, and we contribute more while perceiving more.

"Gute Nacht," the first Lied of *Winterreise*, offers an even greater interpretive challenge. Embodying modified strophic form – ||:A(+A′):||A″A‴ – its first three sections all feature tonal flow from D minor, to F major, to B♭ major before D minor returns, underscoring the fluidly shifting moods of the ex-suitor in front of his beloved's house. The third presents changes in the main melody, plus an extension with a more prominent piano part, to portray rising regret as the protagonist prepares to leave. The final section brings a surprising switch to D major to convey rueful acceptance, though the postlude's minor close bears (and bares!) genuine grief. For engaged listeners, the changes require more, we invest more, and we gain more.

"Der Lindenbaum," from *Winterreise*, presents a design – **AA′A″** – that might be considered either modified strophic or three-part form. Its piano part becomes increasingly energetic and expansive to portray enveloping elements and emotions as the wanderer weighs the tree's offer of rest. The song's contrasting central variant, which starts in minor, moves to major, and concludes with an extension (mm. 45–58), communicates the wanderer's determination to reject the linden tree's comfort and move on, even as cold winds blow off his hat. The final section of "Der Lindenbaum," all in major, captures the diminishing pull of memory dominated by the ex-suitor's desire to get away. The composition's individuality and suggestiveness impel us to seek meaning, infer, recognize, connect, and understand. In turn, we cannot help but resonate with the emotions expressed by the wanderer character.

While the formal diversity and structural complexity of Schubert's song cycles may only be generally compared, it would seem that *Winterreise*'s interpretive demands require considerable conscious concentration from engaged listeners and are apt to elicit substantial background processing of its narrative that may encourage identification with its protagonist. Texture appears to bear similar implications.

Texture and Identification in Schubert's Song Cycles

The textures of *Die schöne Müllerin* and *Winterreise*, like much Western art music, may be characterized using visual terms. More specifically, textural elements within a given span of music may be interpreted as belonging to its foreground, middleground, or background.[4] A Lied's vocal melody, when present, predominates in the foreground. We focus on it like a painting's subject. A bass line in the piano's accompaniment, when conceived as a counterpoint to the vocal melody, belongs to the song's middleground. It complements the more prominent part, enriching the structure while informing interpretation. If the bass is less distinguished, it may recede into the Lied's background. Yet a bass line or an upper accompaniment strand may project into the foreground when the voice is absent or when the bass doubles the voice, or strive for attention within the middleground when interacting with the vocal melody. Harmonic accompaniment elements belong to the background. As this general overview suggests, the components of a song's aural field may change roles rapidly in real time – they're not always static. Texture enhances identification with the primary personae in various ways within *Die schöne Müllerin* and *Winterreise*, usually in conjunction with other elements, and sometimes achieves

Example 9.1 *Die schöne Müllerin*, "Das Wandern," mm. 1–12[5]

remarkable effects through brief and/or inconspicuous details in the middle-ground or even in the background. Let's see how.

For instance, at the start of *Die schöne Müllerin*, the journeyman's infectious energy may be perceived within the opening vocal phrases in mm. 4–7 and 8–11 of the first Lied, "Das Wandern," which seem a bit rushed at three measures plus a pickup. Example 9.1 offers illustration.

Answered by the piano's brief melodic responses (d′-f′-d′) that emerge from the rolling background in the right-hand part of mm. 7–8 and 11–12, these foreground/middleground textural alternations communicate youthful enthusiasm anyone can sense. The third phrase brings textural contrast through a seemingly more expansive and invigorating voice/bass duet that's sequential in nature, while the last phrase highlights the voice's repetitive and diminishing melody with undulating harmony in the background. Repeated four more times via the song's strophic structure, the music of this song, with its jaunty physicality, visual suggestion, and textural variety, snags us for the rest of the cycle. Yes, there's more than just texture involved here, but the shifts within "Das Wandern" contribute to its engaging and exhilarating impression.

Surely the shifting textures of "Der Neugierige" intimate the journeyman's interiority in ways that inspire identification. Example 9.2 offers its first twelve measures.

Example 9.2 *Die schöne Müllerin*, "Der Neugierige," mm. 1–12[6]

Gradually moving three times in its opening section (mm. 1–22) from a relatively thin, high, and delicate texture to a thicker, lower, and more resonant one, the Lied initially communicates his fluctuating curiosity by textural expansions in the middleground and background. The texture expands, flourishes, and then recedes. With the emergence of triple meter and undulating arpeggios of the second section, ushered in by the void of m. 22 which conveys a shift of focus that heightens tension, we can virtually see and share in the character's contemplation as he queries the brook about his beloved's feelings. And the recitative-like texture of mm. 33–40 seems to come out of nowhere, portraying a dramatic flight of imagination as he asks for a "yes" or "no" whether the miller's daughter loves him, turning the request over and over in his mind as he wonders. Varying and evolving texture tells what's going on inside the young man, which, in turn, encourages our identification with him.

Other textural features within *Die schöne Müllerin* portray interiority. For instance, the delicate, charming, and unexpected echo in the middleground of mm. 16–21 of "Morgengruss" would seem to suggest an ethereal image passing through the journeyman's mind, at least on first hearing. The accompaniment of "Pause" evokes the lute, much of it unfolding so independently of the voice, mostly within the middleground, that the latter gains a distant, lost-in-thought quality indicative of the character's reverie. Yet on three occasions (see mm. 33–35, 53–55, and 63–69), the piano part of "Pause" defers to the voice by retreating into the background, supporting brief recitative-like spans that suggest clear-minded thought. And while the accompaniment of "Mit dem grünen Lautenbande" also evokes the lute, its closer relationship with the foregrounded vocal line gives the Lied a more retrospective, even archaic quality, as if the young man had imagined himself somewhere in ages past. In contrast, the continuously-reiterated f#′ of "Die liebe Farbe," a persistent, even obsessive textural detail in the background, contributes to that song's striking immediacy and savage irony. The series of changing and contrasting two-measure textural units within the first third of "Die böse Farbe" surely suggests internal anxiety – through texture we sense restlessness and anger. Finally, the inner-voice motion through most of "Des Baches Wiegenlied" surely portrays the murmuring and gentle flow associable with a lullaby, and because of its melodic independence, seems to reside in the middleground. Yet the compound perfect fifths and perfect octaves, expressed via half notes in mm. 1–15 and 20–25 within the background, are no less important to the closing Lied's effect. Indeed, they produce an ambient spatiality unlike any heard earlier in the cycle, perhaps providing a hint of the journeyman's repose. We sense some of what the fellow would seem to perceive through texture within the middlegrounds and backgrounds of *Die schöne Müllerin*. *Winterreise* exploits texture similarly.

However, the middlegrounds conveyed by the piano within Schubert's second song cycle may seem even more teeming and individuated than those of *Die schöne Müllerin*. Their contents may change frequently and unpredictably, interacting with their foregrounds while maintaining considerable independence. Indeed, at times the middlegrounds of *Winterreise* even seem to provide competition with and distraction from the voice. Curiously, this seems to increase our focus on the Lied's texted content and its nuances in the foreground. Engaged by the compelling narrative, the rich content, and Schubert's intriguing style, we lean in. Remarkably, this seems to enhance our engagement and intensify our identification with the wanderer. Let's examine evidence with illustrations.

Consider Example 9.3, a selective excerpt drawn from "Gute Nacht," the first Lied of *Winterreise*, that presents essential foreground and middleground elements from an early span.

As this suggests, separate accompanimental strands, each with its own melodic integrity, compete with the voice for our attention. The contrapuntal web they create with the foregrounded vocal melody places demands on the listener similar to that of fugue. Here, the aural portrait would seem to reflect the soon-to-be wanderer's internal debate and

Example 9.3 *Winterreise*, "Gute Nacht," mm. 15–26 (selective excerpt)[7]

anxiety as he prepares to leave. Our aural filtering here provides an analogous experience.

In Example 9.4, a full-content excerpt drawn from "Irrlicht," the ninth Lied of *Winterreise*, the piano's music certainly defers to the voice, yet is so individuated, as well as interactive with its more prominent partner, that their sum seems to represent concurrent dialogue.

Here, the registrally shifting, distinctively articulated, texturally fluctuating, and orchestrally conceived piano part – much of which sounds higher than the tenor voice – attracts so much attention to itself in the middleground, that we must apply considerable concentration just to follow the quickly unfolding and densely expressive text. In this passage, which presents the second stanza of Müller's poem, we're able to share the wanderer's perception of the darting will-o'-the-wisp as well as his recognition of its correspondence to the randomness of Fate. Our aural experience offers a hint of the journeyman's visual experience.

In "Letzte Hoffnung," the first vocal phrases almost seem to unfold in a separate channel, enveloped by metrically ambiguous activity in the middleground. Example 9.5 illustrates this.

A listener's ear is attracted from register to register in this span as the voice's largely conjunct line holds sway. Capturing the wanderer's visual observations and internal musings about the fate of leaves whipped by the wind and about to fall from their trees, which strike

Example 9.4 *Winterreise*, "Irrlicht," mm. 17–28[8]

Example 9.5 *Winterreise*, "Letzte Hoffnung," mm. 4–15[9]

him as parallel to his own, this music demonstrates Schubert's profound understanding of human psychology as well as any other in *Winterreise*.

Contrary to what one might imagine, increased textural complexity in Schubert's Lieder seems to engage and intrigue more than it deters or fatigues, and this may have something to do with the composer's personal style, which seems endlessly innovative and intrinsically evocative. However, his music also elicits expectations whose fulfillment is less immediate and more cumulative. Let's look closer.

Contextual Processes and Identification in Schubert's Song Cycles

Contextual processes – structural sequences that generate anticipation in advance of a climactic fulfilling event – appear more commonly in Schubert's music than one might imagine.[10] Within *Die schöne Müllerin* and *Winterreise*, contextual processes enhance identification in intriguing and idiosyncratic ways as they contribute to perceptions of momentum and unity.[11] Let's observe several.

For instance, certain contextual processes feature a gradually ascending vocal ceiling.[12] In "Wohin?," the second Lied of *Die schöne Müllerin*, the initially highest vocal pitch, notated as d″ in m. 3, soon is exceeded by the notated e″ in m. 13, which later is surpassed by the notated f♯″ in m. 33.[13] But the then-expected g″ that would complete this rising perfect fourth and resolve the leading tone in the voice of m. 33 waits until m. 71, just ten from the end. During this span, sensitive listeners experience their own subliminal expectation that parallels the uncertainty being conveyed by the character of the journeyman, portrayed by the singer, who describes being led along by a babbling brook, unsure where he is going, only to realize near the Lied's conclusion that the water may be guiding him to another mill. Complemented by other musical factors, of course, this rising registral ceiling adds to the Lied's dramatic momentum while encouraging listeners to identify with the character's anticipation.[14]

In the next Lied, "Halt!," an ascent from a notated e″ in m. 12 to an f″ in m. 16 would seem to have stalled by m. 35 with a repetition of that f″. However, the pitch g″, reached in m. 40 and reiterated in m. 44, enables a coincidence of the vocal line's apex with the word "Himmel" (sky). There within the text's narrative, a shining sun seems to confirm that the millhouse where the still-searching young man has stopped is where he was meant to be. As listeners, we experience an arrival effect contributed in part by this rising vocal ceiling.

And in the seventh Lied of *Die schöne Müllerin*, "Ungeduld," an even more anxious and agitated stepwise rise in the vocal ceiling from a notated c♯" (m. 9) to d" (m. 11) to e" (m. 13) to f♯" (m. 14) to g♮" (m. 15) and – after a bit of a delay – finally to a" (mm. 21, 23), conveys the fellow's waves of impatience that unfold over the four verses. In these songs from *Die schöne Müllerin*, rising vocal ceilings elicit subtle effects of anticipation and arrival, portraying the persona's interiority via expectations whose fulfillment we may share.

Contextual processes founded on rising vocal ceilings communicate interiority within *Winterreise* too. For instance, in "Letzte Hoffnung," a gradual ascent involving the notated pitches c♭", c", d", (e♭"'s skipped!), f", g♭", and g" communicates the height of anguish as the wanderer speaks (via the singer!) of weeping on the grave of his hopes as he waits to see if a leaf will fall. And in "Der Wegweiser," a determined rise over a longer span involving the sequence g'-a'-b♭'-c"-d"-e"-g♭"(=f♯")-g" reaches its height in m. 52 as the character speaks of wandering on relentlessly and restlessly, seeking yet not finding rest. There the final pitch sounds over a climactic cadential six-four, never to be stabilized through harmonization by the tonic triad within the space of the song. We, as listeners, can identify with the wanderer's anxiety through our own unfulfilled expectations, since the resolution of the song's expansive ascent only may be imagined over a later instance of the tonic triad.

Certain other rising vocal ceilings, including those in "Die Wetterfahne" and "Gefror'ne Tränen," fade without ever reaching climactic arrivals at anticipated tonic triad tones in the voice. Similarly, all four sections of "Die Post" seem to suggest that the voice eventually will achieve the notated pitch g" – the third of the E♭ major tonic triad – yet the goal remains tantalizingly out of reach. Frustrating expectations to communicate impressions of inadequacy, these ascents underscore the cycle's narrative as they reflect the wanderer's dejection. It would seem that, following *Die schöne Müllerin*, Schubert continued to explore the expectation-engendering potential of rising registral ceilings in *Winterreise*, creating ever more subtle instances that communicate frustration felt by the wanderer by not providing anticipated arrivals within the music. Along with the matters of form and texture, it seems clear that much remains to be discovered regarding Schubert's rising registral ceilings, as well as his incorporation of contextual processes more generally.

A master of manipulating his listener's responses, Franz Schubert employs subtle musical means in his song cycles to enable us to sense emotions and reactions similar to those portrayed by his characters. If we're engaged, we identify with them even more through what we perceive as shared experience. In turn, our immersion within his narratives is all the more vivid.[15]

Afterthoughts

Perhaps the most admirable achievements of *Die schöne Müllerin* and *Winterreise* are their persuasive prompts to sympathize and empathize with their central characters. Each encourages us to descend deeper into our own imaginations and reflect upon our own responses to their stories. In turn, these masterpieces may be interpreted as entreaties to become more sympathetic and empathetic human beings. Within today's turbulent world and dimming future, such sensitivity seems in short supply. Indeed, the pleas for compassion within *Die schöne Müllerin* and *Winterreise* may be among the greatest legacies of Franz Schubert's Romanticism.

Notes

1. After apprenticing to a master miller for seven years, one became a *journeyman* – a laborer employed by another master. The protagonist of *Die schöne Müllerin* initially could have been an apprentice, though more likely a journeyman, since he was able to take leave of his master.
2. For more on narrative, see: Wayne C. Booth, *The Rhetoric of Fiction*, 2nd ed. (Chicago: University of Chicago Press, 1983); H. Porter Abbott, *The Cambridge Introduction to Narrative*, 2nd ed. (Cambridge: Cambridge University Press, 2008); Matthew Garrett (ed.), *The Cambridge Companion to Narrative Theory* (Cambridge: Cambridge University Press, 2018).
3. In the system of form representation here, subsequent verses featuring new text conveyed by repeated accompaniment are symbolized using parentheses enclosed by repeat signs, and bolded letters with primes indicate textual variation. Unenclosed bolded letters with one or more primes communicate more substantial variation. Repeated letters identify corresponding content, while different letters identify contrasting content. Subordinate spans within individual Lieder, like introductions, links, transitions, and codettas, are not represented by these patterns so as to enable the highlighting of broad similarities.
4. Heinrich Schenker used the terms *foreground*, *middleground*, and *background* in reference to tonal voice-leading structure, but here these terms characterize more immediate perceptions. My own approach derives from the discussion in Samuel Adler, *The Study of Orchestration*, 4th ed. (New York: Norton, 2016), 126–32.
5. Franz Schubert: *Die schöne Müllerin* op. 25 (High Voice), ed. Walther Dürr, BA 9117 (Kassel: Bärenreiter-Verlag Karl Vötterle GmbH & Co. KG, 2010), 1. Cordial thanks are extended to Katharina Malecki of Bärenreiter for her kind help with these musical examples.
6. Ibid., 15.
7. Franz Schubert: *Winterreise* op. 89 (High Voice), ed. Walther Dürr, BA 9118 (Kassel: Bärenreiter-Verlag Karl Vötterle GmbH & Co. KG, 2009), 2. This excerpt is termed "selective" because some inner elements of the accompaniment are omitted to highlight the contrapuntal strands.
8. Ibid., 30–31.
9. Ibid, 48.
10. Edward T. Cone's essay, "Schubert's Promissory Note: An Exercise in Musical Hermeneutics," *19th-Century Music* 5/3 (1982): 233–41, offered the first description of a contextual process within the music of Franz Schubert, though it did not use that term to describe the composer's systematic delay of a prominent and persistent chromatic pitch's resolution in his *Moment musical* in A♭ major (D780). Richard Kurth described a contextual process involving meter in his "On the Subject of Schubert's 'Unfinished' Symphony: Was bedeutet die Bewegung?," *19th-Century Music* 23/1 (1999): 3–32.
11. I have discussed a variety of contextual processes in Schubert's music; see: " Tonal Implication and the Gestural Dialectic in Schubert's A Minor Quartet," in Brian Newbould (ed.), *Schubert the Progressive: History, Performance Practice, Analysis* (Aldershot: Ashgate, 2003), 53–79; " The 'Problem' of Schubert's String Quintet," *Nineteenth-Century Music Review* 2/1 (2005), 57–92;

"Schubert's Self-Elegies," *Nineteenth-Century Music Review* 5/2 (2008), 71–105; "Conversations Within and Between Two Early Lieder of Schubert," *Nineteenth-Century Music Review* 13/1 (2016), 83–102; "The Dramatic Strategy in Two of Schubert's Serenades," in *DMFS*, 133–50.

12. I have observed similar instances of rising registral ceilings in Schubert's choral music; see my chapter, "Contextual Processes in Schubert's Late Sacred Music," in *RS*, 295–332, especially 297–99.

13. References to the voice's pitches are qualified here by the term "notated" pitches (e.g., "notated as d‴") since a tenor's voice actually sounds an octave lower than written. Of course, *Die schöne Müllerin* has been performed by sopranos at the notated pitch.

14. The high g″ in m. 71 of "Wohin?" isn't supported by the tonic harmony, sounds only briefly, and appears off the beat, so its arrival remains somewhat tentative.

15. *Winterreise* also holds other kinds of contextual processes. Readers may wish to examine Arnold Feil's analysis of Schubert's "Im Dorfe," which illuminates an intriguing contextual process involving metric conflict whose resolution seems imminent in mm. 37–40, yet requires a second attempt in mm. 42–46. See *FSSMW*, 29–38.

10 Text–Music Relationships

SUSAN WOLLENBERG

This chapter explores Schubert's *Winterreise* from a number of angles. First, under the heading of "Connecting Threads," I consider overarching elements in text and music. Text and music do not necessarily coincide in all dimensions (such as their timeframe, or their structure), but may gain added power from being non-congruent. Secondly, I examine Schubert's deployment of the "fingerprints" of his personal style: these too contribute to the intense impact of *Winterreise*.[1] In setting the twenty-four poems of the finished cycle, Schubert not only created an alliance between music newly conceived for the purpose and Müller's words; he also, importantly, formed an alliance of the words with core features of his compositional style at a ripe stage of its development.

In highlighting the detail of Schubert's settings, I identify in some songs what I call the "crux," containing the nub of what is expressed in the poetic text. Where the musical response to the poetry coincides with the crucial words uttered by the voice, such examples are among the most powerful in this category. Under various headings, I pinpoint specific topical references that help form the fabric of text and music.[2] The intricacy of that combined fabric means that only a selection of examples can be discussed in detail. Table 10.1 provides an overview of all twenty-four songs for reference.

We might pause to consider the characters peopling the narrative of *Winterreise*. The cycle is remarkable in its intensive focus on the protagonist, so that as listeners we may feel almost as if we experience something of the hardship he goes through on his journey. The landscape itself is a quasi-figure in the narrative, its features vividly delineated; its presence is constantly impressed on our senses, as it is on the protagonist's. In a work founded on paired opposites, this strenuous winter's journey represents a negative version of the Grand Tour (in the sense of a photographic negative). In place of the kind of *Bildung* whereby the traveler on the Grand Tour absorbs the culture of the wider world beyond his own experience, the landscape traversed by the protagonist in *Winterreise* makes his awareness turn inward onto his private feelings and experiences.[3]

[165]

Table 10.1 *Overview of text and music*

Song number/Title	Key/Tempo	Mood/Musical topics	Motifs/Devices (text)	Motifs/Devices (music)
1 Gute Nacht (Good Night)	d / *Mässig*	Somber/slow march; hymn-like (F, B flat); dreams (D)	Winter landscape, enforced journey; hope/disappointment; lost love/isolation; past/present; dreaming	Drone/trudging footsteps; neighbor-note motif ("x"); falling third motif ("y"); falling fourths; arpeggiation; minor/major
2 Die Wetterfahne (The Weathervane)	a / *Ziemlich geschwind*	Ominous; grotesque; dance (*Konzertstück*)	Wind blowing; her house; mockery; faithlessness	Arpeggiation; trills; motif x; chromatic thread; minor/major
3 Gefror'ne Tränen (Frozen Tears)	f / *Nicht zu langsam*	Grotesque march; Viennoiserie/dance; recitative	Tears falling; ice/heat; his heart	Semitonal motif; aug./dim. intervals
4 Erstarrung (Numbness)	c / *Ziemlich schnell*	Antique style/canon, augmentation (mm. 26 ff.)	Ice and snow; frozen/melting; tears; his heart; past/present/memory	Motif x; moto perpetuo; chromatic threads; cadential delaying (v. 2); Neapolitan figure
5 Der Lindenbaum (The Linden Tree)	E / *Mässig*	Hymnlike (E); storm; lullaby	Linden tree; dreaming; love; wind blowing	Major/minor
6 Wasserflut (Flood Water)	e / *Langsam*	Slow quasi-march/dirge; lullaby	Ice and snow, wind; burning, melting; tears; her house	Arpeggiation; cadential delaying
7 Auf dem Flusse (On the River)	e / *Langsam*	Slow march; antique style; lyrical (central episode)	[Water] rushing/still; past/present; memories; his heart	Partimento-type bass; remote modulations; motif x; minor/major
8 Rückblick (A Look Backward)	g / *Nicht zu geschwind*	Impulsive motion (vs. 1 & 2, v. 5); fragility/ lullaby (vs. 3 & 4)	Ice and snow; birds, linden trees; past/present; inconstancy; her house	Rocking octaves; chromatic threads; motif y; hemiola; minor/major
9 Irrlicht (Will-o'-the-Wisp)	b / *Langsam*	Grotesque march	Illusion (*ignis fatuus*); mockery; the grave	Falling fourths; Neapolitan figure (v. 3)
10 Rast (Rest)	c / *Mässig*	Dirge/antique style/ground; "folk" style (voice, vs. 1, 3)	Freezing/burning; storm; his heart	Chromatic threads; cadential delaying
11 Frühlingstraum (Dream of Spring)	A / *Etwas bewegt/Schnell/Langsam*	Musical box/ Viennoiserie/dance; dreams; grotesque; lullaby	Dreaming/awakening; birds; illusion; his heart	Motif x; dissonance; rocking octaves; major/minor
12 Einsamkeit (Solitude)	b / *Langsam*	Dirge, "folk" style; storm (v. 3)	Alienation; gentle breeze/raging storms	Drone/slow footsteps; accompanied recit.

No. Title	Key / Tempo	Motifs/Devices (topic)	Mood/Musical topics	Motifs/Devices (music)
13 Die Post (The Post)	E flat / *Etwas geschwind*	Horn calls (posthorn)	Hope/disappointment; his heart	Moto perpetuo
14 Der greise Kopf (The Old Man's Head)	c / *Etwas langsam*	Antique style/ground; recit. (v. 2)	Illusion; frost/melting; death	Arpeggiation/ dim. sevenths
15 Die Krähe (The Crow)	c / *Etwas langsam*	"Folk" style (v. 1, v. 3 ll. 1–2)	Faithfulness; the grave	Moto perpetuo; motif x; drama (v. 2, v. 3 ll. 3–4)
16 Letzte Hoffnung (Last Hope)	E flat / *Nicht zu geschwind*	"Pizzicato"-style acc. (v. 3, final line)	Wind/fall of a leaf; loss of hope	Arpeggiation/ dim. sevenths; semitonal motif; major/minor
17 Im Dorfe (In the Village)	D / *Etwas langsam*	Hymn-like/antique style (final line)	Barking dogs; dreams; alienation	Tremolo figuration; 4-3 suspensions; Mozartian buffo style
18 Der stürmische Morgen (The Stormy Morning)	d / *Ziemlich geschwind, doch kräftig*	March; theatricality/impulsiveness	Extreme weather; his heart	Arpeggiation/dim. sevenths; Neapolitan figure (v. 3 ll. 3–4)
19 Täuschung (Illusion)	A / *Etwas geschwind*	Waltz/Viennoiserie /barcarolle	Illusion; ice; warm house/beloved soul	Ostinato; motif x; chromatic thread
20 Der Wegweiser (The Sign Post)	g / *Mässig*	Dirge; antique style incl. "lament bass" and "wedge," chant (v. 4)	Isolation; death	Trudging footsteps; chromatic thread; remote modulations; Neapolitan figure
21 Das Wirtshaus (The Inn)	F / *Sehr langsam*	Hymn-like, slow march	Mortally wounded (v. 3, l. 4); the graveyard ("no room at the inn")	Motif y; dactylic figure; major/minor incl. echo (v. 3, l. 4)
22 Mut (Courage)	g / *Ziemlich geschwind, kräftig*	March/"folk dance"	Defiance; snow/wind; his heart; singing	Major/minor
23 Die Nebensonnen (The False Suns)	A / *Nicht zu langsam*	Hymn-like, antique style/sarabande	Illusion; death wish	Major/minor
24 Der Leiermann (The Hurdy-Gurdy Man)	a / *Etwas langsam*	"Folk" style; grotesque lullaby	Ice; dogs growling; traveler/musician; singing	Drone; ostinato

Key

Acc. = accompaniment; Capitals for major, lower case for minor keys; aug. = augmented; dim. = diminished; l. = line, ll. = lines; v. = verse, vs. = verses. In "Mood/Musical topics," "*Konzertstück*" indicates "brilliant" topic (virtuoso display); "*Viennoiserie*" denotes stylised Viennese dance figures. In "Motifs/Devices (music)," "chromatic thread" refers to the melodic line; "minor/major" (or vice versa) is indicated only in cases of parallel rather than relative keys; "motif x" refers to its original or inverted form; "Neapolitan figure" is the three- or four-note motif with flattened supertonic and leading-note turning around the tonic note or flattened sixth and augmented fourth turning around the dominant note.

Other characters are figures from the past: the girl he longs for, her mother, and by implication her father, and the bridegroom who has replaced the protagonist in her affections. Those telling lines in "Gute Nacht," "Das Mädchen sprach von Liebe, / Die Mutter gar von Eh'" (The girl spoke of love, / Her mother even of marriage), accompanied in the music by the turn to the relative major, have the power to remain imprinted on our minds. Indicative of a poetic thread running through the cycle, their import is full of hope, yet weighted with the danger of hope's defeat. We might recognize their echo in "Die Post" at the start of Part II, when the sound of the posthorn raises hopes doomed to be betrayed. There too Schubert matches the opposing states by contrast of mode, in the parallel minor at the start of verse 2 where the traveler imagines that the post brings him no letter.[4]

While the girl and her family remain in his memory, the only other characters introduced during the course of the winter journey belong to the present rather than the past. First of these is the charcoal-burner in "Rast," whose cramped home the wanderer enters for shelter. This character apparently exists only in absentia, or – if he is in residence – as a silent and unseen presence.[5] The hurdy-gurdy man introduced in the final song ("Der Leiermann") provokes speculation as to whether he represents an illusory or a real figure, and whether he functions literally as a traveling performer, or symbolically as a manifestation of Death. The Leiermann's instrument suggests that he could represent an immigrant, set apart, like the protagonist. Susan Youens characterizes him as the protagonist's *Doppelgänger*, a figure traditionally taken to be a premonition of death;[6] this chimes with the duality in the constructions of both text and music throughout the cycle.

Connecting Threads

Arguably the most fundamental element linking text and music across the cycle is the intimation that the central figure is a musician. His appeal to the hurdy-gurdy man in the final three lines: "Soll ich mit dir geh'n? / Willst zu meinen Liedern / Deine Leier dreh'n?" (Shall I go with you? / Will you play your organ / To my songs?), can be taken as an indication of the protagonist's calling rather than as metaphorical. Ian Bostridge has explored the traveler's possible status as a music tutor in the girl's household, while emphasizing Müller's wish to avoid defining the character too precisely.[7] Further indication is planted in "Mut!," where the protagonist sings in defiance of the harsh conditions through which he journeys (and the depressive side of his own feelings): "Wenn mein Herz im Busen spricht, / Sing' ich hell und munter" (When my heart speaks in my breast, / I sing loudly and gaily).

Another overarching element is the intensity with which the poet's words portray the winter journey. The effects involved include extreme contrast and the evocation of startling images. Schubert's setting creates a comparable intensity from across the spectrum at his disposal, including rhythmic profile, melodic shaping, motivic usage, harmony, texture, dynamics, relationship of voice and piano, and function of the piano accompaniment. All these, overlapping with topical reference, have the power to convey what words alone could not achieve, and to enhance or affirm what the words express. Additional details such as a specific contrapuntal device, or fragment of word-painting, can throw a spotlight on the text at individual moments.

Used in these ways, the music may add to the text Schubert's personal reading of it, especially where the poet has created ambiguity or uncertainty rather than giving explicit definition to his ideas. In "Gute Nacht," where the girl speaks of love and the mother "even of marriage," with the move from the tonic minor to the relative major and then into its subdominant (see Example 10.1, mm. 15–23), Schubert allies the major mode with a diatonic chordal style of hymn-like serenity.[8] This passage gains a touching hopefulness, expressed musically in the upwards reach of the melody and its sequentially related phrases. Notably absent from Schubert's setting here is any trace of the bitterness associated with the betrayal that followed those promising signals from mother and daughter. Schubert's music recaptures the moments of pure hope, untainted by hindsight.

That excursus into the major throws into sharper relief the return to the tonic minor for the ensuing lines: "Nun ist die Welt so trübe, / Der Weg gehüllt in Schnee" (Now the world is so gloomy, / The road shrouded in snow). Here Schubert's repeat of the paired lines is unable to move in key, remaining mired in the protagonist's mood and the surrounding scene. In both text and music, "Gute Nacht" prepares us for many other instances where references to past happiness and comfort are contrasted with present hardship and misery. Schubert's musical treatment gives love remembered a distinctive profile, as he does variously with the other main themes of *Winterreise*: loss, loneliness, death, and the winter journey itself. "Gute Nacht" introduces elements in both words and music that will be fundamental to the cycle as a whole.

Altogether a sense of the magnitude of the protagonist's situation, and of the epic journey he undertakes, issues from the cycle in both text and music. The prolonging of harmonic progressions, as in "Rast," at the matching ends of verses 2 and 4 in each paired set of verses, corresponds

Example 10.1 "Gute Nacht," mm. 15–29[9]

to the prolonged agony the wanderer carries with him. The extended diminished seventh chord heard at mm. 21–23 (see Example 10.2) and again at mm. 51–53, prefacing the approach to the cadence, is exploited for its disturbing properties. Its configuration, with notes crowded low in the piano accompaniment, together with the dissonant appoggiaturas in the voice (arrowed on Example 10.2), contributes to the harsh, grinding effect.

Within each of these passages, the harmony is twice denied resolution before it is accomplished. Delay first sets in with the prolongation of the diminished seventh beyond normal expectations (as indicated on Example 10.2). An escape route is offered by the move to an augmented sixth (marked on the example in m. 23), with potential to trigger the cadential progression towards closure; but the music stalls, forming an interrupted rather than perfect cadence at m. 25. Only after a varied rerun, to a repeat of the last two lines of text, now prolonging the augmented sixth harmony (at mm. 26–29), does it finally resolve in a perfect cadence. In tandem with

Example 10.2 "Rast," mm. 20–31

these proceedings, the vocal line soars beyond the confines of its contours earlier in the song. Schubert adds a tiny, affecting detail to the vocal part in the final version of the passage, inserting an anticipatory note at m. 55, before the upwards resolution of the appoggiatura on the word "regen" (stir).

These tactics lift the music of "Rast" above the level of the quasi-folk style with which Schubert delineated the humble scene in the vocal melody at the start. (That folk-like idiom forms another recurrent feature of the cycle, matching the equivalent element in Müller's poetry). At the same time, and a measure of Schubert's mastery, the disruptive surface created here rests on an underlying harmonic logic. Schubert's dynamics add to the dramatic effect. He marks *pianissimo* for those uncertain approaches to the cadence, poised in each case on an enigmatic chord. *Forte* is marked for each of the postponed cadential resolutions, where in verse 2 the storm blows the traveler uncomfortably, even dangerously, along (a sensation he

Example 10.3 "Gute Nacht," mm. 1–11

later tells us he welcomes), and where in the painful closing words of the final verse, his heart burns with the serpent that stirs within his breast.

At the opposite end of the spectrum from this drawn-out effect is the sudden stab of pain, as in "Wasserflut" towards the end of verse 1 in the repeated double-verse setting. After climbing precipitately through a tenth (m. 11), the vocal line seems to overshoot its target. What could have been the expected end of the phrase, on the E, is harmonized not with the tonic chord but with a dominant seventh of A minor transformed to a diminished seventh, against which the voice utters an anguished cry (m. 12) on the word "Weh" (woe). The melisma here, tracing the interval of a descending minor third over the sustained dissonant harmony, leaves the music open, responding to the sound of the word, which with its soft ending rather than hard consonant leaves the line of poetry similarly open-ended. (This plangent minor third was predicted at the start of the cycle in the opening three notes of the piano's RH melody, echoed in the voice, filling in the interval stepwise in what constitutes the recurrent motif marked "y" in Example 10.3.) Schubert's sensitivity to what Stephen Rodgers has referred to as the "sonic dimension of poetry" is a feature in evidence throughout D911.[10]

In "Wasserflut," with the ensuing repetition of the text, the vocal line plummets towards closure (mm. 13–14), a gesture that can be seen as reflecting the traveler's volatile mood. At the end of the second half, the vocal line achieves closure on the e″ but approaches it differently, in a passage marked *forte*. With these strongly projected passages we can imagine the wanderer shouting into the snow-covered landscape as he conjures up first a vision of the snow melting away (verse 2), and finally his hot tears flowing with the brook past his beloved's house (verse 4). Throughout the cycle Schubert uses the directional curve of his melodic lines (sometimes, as here, looping round as they climb up or plunge down) to dramatic effect. In "Der greise Kopf," the piano introduction is launched with a precipitate ascent, followed by an abrupt descent tracing the outline of a diminished seventh, a harmony that resonates through the cycle. It featured as the first dissonant harmony at the opening of "Gute Nacht," associated with the semitonal fall formed by the first two notes of motif y′ (see Example 10.3, m. 2). That two-note fragment creates the lamenting "sigh" figure noted by Youens; it too threads its way through the songs.

Unexpectedly, in "Der greise Kopf," the voice takes up the piano's sweeping opening gesture, peaking a third lower. This unlocks the theatrical character of the music that follows. Its expressive zone, drawing on the language of recitative, matches the drama enacted in the words. The traveler thinks jubilantly that he has grown old suddenly, and is horrified to realize that the white sheen spread by the frost over his hair has melted away. This strange reversal of the wish to stay young, resisting the encroachment of old age, is destabilizing and yet understandable in the context of his longing for death. The build up to the crux at the words "Wie weit noch bis zur Bahre!" (How long still to the grave!) is couched in the ominous chromatic language with which Schubert portrayed elements of plot and character in his early dramatic Lieder.[11] More ominous still is the octave/unison texture that follows in piano and voice for that crucial line where the traveler contemplates the grave.

Allied to the intensity felt in both text and music at a single moment is the prevailing sense of obsessiveness and circularity characterizing the protagonist's pronouncements as he reflects on his condition. Schubert's setting produces an equivalent to this poetic trope. The devices of ostinato and moto perpetuo, hallowed by centuries of use and finding new life in the nineteenth-century Lied, are exploited to this purpose throughout *Winterreise* (see Table 10.1 for songs employing the techniques). Schubert draws on them in a myriad of ways. (Examples discussed under the heading of "Topical Genres" below include "Gute Nacht" and "Wasserflut".)

Besides its psychological implications, circularity serves in *Winterreise* to reinforce the work's cyclic status, linking individual songs more than casually within the whole structure. Schubert's compositional choices enable the music to support this element in the poetry, as well as building a strong overall structure in itself. At its most readily perceptible, this process operates where melodic and rhythmic figures heard at the end of one song are picked up at the beginning of the next. As Bostridge puts it, these connections create "an elective affinity between certain songs (the way the impetuous triplets of "Erstarrung" segue into the rustling triplets of "Der Lindenbaum" ... [and] the repetitive ... dotted figure of the last verse of "Lindenbaum" is transmuted into the opening of "Wasserflut")."[12]

Schubert's Fingerprints

By the time of writing *Winterreise*, Schubert had the elements of his style well-honed and readily at his disposal. Traces of intertextuality are threaded through in tandem with these Schubertian "fingerprints." They range from the innermost connections within the cycle through analogies with others of his Lieder; further across his oeuvre to parallels with his instrumental and sacred vocal works; and also, beyond all those, to echoes of other composers. Mozart is in the background to Schubert's music throughout his oeuvre. Mozartian echoes in *Winterreise* include the repeated-note patter (on the note D) in "Im Dorfe" at mm. 19–23, with the playful vocal interjections against it, and the bass in parallel with the voice, which sounds like a passage from the Act II finale of Mozart's *Le Nozze di Figaro*.[13] The choice of key for a song also sets up associations. By Schubert's time, the key of "Gute Nacht," D minor, carried with it an aura of tragedy, horror, and death from its usage in opera and requiem: Mozart again comes to mind.

Beginnings and Endings
Schubert invests the opening and closing music of *Winterreise* with special significance. Songs 1–5 and 20–24 provide in many respects a microcosm of the cycle. The two bookends (songs 1 and 24) resonate with each other, possessing musical figures rich with import. As Youens put it, the closing measures of "Letzte Hoffnung" present a "gesture with a history that begins in the first measures of the cycle."[14] This certainly applies to the final song. The drone bass at the start of "Gute Nacht," with its topical reference to rustic culture, evokes the traveler's footsteps as he trudges across the wintry landscape. In retrospect it can be seen as prophesying the hurdy-gurdy man's music at the end of the cycle. (As commentators have noted, Schubert plants references to it in the intervening songs.)[15] Heard in the opening measures of "Gute Nacht," this trudging drone has an inexorable quality reflecting the traveler's intense compulsion to embark on the journey. In one possible reading of the final song, it may indicate the transformation of his journey into a life of eternal wandering.

Within the casing formed by the songs at start and finish, each individual song contains a sharply drawn vignette, in some cases focusing more steadily on a particular scene, in others more hectically dramatic, and typically framed by both piano introduction and postlude. As Youens notes, only one song, "Rückblick," lacks a postlude.[16] The purposes to which these textless opening and closing passages lend themselves are rich with possibilities in relation to structure and expression. When the piano postlude in "Gute Nacht" echoes the voice's closing phrases, where the traveler wants his beloved to know he thought of her as he departed ("an dich hab' ich gedacht"), those echoes in the piano are placed in an inner voice within the trudging chords, as if to indicate the persistence of her presence deep in his mind. They convey his ambivalence: while he knows he must leave, he nurtures an abiding reluctance to part from her.

These psychological implications resurface later, for instance in "Rückblick," where at the end he wants to stand still outside her house (hence, as Youens observes, the lack of a piano postlude, since the music too must stand still).[17] Here the crux comes at the end (as in "Erlkönig," D328): the ensuing silence, shorn of a postlude, is telling. Those last wishful thoughts the protagonist expresses contain the seeds of what would now be called stalking; the urge remains in his imagination, where it contributes to the burden of emotional pressure he carries. The words and music at the end of "Rückblick" tell us that he has not yet managed to separate from her psychologically. When he does so, in Part II (which, as commentators have noted, remains free of direct reference to the beloved after the first song, "Die Post"), it is a sign that his obsession with her has been replaced by an equally strong fixation on a desire for death. The words of Death personified in Schubert's "Der Tod und das Mädchen" (D531) come to mind, when he reassures the maiden that he comes to comfort and not to punish her. The traveler in Part II of *Winterreise*, contemplating death, pleads that he is not deserving of punishment: "Habe ja doch nichts begangen, / Dass ich Menschen sollte scheu'n" (I've committed no crime / That I should hide from other men).[18] The songs towards the close, bringing to the fore intimations planted earlier, suggest that his hopes are increasingly fixed on the release from suffering offered by eternal rest.

Motivic Networking

From the start, with "Gute Nacht," Schubert's characteristic fashioning of melodic lines from a few intervallic cells helps to give the opening measures an intensity that not only sets up the mood of the whole cycle, but also introduces significant motivic elements. The motifs packed into those measures suggest in miniature a kinship with the principle of "developing variation" that has been attributed to Brahms.[19] The falling fourths (numbered on Example 10.3) already contained in the continuation of motif y and its variant form y', are detached in mm. 4–5, then heard in diminution and filled-in at m. 5^2. Schubert's song melodies, far from spreading luxuriantly, tend to make economical use of tiny seeds that grow into a unified yet variegated line.

The genre of song cycle lends itself to the creation of a network of motivic material linking individual songs and responding to the intertextuality within the poetic sequence.[20] While a motif may not necessarily be associated with the same or similar poetic ideas on its recurrence, there may be a shared poetic context among its appearances. A particularly prominent Schubertian fingerprint heard at the beginning of *Winterreise* is the palindromic neighbor-note motif (marked "x" on Example 10.1) which, together with its inverted form, recurs in voice and piano throughout "Gute Nacht." The motif is found among songs from earlier in Schubert's life. The obsessive quality that infuses his remarkable setting of "Gretchen am Spinnrade" (D118; 1814) derives partly from its use in both the spinning piano accompaniment and the vocal line, in its original (here with lower neighbor-note) as well as its inverted form, throughout. Among a plethora of examples in the instrumental works, the late string quartets show a similarly obsessive use of this motif. In *Winterreise*, its occurrence in a variety of contexts mirrors the protagonist's obsessive musings at different stages of his journey (see Table 10.1, shown as "motif x").

Major–Minor Juxtapositions

The most familiar major–minor effect, the echo, where a passage in the major is repeated in the parallel minor (or vice versa), has the power to transform mood as well as mode. This is but one of an array of devices along the spectrum Schubert explored with regard to modal mixture. In his Lieder, he used the major–minor echo with sensitivity to the implications of a variety of textual prompts.[21] Some of its most powerful manifestations occur with the reverse Picardy third, a Schubertian specialty (inherited by Brahms) whereby after apparently signaling closure, the major is followed by a minor resolution, as in two of D911's "dream songs": "Gute Nacht" and "Frühlingstraum," conveying the return from the dream-world (or thoughts of it) to reality.

During the course of a song, Schubert's injection of major into minor-key surroundings ranges from a brief flash of color (as occurs towards the end of "Die Wetterfahne") to an extended section, as in verse 7 of "Gute Nacht." Its adaptability as an emotional signifier ranges from the bitter resentment expressed in the final lines of "Die Wetterfahne" ("Was fragen sie nach meinen Schmerzen? / Ihr Kind ist eine reiche Braut." [Why should they care about my grief? / Their child is a rich bride.]) to the tenderness with which the music in "Gute Nacht" suggests that the traveler imagines her sleeping and dreaming.

Variations and Transformations

In Schubert's songs, as well as his instrumental works, variation principles at their most sophisticated reflect his vision of a range of possibilities operating at different levels of the music.[22] Among the song-structures Schubert builds (exercising some flexibility in relation to Müller's verse structures), the modified strophic form (as in "Gute Nacht") and bar form (AA'B, as in "Irrlicht") can accommodate variations in voice and piano responding to nuances, or more extended changes of mood, in the text. This applies also to more freely built song forms possessing an element of refrain, such as those in "Die Wetterfahne" and "Der Lindenbaum," with their varied treatment of the recurring passages.

Among Schubert's characteristic ploys is the playfulness he brings to varying his material. In *Winterreise*, this is manifested not in the lighter vein of such works as the "Trout" Quintet (D667), but in cruel travesty. The trickery that characterizes the *ignis fatuus* in "Irrlicht" is established at the start in the piano introduction with its consequent at mm. 3–4 mocking the falling fourths of mm. 1–2. That falling fourth motif is subjected to further mockery in the voice's entry, first with the dotted rhythm developed into a kind of anti-march figure at m. 5, filtering into a grotesquely leaping figure in m. 6; then on its next appearance turned into a misshapen diminished fourth (m. 9). These proceedings constitute a distortion of Schubert's customary practice of echoing the piano's introductory melody in variant form in the voice's first entry (as in "Gute Nacht," to the enrichment of the motivic network). In "Irrlicht," what follows in m. 11 distorts the arpeggio figure from mm. 25–26 of "Gute Nacht." It is as if in his febrile state the traveler takes on something of the character of the *Irrlicht* as he describes its effect on him. In the verses that follow, Schubert develops the bar form, featuring a variant A section for verse 2; the B section for verse 3 responds with a new, profound seriousness to the text (its crux in the final lines introducing the first reference to the grave in the cycle). The piano postlude allows the *Irrlicht* to have the last word.

Like the musical motifs, recurrent motifs in the poetic text appear in different contexts. The memory of the "green meadow" through which the protagonist walked with his sweetheart, recalled in "Erstarrung," verse 1, triggers a move to the relative major (E♭) at mm. 20–23. His (fruitless) wish in verse 3 to recapture it ("wo find ich grünes Gras?") again triggers a passage in a related major key, this time the submediant (A♭). "Frühlingstraum" allows him the idyllic vision of green meadows in his dreams, set in a brightly configured A major. The color green appears transformed in Part II. In "Das Wirtshaus," instead of the association with happier memories of lush meadows, he sees green wreaths ("grüne Totenkränze") as a sign inviting him into the graveyard: the setting moves at this point from F major into G minor, as it did at the beginning of the song when his steps turned towards the graveyard.

A particular Schubertian speciality is the transformation of lyrical into dramatic and violent expression, found among the late instrumental works at its most extreme in the slow movement of the A Major Sonata (D959).[23] In *Winterreise*, this aspect of the music, like Schubert's major–minor juxtapositions, is harnessed to Müller's penchant for binary constructions. In verse 1 of "Frühlingstraum," the idealized dream scene painted by the poet is matched by the artificiality of the Viennese waltz, fashioned in music-box style, its only chromatic touch a fleeting neighbor-note decoration. Birds reappear grotesquely transformed, when the twittering creatures incorporated gracefully into the opening section's dance topic find their alter egos in the stormy B section that follows, with the harsh cockcrow, and the ravens shrieking from the roof, marking the abrupt awakening from the dream. Here the elegant neighbor-note motif associated with major-key sweetness in the opening section is embedded within the language of dissonance and distortion, as the music rises hectically in pitch and volume.[24]

Topical Genres: March, Dance, and Lullaby

Schubert's contribution to the genres of march and waltz belongs largely to the sociable, popular side of his oeuvre.[25] Their infiltration into the late chamber and piano works involves the expression of darker moods. In *Winterreise*, too, they take on a sinister character. The pressure on the protagonist to pursue his journey, reinforced musically by the recurrent march topic initiated in "Gute Nacht," and poetically by the winter imagery, has echoes in the forced marches made throughout history. Also recurrent is the dirge or funeral march topic, linked with oppressive ostinato patterns and antique style, and evoked in a variety of contexts, ranging from "Wasserflut" to "Der Wegweiser" (see Table 10.1). The Viennese waltz topic characterizing the A sections of "Frühlingstraum," with its air of unreality, extends to grotesque effect in "Täuschung," where it persists manically throughout the song, prefiguring the glittering ball scene in the same key in Berlioz's *Symphonie fantastique*, and confirming the sentiment that concludes Müller's text: "Nur Täuschung ist für mich Gewinn!" (Only illusion lets me win!).

Besides the handful of songs Schubert produced under the title of "Wiegenlied" (Cradle Song) or "Schlaflied" (Lullaby), this topic is discernible in numerous others of his Lieder. While the final song of *Winterreise* ("Der Leiermann") is less obviously a lullaby than that of *Die schöne Müllerin* ("Des Baches Wiegenlied," D795/20), it possesses the hypnotic qualities associated with that genre, with its steady harmonic grounding and the repetitive looping figures in the melodic line. But in its angularity and eschewal of comfort, "Der Leiermann" forms a grotesque version of lullaby.[26] In more muted form, lullaby is threaded through the cycle. "Wasserflut" mixes its piano LH topic (its dotted-rhythm dirge conveying an aura of funeral march, albeit in triple time) with a distinctly different RH topic, whose hypnotic rocking arpeggio figures signal lullaby, demonstrating the power of music to express two or more contrasting items simultaneously. Bostridge's argument for non-assimilation of the differing rhythmic elements in the piano LH and RH receives support from the presence of these two topics.[27]

Schubert has taken his cue for the more restful lullaby topic in "Wasserflut" and in the final verse of its predecessor, "Der Lindenbaum," from the protagonist's expressions of yearning for peace and rest ("Ruh"). These form a poetic motif throughout the cycle. In the ABCABC form of "Frühlingstraum," the C section exhibits lullaby properties as the protagonist reflects on his dreams with a profound sense of loss: "Wann halt' ich mein Liebchen im Arm?" (When will I hold my love in my arms?). The rocking octaves in the piano accompaniment soothe rather than disturb. Here, as elsewhere, the piano is a sympathetic responder to the protagonist's mood.

Antique Style

Contributing to the profundity of *Winterreise* is Schubert's frequent turning toward antique models of musical material, a phenomenon rife also in the instrumental music of his last decade. In D911, such references appear in a variety of shapes and contexts: some instances are clearly audible on the surface, while others are embedded more subliminally. Their use contributes to the dual-facing impression that pervades *Winterreise*. Both Müller and Schubert show allegiance to inherited forms of expression, as well as an experimental modernity. The ancient formulae come loaded with meaning. Most loaded of all is the chromatic fourth, the lament bass familiar from Purcell's *Dido and Aeneas*, and widely used in seventeenth- and eighteenth-century instrumental as well as vocal genres. The chromatically filled-in fourth, or fragments of it, threaded through the musical texture in D911 (see Table 10.1 and Example 10.4) is a constant reminder of the protagonist's incurable sense of loss. In Part II its traditional association with death emerges more strongly.

Example 10.4 "Der Wegweiser," mm. 65–83

Linked to antique style is the *religioso* topic present from the start of the cycle with the turn to F major (and its subdominant B♭) in verse 1 of "Gute Nacht." The hymn-like veneer added to a variant of the trudging motif in the accompaniment there comes to the surface (like much else) towards the end of the cycle. Graham Johnson sees the key of F major, inflected with subdominant color, that Schubert chose for "Das Wirtshaus" as an anomaly, illogically poised between the G minor songs on either side.[28] But we could interpret it as a reference to the original manifestation of that topic in "Gute Nacht," in those same keys (F and B♭). Seen in this light, in "Das Wirtshaus," they serve simultaneously as a reminder of the hope of lasting love that was lost at the origin of the journey, and a signal of the hope for death that has replaced it.

Commentators have not failed to notice parallels in the poetic text of "Das Wirtshaus" to the Nativity story, and also in that text, as in the winter journey altogether, to the Passion story. Schubert's music in "Das Wirtshaus" endows the funereal scene, and the protagonist's response to it, with dignity, reinforcing the idea conveyed in the words of the preceding song, "Der Wegweiser," of his purity of character. Whatever the protagonist's theological stance may be, reference to antique models, and hymn-like style, confer a seemingly genuine aura of the sacred on the music of *Winterreise*. It gains added gravitas when infused with counterpoint. Among Schubert's references to antique style, and a personal fingerprint shared across the range of genres he cultivated, is the 4–3 suspension, first heard in "Gute Nacht" together with the hymn-like topic at mm. 16–17 (Example 10.1). This ancient contrapuntal formation becomes a pervasive element thereafter.

Schubert's penchant for canonic technique contributes to the seriousness evoked in particularly portentous passages of the text. The archaic references in "Der Wegweiser" present the most intense example, ranging from the canonic reflections of the funereal opening phrases between voice and piano, threaded through the minor-key A sections (the brief memory of the traveler's blameless past in the central B section is free of such artifice), to the building of tension in the final measures, with their combination of chromatic fourth (lament figure) and wedge (chromatic contrary motion), as marked on Example 10.4. Both those figures are weighted with a history of fugal counterpoint. Their inexorable move towards collapse, followed by the unmistakable quotation from "Der Tod und das Mädchen" (the dactylic repeated-note figure associated with death), forms one of the most ominous endings in *Winterreise*.

Epilogue

Schubert's scene-painting in *Winterreise* has a vividness fueled by his evident belief in music's power to bring words to life – a belief shared by Müller. In joining his art to Müller's, Schubert conjured up the swinging weathervane (sign of the girl's faithlessness) in "Die Wetterfahne," the descent to the rocky depths in "Irrlicht," the shrieking ravens in "Frühlingstraum," the falling leaves in "Letzte Hoffnung," the dogs barking in "Im Dorfe," the hurdy-gurdy playing in "Der Leiermann," and much else. Beyond this, Schubert's settings convey his profound feeling for the central character. Because Schubert was deeply moved by the protagonist's sufferings, his music for *Winterreise*, working with the poetry, has the power to move us.

Noticeable in Müller's text is the evidence of the human urge to leave some trace of a person and a life, expressed in the traveler's memories of carving names in happier times into tree bark, and his wish, as he makes his winter journey, to etch them on the icy surface of the water. Schubert, writing his name as a composer on the surface of the poetry, allows us access to the depths that lie beneath.

Notes

1. On the notion of "fingerprints," see *SF*.
2. For an introduction to topic in music, see Danuta Mirka (ed.), *The Oxford Handbook of Topic Theory* (Oxford and New York: Oxford University Press, 2014). Further on topical analysis, see Kofi Agawu, *Music as Discourse: Semiotic Adventures in Romantic Music* (New York: Oxford University Press, 2008); and Robert Hatten, *Interpreting Musical Topics, Tropes, and Gestures: Mozart, Beethoven, and Schubert* (Bloomington: Indiana University Press, 2004).
3. On travel narratives in the song cycle, see Barbara Turchin, "The Nineteenth-Century *Wanderlieder* Cycle," *Journal of Musicology* 5/4 (1987): 498–525.
4. Further on modal mixture, see under the heading of "Major–Minor Juxtapositions" below.
5. On the implications of this "lowly figure," see *SWJ*, 213–19.
6. See *RWJ*, 62.
7. *SWJ*, 34–38.
8. For a study of this phenomenon, see Stephen Rodgers, "Schubert's Idyllic Periods," *Music Theory Spectrum*, 39/2 (2017): 223–46.
9. The original scores of the examples in this chapter, appearing in *Neue Schubert-Ausgabe*: Series IV: *Lieder*, Band 4, Teil a, *Winterreise* Op. 89, ed. Walther Dürr, BA 5516 (Kassel: Bärenreiter, 1979), 110–11, 148, and 181, have been reset with kind permission from Bärenreiter.
10. Stephen Rodgers, "Song and the Music of Poetry," *Music Analysis* 36/3 (2017): 315–49 (316).
11. See Susan Wollenberg, "Schubert's Dramatic Lieder: Rehabilitating 'Adelwold und Emma,' D.211," in *DMFS*, 85–105.
12. *SWJ*, 302–3.
13. Müller's words here are: "Je nun, sie haben ihr Teil genossen / Und hoffen, was sie noch übrig ließen, / [Doch wieder zu finden auf ihren Kissen]" (Oh well, they had their share of pleasure / And hope that what they missed / [Can be found again on their pillows]).
14. *RWJ*, 88.
15. See especially *RWJ*, *passim* on what Youens terms the "journeying motif."
16. *RWJ*, 106. Youens (ibid., 105–7) provides detailed discussion of the functions of the piano introductions and postludes.
17. *RWJ*, 106.
18. "Der Wegweiser," verse 2.
19. See Walter Frisch, *Brahms and the Principle of Developing Variation* (Berkeley: University of California Press, 1984).
20. On the generic properties of song cycle, see Laura Tunbridge, *The Song Cycle*, Cambridge Introductions to Music (Cambridge: Cambridge University Press, 2010), Chapter 1, "Concepts," 1–5.
21. See Eric Blom, "[Franz Schubert:] His Favourite Device," *Music & Letters* 9/4 (1928): 372–80.
22. See *SF*, Chapter 8, "Schubert's Variations," 213–43.
23. On these episodes, see *SF*, Chapter 6, "Schubert's Violent Nature," 161–89.
24. See *SF*, 171–74.
25. See Martin Chusid, *Schubert's Dances: Music for Family, Friends, and Posterity* (Hillsdale: Pendragon Press, 2013); and Scott Messing, *Marching to the Canon: The Life of Schubert's*

Marche militaire (Rochester: University of Rochester Press; Woodbridge: Boydell & Brewer, 2014).

26. On the grotesque in Schubert's music, see Joe Davies, "Stylistic Disjuncture as a Source of Drama in Schubert's Late Instrumental Works," in *DMFS*, 303–30 (324–30).

27. *SWJ*, 152–63.

28. *FSCS*, vol. 3, 712.

11 A Winter of Poetry: Connections Among the Songs in Schubert's *Winterreise*

XAVIER HASCHER

One inhabits, with a full heart, an empty world. – CHATEAUBRIAND

While impressions can be deceptive, more often than not that very decep-tiveness is significant.[1] At a surface glance, Schubert's *Winterreise* (D911) might appear to the imagination as a landscape in twenty-four mono-chrome studies with only the dark bark of the trees and a few black strokes, representing the crows perching on them, to contrast with the ubiquitous wintry white. Yet, on further inspection, one gradually perceives variations in shades and perspective, so that each part of the whole acquires definition and can be viewed separately. Aurally, one is struck by the unremitting bleakness and severity of the ensemble, which evokes a barren expanse where the flowers of melody seem unable to grow or, if they do, are soon condemned to wither. Sheer quantity is of consequence: twelve parts may be considered and recollected individually, but confronted with double that number, perception shifts towards a more global grasp of its object. This is even truer of memory; as one component part cancels its predeces-sor and is in turn obliterated by its successor, the cumulative traces that subsist in the mind tend to be of a diffuse, qualitative nature rather than constitute a series of precise items stored in a continuous way. It takes a while before we can remember each particular song in such a long sequence. But we surely retain the overall effect of the sequence, where echoes of salient passages emerge, framed by the more lasting impact made by the first and last songs. As we penetrate deeper into *Winterreise* by focusing on the individual songs and learning to differentiate them, that overall effect remains with us.

Indeed, *Winterreise* makes a very powerful impression on the listener. The cycle coheres because of its singular tone – the recognizable voice that pervades and unites the songs. One recognizes not only Schubert's voice, but a particular modulation of it, altered, and with a contracted expressive range. Such a tone is encountered episodically in his music – especially his instrumental works – from the *Unfinished Symphony* (D759) onwards in the form of acute grief and violent eruptions of anxiety. Yet nowhere is it met in such concentration as here. In *Winterreise*, specific Schubertian gestures are transposed into more remote and rarefied regions than in any previous work. The cycle is a cry of pain and a renunciation, starting with what amounts to a renunciation of singing. Indeed, for a song cycle, *Winterreise* "sings" remarkably little – far less, for instance, than its obvious counterpart, *Die schöne Müllerin* (D795). Even such songs of desolation as the *Gesänge des Harfners*, Op. 12 (D478), which Schubert revised in 1822, and which resemble *Winterreise* thematically, sing admirably and project a very different aural image from that of the later cycle. The particular treatment of the voice in *Winterreise* is reflected in the accompaniment; here, Schubert achieves a novel and distinctive combination of voice and piano that departs from the model of accompanied melody.

Beyond pain and anger, the cycle exhibits both rebellion against and acceptance of fate, nostalgia coupled with distressing return to the present and the abandonment of hope. Noticeably absent is the kind of ecstatic vision expressed by such songs as "Nacht und Träume" (D827) or "Im Abendrot" (D799), where nature and the elements are propitious rather than hostile. Gone, too, is the popular dimension of the traditional Lied; nothing could be less folkish than *Winterreise*. The harmony between the self and the people has been broken, as has that between the self and the cosmos. Nature, though omnipresent, has undergone a negative metamorphosis through which she has become inaccessible and her bounties out of reach. Unlike the miller of *Die schöne Müllerin*, the protagonist of *Winterreise* does not exemplify the German communal simplicity epitomized by the characters of fairy tales, which Novalis equates with "true popularity, and therefore an ideal."[2] Instead, the cycle is a rumination on unhappiness, solitude, and estrangement, from which any utopian aspiration or religious consolation has been banished. *Winterreise* depicts a journey through a world bereft not only of life, but also of any prospect of an after-life – in short, an underworld.[3] Dante's inscription on the gate of his inferno, "*Lasciate ogni speranza*," could also apply to the condition of Müller's and Schubert's character as he trudges aimlessly though icy, arid stretches.[4] The songs themselves, frequently interrupted as they are by recitative-like passages, do not offer the comfort of continuity, the solace that music may provide. The wanderer's curse affords him no rest, or insufficient one.

Yet this ostensible singleness of mood is not reflected in the musical material of the cycle or its harmonic scheme, that is, in the interconnection of motives across the songs or a concatenation of functionally related keys. No song in *Winterreise* quotes from another in a clear, identifiable way; yet throughout the cycle one hears internal resonances that are at once recognizable and difficult to pinpoint as they act on a sub-motivic, sometimes textural or gestural level, distinct in scale or nature from that of ordinary, foreground events. These resonances have no primary, original form to which further transformations or developments can be traced, but instead seem to infuse the cycle almost furtively, as if to escape direct attention. They contribute to the overall impression of uniformity without constituting a factor of unity in the consecrated sense, as within the function typically attributed to motives and themes.

Organicism, Form, and the Fallacy of Necessity in the Artwork

In *The Romantic Generation*, Charles Rosen argues that even though each song in *Winterreise* might stand independently as a coherent, sufficient whole, it partly loses its "character and significance" and makes "imperfect sense" when considered in isolation.[5] This amounts to admitting indirectly that the cycle exerts a binding force on its components and forms a greater whole, despite the apparent looseness of the relationships among the songs.[6] The global light projected by this overarching whole – its "resonance" – is created not from the mere addition but rather from the combination, or admixture, of the different shades and qualities of the lights emitted by the various parts; each part interacts with its neighbors and contributes to the overall effect. The cycle provides a context for understanding the "sense" of every individual song as well as modifies our perception of it, as though some chemical reaction resulted from the song's placement among the collection, a reaction that affected its substance.

A long-standing presupposition in music criticism is that, in order to deserve praise or attention, a musical work has to be "organic" – so tightly organized that no limb might be added to or removed from the work's body without causing it irretrievable damage. Deemed especially meritorious are works where almost every part or element demonstrably originates from a single primary cell that germinates and reproduces itself throughout, permeating every subdivision of the whole either overtly or covertly. The chagrin experienced by music analysts in relation to *Winterreise* stems from their wish to view it as more than a mere aggregate of songs despite the difficulty of establishing such organicism at the level of the cycle. Analysts depend on the assumption of coherence. As in every academic field of inquiry, they set out to uncover patterns where there seems to be only lesser or greater randomness; they seek manifestations of sameness, recurrences of a given feature or phenomenon, usually a melodic contour or harmonic progression. Such an approach is entirely legitimate assuming that a pertinent choice is made of what features to track – a choice that is crucial and can become delicate when the obvious categories refuse to yield the expected results.

This approach appears less exclusive, though, when we take into account the artistic nature of music, whereby the exceptional, the unexpected, that which falls outside any pattern, is at least as significant as similarity or repetition. No valid piece of music could exist without an element of unpredictability, even surprise. Works of art are unique occurrences, and to reduce them to a set of common, replicating features (within a single work a well as from one work to another) is also to ignore what precisely makes them unique. Moreover, concentrating on sameness and repetition risks blinding us to contrast, opposition, diversity, and complementarity, which are as essential to artistic elaboration as repetition. A sense of completeness may be derived from complementarity, or the exhaustion of a certain number of discrete possibilities within a limited array (in modulation, for instance), which strict adherence to a monochromatic type of consistency may be unable to provide. When asking what in music makes something – a piece or a sequence of pieces – a "whole," we thus have alternative ways of answering, although the analytical tools at our disposal are far more suited to highlighting unity than diversity.

Another objection lies in what may be called the "fallacy of necessity" in the artwork. Notions such as organicism, as often understood, tend to make us see works as perfect and therefore inalterable, and the creative process as unerring, as though governed by certainty and inevitability. Every part, every development, purportedly proceeds from that inner necessity manifested through internal coherence, which analysis seeks to reveal. Analytical theories such as Heinrich Schenker's reinforce this belief by positing an underlying framework that obeys its own genetic program, so to speak, and placing a moral blemish on any type of music embodying a less rigorous conception of unity. The general analytical vocabulary, perhaps under the modernist influence, has for decades been replete with such terms as "functional" and "structural." Yet artworks, including pieces of music, are neither objects found in nature nor entities designed supernaturally and merely transmitted through their author or composer. How we approach these works should therefore be free of the pseudo-scientificity mixed with superstition that can be detected in some attitudes to analysis. Art is largely arbitrary, and to acknowledge this is a necessary step. Works are shaped a certain way: but every juncture in them reveals a choice that could have been made differently. The result of such a series of choices is contingent rather than predictable. Once a work has been delivered into the world, though, its seeming permanence creates the illusion that it has always been there, and could not have been otherwise than it is.

If the composer is not a passive medium through which some impersonal "will of the tone" expresses itself, but rather a creator who wills every detail of the work, we as receivers are likewise not passive receptacles into which that expression is poured. Coherence and relations are things that we establish each time we "activate" a work of art, that is, look at it with some intention of interpreting it, thereby turning reception into an act. Some of these relations depend on clues unambiguously laid out by the composer, but others are dependent on elements that we distinguish and elect as clues. If any "sense" is to be made, it is always our making. If beauty, as commonly said, is in the eye of the beholder, coherence is in the ear and mind of the listener.

Journeying Through Keys

Such considerations have a bearing on how we identify coherence in *Winterreise*. Within the Classical style, principles of distribution, symmetry, convention, and topicality assisted composers in framing their works. However, by the early nineteenth century, these principles had weakened. With *Winterreise*, a first analytical challenge arises from the fact that while Schubert did not alter the order of the initial twelve songs to accommodate his setting of Müller's additional twelve poems, he nevertheless transposed some of these songs (most notably No. 12, "Einsamkeit," no longer in the opening D minor of "Gute Nacht") and demoted what was once a complete cycle to the status of a half cycle.[7] While Schubert himself certainly intended the transpositions in the first part of *Winterreise*,[8] the publisher Haslinger may well have proposed those in the second part or even, as Richard Kramer suggests,[9] decided upon them. (However, these transpositions are sufficiently coherent for Schubert's assent not to be ruled out.) Even if we accept this hypothesis, Schubert's modifications question that inner necessity commonly linked with organicism, and which we associate with masterpieces.

To address these issues, Table 11.1 shows the keys of the cycle distributed among four columns representing harmonic "quadrants," or subdivisions of the circle of fifths. For the transposed songs, the original key appears in parentheses with an arrow pointing towards the transposed key. In the second row of the table, the tonic key (F, D, B, A♭, respectively) of the harmonic quadrant appears at the center of each column, flanked by its subdominant (B♭, G, E, D♭) and dominant (C, A, F♯, E♭) keys. Each quadrant is named after its tonic key, as shown in the top row of the table. Keys within each quadrant can be either minor or major in accordance with the modal interchangeability so often encountered in Schubert's music. The choice of D as tonic in column I is justified by it being the

Table 11.1 *The keys of the songs distributed among the tonal quadrants*

Harmonic quadrants	F(II)			D(I)			B(III)			A♭(IV)		
Keys	B♭	F	C	G	D	A	E	B	F♯	D♭	A♭	E♭
Songs: *1. Gute Nacht*					D⁻							
2. Die Wetterfahne						A⁻						
3. Gefror'ne Tränen		F⁻										
4. Erstarrung			C⁻									
5. Der Lindenbaum							E⁺					
6. Wasserflut							E⁻		(←F♯⁻)			
7. Auf dem Flusse							E⁻					
8. Rückblick				G⁻								
9. Irrlicht								B⁻				
10. Rast			C⁻	(←D⁻)								
11. Frühlingstraum						A^{+/-}						
12. Einsamkeit				(D⁻→)				B⁻				
13. Die Post												E♭⁺
14. Der greise Kopf			C⁻									
15. Die Krähe			C⁻									
16. Letzte Hoffnung												E♭⁺
17. Im Dorfe					D⁺							
18. Der stürmische Morgen					D⁻							
19. Täuschung						A⁺						
20. Der Wegweiser				G⁻								
21. Das Wirtshaus		F⁺										
22. Mut				G⁻	(←A⁻)							
23. Die Nebensonnen						A⁺						
24. Der Leiermann						A⁻	(←B⁻)					

key of the first and last songs of the earlier, twelve-song cycle, while yielding the most balanced distribution of keys for the whole of *Winterreise* with respect to the first quadrant in terms of harmonic function, and also between both adjacent quadrants.[10]

In Figure 11.1, which recalls Ernő Lendvai's axis system,[11] the twelve (major or minor) keys in the second row of Table 11.1 are displayed more traditionally in a circle. Passage from one quadrant to the next is made possible by equating the subdominant key of a given quadrant with the supertonic, or the "dominant of the dominant" ($^{\mathbf{D}}\mathbf{D}$), of its counterclockwise successor. Figure 11.1 also permits us to measure the distance of the various song keys from the initial D in fifths.

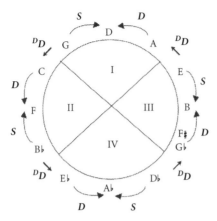

Figure 11.1 The circle of fifths and the tonal quadrants

Table 11.1 shows that, while most songs in the cycle belong to the first quadrant (I), a significant number belong to the adjacent quadrants (II) and (III). Precise numbers are inessential here; what matters is the overall balance inherent to Schubert's choice of keys. In the final version of *Winterreise*, the number of songs in the first quadrant equals that of the second and third quadrants combined, and the number of songs in the third quadrant approximates that in the second quadrant. Traveling leftwards, or in the flat direction, from the first quadrant towards the second quadrant, is usually perceived as a darkening of tone color, while traveling rightwards, or in the sharp direction, towards the third quadrant, creates a sense of tonal brightening. More generally, keys are perceived differently according to how they relate to each other. What one observes in *Winterreise* is Schubert's attempt to establish a tonal core, on both sides of which are disposed songs in complementary, contrasting keys. The tonal "journey" thus essentially explores three quadrants out of four. The more remote fourth quadrant (situated opposite the first quadrant in Figure 11.1) is visited only twice – both times in the second half of the cycle, this moment being delayed until a certain degree of harmonic richness has been reached. Schubert's reason for visiting the fourth quadrant at this point may have been to add further contrast before reaffirming the centrality of the first quadrant.

Schubert's transposition of songs considerably modifies the tonal balance of the first part of *Winterreise* by increasing its harmonic diversity. These changes were no doubt motivated by the introduction of the twelve new songs of the second part, as Schubert must have felt that the resulting collection would otherwise have been too uniform. Indeed, the expanded proportions of the cycle called for a wider harmonic scope, itself yielding a broader expressive range.

Already in his original conception, Schubert paralleled the move from D minor in "Gute Nacht" (No. 1) a fifth upwards to A, its minor dominant, in "Die Wetterfahne" (No. 2), in the first quadrant, with the similar move from F minor in "Gefror'ne Tränen" (No. 3) to C minor in "Erstarrung" (No. 4) in the second quadrant. He then shifted to the highly contrasting E major of "Der Lindenbaum" (No. 5) in the third quadrant. Moving from A minor to F minor implies one chromatic transformation, that of A into A♭, appended to the plain, diatonic succession from A minor to F major, with the common note C held throughout. The progression thus follows this simple underlying pattern:

$$A^-$$
$$\downarrow$$
$$F^+ \rightarrow F^-$$

F and C are the relative major of D minor and the dominant of the relative, respectively (thus harmonically close to D), yet which have been rendered minor in order to fit the mood of the poems. While all the keys up through No. 4 have been minor ones, a more somber shade is introduced with "Gefror'ne Tränen" and "Erstarrung," so that even within the overall category of the minor, nuances and opposition obtain. Conversely, E – the subdominant of B minor, the relative of D major – should itself have been a minor key; instead, Schubert chose to accentuate the harmonic contrast provided by the move to the third quadrant by making the key major, again in accordance with the poem. The progression from C minor to E major offers two chromatic transformations (E♭ to E and G to G♯) and no common notes. It can be decomposed as follows:

$$C^- \rightarrow C^+$$
$$\downarrow$$
$$E^+ \leftarrow E^-$$

Despite the modal changes, it is worth noting that both lines of development so far – one towards the second quadrant, the other towards the third, whose tonic keys are F and B respectively – derive from the first song's hesitation, in mm. 70–71, between D minor (whose relative is F major) and D major (whose relative is B minor). Rather than superficial and theoretical, the relations between the song keys are poetic in nature and rooted in the very dialectic of *Winterreise* displayed at the outset.

The relationship of E major to F♯ minor between "Der Lindenbaum" (No. 5) and "Wasserflut" (No. 6) in the original version of the cycle is straightforward: V to vi in a major key. The position of "Wasserflut" inside the third quadrant is not affected by the transposition to E minor, even though the change has an impact on the song's sonority and distance from D (F♯ minor being on the further border of the quadrant). The motivation for this transposition remains unclear, apart from simplifying the transition to the next song, "Auf dem Flusse" (No. 7), by staying in the same key instead of descending a whole tone from F♯ minor to E minor – a rather abrupt, unusual succession. Song Nos. 5, 6, and 7 therefore help to establish a tonal pole around the key of E within the first half of the cycle. Yet "Auf dem Flusse" is a very rich song, above all harmonically; after temporarily re-establishing the E major of "Der Lindenbaum" in its course, for the first time in the cycle it ventures into the fourth quadrant by modulating to G♯ minor before regressing into the first quadrant with G minor. This modulation prepares for the shift to G minor with "Rückblick" (No. 8). E minor to G minor is another chromatic third progression; G, the relative major of E minor, is itself made minor, thus standing in a similar relation to it as F minor to D minor previously. "Irrlicht" (No. 9) at last establishes B minor, the relative of D major, thus returning to the third quadrant. The progression from G minor to B minor transposes and reverses that from A minor to F minor discussed above.

In the original twelve-song version of *Winterreise*, the last three songs returned to the first quadrant and remained there with the tonic–dominant–tonic succession of D minor in "Rast" (No. 10), A major-minor in "Frühlingstraum" (No. 11), and finally D minor in "Einsamkeit" (No. 12). The cycle thus closed in the same key in which it began by reversing the initial progression. But the transposition of "Rast" to C minor and "Einsamkeit" to B minor, in the second and third quadrants, respectively, testify to Schubert's intention, with the composition of his *Fortsetzung*, of broadening the tonal scope of the first half and avoiding cadential resolution into the initial key, or even the initial quadrant; the transpositions invite a continuation. Whereas the original version of the cycle was strongly centered around the first quadrant, the second version offers a richer and more balanced sequence of keys. The transposition of "Rast" to C minor, for example, was evidently motivated by the need to compensate for the predominance of keys in the third quadrant.

The relation of B minor to C minor between "Irrlicht" and "Rast" is the most distant of the whole cycle. It can be understood as the mediant to the minor subdominant of a major key (or "schlichter Halbtonschritt" in Riemann's nomenclature)[12] and, here again, implies a mode transformation from an expected major key to a minor one. Given our habituation to the tonal system, such alterations affect our perception of the transition from one song to the next. The succession is rendered more intense by the semitone step between the two keys – a dissonance, instead of a consonant third or fifth. Schubert thus not only varies the transitions between the songs, but also intensifies them. Whereas the succession from B minor to D minor would have transposed that from "Auf dem Flusse" to "Rückblick" (E minor to G minor), the succession from B minor to C minor introduces an element of mystery and tension. Music does not merely reflect the drama of the words: it also projects its own drama onto them. Here the progression not only accords with the first lines of "Rast" ("I only notice now how tired I am / As I lie down to rest") but also sets them in striking relief. The ensuing path from C minor to A major between "Rast" and "Frühlingstraum" is reminiscent of that from C minor to E major above. Likewise implying two chromatic, modal transformations and including no common note, it can be broken down as follows:

$$C^- \rightarrow C^+$$
$$\downarrow$$
$$A^+ \leftarrow A^-$$

Finally, the succession from A minor to B minor, from the end of "Frühlingstraum" to the beginning of "Einsamkeit," shows another, less stringent, stepwise progression, this time by a whole tone, aptly ending the first half of *Winterreise* by evading the set of progressions so far established. Thus, as this discussion of Part I of the cycle reveals, not only does the choice of keys demonstrate variety, complementarity, and unexpectedness, but so also does the choice of progression from one song to another.

Relation of Keys to Poetic Content

In his essay on *Winterreise*, Walther Dürr interprets the motion towards F minor and C minor ("Gefror'ne Tränen" and "Erstarrung") as a trajectory from reality – represented by D minor ("Gute Nacht") – into inwardness. The cycle, he posits, then moves into the region of dreams with the shift to E major ("Der Lindenbaum") and remains there for both subsequent numbers ("Wasserflut" and "Auf dem Flusse").[13] For reasons to be disclosed later, I resist associating D minor, or any other key, with "reality," even if it is linked (in Dürr's words) with "melancholy and resignation."[14] Yet I accept this premise provisionally. Songs whose keys lie in the first quadrant appear to be most closely related to the journey itself: these are, in the first half, "Gute Nacht," "Die Wetterfahne," and "Rückblick." They tend to be more descriptive than other songs of what is given as the outside world. "Gefror'ne Tränen" and "Erstarrung," in the second quadrant, on the other hand, suggest a retreat from this journey, a pause not so much *in* it as *beside* it. They imply a poetic displacement into interiority, a concentration on the self marked by sadness and brooding, but also passion, whether repressed or partly expressed. In reaction, the protagonist recalls memories of long ago in "Der Lindenbaum"; the magical resurrection of the past in the glory of E major, brought about by the rustling of the linden tree's branches, soon transforms into a hallucinated, deadly lure. Even more than into dreams, songs in the third quadrant thus betray a flight into the imaginary. The tragic fantasy of "Wasserflut" is followed by further remembrances of the past in "Auf dem Flusse," memories that contrast sharply with the transfigured state of the present, rendered unrecognizable by winter. The slip from E minor down to D♯ minor at m. 9 – the cycle's first foray into the fourth quadrant – alludes to a present that has become alien, unfamiliar, *unheimlich*.

While it is not difficult to associate "Irrlicht" with the imaginary, "Einsamkeit" is more problematic because of its transposition. Indeed, the original key of D minor seems more suited to a song that reverts to the theme of the journey. Yet the the transposed key of B minor throws a different light on "Einsamkeit," differentiating its atmosphere from that of "Gute Nacht." The transposition of "Rast" from D minor to C minor emphasizes the inwardness of the poem and the interruption of the journey, as opposed to its resumption. Finally, despite belonging to the first quadrant, the A major of "Frühlingstraum" brings the song closer to "Der Lindenbaum" and E major, although the "dream of spring" does not hold the same fascination as the linden tree. Schubert's choice of keys for the final songs of the first part of the cycle is dependent on the overall tonal construction. However, the contrast within the poetic text of "Frühlingstraum" between illusion and the reality of the journey, reflected in the parallel minor ending of each half of Schubert's setting, connects this song with the previous ones in the first quadrant.

It is striking that Schubert starts the second half of the cycle in E♭ major with "Die Post" (No. 13) – the first song belonging to the fourth quadrant, and a sharp contrast to all of the preceding songs in terms of key, tempo, figuration, and atmosphere. Its tonal distance parallels the physical distance traveled by the post carrying news from the far-flung town, while the shift to E♭ minor at mm. 27 and 72 again plunges us into an alien reality. As a new beginning, the song is highly effective; it is also more expansive melodically than most of the earlier songs, and allows the voice to soar and sing more fully. "Letzte Hoffnung" (No. 16) is again in the key of E♭ major, though it is very much colored by its parallel minor and its relative, C minor, in which both intervening songs, "Der greise Kopf" (No. 14) and "Die Krähe" (No. 15), are placed. (Fig. 11.1 shows that the fourth quadrant borders on the second, whereas Table 11.1 suggests a degree of remoteness contradicted by the simplicity of the actual relationship between E♭ major and C minor.)

Transitions between songs in the second half of *Winterreise* are less chromatically inflected than those in the first half, but make more use of stepwise relations. Thus the descending semitone from E♭ major in "Letzte Hoffnung" to D major in "Im Dorfe" (No. 17) sounds abrupt even though it is easily explained in terms of a VI–V progression in a minor key. With the exception of "Das Wirtshaus" (No. 21) in the second quadrant, all songs from "Im Dorfe" until the end of the cycle remain in the first quadrant, therefore in the orbit of the opening key of D minor, in which "Der stürmische Morgen" (No. 18) is set. Regarding tonal balance, the reinstatement of the first quadrant at this point in the cycle creates a final area of stability that resolves the previous venturing into the fourth quadrant and the instability of the first half of the cycle. The anticipated return to the "tonic" key of D makes it possible for Schubert to prepare the cycle's dominant ending in A. The original key of "Der Leiermann" (No. 24), B minor, counterbalanced at a tritone's distance the F major of "Das Wirtshaus," but made the conclusion of the cycle too similar to that of its first half. By moving "Der Leiermann" down a whole tone to A minor, Schubert preserved the benefit of an open ending, endowing the cycle with the qualities of a fragment calling for completion rather than a closed, finished work. The succession of A major, G minor, F major, and a symmetrical ascent back to A major in Nos. 19–23 is remarkable in that it involves only whole tones and mode changes; it can be understood in the weakly functional terms of a modal exchange between the dominant and the mediant of D minor via the subdominant.

Such stepwise transitions – generally unthinkable between the movements of an instrumental work – together with the indirect, chromatic third relationships in the first half of the cycle, reinforce the apparent disconnectedness that characterizes the sequence of songs in *Winterreise*. The notion of "parataxis" has been introduced in relation to Schubert's music. This term refers to a syntactic construction in which clauses are placed side by side through simple juxtaposition or coordination without subordination, that is, without establishing a hierarchy between them.[15] Such a notion, however, seems partly reductionist – it disregards the analogical, subjacent relationships and the underlying continuity between parts of a movement, for instance – and partly inaccurate – as Schubert maintains a certain hierarchy in his music, if by different means than those employed by his predecessors. This disconnectedness relates back to the poetic nature of Müller's original cycle, which is not canceled by its being set to music. In Roman Jakobson's words, "poeticalness is not a supplementation of discourse with rhetorical adornment but a total re-evaluation of the discourse and of all its components whatsoever."[16] Poetry is not merely a kind of decorated prose. It differs from prose in that its fundamental purpose is not to take part in a transitive information chain between an addresser and an addressee where the focus is on the denotative meaning of the message in reference to the outside world, and even less where decision and action are to follow. Instead, as Jakobson puts it, "the focus" of poetic discourse "is on the message for its own sake."[17]

In the aesthetic of early Romanticism, music *is* a form of poetry, and the stance taken here is to consider Schubert as aware of and partaking, even if critically, in that aesthetic – thus considering his music as poetic in essence but also in form. It would equally amount to ignoring this quality to reorder the songs of *Winterreise* with the idea of yielding a clearer narrative, as it would to transpose them according to a sequence of perfect fifth or common-note third progressions. Poetry is not about the telling of a story; poetry of early Romanticism in particular welcomes incoherence and disjointedness. In the summer of 1799, Novalis could thus summarize his program for a new literature:

> Narratives, disconnected and incoherent, but which contain associations, like *dreams*. Poems – wholly *harmonious* and teeming with beautiful words – yet also entirely without meaning or connection – where, at most, only individual stanzas are intelligible – which must be like nothing but fragments of the most diverse things. True poetry can at best have a general *allegorical* meaning or exert an indirect effect, as does music, etc. This is why nature is so completely *poetic*, in the same way as a magician's chamber – a physicist's office – a nursery – a storage room filled with bric-a-brac.[18]

Nearly three decades into the nineteenth century, *Winterreise* (both Müller's poetry and Schubert's songs) also formulates a critique of early Romanticism, notably by rejecting the harmoniousness of the dream world and avoiding the beauty of words that Novalis desired. The prosaic quality of Müller's verse has commonly been noted, often to criticize it.[19] This quality is matched by Schubert's unwillingness, as mentioned earlier, to let the songs fully "sing." Schubert dismisses the aestheticizing power of melody in order to leave the protagonist's cries almost raw and unadorned; he utters his anguish through uneasy, dissonant intervals.

Associative Relations

Contributing to the overall perception of *Winterreise* as a cycle is a web of associative – rather than transitive – relations. Far more than actual motives, these relations involve texture, timbre, register, articulation, or even general dimensions such as tempo, key, and meter that have a direct impact on perception – hence the greater difficulty in bringing them to light. Their number is potentially unlimited. As with every piece of music, *Winterreise* is a finished sequence that can be interpreted in a multitude of ways. Each hearing generates associations in the mind in the form of analogies, resemblances, and correspondences that impress themselves on us and seem to bear greater or lesser significance.

A number of writers, notably Feil and Youens, have pointed out that the *in gehender Bewegung* tempo of "Gute Nacht" (Example 11.1a) establishes

Example 11.1 (a) "Walking" rhythm and F–E motif in "Gute Nacht," mm. 1–3; (b) "walking" rhythm in "Einsamkeit," mm. 1–3; (c) "rushing wind" and F–E motif in "Die Wetterfahne," mm. 1–4; (d) "rushing wind" in "Rückblick," mm. 1–2; (e) slow, arrested rhythm in "Wasserflut," mm. 1–2; (f) "lulling" rhythm in "Frühlingstraum," mm. 1–2

Example 11.1 (cont.)

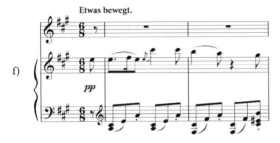

a pattern for other "walking" songs in the cycle, such as Nos. 3, 7, 10, and 12 (Example 11.1b). Likewise, the rushing wind of "Die Wetterfahne" (Example 11.1c) is perceptible in other fast, even chase-like songs, as, for instance, Nos. 4, 8, and 18 (Example 11.1d). *Winterreise* is especially remarkable for its slow songs, in which all movement seems arrested in order to give way to some fantastic, vision-like character, as in "Wasserflut" (Example 11.1e). Slow songs may follow each other to create a profound feeling of standstill, as with Nos. 6 and 7, or form a group, as with Nos. 14, 15, and 17. Finally, a last category might embrace "lulling" songs in 6/8 time, such as "Frühlingstraum" (Example 11.1f). These characterizations may be disputable, and some songs that are not unified with regard to tempo or time signature may relate to several categories. Interestingly, these categories do not quite tally with the placement of songs in the harmonic quadrants, thus contributing to the cycle's rich yet unsystematic set of relationships.

Remarkably, the main recurring motif in *Winterreise* consists of a mere minimal figure, namely the minor $\flat\hat{6}-\hat{5}$ descending semitone, which is also echoed across the cycle by other semitonal relationships, notably $\flat\hat{3}-\hat{2}$, or sometimes $\hat{8}-\natural\hat{7}$. Thus the F–E semitone of "Die Wetterfahne" (mm. 1–2) (Example 11.1c) is anticipated in "Gute Nacht" (mm. 1–2) (Example 11.1a), and the C–B semitone in "Der Lindenbaum" (m. 26) (Example 11.2a) finds its final resonance in "Der Leiermann" (m. 4) (Example 11.2b).[20] The motif is particularly pervasive in such songs as "Rast" and "Letzte Hoffnung," although, because it is so elemental, it can be traced almost everywhere in the cycle, especially in relation to the minor mode or the diminished seventh chord. While this motif is not unique to Schubert, it does carry particular meaning in his work as being the semitone that, in the piano part, marks the dramatic climax of "Gretchen am Spinnrade" (D118), where the music temporarily halts. A similar heart-rending effect can be heard in "Wasserflut" (m. 12) (Example 11.2c). In "Gute Nacht," the F–E oscillation is harmonized by a singular I–II$_2^4$–I succession (mm. 8–10) (Example 11.2d), which is

Example 11.2 (a) C–B motif in "Der Lindenbaum," m. 26; (b) and in "Der Leiermann," m. 4; (c) E–F sorrowful climax in "Wasserflut," m. 12; (d) F–E motif and I–II$_2^4$–I progression in "Gute Nacht," mm. 8–10; (e) II$_5^{\#6}$–I^6 progression in "Die Wetterfahne," mm. 31–32; (f) apparent I–V–IV–I regression in "Irrlicht," mm. 1–2; (g) and in mm. 5–6

later replicated in "Einsamkeit" (mm. 9–10), but it also bears a kinship with the striking II$_5^{\#6}$–I^6 progression of "Die Wetterfahne" (mm. 31–32) (Example 11.2e) – a passage highlighted by Ernst Kurth.[21] Equally related is the seeming I–V–IV–I regression in "Irrlicht" (mm. 1–2, 5–6) (Example 11.2f, g), though it is never actually articulated as such by Schubert.

Other resemblances arise from manifestations of tone painting: tramping steps, bursts of wind, posthorn calls, tears seized by frost, a horse galloping, cocks crowing, wings fluttering, leaves falling, etc. Even the horns of "Der Lindenbaum" partake of a related form of evocation that transforms absence and the abstraction of remembrance into poetic presence and fullness. Despite the permanence of the principle, only a few of these figures recur in more than one song, and always in a different, metamorphosed shape.

Recitative passages and dissonant melodic intervals both occur in "Die Wetterfahne" (mm. 11–13, 15–17) (Example 11.3a, b). Unison textures between piano and voice are found repeatedly, as again exemplified in "Die Wetterfahne" (mm. 6–9) (Example 11.3c), as if to signify a renunciation of accompanying that parallels the periodic repudiation of singing. In contrast, a quasi-religious, chorale-like texture appears in places, as in "Im Dorfe" (mm. 37–39) (Example 11.3d). Noticeable, too, are sudden harmonic changes that alter the prevalent color dramatically ("Auf dem Flusse," mm. 8–9) (Example 11.3e) or move towards greater lightness ("Der greise Kopf," mm. 10–12) (Example 11.3f). Vocal outbursts in the top register punctuate a number of songs, e.g. "Gefror'ne Tränen," mm. 47–49 (Example 11.3g). Schubert frequently opposes the voice's lower and upper range, often favoring high, tense notes. While the diction is primarily syllabic, occasional, rapid melismas can express anger or anguish ("Die Wetterfahne," m. 18) (Example 11.3h).

Also returning intermittently are martial-sounding dotted rhythms or other inexorable rhythms in the piano part ("Wasserflut," mm. 5–7, 9–11) (Example 11.4a), embodying both the protagonist's surges of resoluteness and the implacability of his situation. Rising $\hat{5}$–$\hat{8}$ motions in the voice or piano reinforce this implacability as well as allude to some strenuous surpassing of the self ("Wasserflut," mm. 11, 13, 27) (Example 11.4b, c). At times, the piano part, in repeated notes, swells to such an extent that it almost swamps the voice, as though the traveler were overcome by his condition ("Einsamkeit," mm. 28–30) (Example 11.4d). Finally, it is worth noting how the modulation from the key of ♭II (over a dominant pedal) back to the dominant of the main key in "Gefror'ne Tränen" (mm. 34–38) (Example 11.4e) comes back almost literally in "Einsamkeit" (mm. 30–34) (Example 11.4f),[22] and how more subtle echoes of "Frühlingstraum" can be heard in "Täuschung."

Major–minor exchange is a feature common to many songs in *Winterreise*, starting with "Gute Nacht."[23] More generally, the cycle is characterized by a refusal to let music "flower" in the sense, described by Goethe in his 1790 *Versuch die Metamorphose der Pflanzen zu erklären*, of

Example 11.3 (a) Recitative passage in "Die Wetterfahne," mm. 11–13; (b) dissonant intervals, mm. 15–17; (c) unisons between piano and voice, mm. 6–9; (d) chorale-like texture in "Im Dorfe," mm. 37–39; (e) distant, rapid harmonic changes in "Auf dem Flusse," mm. 8–9; (f) and in "Der greise Kopf," mm. 10–12; (g) vocal outburst in the higher register in "Gefror'ne Tränen," mm. 47–49; (h) rapid melisma in "Die Wetterfahne," mm. 17–18

Example 11.3 (cont.)

progressive elevation, differentiation, and refinement; most songs shun any real development or growth, so that very few, for instance, can be exploited individually in a recital program. Some, such as "Frühlingstraum," even display a pattern of retrogressive growth, shifting from a richer, more melodic texture to a barer, more declamatory one, from major to minor, and from warmth to cold.

Ultimately, our expectations about connectedness between the songs and the way we conceive connections are dependent on our understanding of the cycle. If, according to Novalis, nature is but a construction of the mind, or, in Schelling's words, "a poem lying pent in a mysterious and wonderful script . . . a world existing, not outside" the artist "but within,"[24] then we should reconsider the relation of reality to illusion in *Winterreise*, if only because illusions are the very stuff of reality in Romantic poetry, while reality is degraded to a mere illusion. But there is nothing "realistic" in the cycle, and what is more, no "reality." Hence, there is no actual winter, no snow, no crows, no dogs, no unlucky love, and also no death (at least in a physical sense). Above all, no narrative is to be sought. Everything

Example 11.4 (a) Dotted rhythms in "Wasserflut," mm. 5–7; (b) $\hat{5}$–$\hat{8}$ motion, mm. 11–12; (c) and in mm. 13–14; (d) piano accompaniment overpowering the voice in "Einsamkeit," mm. 28–30; (e) modulation to ♭II over a dominant pedal point and return to V of the main key in "Gefror'ne Tränen," mm. 34–38; (f) and in "Einsamkeit," mm. 30–34

is to be taken, as Novalis writes, "allegorically." In that respect, if flowers – especially blue ones – that were so essential to *Die schöne Müllerin* are the attribute of the poet and representative of poetry, their disappearance in *Winterreise* takes on a significance that involves the disappearance of poetry itself, or of the possibility of it. What this winter of poetry meant for Schubert cannot be surmised from any literal reading of the cycle. The apparent disconnectedness of the latter is at once a manifestation of, and a pointer to that symbolic riddle.

Notes

1. My gratitude goes to the late David Lewin, of Harvard University – a model of a scholar, man, and friend – who introduced me to the analytical challenges of *Winterreise*; I am also indebted to Lorraine Byrne Bodley, of Maynooth University, for her warm endorsement of my work and sharing her extraordinary knowledge of Schubert's life and music.
2. Novalis, *Philosophical Writings*, trans. and ed. M. M. Stoljar (Albany, NY: State University of New York Press, 1997), 33.
3. For an intriguing reading of *Winterreise* in relation to the Ancient Greek myths, see Carlo Lo Presti, *Franz Schubert, il viandante e gli inferi. Trasformazioni del mito nel Lied schubertiano* (Turin: Le Lettere, 1995).
4. The protagonist of *Winterreise* borrows features of the Wandering Jew. Müller's poem "Der ewige Jude" (*Taschenbuch zum geselligen Vergnügen auf das Jahr 1823* [Leipzig: J. F. Gleditsch, 1823], 10–12) uses vocabulary that matches that of certain poems in the cycle. See *RWJ*, 17, n. 20.
5. Charles Rosen, *The Romantic Generation* (Cambridge, MA: Harvard University Press, 1995), 203–4.
6. See ibid., 195–6.
7. On Müller's and Schubert's different orders of poems and songs, see Chapter 5 in this volume. On the song transpositions, see also Chapter 12 and Table 12.1.
8. See Walther Dürr's critical notes in Dürr (ed.), *Franz Schubert. Neue Ausgabe sämtlicher Werke*, Series IV: Lieder, vol. 4b (Kassel: Bärenreiter, 1979), 306, 310, 312, and 315–16.
9. *DC*, 165.
10. Deborah Stein proposes a different table in "The End of the Road in Schubert's *Winterreise*," in *RS*, 355–82 (372).
11. See Ernő Lendvai, *Béla Bartók: An Analysis of His Music* (London: Kahn & Averill, 1971), 1–16. See also Hermann Beckh, *Die Sprache der Tonart* (Stuttgart: Urachhaus, 1937). Beckh's tonal "crosses" indirectly anticipate Lendvai's representation.
12. Hugo Riemann, *Skizze einer neuen Methode der Harmonielehre* (Leipzig: Breitkopf & Härtel, 1880), 27.
13. Walther Dürr, "Zyklische Ordnung und Liederzyklus. Schuberts 'Winterreise,'" in *Programmbuch Schubertiade Hohenems* 1984, s. l. [1984], 79–80.
14. Ibid., 79.
15. See Su Yin Mak, *Schubert's Lyricism Reconsidered: Structure, Design and Rhetoric* (Saarbrücken: Lambert, 2010), 31.
16. Roman Jakobson, "Closing Statement: Linguistics and Poetics," in Thomas A. Sebeok (ed.), *Style in Language* (Cambridge, MA: MIT Press, 1960), 350–77 (377).
17. Ibid., 356.
18. Novalis, *Schriften*, vol. 3. *Das philosophische Werk II*, ed. R. Samuel et al. (Stuttgart: Kohlhammer, 1968), 572. (My translation.)
19. See, for instance, Rolf Vollmann's concluding chapter on "Wilhelm Müller and Romanticism" in *FSSMW*, 153–63.
20. The latter connection was brought to my attention by Michael Spitzer, of the University of Liverpool.

21. See Ernst Kurth, *Romantische Harmonik und ihre Krise in Wagners "Tristan"* (Berlin: Max Hesse, 1920), 128–29.

22. I am grateful to Georges Bloch, of the University of Strasbourg, for mentioning this resemblance to me.

23. *DW*, 181.

24. Friedrich Schelling, *System of Transcendental Idealism (1800)*, trans. Peter Heath (Charlottesville, VA: University of Virginia Press, 1993), 232.

12 Discontinuity in *Winterreise*

DEBORAH STEIN

This essay explores the distinction between "continuity" and "discontinuity" in the poetry and music of *Winterreise*. In a continuous poetic cycle, the poems progress in a logical, recognizable process where we know where we begin and end, and everything in between relates to the whole. Musical continuity likewise involves a clear sense of motion forward and reaching a goal – such as beginning and ending in the same key, or tonal coherence. In a discontinuous poetic or musical cycle, on the other hand, there is no clear motion forward from beginning to end, no clear end point, and a lack of cohesion or interconnectedness (recurring elements) over the whole. But the distinction is not altogether clear. Within a continuous cycle, interruptions do occur, and within a discontinuous cycle, elements of continuity occur as well. Ultimately, a cycle is experienced primarily one way or the other based on a number of factors, including the presence of repeated elements (continuous) or lack of repeated elements (discontinuous).

I propose that *Winterreise* is characterized by discontinuity, i.e., a pervasive lack of forward motion and coherence in the poetry and in Schubert's transformations of it within his musical settings. Yet, as I will show, the cycle also features some elements of continuity and coherence.

The poetry traces a wanderer who leaves his rejecting love and grapples with emotional and psychological anguish. The wanderer is overwhelmed with a mixture of difficult emotions – hurt, anger, alienation, anxiety – and he staggers about in a state of painful confusion. The first part of this essay examines the poetic narrative with a focus on the inherent disconnections – how each poem is a distinct moment in the journey and may not be related to those that precede or follow it.

When Schubert began to set this seemingly discontinuous text, he faced the challenge of creating musical disconnection while at the same time shaping a work that had some measure of musical comprehensibility. The second part explores how Schubert transformed the poetic discontinuity in terms of tonal design, and the third part details how he used elements of temporality (rhythm, meter, and tempo) to depict the disjointed poetic narrative.[1] The fourth part addresses the end of the cycle.

Müller's Poetry

German Romanticism

My interpretation of Schubert's *Winterreise* is founded on several aspects of German Romanticism, the most common poetic subject of which is the very wanderer found in *Winterreise*: an alienated man overwhelmed with despair about a grievous loss, usually a lost love, but perhaps a lost homeland.[2] He roams about in nature, especially at night, in order to *feel* his pain and thus to somehow reconnect with his loss, usually through memory.

German Romantic works often focus on the inner world of human emotions and psychological states, including inner conflicts, dreams, fantasies, and the subconscious. The outer world of nature, meanwhile, provides a dramatic stage for the wanderer. Nature enables him to access difficult feelings through a complex, circular process of projecting his feelings onto it, e.g., night violets are melancholy or the forest is lonely. The wanderer then feels empathy for nature and internalizes the emotions: *he* is melancholy and lonely.[3]

The natural world also engages another important poetic issue: the element of time. On a large scale are the different seasons (in *Winterreise,* the contrast of spring vs. winter) and on a smaller scale, the past (remembering happier days), present (feeling oppressed and hurt), and future (often longing for release from pain through death). The shifting of time in *Winterreise* is a critical factor: the miserable wanderer in the cold present seeks warmth and happiness through memories of the past. Questions about the "future" are persistent as well: Where will he go next? What is the goal of his wandering? Can he escape his turmoil through death?

Three other concepts are particularly pertinent to *Winterreise*. First is what I call the Romantic soul's "insatiable quest to go beyond what is known."[4] This quest takes the wanderer outside normative boundaries (for example, outside the village of his lost love) and into the infinite (the wanderer's journey without direction or end). Second is "the embrace of the contradictory or dichotomous, the mingling of two seemingly incompatible, opposing elements."[5] Part of the impact of poetry in general arises from the juxtaposition of contrasting elements, and, as noted by many, dichotomy is an important feature of *Winterreise*. For example, the recurring opposition of fire and ice (beginning in poem 3 and continuing through poem 8) has the paradoxical effect of intensifying the two images because of their stark contrast: the wanderer's hot tears melt in the frozen ice, leaving him to wonder if his tears also will thaw his frozen heart.

Finally, German Romantics savored how tensions and powerful feelings can remain unresolved. The *romantische Sehnsucht*, or longing for the unattainable, is a critical poetic element; *yearning* is the goal, not attainment of what is irretrievably gone. Longing for the unattainable is captured in the German Romantic concept of "fragment," where a work is inherently incomplete and unresolved.[6] This bold idea threatened the artistic notions of continuity and closure and, indeed, an important aspect of Schubert's *Winterreise* is the lack of a definitive ending, both in many of the poems and at the cycle's conclusion. We will return to this issue presently.[7]

The Poetic Narrative

While the poetic cycle depicts a winter's journey, there is neither a clear purpose nor a trajectory to this wandering. Indeed, the poems do not all follow one another in a logical order, and the cycle does not arrive at a clear destination. There are two different ways to understand the poetic narrative: (1) that the cycle is at least somewhat coherent, with many recurring elements that link poems with one another, and (2) that the cycle lacks overall coherence. Susan Youens finds some coherence, especially in Part I, where one poem follows another as a reaction to the latter.[8] As noted, I prefer the second understanding, which emphasizes "discontinuity" or a general lack of connectedness between poems. Other scholars have also adopted this view. Arnold Feil states, "The text of *Winterreise* lacks the element of plot," and Brian Newbould says, "The poems do not form a continuous narrative . . . [but present] . . . a series of episodes in a psychological soliloquy." Lauri Suurpää concurs that "discontinuity . . . play[s] a significant role in *Winterreise*."[9]

Two factors encourage this interpretation: the uncertainty of poetic time and the chaos of the wanderer's emotional struggles. First, the poetic time between individual poems is unclear; we do not know how much time passes, only that we remain in winter. Is the timing from one poem to another immediate, suggesting a direct response? Does one poem follow another? Or is it after a while? Or not at all? In addition, while one poem may occur after another, the emotions may be drastically different, and the movement away from one poem is not necessarily toward the next. The nature of the wanderer's psychological state is tumultuous and complicated, and he struggles with many conflicts and confusions. The wanderer does not choose a continuous path; he stumbles about, pauses to feel or ruminate, and trudges on. The poetic narrative thus can be characterized as unpredictable and unsettled.

It may prove helpful to review the central issue of grieving in *Winterreise* before examining the poetic cycle in detail. As is well known, grieving a loss involves several different stages, from denial (avoidance, confusion, shock, fear) to anger (frustration, annoyance, anxiety) to attempts to reframe issues called "bargaining" (struggling to find different meanings) to depression (feeling overwhelmed, helpless, hostile, or impelled to flee) to eventual acceptance.[10] Both in real life and in *Winterreise,* grieving is neither linear nor fluid; rather, those who grieve, including the wanderer, move in and out of the various stages.

Poetic Interpretation

Like much poetry, Müller's poetic cycle depicts both external events (wandering) and internal experiences (dreams, emotions, confusions). Two different interpretive approaches are possible. First is a literal level of interpretation, where the images (the girl's house, the linden tree, etc.) depict a real, outer world through which the wanderer journeys, and second is a metaphorical level, where imagery helps to conjure an *inner* journey within his mind.[11] In a literal interpretation, the wanderer passes by places important to his lost love: her house, the linden tree, the river, etc. In between these places, other poems depict his inner life, where he poses questions to himself, his heart, the village dogs, or the crow. At the various places where the wanderer pauses, nature prompts him to think about and feel different aspects of his struggle. Indeed, the powerful images of the linden tree and the frozen river bring out critical moments of the journey: in poem 5, "Der Lindenbaum," the possibility of an escape through death occurs for the first time, while in poem 7, "Auf dem Flusse," the wanderer experiences the flowing river beneath its frozen crust as representing the torrents within his frozen heart.[12] In the literal interpretation, the performers may present the travels as occurring in real time or may in essence re-enact the journey, as if in an immense recollection.

While it is possible to imagine the protagonist wandering through an actual frozen landscape, my interpretation focuses on the second, metaphorical approach: the wanderer's journey takes place *within* his tortured mind and soul. In this case, the wanderer is not remembering an actual journey, but rather is *imagining* one.[13] His journey involves struggling with many complex emotional and psychological issues and is fraught with difficulty. He often experiences several different emotions (e.g., hurt and anger) simultaneously, or he may start out feeling one way and another feeling takes over. With this interpretive approach, images from his life can be understood as not real or external, but rather as fantasies in the wanderer's mind of people or places from his earlier life. The poetic imagery has the same profound effect as if the wanderer was taking an actual journey, but his experience of them is internal. In this interpretation, the performers recreate the lengthy fantasy as if it was an actual journey.

It might be best, then, to think of the cycle as a series of vignettes, where each poem represents a separate moment of the wanderer's inner journey.[14] The poetic cycle vacillates between two types of experience: he recalls past images of the outside world in poems 1, 2, 4, 5, 7, 8, 9, and 13, and he dwells on deep emotions and ponders his confusions in poems 3, 4, 6, 10–12, 14–16 18, 19, and 21–24.

Poetic Meaning Through Dichotomy

The challenge in understanding a discontinuous cycle of poems is immense. What can help is finding recurring elements that group poems together, if not immediately, then over time. These interrelationships among poems do not create stability or coherence; rather, they offer a small measure of order within an essentially disordered world. Recurring dichotomies or oppositions serve this function. For example, the important metaphor of a happy past vs. the painful present occurs throughout Part I of *Winterreise*, as the wanderer's memories and dreams of a joyful past contrast with his present state of hurt and despair. Happy reminiscences emphasize present misery, and present despair intensifies longing for the past; the opposition reinforces both. Müller's poetic cycle includes a wealth of such dichotomies that emphasize the protagonist's feelings and highlight his inner conflicts.

The most complex dichotomy, one that permeates German Romantic poetry, is spring vs. winter. Both of these seasons carry numerous meanings. Spring holds the promise of love; it is warm, with flowers and fields, bright skies and babbling brooks. Winter, on the other hand, is a time of loss and death; it is cold with snow and ice, gloomy skies, and menacing storms. Poems with fantasies and memories of spring occur mostly in Part I, e.g., nos. 1, 4, 5, 6, 7, 8, 11, and 12. The continuous recollection of spring (i.e., past happiness) intensifies the cold and dark of winter (present despair), and, conversely, winter's icy storms underscore the warm gentleness of spring remembrances.

Another recurring dichotomy is rejection vs. acceptance (wanting acceptance and fearing rejection are embodied in alienation). In poems 1, 2, 8, 12, 17, and 20, the wanderer experiences feelings of isolation and alienation from the village and the world beyond.[15] These poems involve his anger at the village around him; he begins by feeling disdain for his lost love's family (poems 1 and 2), continues feeling shunned by villagers (poems 8 and 12), and is able to ironically reject the villagers themselves (poems 17 and 20).

Dichotomies embody emotional and psychological conflicts. For example, the wanderer's desire to escape his pain through death includes both yearning and anxiety. Another recurring conflict is the wanderer's ambivalence about continuing his journey. In poem 8, "Rückblick," Richard Capell notes a "hastening and delaying," that is, a need to keep going vs. a wish to stop wandering and turn back.[16] In poem 10, "Rast," the wanderer is similarly caught between a "compulsion to move" and exhaustion.

Obsessions and Fears

The wanderer has several profound obsessions and anxieties throughout the cycle. Part I involves his struggles to search for or let go of his rejecting love. In poem 4, he frantically tries to find traces of her in his icy world and fears he will lose even his memory of her, while in poem 7, he acknowledges that their love is dead as he carves the beginning and ending dates of their relationship in the river's frozen crust. The most powerful obsession is with the notion of death as an escape from his torment. This common German Romantic theme occurs in Müller's *Die schöne Müllerin* cycle and in many single poems set by composers.[17] In Part I of *Winterreise*, poem 5 offers the first inkling of the wanderer thinking about death, and poems 7 and 9 continue these initial thoughts. In Part II, then, the drive toward death becomes obsessive, intensifying in poems 14, 15, 16, 20, and 21. Interestingly, before the wanderer's obsession with death begins, his fixation on loss *as* a kind of death recurs often. His "frozen" heart is as if dead in poem 4;[18] he carves "a makeshift tombstone for his love" in poem 7;[19] "everything, joy and sorrow alike, culminates in death" in poem 9;[20] and he experiences the death of hope in poem 16.[21]

Death proves elusive, however. Although it seems inevitable by poem 20, with poem 21, the wanderer's search for death is "denied." This denial is ironic given the wanderer's obsession; it is a dramatic example of his ambivalence about stopping vs. moving on. The intensification of this yearning for death in *Winterreise* from poems 5 through 20 is dramatic, and the denial in poem 21 is a shock, a powerful disruption in the cycle.

The Tonal Design of Schubert's Cycle

Schubert faced the challenge of setting Müller's poems in a way that incorporated both the poetic discontinuity and, where possible, any interconnections among the poems. He created musical disruptions through several musical means: a chaotic tonal design and the use of unpredictable rhythms, meters, and tempi.[22]

Large tonal works, including multi-movement pieces and cycles, tend to have an underlying tonal design that provides a point of

Table 12.1 *Tonality in* Winterreise

Song	Key	P or R	♯s/♭s	Orig key
Part I				
1	d/D	P	1♭/2♯	
2	a/A	P	0/3♯	
3	f/A♭	R	4♭	
4	c		3♭	
5	E/e	P	4♯/1♯	
6	e		1♯	f♯ (3♯)
7	e/E	P	1♯/4♯	
8	g/G	P	2♭/1♯	
9	b/D	R	2♯	
10	c/E♭	R	3♭	d (1♭)
11	A/a	P	3♯/0	
12	b		2♯	d (1♭)
Part II				
13	E♭		3♭	
14	c		3♭	
15	c/E♭	R	3♭	
16	E♭/e♭	P	3♭/6♭	
17	D	P	2♯	
18	d		1♭	
19	A		3♯	
20	g/G	P	2♭/1♯	
21	F	P	1♭	
22	g/G	PR	2♭/1♯	a (0)
23	A/C/a	PR	3♯/0	
24	a		0	b (2♯)

Notes:
(1) Upper-case letters show major keys; lower-case show minor keys
(2) P is parallel major/minor pair and R is relative major/minor pair

reference (a governing tonic) and clear tonal closure (a strong Perfect Authentic Cadence, or PAC). The large-scale musical space is thus created through a tonal frame that ensures continuity and coherence. In *Winterreise*, however, the tonal design imparts neither a sense of continuity (i.e., of moving within a comprehensible space) nor of coherence (beginning and ending in the same tonal space). Instead, Schubert conveys the cycle's poetic discontinuity through a seemingly disorganized choice of keys and, with a few exceptions, a general lack of interrelationships among keys. An additional issue involving the cycle's tonal design is that the keys of five songs (nos. 6, 10, 12, 22, and 24) were changed prior to publication. Table 12.1 shows the keys Schubert used in his first version as well as the publication keys. The original keys of songs 10 and 12 provided coherence in that Part I of the cycle ended in D minor, the same key in which it began. Meanwhile, song 6, in F♯ minor rather than the later key of E minor, broke up a three-song grouping in E major/minor. In Part II, the key changes are toward the end, songs 22 in A minor and 24 in B minor.[23]

For most of the cycle, the keys shift back and forth between sharp and flat keys, creating constant tonal disruptions, especially, as will be shown, with more remotely related keys. Table 12.1 highlights this shifting. Given the grim poetic narrative, it is not surprising that minor keys appear far more frequently than major ones. Also, while closely related major-mode songs occur over time in E major (song 5), A major (songs 11, 19, and 23), and D major (song 17), they are too dispersed over the cycle to create any tonal closeness or continuity.

Schubert's tonal choices are, of course, deeply related to the poetic text. For example, song 1 is in D minor/major, and song 2 is in a close relation, A minor/major. Both songs involve the wanderer standing outside the house of his lost love. Song 3, "Gefror'ne Tränen," however, where he acutely feels the pain of rejection and alienation, is farther removed: F minor and its relative, A♭ major, are a distinctly different tonal world. Similar disconnections occur between songs 10 and 11. In song 10, "Rast," the wanderer deals with his ambivalence of finding rest vs. moving on in C minor. Then song 11, "Frühlingstraum," where the wanderer seeks solace in dreams of love and spring only to awaken to the cold, dark reality, occurs in A major/minor. The two songs are thus tonally disconnected.

Schubert does allow some songs to group together within recurring, closely related keys, and there is one such group in each part of the cycle. In Part I, songs 5–7 are in E major or minor. All intensify the wanderer's pain and despair and thus form a poetic unit within the journey: song 5, "Der Lindenbaum," with the first lure toward death; song 6, "Wasserflut," where he weeps and recalls the girl's house once more; and song 7, "Auf dem Flusse," where he carves the ending date of their love. The same intensification occurs at the opening of Part II, where songs 13–16 are in the relative pair, C minor and E♭ major. By keeping to the relative major/minor pair, Schubert groups these songs together tonally as the poems and songs proceed from his last temptation to think of his lost love (song 13) to his increased yearning for death (songs 14 and 15) to finally his abandonment of hope (song 16).[24]

However, these groups occur within *larger* disconnections. Songs 5–7 in E major/minor are flanked by song 4 (C minor) and song 8 (G minor). Thus C minor (three flats) goes to E major (four sharps), and E minor (one sharp) goes to G minor (two flats): C minor–E major/minor–G minor. In a similar way, songs 13–16, in E♭ major/C minor, occur between B minor (song 12) and D major (song 17): B minor (two sharps) goes to E♭ major/C minor (three flats), which goes to D major (two sharps): B minor–E♭ major/C minor–D major. A similar disconnection occurs with songs 19–23: both songs 19 and 23 are in the sharp key of A major. But in between these songs are the flat keys of G minor and F major: A major–G minor–F major–G minor–A major. The A major songs depict the wanderer's retreat to fantasy, while the G minor and F major songs convey the reality of the wanderer's ongoing struggle.

One final issue involving discontinuity in the tonal design is Schubert's well-known use of parallel major/minor and relative major/minor pairs. In a sea of tonal discontinuity, the use of closely connected major/minor pairs enables contrasting issues *within* a poem to be easily distinguished without a more dramatic change in tonal center. Table 12.1 shows Schubert's use of these modal shifts. For one third of the cycle, a prevailing minor mode shifts to major, where the major mode depicts escape through dream, memory, or illusion. A few songs involve the relative pair: in Part I, songs 3, 9, and 10, and in Part II, songs 15, 22, and 23. The most dramatic use of the relative pair is in song 3, "Gefror'ne Tränen," which vacillates between the keys of F minor and A♭ major to dramatize the wanderer's conflicts. The vacillation between two closely related keys creates tonal ambiguity, which in turn illustrates the wanderer's emotional distress.

Temporality in Schubert's Cycle

Pacing and Tempo

In response to Müller's poetic discontinuity, Schubert creates temporal disorder through the use of diverse meters, rhythms, and tempo indications. These basic elements create "temporality," or the passage of time: how fast or slow the cycle moves and over what span of time. For the most part, Schubert uses simple meters. There are eleven songs in duple meter: 4/4 (including one in cut time) and 2/4; eight songs in triple meter: 3/4 and 3/8; and three songs in the compound meter of 6/8. In addition, two songs use more unusual signatures: a juxtaposition of two different time signatures, 6/8 and 2/4, in song 11; and the carefully notated 12/8 in song 17. Metric changes within the cycle do not create the same disruptions as do keys in the tonal design. Even so, Table 12.2 shows the frequent metric shifts between duple and triple with only occasional consecutive songs of the same metric type.

Schubert's meters work in concert with his tempo indications, which span from *Sehr langsam* (very slow) to *Ziemlich schnell* (quite fast).[25] Schubert's tempo choices suggest concerns about pacing. He constantly modifies his tempo markings to avoid extremely slow or fast tempi. In contrast to the definitive *Sehr langsam* of song 21, seven songs have "*Etwas*" (somewhat) applied to either *geschwind* (fast) or *langsam*, or "*Ziemlich*" (quite, somewhat, rather) applied to *geschwind* and *schnell*. He uses other qualifiers as well, e.g., in songs 2, 3, 8, 16, 18, and 21–23.

Table 12.2 *Temporality in* Winterreise

Song	Meter	Tempo		Triplets	Rests	Beat 2
Part I						
1	2/4	Mässig,	moderate			
		in gehender Bewegung	walking motion			
2	6/8	Ziemlich geschwind,	somewhat fast			
		unruhig	restless			
3	Cut	Nicht zu langsam	not too slow			
4	C	Ziemlich schnell	somewhat fast	✓		
5	3/4	Mässig	moderate	✓	44, 58	✓
6	3/4	Langsam	slow	✓		✓
7	2/4	Langsam	slow		40	
8	3/4	Nicht zu geschwind	not too fast			
9	3/8	Langsam	slow	✓	12, 16, 24, 26	
10	2/4	Mässig	moderate			✓
11	6/8	Etwas bewegt	somewhat moving		14, 26, 48, 58, 70	
	2/4					
12	2/4	Langsam	slow		27, 30, 39, 42	
Part II						
13	6/8	Etwas geschwind	somewhat fast		26, 71	✓
14	3/4	Etwas langsam	somewhat slow	✓	4, 12, 14, 16, 20, 24, 39	
15	2/4	Etwas langsam	somewhat slow	✓		✓
16	3/4	Nicht zu geschwind	not too fast		24, 38, 40	✓
17	12/8	Etwas langsam	somewhat slow		10, 15, 30, 35	
18	C	Ziemlich geschwind,	rather fast		3, 9	
		doch kräftig	yet strongly			
19	6/8	Etwas geschwind	somewhat fast			✓
20	2/4	Mässig	moderate		40	
21	C	Sehr langsam	very slow			
22	2/4	Ziemlich geschwind,	somewhat fast			
		kräftig	strongly			✓
23	3/4	Nicht zu langsam	not too slow		15, 25	✓
24	3/4	Etwas langsam	somewhat slow			✓

A special temporal feature of the cycle is its "walking motion," a continuous rhythmic motion that suggests the wanderer moving along on his journey.[26] Feil discusses this feature at length, identifying songs 1, 3, 7, 9, 10, 12, 15, 20, and 22 as "walking songs." He draws particular attention to song 1, "Gute Nacht," as well as to the important point of arrival, song 20, "Der Wegweiser."[27] The walking songs occur at different moments in the journey, and thus Schubert used different rhythmic notations. This raises some questions. Does a song written in continuous eighth notes suggest a faster pace than one written in quarters? Do quarters suggest a slower tempo?[28] If song 1, with the tempo indication "*Mässig, in gehender Bewegung*" (moderate, with walking motion) was notated in quarters rather than eighths, might it be too slow for setting the cycle in motion? Two walking songs illustrate: song 1, "Gute Nacht," notated in eighths, and song 3, "Gefror'ne Tränen," marked "*Nicht zu langsam*" (not too slow) and notated in quarters. While the eighth notes in song 1 initiate the journey at a reasonable walking pace, the continuous quarters in song 3 tend to slow down the pacing in order to depict the wanderer's pause to turn inward and weep.

While the wanderer continues "walking" at various moments throughout the cycle, the *way* he walks, whether literally or metaphorically, changes, from depressed walking (*Mässig*) in song 1 to belabored walking (*Langsam*) in song 7 to a more driven walking (*Mässig*) in song 20. In between the walking songs, when the wanderer focuses on inner feelings, the dichotomous vacillation between moving ahead and pausing emerges, adding to the temporal disruptions throughout. The pacing for the entire cycle, therefore, is unpredictable, with shifts between slower and faster songs.

Table 12.2 also shows Schubert's use of *Mässig* (moderate) tempo to facilitate subtle accelerations or decelerations between songs. For example, after song 1, two other *Mässig* occurrences in Part I assist in the shifts between slower and faster songs. After the *Ziemlich schnell* of song 4, song 5's *Mässig* decelerates to prepare for the *Langsam* of song 6; similarly, the *Langsam* of song 9 is followed by the *Mässig* of song 10, which accelerates to the *Etwas bewegt* (somewhat moving) of song 11. In Part II, after the *Etwas geschwind* of song 19, the *Mässig* tempo of song 20 decelerates the motion to prepare for song 21 (*Sehr langsam*).

Triplets

Schubert also employs other temporal devices to depict the poetic verse. He uses triplet rhythms for this purpose in songs 4, 5, 6, 9, 14, and 15. Sometimes triplets are pervasive, such as in song 4, "Erstarrung" (*Ziemlich schnell*), where the wanderer's frenzy to find keepsakes of his lost love is expressed through rhythmic agitation. Triplets also occur as part of a more complex use of rhythm, such as in song 14, "Der greise Kopf," a meditation on yearning for death, as illustrated in Example 12.1. The piano introduction in mm. 1–4 comprises two 2-measure units, and the second of these units recurs in the interludes in mm. 9–10, 15–16, 34–35, and the postlude in mm. 43–44. The piano's recurring solo gesture is dramatic: a crying out in a relatively high register that immediately descends more than an octave with an arpeggio in triplet eighth notes. The rests that follow these

Example 12.1 *"Der greise Kopf"*: Triplets

outbursts separate the poignant piano gestures (depicting the wanderer's anxiety) from the words that follow as he dwells on his desire for death.

Silence (Rests)

Recurring rests can have diverse effects in music. In *Winterreise,* the use of rests for expressive effects is exemplified in the much-explored song 7, "Auf dem Flusse," where the constant eighth-note rests portray a hesitation or tentative feeling.[29] The constant use of eighth-note rests in the piano in mm. 1–12 depicts the wanderer questioning the river, from which he feels estranged, with short vocal phrases using dotted rhythms. In mm. 13 and 22, the rests cease for one measure, to be replaced by continuous sixteenth notes that accelerate the song's motion. When the poem shifts to focus on the river's frozen crust in m. 14, the initial rest usage resumes. After the sixteenths in m. 22, Schubert shifts to the parallel key of E major, as the accompaniment adopts a new rhythmic profile (mm. 23–39): in the LH, one beat of eighth note and eighth rest followed by another beat of four sixteenth notes. This conveys the dramatic tension of what Youens calls "the attempt to carve a makeshift tombstone for the love."[30] The pain of this carving is depicted by combining two previously separated rhythms that illustrate the dichotomy of moving on vs. pausing: the sixteenth notes suggest accelerated motion showing the wanderer's increasing tension, while the eighth rests undermine that motion, suggesting he is in too much pain to move ahead. In the next stanza, the wanderer questions whether his frozen heart, like the frozen river, internalizes a "raging torrent" of pain. Schubert portrays this climactic moment in two ways. First, he combines the two rhythmic elements: the piano's eighth rests and the dotted rhythms from the opening vocal line in the accompaniment to express the accumulation of anxieties from the song's opening. Second, he gives the vocal line a recitative-like style, with many rests fracturing the line into two-measure units, almost as if the wanderer's pain causes a breathless weariness.

The constant use of rests in song 8, "Rückblick," meanwhile, expresses agitation rather than trepidation as the wanderer pushes forward against the temptation to turn back to his lost love. Indeed, throughout the cycle, songs 2, 7, 10, 11, 13, 17, and 20 use rests in either voice or piano to create various effects.[31]

Example 12.2 "Frühlingstraum": Disruptive rests in piano accompaniment

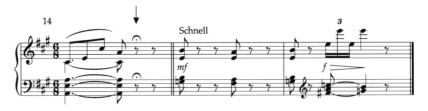

As noted, in song 7, "Auf dem Flusse," Schubert also uses rests in *both* performers' parts to create formal disjunctions: separations between sung verses and piano solos. These rests in all parts disrupt the musical flow throughout one half of the cycle: songs 5, 7, 9, 11–14, 16–18, 20, and 23. Song 5, "Der Lindenbaum," has two such formal divisions: in m. 44, at the end of stanza 4 ("Here you'll find peace [death]!") and in m. 58, at the end of stanza 5 ("The cold winds blew / Right into my face; / . . . I didn't turn around"). Eighth rests with fermatas stop motion before each of the last two stanzas as the wanderer reacts to the call of death in stanza 4 and the fury of winter winds in stanza 5.

Several songs use rests for both formal interruptions and expressive effects. In song 11, "Frühlingstraum," piano solos (introduction and interludes) and the poem's six stanzas are all separated by eighth-note rests in both voice and accompaniment. These pauses underscore the dramatic changes in the text. After the hopeful dream of spring in mm. 5–14 (downbeat), the eighth rests at the end of m. 14 in both vocal line and accompaniment occur with fermatas as the wanderer is brutally awakened. Similarly abrupt shifts between dream or illusions (e.g., painted windows) and reality recur in mm. 26, 58, and 70. In addition to the formal separations in "Frühlingstraum," Schubert uses rests in the accompaniment to portray the text in other ways. After offbeat rests in mm. 5–13, the eighth rests in mm. 15–21, a passage marked Schnell (fast) and *mf,* portray this devastating awakening (see Example 12.2).

In Part I of the cycle, the discontinuity produced by silence is extremely suggestive of the wanderer's struggles with his pain, anger, and alienation, and in Part II, of his obsession with death and psychological disintegration. His increasing despair leads to a diminishing sense of reality throughout, but especially in songs 19 and 23. Note that seven songs creating tensions through the use of rests occur in Part II, where the wanderer becomes both obsessive and unhinged.

Accents on Beat 2

Another way that Schubert destabilizes rhythm and meter is to accent beat 2 rather than the downbeat, especially through agogic accents (accents on

Example 12.3 "Wasserflut": Agogic accent on beat 2

a) as notated: b) re-barred for accent on downbeat

normally weak beats due to longer duration).[32] This technique, occuring in songs 5, 6, 10, 14–16, 19, and 22–24, creates metric ambiguity and a general unsteadiness as the ear searches for the "real" downbeat. In addition, three songs (2, 5, and 23) end on beat 2 rather than a downbeat, and song 18 ends on beat 3 of a 4/4 meter. These accents weaken the songs' endings, as will be discussed below.

Song 6, "Wasserflut" (*Langsam*), elegantly exemplifies the use of both triplets and accents on beat 2. In the piano introduction, an ascending sweep of triplet eighths on the downbeat suggests motion that is immediately undermined by the longer dotted quarters that emphasize beat 2. This vividly depicts the wanderer's struggling with his unremitting tears. The mix of triplets and agogic emphasis on beat 2 is unsettling, as it is possible to hear the arpeggio as an upbeat to a downbeat on the longer dotted quarter. Example 12.3 shows (a) the beat 2 accent in m. 1 as notated, and (b) a re-barring of m. 1 showing the triplets as an upbeat followed by the accented dotted quarter as a downbeat. Beat 2 emphasis continues in many measures of the vocal strophe as well as the recurring piano solos: mm. 1–2, 15–16, and 29–30.

Recitative Style

The musical fragmentation or disjunction caused by silence is especially poignant when the vocal line shifts to a recitative-like style that uses silence to create either more emphatic or more tentative speech-like statements. Song 7, "Auf dem Flusse," where Schubert uses a dramatic recitative (mm. 41–70), is full of rests, shifting dynamics (spanning *ppp* to *f*), and high register. Songs 2, 3, 7, 5, 12, 15, 23, and 24 use some form of the recitative style, with vocal lines fragmented by rests.[33]

Lack of Closure

Another factor that contributes to the cycle's discontinuous temporality is a lack of closure for many of the songs. Closure in a Lied generally involves both tonal and temporal factors. A clear, definitive ending is illustrated in song 1, "Gute Nacht": the vocal line and piano conclude with a PAC in

m. 99; the piano postlude varies or echoes the PAC until m. 105. Other songs have clear endings as well, especially song 20, "Der Wegweiser."[34]

However, many songs begin and end in a given key, but fail to produce closure with a strong PAC in both vocal line and accompaniment. In effect, a song simply stops and motion ceases. This contributes to the temporal ambiguity of the cycle, where boundaries separating one song from the next are vague or unclear. Feil notes that this lack of closure, in one third of the songs, occurs in two ways: (a) the opening prelude returns as a postlude, suggesting a possible continuation, or (b) the song "goes nowhere."[35] While songs 2, 4, 5, 7, 10, 12, 15, and 21 appear to have a strong *vocal* close, the return of a recurring piano solo extends beyond the voice in a less conclusive way. Postludes of this type express what the wanderer is thinking or feeling at the end of the vocal line; the thoughts can be vague and incomplete, and the feelings can remain unresolved. For example, in song 2, "Die Wetterfahne," the voice ends with a PAC in m. 46. The introduction then returns, slightly modified for five measures, and ends inconclusively in low octaves with no tonal cadence. The effect is a cessation of motion *without* a conclusion, as the emotions linger in the wanderer's mind and heart. Feil notes this with song 5, "Der Lindenbaum," which "ends as it began; the introduction, with very little change, serves as closing; no progress is made."[36]

In the Lied repertory, songs with introductions that recur as postludes often suggest incompletion and irresolution because of the inherent lingering in the poetic text stemming from unresolved tensions and yearnings. The fact that many songs in *Winterreise* do not really "end" adds another dimension to a cycle full of discontinuity and confusion.

The impression of "going nowhere" also undermines a sense of closure. The chronic triplets and fast tempo of song 4, "Erstarrung," propel it forward but without any goal. This impression is enhanced by the constant repetition of text and music, which provides a sense of going in a circular rather than a linear direction. Feil states, "The ending, which seems to be tacked on and not really to conclude, and the piano closing, in which all trace of the song seems to be obliterated, make the mood all the more hopeless."[37]

The lack of closure in both individual songs and the cycle as a whole leads to formal ambiguity, a disconnectedness that is related to the German Romantic fragment. As stated earlier, the fragment involves the twin concepts of incompletion and irresolution, and the sense of lingering in the piano after the vocal close suggests both. While the two concepts are similar, lack of closure, or incompletion, may result from the wanderer's physical or emotional state (for example, his exhaustion or sense of being overwhelmed by pain and unable to continue), while irresolution denotes a lingering of emotions that cannot cease (for example, unending despair or *Sehnsucht*). The vocal close often suggests irresolution by ending on the third or fifth of the tonic chord (Imperfect Authentic Cadence, or IAC), rather than the tonic note itself (PAC). In this cycle, several songs end on a perfunctory tonic after a more emphasized scale degree five: songs 2, 9, 12, 14, 15, 17, 19, 22, and 24. For example, the frenzy of song 4, "Erstarrung," can neither be completed nor resolved. The vocal close ends the text but not the emotions that continue in the accompaniment.

Timelessness

One final aspect of disconnection within *Winterreise* is its inherent time-lessness. Whether we understand the cycle as literal or metaphorical, the flow in time is ambiguous. The cycle presents a series of experiences: a movement away from the village, especially in Part I, for example, but with no clarity about how much time elapses between songs. The disruption resulting from the dichotomy of moving on vs. pausing interrupts the temporal flow established by the walking songs, and the moments of feeling and pondering create a kind of timelessness: when does weeping or raging begin and when does it end? This is part of the elegance of temporal artistic expression: time can seem to stand still, or become suspended. From the present, we can move back in time through memory or ahead into the future, outside the boundaries of time.

The lack of temporal clarity in the wanderer's journey underscores the overall sense of discontinuity in the poetry, the tonal design, and the use of temporal elements. This becomes even more significant when the cycle reaches the final song 24, "Der Leiermann," and the wanderer continues on, outside the confines of the cycle itself.

The Ending of *Winterreise*

The premise of disruption and incoherence in *Winterreise* is especially powerful because we do not know how the cycle ends: when and where – or whether – our wanderer arrives at a destination. Numerous scholars have acknowledged this elusive ending, and two different interpretations have emerged. First, many believe that the wanderer achieves his long-desired escape through death – a desire that begins in song 5 and becomes an obsession in Part II of the cycle. This drive towards death culminates in song 20, "Der Wegweiser," where he chooses the "road from which no one ever returned." For many scholars, this intense yearning for death seems convincing, despite the "denial" of death in song 21, "Das Wirtshaus."[38] In *Death in Winterreise,* Suurpää discusses the issue of death in detail, proposing that the wanderer seeks death not of his physical self but rather of his emotional self.[39]

A second interpretation of the wanderer's fate is that he joins the hurdy-gurdy man in madness. Richard Capell adopts this view, noting, "The final songs of the 'Winterreise' are indicative of the overwrought mind's derangement ... The madman meets a beggar, links with him his fortune; and the two disappear into the snowy landscape."[40] John Reed agrees that "[the wanderer] is denied the consolation of death . . . . his fate is a life in death, relieved only by the comradeship of the pathetic hurdy-gurdy man."[41] As Youens indicates, this notion of madness is supported in several earlier songs: song 9, "Irrlicht," where the wanderer's "depths of depression" lead to distraction with the illusory "will-o'-the-wisp"; song 16, "Letzte Hoffnung," which is a "psychologically accurate portrayal of . . . a state of panic and obsession ... barely this side of a psychotic break"; and song 19, "Täuschung," where "[t]he 'death' that threatens the wanderer is the dissolution of his sanity under the burden of despair."[42] Finally, song 23, "Die Nebensonnen," highlights the wanderer's mental frailty as he mourns his loss through a hallucination of multiple suns.

Both proposed "endings" of *Winterreise* are viable, even if clouded in uncertainty. My interpretation, which also involves uncertainty, derives from the German Romantic fragment, with its incompletion and irresolution. The lack of closure for the cycle is consistent with the nature of the poetry: the wanderer stumbles about, overwhelmed by despair and confusion, and his journey continues into the indefinite future, his struggles unresolved. Neither escape through death nor succumbing to madness resolves the ache of his heartbreak and his psychological torment; maybe resolution will come in the future, but we will only know this in our imaginations.

Notes

1. Among others, Lauri Suurpää examines disruption in both the poetry and the songs in *DW*, 188.
2. See Deborah Stein and Robert Spillman, *Poetry into Song: Performance and Analysis of Lieder* (New York and Oxford: Oxford University Press, 1996), 3–16. Lieder examples about mourning a lost homeland include Schubert's "Der Wanderer" (Schmidt von Lübeck, Op. 4, No. 1, 1816) and Schumann's "Sehnsucht nach der Waldgegend" (Kerner, Op. 35, No. 5, 1840).
3. Barbara Barry discusses a similar idea (the "reflective element") in "'Sehnsucht' and Melancholy," *The Philosopher's Stone* (New York: Pendragon Press, 2000), 182. Vivid examples that illustrate this process are Schubert's "Nachtviolen" (Mayrhofer, 1822); Schumann's "In der Fremde" (Eichendorff, *Liederkreis*, Op. 39, No. 1, 1840); and Brahms's "Die Mainacht" (Hölty, Op. 43, No. 2, 1864). See also Stein and Spillman, *Poetry into Song,* 40–43, 78–79, 91–93, 114–15.
4. Stein and Spillman, *Poetry into Song,* 5.
5. Ibid.
6. This study is particularly indebted to David Ferris, *Schumann's Eichendorff Liederkreis and the Genre of the Romantic Cycle* (Oxford: Oxford University Press, 2000), which challenges the notion of cyclic coherence in Schumann's *Liederkreis*, Op. 39.
7. The German Romantic fragment is explored in: John Daverio, *Nineteenth-Century Music and the German Romantic Ideology* (New York: Schirmer, 1993); *DC*; Kramer, "The Hedgehog: Of Fragments Finished and Unfinished," *19th-Century Music* 21/2 (1997): 134–48; and Charles

Rosen, *The Romantic Generation* (Cambridge, MA: Harvard University Press, 1995). See also Beate Julia Perrey, *Schumann's* Dichterliebe *and Early Romantic Poetics: Fragmentation of Desire* (Cambridge: Cambridge University Press, 2002); and Berthold Hoeckner, "Paths through Dichterliebe," *19th-Century Music* 30/1 (2006): 65–80. Suurpää cites many such studies of Schumann's use of the fragment but does not find similar usage in Schubert's cycles. *DW,* 188.

8. *RWJ*: 145–46, 153, 209, 217, 224, 262, and 267. Anthony Newcomb also connects "adjacent songs" in "Structure and Expression in a Schubert Song," in Walter Frisch (ed.), *Schubert Critical and Analytical Studies* (Lincoln: University of Nebraska Press, 1986), 166–67.

9. *FSSMW,* 87; Newbould, in *Schubert: The Music and the Man* (Berkeley and Los Angeles: University of California Press, 1997), 299; and *DW,* 188.

10. The classic study of grieving is Elizabeth Kübler-Ross, *On Death and Dying* (New York: Scribner, 1969).

11. Youens discusses the inner understanding of *Winterreise* in *RWJ*, 55–58, and Richard Kramer states that "[t]he action of 'Winterreise' is interior, a play of the mind caught in the inexorable trudge toward solitude and alienation" in *DC,* 172.

12. The poem numbers given here reflect Schubert's order in his cycle.

13. See Stein, "The End of the Road in Schubert's *Winterreise*: The Contradiction of Coherence and Fragmentation," in *RS*, 356–59.

14. Ibid., 376.

15. This is an important theme in *RWJ*, e.g., 120, 124–25, 132.

16. Richard Capell, *Schubert's Songs* (Old Woking, Surrey: The Gresham Press, 1928; 3rd ed., 1973), 235.

17. For example, Schubert's "Der Jüngling und der Tod" (D545), and Brahms's "Der Tod das ist die kühle Nacht" (Op. 96, No. 1) and "Immer leiser wird mein Schlummer" (Op. 105, No. 2).

18. Capell, *Schubert's Songs,* 234.

19. *RWJ,* 177.

20. Ibid, 197–98.

21. *DC,* 179.

22. Many authors have sought logic and coherence using a Schenkerian approach, including Kramer, *DC,* 153ff and Suurpää, *DW*. This approach will not be discussed here.

23. For more discussion of the key changes, see *RWJ*, 96–99, *DC,* 165–71, and Chapter 11 in this volume.

24. See also Barbara Turchin, "The Nineteenth-Century *Wanderlieder* Cycle," *The Journal of Musicology* 5/4 (1987): 514.

25. See *FSSMW,* 87 and *RWJ,* 111.

26. Youens refers to this rhythmic idea as a "journeying" motive, *RWJ,* 127, and 242.

27. *FSSMW,* 118–20.

28. Stein and Spillman, *Poetry into Song,* 70–72.

29. See David Lewin, "*Auf dem Fluße*: Image and Background," *19th-Century Music* 6/1 (1982): 47–59; Anthony Newcomb, "Structure and Expression," 153–74; and *DC,* 153–56.

30. *RWJ,* 177.

31. In *RWJ*, Youens includes the use of fermatas as a form of rest, 137, 180, 193, 205, 211–12, 230, 256, 274–75. For the rhythmic complexities of "Rückblick," see also *FSSMW,* 38–44.

32. Agogic accent is defined in Stein and Spillman, *Poetry into Song,* 70.

33. See *FSSMW,* 92, 94, 96, 100, 106, 111, 125, 127. See also *RWJ,* 81–82.

34. See *DC,* 181.

35. *FSSMW,* 87.

36. Ibid., 96.

37. Ibid., 95.

38. See Rosen, *Romantic Generation,* 194–95, and Barry, "'Sehnsucht' and Melancholy," 183.

39. *DW,* 195.

40. Capell, *Schubert's Songs,* 238–39.

41. *SSC,* 443.

42. *RWJ,* 196, 247, 268.

PART V

Winterreise After 1827

13 Performance and Reception

BENJAMIN BINDER

We think we know what *Winterreise* is: a formal live performance by a classically trained baritone and concert pianist in a recital or concert hall, featuring all twenty-four songs of the cycle presented without interruption or deviation from the printed score in Schubert's original publication order. But in the full sweep of *Winterreise*'s reception history since 1827, performances satisfying all or even most of these conditions have been much less common than we might assume. The fact is that there are just as many *Winterreise*s as there are performances, each informed by its own set of social, cultural, personal, historical, and technological factors. In this survey of *Winterreise*'s life in performance from Schubert's day up until the present, we will observe how the cycle's meaning is fundamentally dependent upon the manner and context of its presentation: performance as reception.

Winterreise During Schubert's Lifetime

In early March 1827, shortly after writing the first twelve songs of *Winterreise* – at that time, we should remember, Schubert believed the cycle to be complete – the composer had just moved into Franz von Schober's apartment at the Blue Hedgehog and invited a few friends over to hear some new works of his. They came to Schober's at the appointed time, but Schubert never showed. It was only some time later in the year that Schubert felt ready to reveal the fruits of his labor, as we learn from the 1858 reminiscences of Joseph von Spaun, one of Schubert's oldest and most trusted friends:

> For a time Schubert's mood became gloomy and he seemed exhausted. When I asked him what was the matter he merely said to me, "Well, you will soon hear it and understand." One day he said to me, "Come to Schober's today – I will sing you a cycle of terrifying songs. I am anxious to see what you will say about them. They have affected me more than has been the case with any other songs." So, in a voice wrought with emotion, he sang the whole of *Winterreise* through to us. We were quite dumbfounded by the gloomy mood of these songs and Schober said he had only liked one song, "Der Lindenbaum." To which

Schubert only said, "I like these songs more than all the others, and you will get to like them too."[1]

If it was indeed songs from *Winterreise* that Schubert hesitated to share with his friends back in March, then Spaun's account helps us understand why. These songs were uniquely challenging and pervasively "gloomy," perplexing even Schubert's most intimate confidantes. If Spaun's memory serves, and we draw upon other first-hand descriptions of Schubert singing, then we can imagine Schubert at the piano in the Schobers' music room, alone with two dear friends in the most private of settings, singing through these "terrifying songs" (perhaps the first twelve, perhaps all twenty-four) with his thin but agreeable voice of middling range, going into falsetto when the tessitura was too high, singing plainly and without theatrical affectation, all while accompanying himself on one of the era's fortepianos, with its more intimate dynamic range and variegated timbral palette in comparison with today's instruments. Above all, Schubert seems to have communicated a powerful sense through his performance ("wrought with emotion") that his own suffering was expressed in the work: "you will hear it and understand." This first performance of *Winterreise* was an intensely personal and vulnerable act for Schubert, forging a direct link between Schubert himself and the protagonist of *Winterreise*, and it made a deep impression on Spaun. Throughout his 1858 narrative, Spaun draws a close connection between Schubert's deteriorating physical and psychological condition and the creation of *Winterreise*, a connection set in motion by Schubert's memorable embodiment of *Winterreise*'s wanderer in Schober's apartment. Scholars often suggest that it was Schubert's death in 1828, so soon after the creation of *Winterreise*, that made it irresistible for his contemporaries to hear the cycle in autobiographical terms, but we cannot underestimate the authoritative power of Schubert's own performance of the cycle to have played a key role in cementing these associations as well.

Another reason why Spaun and Schober may have been initially put off by *Winterreise* was that Schubert decided to perform the entire thing straight through. With rare exception, song cycles up until the last third of the nineteenth century were virtually always treated as collections to be sampled from at the consumer's discretion rather than as integral works. It may have been the unremitting aspect of *Winterreise*'s gloominess that posed a problem, not the gloominess itself. The same principle governed the presentation of song on the public stage. The first (and only) concert performance of a song from *Winterreise* during Schubert's lifetime took place on January 10, 1828, when the tenor Ludwig Tietze sang "Gute Nacht" at one of the *Abendunterhaltungen* (Evening Entertainments) for members of Vienna's *Gesellschaft der Musikfreunde* (Society for Friends of Music). Given the norms of nineteenth-century public concert programming, "Gute Nacht" would have been one of the only songs on offer – probably the only one, in fact – along with a smorgasbord of operatic numbers, a concerto, and some showpieces for solo instrumentalists and orchestra; for the somewhat more earnest and musically sophisticated audience of the *Gesellschaft*, chamber music would also have appeared. Audiences expected variety, so an entire song cycle would have been too taxing on attention spans, and, in any event, Lieder were considered to be too diminutive to warrant extensive inclusion in concert programs. One or two would suffice as palate cleansers in between the larger courses.

As a result, the individual songs of *Winterreise* tended to live lives of their own in the first half of the nineteenth century, and each life depended upon the specific performers, audience, and context at hand. As part of the *Abendunterhaltung* from January 1828, "Gute Nacht" may have been heard as a self-contained narrative aria of sorts, perhaps drawing associations with the oratorio roles Tietze was also known to perform in public concerts. Four days earlier, however, Tietze sang several Schubert songs "movingly and soulfully" at a musical house party hosted by the lawyer Dr. Kaspar Wagner, as described by Wagner's twenty-four-year-old niece Marie von Pratobevera in a letter to her fiancé, Josef Bergmann:

> I could have wished, my friend, I might conjure you here, so beautiful and glorious was this celebration; and I was especially enraptured by the transfiguration of [Wagner's daughter] Marie, who forgot all her pains and sorrows [from the death of her fiancé three years prior] and was once again as if transported into the earliest years of fair youth from sheer musical enthusiasm . . . [O]ur little domestic nightingale Fanni [Marie von Pratobevera's younger sister] also sang two songs. She really has a very pleasant voice and feels what she sings.[2]

Presuming that Tietze gave "Gute Nacht" a trial run at this party, we can imagine that the song meant something quite different here, grouped together with other Schubert songs for the delectation of listeners who were already familiar with the composer and his music. At this private family get-together, the romantic betrayal and tender farewell depicted in "Gute Nacht" may have reminded Marie Wagner of her own life's tragedy, as the song resonated with personal significance far removed from the particulars of the cycle's plot.

The "domestic nightingale" Franziska ("Fanni") Pratobevera also enjoyed singing songs from *Winterreise*, as her sister wrote to Josef Bergmann a few weeks later. In that letter, Marie singles out "Wasserflut" as her favorite song in the cycle and characterizes *Winterreise* as "a companion piece to *Die schöne Müllerin*, by the same poet, and also nearly identical in content. Laments over the unfaithfulness of a beloved."[3] Today we would not be inclined to equate the two cycles so readily. The sudden surges of vocal range and volume in "Wasserflut," for example, are usually performed by modern singers (and heard by commentators) as volcanic eruptions of harrowing despair and even deranged madness, typifying the existential angst that is supposed to distinguish *Winterreise* from its predecessor. But as embodied by Fanni, with her young, delicate amateur voice, and in the context of her own naïve and tender stage of life ("she feels what she sings"), "Wasserflut" was a tearful, sentimental song of lost love, at least for Marie, who wrote that "the music [of "Wasserflut"] is just as melancholy [as the poem], it completely suits the text and to hear it sung beautifully makes an infinite impression."[4] A few months later, in May, Marie reported to her fiancé that Fanni made another impression with Schubert's songs, this time on her own future fiancé, Josef Tremier, who was "enraptured by Fanni's singing."[5] It is entirely possible that songs from *Winterreise* figured into their courtship rituals.

Winterreise in the Nineteenth Century

According to Spaun, we recall, Schubert declared that his friends would eventually come to like *Winterreise* despite their initial trepidation. Spaun continues:

> He was right – soon we were enthusiastic over the effect of these melancholy songs, which Vogl performed in a masterly way.[6]

Johann Michael Vogl, renowned baritone of the Vienna Court Opera and some thirty years Schubert's senior, became a staunch advocate of Schubert's songs after first meeting the composer in 1817. By the time Schubert came to write *Winterreise*, Vogl had been singing his songs regularly in public and in private for ten years, sometimes with the composer at the piano, and he had become inextricably woven into the composer's creative process. The composer Johann Vesque von Püttlingen once recalled that during the summer of 1827, while Schubert was working on the second half of the cycle, he and Schubert would visit Vogl's apartment on Tuesday afternoons, "where [Vogl] would sing Schubert songs for us and sometimes a brand-new song as well, which Schubert had just brought with the ink hardly dry."[7]

Whereas *Die schöne Müllerin* was dedicated to and associated most closely with Karl Freiherr von Schönstein, an amateur singer who was widely praised for his noble voice and the genteel sensitivity of his interpretation, *Winterreise* became the property of Vogl, the imperious and cultured man of the theater. His song performances were dramatic and declamatory; they came across as heightened recitations of the poetry, with textual clarity and meaning front and center. According to Vesque, "[Vogl's] motto was: if you have nothing to say to me, then you have nothing to sing to me either."[8] Vogl therefore took an actor's liberties with the musical script: he might lapse into speech or use falsetto, alter notes and rhythms, adjust dynamics, or add embellishments, all in order to intensify the theatrical impact of his performance. The practice was by no means unusual at the time, even if it would soon fall out of favor, and virtually everyone who wrote about hearing Vogl sing Schubert was profoundly touched by the experience.

Vogl's last performance of any kind took place in 1839, five years after his final concert appearance and a year before his death at age 72. Spaun described it thus:

> The noble old man was so obliging as to perform the complete cycle of *Winterreise* one evening for a gathering [*Gesellschaft*] at Privy Councillor [Karl von] Enderes', in such a way that, notwithstanding [Vogl's] greatly weakened vocal resources, the entire company [*Gesellschaft*] was moved to the very depths by it.[9]

Enderes was a close friend of both Spaun and Vogl and a full participant in the hijinks of Schubert's inner circle during the mid-1820s, including hosting duties for many a musical house party (the so-called "Schubertiades"). Here in his home once again, eleven years after Schubert's passing, an elderly Vogl was persuaded to re-enact a scene from the glory days of the old *Gesellschaft*, his voice a shadow of what it once was. This performance of *Winterreise* was also a performance of collective memory, conjuring up the group's shared history and evoking meditations on mortality and the passage of time. Given the tight connection between *Winterreise* and Schubert's own mortality in the minds of the gathered friends, the composer's absence must have been palpable, the atmosphere séance-like.

Not everyone enjoyed Vogl's performances so unreservedly, however. At the end of the 1850s, the lawyer, musical connoisseur, and Schubert contemporary Leopold Sonnleithner claimed that Schubert's songs were "usually performed these days in a manner that is directly opposed to the intention of their creator" and asserted that "their musical beauty is in no way dependent on a declamatory style of performance," implicating Vogl as the progenitor of this worrisome trend.[10] In his written reflections on the singing of Schubert's songs, Sonnleithner advocated for performances of unaffected simplicity and naturalness that always preserved the integrity of the melody and remained faithful to the composer's conception as notated in the score. In this, Sonnleithner was upholding the ideology of absolute music – the concept of music as an abstract, autonomous art form of "purely musical" values, unbeholden to non-musical concepts or prerogatives – and applying it to Schubert's Lieder in an effort to elevate them alongside the sonata and symphony in the hierarchy of genres.[11] Sonnleithner acknowledged that the singer had a responsibility to the text as well, not just the music, but here is how he defined the singer's role:

> The lieder singer, as a rule, only relates the experiences and emotions of others – he does not himself impersonate the character whose feelings he depicts. Poet, composer, and singer must conceive the song *lyrically*, not *dramatically*.[12]

Whereas Vogl, the great showman and longtime opera singer, fully inhabited the poetic persona of a song and brought this character to life with all the dramatic tools at his disposal, Sonnleithner felt that the singer should use "purely musical" expression to comment on the song's persona from a narrative distance. This debate about song performance – dramatic enactment vs. lyrical narration – gained steam in the twentieth century, as we shall see, and it continues to the present day.

In certain respects, the German baritone Julius Stockhausen would seem to have fulfilled Sonnleithner's wishes for song; Stockhausen once told his students that "you must not exhibit your personality in the concert hall, for there you are nothing but an interpreter of the poet and composer."[13] Stockhausen's teacher had been the legendary vocal pedagogue Manuel Garcia, whose specialty was *bel canto* opera, but in the concert hall, as the pre-eminent Schubert singer of the mid-nineteenth century, Stockhausen used his operatic training as a vehicle for lyricism and precise, meaningful diction, rather than vocal and theatrical display.

Regarding Schubert's song cycles, Stockhausen is most famous for being the first singer to perform them not only in their entirety (as Vogl had been cajoled to do in 1839 as a special occasion) but also in public. After studying *Winterreise* with Garcia in London in 1851, Stockhausen began to include songs from the cycle in his concerts, most notably in a Hamburg soirée given by the great pianist Clara Schumann in 1862. The concert began with Robert Schumann's Piano Quintet, Op. 44, followed by the first thirteen songs of *Winterreise* – that is, the first thirteen songs in Müller's final ordering of his published poems, rather than the order found in Schubert's score (more on this below). The songs were grouped in sets of four or five, interspersed with piano works by Bach, Scarlatti, and Mendelssohn, and there were almost certainly improvised transitions as well. The audience would have expected Schumann to offer some solos in her soirée, and the alternation of genres prevented the audience's attention span (as well as Stockhausen's vocal stamina) from flagging. The result was a fluid dialogue between vocal and instrumental music, with the songs providing a storyline and the piano solos perhaps intended to provide guided reflection upon it, somewhat like the relationship between the Gospel recitative and the arias in a Bach Passion. Here we see the beginnings of the full-scale narrative approach to presenting *Winterreise* in concert, but the narrative itself would have been quite different than what we usually experience today. In the program, the songs were listed as follows:

> **Reisebilder** ["Travel Pictures"] *von* **Wilhelm Müller**, *Winterreise*
> comp[*oniert*] *von* . . . .*F. Schubert.*

The new title was likely to remind the audience of Heinrich Heine's well-known *Reisebilder* (1826–31), a journalistic travelogue interlaced with poetry, fictionalized autobiography, and socio-political commentary, all featuring the author's characteristic wry irony. Stockhausen's framing of *Winterreise* in Heinesque terms might have underlined the dark cynicism of "Der greise Kopf," "Die Krähe," and "Letzte Hoffnung," the penultimate three songs on the program, as well as the biting social criticism of the concluding song, "Im Dorfe," as though *Winterreise* were a subsection of Müller's own (non-existent) *Reisebilder*.

Two years later Stockhausen returned to Hamburg and gave his first public performance of the entire cycle, and once again, he used the poet's final published order. Commentators usually agree that Müller's order has a more linear dramatic structure in comparison to the more inward psychological journey of Schubert's order. In Müller's order, for example, the wanderer climbs mountain paths in song 16, "Der Wegweiser," and two songs later, he descends them in "Irrlicht," which is song 9 in Schubert's order. Stockhausen's preference for Müller's order even extended to musical details that now bolstered the cycle's narrative logic. The mysterious horn calls that suffuse song 5, "Der Lindenbaum," are often heard as mythic emblems of memory and the distant past, but in Müller's order, when this song is followed by the piano introduction of "Die Post," we suddenly hear the very real horn calls of the mail carrier; Stockhausen loved this juxtaposition, noting that "this posthorn that tears the wanderer away from his dreams and his lime tree has a magnificent effect."[14] Despite Sonnleithner's admiration, then, Stockhausen ultimately seems to have been more interested in impersonating a character with a coherent "dramatic" arc than in narrating that character's experiences at a "lyrical" remove.

In the last quarter of the nineteenth century, it was Stockhausen's student Gustav Walter, lyric tenor and veteran of the Vienna State Opera, who inherited the mantle of greatest Schubert singer alive. Walter's legendary all-Schubert recitals (known as *Liederabende*, literally "evenings of song") transfixed a Viennese public eager to celebrate the musical heritage of their city and empire in an era of increasing nationalism. As sung by Walter with a mellifluous yet powerful voice built for Mozart as well as Wagner, Schubert's Lieder were heard as the virtual folksongs of the Austrian people stemming from the pen of their most beloved native son. Walter gave complete performances of both Schubert cycles during his recital years, but as with Stockhausen before him, *Die schöne Müllerin* had much more success with audiences than *Winterreise*. With its tuneful strophic songs and picturesque love story, *Die schöne Müllerin* was much more suitable to the project of Austro-German identity formation, and it remained the darling of the sentimental nineteenth century. The neurotic twentieth century, on the other hand, found itself ineluctably drawn to *Winterreise*.

Winterreise in the Twentieth Century

In 1921, the German music critic Paul Bekker singled out *Winterreise* (along with the six Heine songs of *Schwanengesang*) as most representative of how, in Schubert's hands, the Lied shed its predominantly social character from the eighteenth century and instead became a "monologue of the soul":[15]

> This lyric [song] of Schubert's is confessional music of the most intimate kind. Its uniqueness and inner grandeur arise precisely from the emphasis on the private character of experience, the insulation from the external [world], the conscious avoidance of every call to fraternal feeling.[16]

It was the reclusive, self-absorbed dimension of *Winterreise* that led Bekker to claim it as the quintessence of the entire Lied genre, and in his preference for the cycle he was prescient. Certainly for the latter half of the twentieth century, *Winterreise* captured the radical aloneness and existential alienation of modernity and provided a rich field for the exploration of interior psychological realms in the shadow of Freud.

As a consequence of these priorities, Bekker argued that the concert stage, with its pronounced emphasis on visual presentation and virtuosic performance effects, was no place for the Lied:

> When one relocates a series of Lieder like *Winterreise* or pieces like "[Der] Doppelgänger" or "Die Stadt" [from *Schwanengesang*] into the modern concert

hall, even if the lighting is ever so "atmospheric," there is in this just as much of a flagrant falsification of the fundamental artistic essence as if one had an Adagio from one of Beethoven's string quartets played for a military parade . . . [In Schubert's songs] a solitary soul sings completely for itself, freed from outer dependencies and connections. Schubert's deed rests entirely in this disentanglement, in this unreserved freedom of the most inward disclosure of feeling. Participation in this [inward disclosure of feeling] through listening demands deliberate preservation of the frame contingent upon such requirements, demands absolute suppression of all externalizing, coarsening means of representation, even in the least.[17]

For Bekker, the only way for a listener to truly connect with the emotional and psychological journey of the "solitary soul [that] sings completely for itself" in the Lied meant a total elimination of the communal as well as the visual. The experience had to be not only entirely private but entirely aural as well, going far beyond the intimate conditions of domestic musicmaking that marked Schubert's own era. Bekker seems to be suggesting that Schubert's songs (with the songs of *Winterreise* foremost among them) were still waiting for their proper medium, one in which there would be, strictly speaking, no audience and no performers at all. Seven years after Bekker wrote his essay, the first-ever complete recording of *Winterreise* was released on eight 78rpm discs, featuring Austrian operatic tenor Hans Duhan and pianists Ferdinand Foll and Lene Orthmann. If the apotheosis of the nineteenth-century appreciation of Schubert's song cycles was Stockhausen's nationalistic 1862 *Volkskonzert* (People's Concert) in Cologne, where an appreciative audience of two thousand erupted in applause after each song of *Die schöne Müllerin*, the ideal image for the twentieth century would be a pensive single individual at home by the hi-fi, listening intently to the latest recording of *Winterreise*.

Before Duhan's 1928 release, singers only recorded selections from *Winterreise*, reflecting not only the temporal limitations of the gramophone record but also the continuing traditions of the concert stage. In the ensuing decades, the relationship between concerts and recordings reversed; as unabridged recordings of the cycle became the dominant mode of appreciation, live performance now aimed to replicate that standard, resulting in the familiar norms for the complete concert presentation of *Winterreise* described at the beginning of this chapter. Consumers of recordings could take in the entirety of *Winterreise* much more comfortably and at their own pace, with texts, translations, and liner notes at hand to enhance their deepening understanding of what was now perceived as an integral "work." Bekker may no longer have been horrified by the idea of *Winterreise* in public performance had he lived to see the effects of these developments by the mid-twentieth century, when one of *Winterreise*'s leading exponents, the German lyric baritone Dietrich Fischer-Dieskau, is said to have declared that "only the voice (and therefore the soul) and one's facial expression should speak in a Lied."[18]

We can chart the range of interpretations of *Winterreise* on record using Sonnleithner's nineteenth-century categories of "lyrical" and "dramatic" expression, as applied respectively to the two singers most closely associated with the cycle in the twentieth century: the stentorian German bass-baritone Hans Hotter (1909–2003), known also for his Wagner roles, and Fischer-Dieskau (1925–2012). Both singers performed and recorded *Winterreise* more frequently and with greater authority than anyone else, but their approaches were polar opposites in many respects. Here is how Hotter conceived of his task as a Lieder singer, as framed by his biographer, Penelope Turing:

> [T]he singer can be either subjective or objective in his presentation. He can actually identify himself with the character, or he can reveal him with the knowledge and compassion of the creator of the work, as a storyteller . . . [Hotter] says the second [position] is the better of the two. Perhaps it is because the central character in *Winterreise* or any other song of this genre is too engrossed in himself to belong consciously to his surroundings. When the singer stands outside the character he is more closely identified with the flow of the pianist's accompaniment. Together they show us the unhappy and egocentric hero, both as he feels and as he is.[19]

Hotter's "objective" storyteller is none other than Sonnleithner's "lyrical" narrator who recounts the feelings of the protagonist from the omniscient perspective of the composer, as one part of the composer's composite musical design (voice and piano).

We can get a good sense of Hotter's "lyrical" interpretive style from the rendering of "Letzte Hoffnung" on his 1954 *Winterreise* album with pianist Gerald Moore. In this song, the protagonist describes his habit of gazing at the colored leaves on the trees, pinning his hopes on one leaf as it is buffeted by the wind, only to watch it fall to the ground as a symbol of his own despondency. Schubert's setting contains a striking number of textural juxtapositions and unsettling rhythmic patterns, but Hotter and Moore's performance has a remarkable steadiness and equanimity about it. Their tempo (♩=66) takes Schubert's opening instruction of "not too fast" quite earnestly, and Moore's fat staccato eighths hold to that tempo with metronomic precision – his leaves flutter about in slow motion. Hotter maintains the beauty of his sound throughout, letting the "purely musical" line do the work. His voice is evenly suffused with a pale, doleful timbre that is imperturbably smooth and sustained; a faint sense of worry colors the voice when the wind begins to play with the protagonist's leaf (mm. 18–22), but it dissolves as gently as it had arisen. Apart from where it is required by the score (mm. 29–30), their tempo only changes from m. 35 to the end, when the protagonist weeps over the grave of his hopes. The slower tempo here is indeed funereal, but in the manner of a sympathetic bystander to the graveside scene, not a suffering mourner. Hotter even represses the power of his voice for the high note in m. 39 on "wein" (weep), suggesting that he pities the protagonist but does not actually weep with him. His performance creates the impression that he is reflecting upon the protagonist's plight from a great temporal and psychological distance, as though he were watching these events unfold on film.

In contrast, in their 1966 recording, Fischer-Dieskau and pianist Jörg Demus give us a "dramatic" interpretation in which they appear to be living through the protagonist's harrowing experience in real time. Within their more energetic basic tempo ($\downarrow$=96), Demus plays his eighths with constant rubato – his wind is stronger and more erratic, his leaves more in present danger of falling. In mm. 10–13, Fischer-Dieskau burrows into "oftmals in Gedanken stehn" (stand often in thought) with an intense crescendo and ritardando whose momentum lands in the middle of the word "Gedanken" just as his vibrato suddenly flattens out. The effect is of someone terrifyingly transfixed by an image (the trees mentioned in m. 10) who then drops precipitously into brooding contemplation as a consequence. In mm. 18–22, where Hotter dimly gestures toward the protagonist's anxiety, Fischer-Dieskau sings with an agitated, panicky timbre as the wind plays with his leaf, then meekly withdraws with a bit of a sob on "zittr' ich" (I tremble). Because the contrasts of tempo, dynamics, and expression in the latter part of the song are much more pronounced in Fischer-Dieskau's performance, we feel that he is describing and participating in actions that are now taking place: the leaf falls to the ground, his hope disappears, he falls to the ground, he weeps. The lachrymose plangency of his full-volume "wein'" in m. 39 connotes a character who is actively, even self-consciously, in the throes of grief.

The difference between Hotter's and Fischer-Dieskau's versions of *Winterreise* is also indicative of what is often recognized as a broader shift in performance style around World War II, when naïve simplicity and directness in Schubert singing gave way to psychological complexity and turbulence. As one listens to the full gamut of recordings of "Letzte Hoffnung" across the twentieth century, for example, tempi speed up drastically and the rubato becomes more chaotic, underlining the protagonist's schizoid qualities. Yet alongside this general trend, the "dramatic" and "lyrical" approaches still competed with one another throughout the century and continue to inform performances today. In the early 1940s, at the then-customary slow tempo, Lotte Lehmann sang "Letzte Hoffnung" with a "dramatic," almost expressionist intensity that is comparable to what Ian Bostridge achieves today at a modern fast tempo, and for every Bostridge in the contemporary universe of Lieder singers there is a Matthias Goerne or Christian Gerhaher who offers a more reflective, observant, "lyrical" interpretation. Moreover, the many female singers who have tackled the cycle (again Lehmann, but also Elena Gerhardt, Christa Ludwig, Brigitte Fassbaender, and Christine Schäfer, just to name a few) can be analyzed similarly; the fact that Müller's wanderer is male has not ultimately proven to be an obstacle, even if it has sometimes aroused mild resistance from some critical quarters. As Lehmann once wrote, "why should a singer be denied a vast number of wonderful songs, if she has the power to create an illusion which will make her audience believe in it?"[20]

Winterreise in the Last Twenty-five Years

In recent times, *Winterreise* has been presented in alternative performance formats with ever-increasing frequency, certainly more often than any other song cycle in the repertoire. This is partly a simple function of *Winterreise*'s fame within the canon. But with its relatively undefined protagonist, a narrative with sparse particulars, and its themes of heartbreak, alienation, and self-examination, *Winterreise* has proven to be especially suitable for creative adaptation in our own age. And as always, each performance concept coaxes a different meaning out of Schubert's work.

We can organize unconventional contemporary approaches to performing *Winterreise* into three categories, or at least three tendencies, which sometimes overlap. The first tendency is to universalize the work by condensing its details into an overall concept that gives audience members something to reflect upon but is abstract enough to allow them maximal freedom of interpretation and identification. The forerunner of this strategy is the 1970 BBC concert film directed by John Culshaw, featuring tenor Peter Pears and his partner, the composer Benjamin Britten, offscreen at the piano. Pears wears an antiquated brown wanderer's frock, and for each song he stands in a different location of a staged rocky landscape lit in an appropriate mood; often a relevant pictorial image in white light is projected behind him. In 2002, the choreographer Trisha Brown set this strategy in motion by having three dancers create enigmatic visual metaphors for each song as baritone Simon Keenlyside navigated their space while singing. In his 2004 production, baritone Thomas Guthrie sings in the dark while operating a Bunraku-style puppet with a doleful, moon-like face. Meanwhile, Chris Herbert's 2012 *Winterize* takes the cycle outdoors, asking audience members to carry transistor radios and follow the baritone on a literal winter's journey through an urban environment (originally Brooklyn Botanic Garden) as he sings the cycle with piano accompaniment broadcast through the radios.

A second strategy is to find ways of putting modern audiences more directly in touch with *Winterreise*'s historical dimensions. For example, in several concerts as well as a 2017 recording, tenor Julian Prégardien and pianist Michael Gees took inspiration from Clara Schumann's 1862 soirée with Julius Stockhausen (discussed above) by breaking up their performance of the cycle (this time complete, and in Schubert's order) with intervening piano pieces by Bach, Scarlatti, and Mendelssohn as well as piano improvisations. In 2015, Kathryn Whitney's "*Winterreise* Project" brought twenty-seven amateur singers and pianists together to learn and perform *Winterreise* on their own, in order for them to experience how other non-professionals had engaged with the cycle for at least the first few decades of its existence. The hurdy-gurdy virtuoso Matthias Loibner unearthed the full historical significance of the textual and musical references to his instrument embedded in "Der Leiermann" by recording the entire cycle with folk-pop singer Nataša Mirković in 2010. To unaccustomed ears, the twangy exoticism of his arrangement takes *Winterreise* out of the realm of high art and into the domain of the marginalized class of musicians to which a hurdy-gurdy man would have belonged in Schubert's time. Loibner's arrangement also reframes the cycle so that the protagonist's final question to the hurdy-gurdy man ("Will you play your organ / To my songs?") is anything but rhetorical – the answer is yes, and we have just heard that very performance.

Finally, there are those adaptations of *Winterreise* whose principal aim is to reveal its contemporary relevance. In 1993, the composer and conductor Hans Zender created a "composed interpretation" of *Winterreise* that rehears the piece through the filter of subsequent music history. His wildly colorful orchestration cuts, splices, and replays passages, adds sound effects, and alludes to a variety of musical styles in an attempt to bring out the modernity latent in Schubert's cycle, where in Zender's words, "the expressionism of our time is already announced."[21] In John Neumeier's 2001 choreography for the Hamburg Ballet, set to the Schubert/Zender version, the protagonist is split into multiple dancers, each isolated in their own world, reflecting the sense of disorientation, insecurity, and estrangement caused by the events of September 11 of that year. Neumeier puts a heartbreakingly contemporary spin on "Das Wirtshaus," in which Schubert's protagonist yearns to join the dead and buried in a cemetery but must continue on his journey alone. A glass roof slowly descends on a group of dancers while a few onlookers watch helplessly from outside the glass walls of the space; one by one, the dancers are forced to roll out of the dwindling space as the onlookers impotently bang on the walls, left to carry on with their lives in grief. Peter Härtling's 1997 play *Melchinger Winterreise* is laced with performances of most of the cycle's songs in various formats, juxtaposed provocatively against scenes from Schubert's later life as well as Härtling's own youth as a post–WWII refugee. In Christoph Biermeier's 2017 restaging of the play for Theater Lindenhof, the protagonist's identity as an exile is made even more contemporary when refugees from Afghanistan, Iran, and Eritrea speak the words of the cycle's poetry and share their own stories of fleeing war and persecution.

We can close with *Three Pianos*, a 2010 play by theater artists Rick Burkhardt, Alec Duffy, and Dave Malloy that blends all three approaches. The play contains within itself a nearly complete performance of the cycle to the accompaniment of upright pianos whirled about the stage by its three creators. They sing the songs with ordinary untrained voices, using a mixture of prosaic English and the original German, and their musical arrangements are all over the map: stadium rock for "Rückblick," Tom Waits for "Die Krähe," their own indie pop setting of "Letzte Hoffnung," bluegrass-barbershop a capella for "Die Nebensonnen." Playing host to a Schubertiade for the audience that includes free wine, they recreate the down-to-earth ambience and intimacy of Schubert's debut of the cycle in Schober's apartment. At the same time, they make direct connections between the protagonist's journey and the struggles of modern love and relationships. At the end, as snow gently falls on the three sweater-clad actors, each in their own world, performing "Der Leiermann" in the form of a curious, mechanical waltz, one has the sense that *Winterreise*'s distillation of the loneliness of the human condition will find sympathetic and creative responses for generations to come.

Notes

1. *SEF*, 160–61. My translation is adapted from *SMF*, 137–38. All translations from *SMF* in this chapter are similarly adapted.
2. *SDL*, 475. My translation is adapted from *SDB*, 708. All translations taken from *SDB* are similarly adapted.
3. *SDL*, 481; *SDB*, 716–17.
4. *SDL*, 481; *SDB*, 717.
5. *SDL* 519; *SDB*, 779.
6. *SEF*, 161; *SMF*, 138.
7. *SEF*, 248; *SMF*, 215.
8. *SEF*, 248, *SMF*, 216.
9. *SEF*, 420; *SMF*, 364.
10. *SEF*, 388; *SMF*, 337.
11. For more on this point, see Eric Van Tassel, "'Something Utterly New': Listening to Schubert Lieder. 1: Vogl and the Declamatory Style," *Early Music* 25/4 (Nov. 1997): 705–6.
12. *SEF*, 135–36; *SMF*, 116.

13. As quoted in Edward F. Kravitt, *The Lied: Mirror of Late Romanticism* (New Haven: Yale University Press, 1996), 55.

14. As quoted in Martin Günther, *Kunstlied als Liedkunst: Die Lieder Franz Schuberts in der musikalischen Aufführungskultur des 19. Jahrhunderts* (Stuttgart: Franz Steiner, 2016), 282; the translation is mine.

15. Paul Bekker, "Das Lied: Ein kritisches Fragment," in *Klang und Eros*, vol. 2 (Stuttgart: Deutsche Verlags-Anstalt, 1922), 286; all translations from Bekker are mine.

16. Bekker, "Das Lied," 288–89.

17. Ibid.

18. Laura Tunbridge, *The Song Cycle* (Cambridge: Cambridge University Press, 2010), 147.

19. Penelope Turing, *Hans Hotter: Man and Artist* (London: John Calder, 1983), 206.

20. Lotte Lehmann, *More Than Singing: The Interpretation of Songs*, trans. Frances Holden (New York: Boosey and Hawkes, 1945), 16.

21. Hans Zender, "Schubert's 'Winterreise': Notizen zu meiner 'komponierten Interpretation,'" in Zender, *Wir steigen niemals in denselben Fluß. Wie Musikhören sich wandelt* (Freiburg: Herder, 1996), 86.

14 Canonicity and Influence

LAURA TUNBRIDGE

A book such as this confirms the canonical status of *Winterreise*. The song cycle is widely acknowledged to be a great work, as reflected in its constant presence on concert platforms and in recording catalogues, its influence on other composers, and its continuing fascination for scholars. Yet it took time before *Winterreise* achieved its celebrated status. Schubert's contemporaries were initially uncertain about the merits of the "terrifying songs," and full performances did not take place in public until the 1850s. The 1928 centennial commemoration of the composer's death encouraged multiple live and recorded performances of the cycle, but only after World War II, with the invention of the long-playing record, did recordings by internationally celebrated advocates such as German baritone Dietrich Fischer-Dieskau establish *Winterreise*'s canonic status.

This chapter hunts for the tracks that Schubert's *Winterreise* has left on the musical and cultural imagination. Canonicity implies that the identity of an artwork is so strong that it survives – that it remains recognizable – whatever is done to it.[1] A work's influence is dependent on it being a recognizable source, but the approach to the original can be fairly free: the new work has its own identity even as it refers to the past.[2] Adaptation lies at the heart of many musical practices, as is evident in the history of creative responses to *Winterreise*, which range from forensic transcriptions and reworkings to more loosely conceived homages and updatings.[3] The cycle's significance is also apparent in the marks it has made beyond music, on films, novels, plays, and the visual arts.

Arrangements

Before recordings and radio, musical transcription was the easiest way for music to travel: symphonies and operas were arranged into versions for other instruments, to be played at home.[4] Arrangement might not seem as important for songs for solo voice and piano, but, as mentioned, *Winterreise* was not as popular as other Schubert Lieder. It was appreciated first by other musicians and in public rather than domestic performances.

Arrangements could make the cycle, or at least individual songs from it, more palatable to nineteenth-century ears. Schubert's contemporary, the folk-music collector Friedrich Silcher, produced a version of "Der Lindenbaum" for four-part male chorus that, Reinhold Brinkmann notes, "corrects" the melodic trajectory, making it more conventional.[5] Franz Liszt arranged a selection of twelve songs from the cycle as virtuosic showpieces, reordering them and adding expression marks, extravagant embellishments, and extra musical material for rhetorical emphasis. He also converted some songs into introductions for others to create composite forms.[6] Other composers were freer still: Johannes Brahms used portions of the melody but not the words of "Der Leiermann" for his setting of Friedrich Rückert's "Einförmig ist die Liebe Gram" in his Canons for Female Voices, Op. 113 (published 1891).

More recent transcriptions of *Winterreise* can seem less radical, yet they also reveal changing attitudes to the cycle and Lieder performance more broadly. It is rare now to hear individual songs from the cycle in recital, whether as originally written or in an arrangement, and even relatively experimental renditions generally remain faithful to the poetic text and Schubert's score – orchestrations enhance and expand what is written, rather than rework it. For example, versions arranged by Jens Josef for tenor Christian Elsner with the Henschel Quartett (2002) and by Richard Krug for baritone Johan Reuter with the Copenhagen Quartet (2016) explore the expanded timbral range of string instruments, but stay fairly close to Schubert's figuration. The same is true of singer Daniel Behle's lively arrangement for the Oliver Schnyder Piano Trio (2014). Oboe d'amore player Normand Forget takes a more adventurous approach in his arrangement for French-Canadian wind quintet Pentaèdre with accordion, recorded with Christoph Prégardien (2008). Müller's order is restored, "Die Post" features a "real" horn, the quintet members sing a chorale in "Das Wirtshaus," and the accordion sounds more like a hurdy-gurdy than a piano. Maurice van Bueren arranged the cycle for piano and the female vocal group Coco Collectief (2017), in some ways harking back to the choral style of Silcher, even if presenting the cycle in multiple voices seems more alien in the twenty-first century than it did in the nineteenth. Dispersing the voices makes *Winterreise* less about subjective alienation, particularly as presented in Dave Malloy's playful *Three Pianos* (2010), which switches between German and English, and shares the music among three singer-instrumentalists, lubricated by swigs of bourbon. Making *Winterreise* a happy experience is a drastic re-interpretation, but has been well received.

There are also instrumental versions of the cycle, such as violist Roger Benedict's and pianist Simon Tedeschi's recent *A Winter's Tale* (2018). In

2016, Judith Brandenberg's ensemble La Bicicleta took a much freer approach to the music, transmogrifying Schubert into tango, played by violin, piano, bassoon, and accordion. French-Canadian bass-baritone Philippe Sly has presented *Un voyage d'hiver* (2018), developing the idea of the wanderer into that of the Ashkenazi Jew or figure of the gypsy; the musical arrangement by Samuel Carrier and Félix de l'Etoile replaces the piano with a group of klezmer musicians (trombone, violin, clarinet, accordion).

The most well-established of recent compositional responses to *Winterreise* is Hans Zender's "composed interpretation" (1993). The whole of Schubert's cycle is presented, but accompanied by an ensemble: string sextet, piccolo, cor anglais, oboe d'amore, clarinet, saxophone, double bassoons, horn, timpani and percussion, mouth organ, and wind-machines. Sound effects accentuate the wintry atmosphere. The first song, "Gute Nacht," gradually emerges out of tramping rhythms evoked through brushes on a drum, *col legno* playing from the strings, and breathy sounds from the woodwind. "Die Wetterfahne" makes sonically present the gusts that blow around the weathervane. Zender often interrupts the flow of Schubert's songs, decoupling the melodies of voice and piano so that the latter's music is scattered around the ensemble. Some numbers are sung in a lurching slow motion ("Die Post") while elsewhere the singer resorts to *Sprechstimme* – in "Wasserflut," for instance, the horn plays the tune, on which the singer then seems to comment. Zender's "composed interpretation" includes moments of extreme sweetness, but also passages that intensify the protagonist's anguish. At the start of "Auf dem Flusse," rasping brass and woodwind chords make the opening musical material sound tortured, yet when the singer enters, accompanied by plucked strings, all seems even more normal than usual – only tinnitus-like harmonics hint at anything foreboding.

Zender likened his *Winterreise* to contemplating an object from multiple perspectives, and performances have magnified the score's potential for historical multivalence. In a 2016 production directed by Netia Jones, tenor Ian Bostridge wore white face-paint and tails, making him look like a ghostly cabaret singer from the Weimar era. Projected behind him, in addition to surtitles and hackneyed wintry images, were pictures of Bostridge performing the cycle as a younger man, adding another historical layer from the singer's own biography. The way that Zender's *Winterreise* cross-references styles from different periods is not about "performance practice"; rather, as Jürg Stenzl argues, it demonstrates that "musical interpretation is nothing less than a historical phenomenon."[7] Or, as Simon Emmerson explains, "To quote Schubert in the late 20th century in this manner, reworking, placing against contrasting material, is to say something about difference . . . and we must perceive the character of that difference for 'meaning' to emerge."[8] Whereas in the nineteenth century transcriptions and arrangements were used to disseminate musical works, to widen their familiarity around the world, now their purpose is to defamiliarize them – to make them strange, or stress their "difference," and thereby keep them fresh.

Musical Legacy

Many composers have been inspired by Schubert's Lieder. It is difficult, though, to pinpoint exact stylistic references to *Winterreise*, unless every narrative song cycle about Romantic wanderers, lost love, and death is considered in its debt. The musical style of the cycle is also elusive; individual songs, such as "Der Lindenbaum" and "Der Leiermann," are quoted or alluded to in various works, but attempting to define the musical traits that distinguish *Winterreise* as a whole is confounding because the cycle contains such a broad stylistic range. There may well be Schubertian "fingerprints," to borrow Susan Wollenberg's term, that reveal the composer's influence, such as shifts between major and minor modalities, a predilection for tertiary relationships, or particular kinds of pianistic figuration, but it is sometimes challenging to determine which belong to Schubert, to *Winterreise*, or to a generation of Romantic composers. Other composers may have set poems from Müller's *Die Winterreise* before Schubert, but he was the first to gather his settings into a substantial cycle. A precedent for a song collection centered on a lone wanderer was Conradin Kreutzer's *Neun Wander-Lieder von* [Ludwig] *Uhland*, Op. 34 (1818), which Schubert admired.[9] After Schubert's *Winterreise*, many more composers selected poems from Müller's collection (though not quite as enthusiastically as they had from *Die schöne Müllerin*). Some paid musical homage to Schubert, borrowing and building on nuggets of his songs, as in Carl Banck's sequel to the cycle, *Des Leiermanns Liederbuch* (1838–1839), and Wilhelm Kienzl's "Der Leiermann" from *Zwei Lieder*, Op. 38 (1904). Much later and more radically, artists in the German Democratic Republic used the notion of the "winter journey" to comment on their own political situation and relationship to the musical canon. Thus, according to Elaine Kelly, Reiner Bredemeyer's *Die Winterreise*, composed for baritone, horn, and piano (1984), gives "absolute prominence" to Müller's poems, keeping their original order and eschewing textual repetition. Bredemeyer creates "a sparse atonal, or as he puts it, 'skeletal' texture that reflects the political landscape of winter."[10] Here, Schubert citations are dissociative; for example, a musical fragment of

"Gute Nacht" appears not in Bredemeyer's setting of that poem but rather in the setting of "Der stürmische Morgen." According to Bredemeyer, Schubert had misread or misrepresented Müller's *Die Winterreise* as love poetry, rather than seen it as political commentary. A more musicologically critical approach was taken in Andrea Cavallari's *Winterreise* for Kammeroper Frankfurt (2006–2007), in which settings of Müller's poetry with instrumental accompaniment (accordion, cello, piano) were interleaved with Schubert's songs, original and commentary being brought into dialogue with each other.

Detecting the influence of Schubert's *Winterreise* when composers are setting poetry other than Müller's becomes still more complex. Susan Youens points out that Gustav Mahler never acknowledged the relationship between the four songs of his *Lieder eines fahrenden Gesellen* (1884–1885), composed to his own, *Des Knaben Wunderhorn*-derived poetry, and Schubert's *Winterreise*.[11] However, according to Youens, there are significant thematic connections between the two cycles. Mahler described his *Gesellenlieder* as being about "a wayfaring man, who has been stricken by fate, [and] now sets forth into the world, travelling wherever his road may lead him." Like Schubert's cycle, Mahler's encompasses a solitary farewell, a sweetheart who is married to another man, and longing for death. The same could be said of dozens of nineteenth-century German songs, but, Youens argues, Mahler "inverts elements that could only come from Müller and Schubert." Schubert's "winter journey" thus becomes a "summer journey." The most convincing references to Schubert's cycle occur in Mahler's fourth song, "Die zwei blauen Augen von meinem Schatz" ("The Two Blue Eyes of my Beloved"). Like the wanderer of Schubert's opening song, Mahler's wayfarer sets out alone, at night. Their journeys' companions are similarly mostly mute and non-human: birds, the moon, a river. Youens compares the beloved's blue eyes in Mahler's poem to the suns of Müller's "Die Nebensonnen." Perhaps more obviously, at the end of the song, Mahler's protagonist falls asleep beneath a linden tree. The symbolism of the linden tree as a meeting-point for lovers extends back centuries to the Minnesingers. In "Erstarrung" and "Der Lindenbaum" from *Winterreise*, the linden tree becomes associated with the unending sleep of death. Yet Mahler's wanderer might here defy historical precedent, for he could refuse to stay under the tree and instead choose life.

The 1928 centenary of Schubert's death encouraged not only more performances of and scholarship on his music, but also more responses from composers. For Ernst Krenek, it was important to reclaim Schubert as an Austrian as a means to resist the pan-German nationalism that was becoming politically dominant. His song cycle *Reisebuch aus den österreichischen Alpen* (*Travel Book from the Austrian Alps*) (1929) begins

"Ich reise aus, meine Heimat zu entdecken" (I set out traveling in order to discover my homeland). Although again the protagonist is a lone wanderer, the poetry of Krenek's *Reisebuch* is more place- and time-specific than Schubert's *Winterreise*. Krenek name-checks particular locations and current fashions and technologies (gramophones and automobiles), thereby marking the difference between his era and Schubert's. Similarly, his music mixes Schubertian tonal devices, including major/minor fluctuations and tertiary relationships, with more dissonant passages, the juxtaposition of sweet lyricism and consonance with disjunct melodies and dissonance conveying his dissatisfaction with the modern world.

Schubert's music also functioned as a nostalgic cipher for earlier, less troubled times in Hanns Eisler's *Hollywood Liederbuch* (1942–1947). Eisler fled Nazi-occupied Europe, eventually arriving in Hollywood in 1942. In the forty-seven songs of the *Hollywood Liederbuch* (more a collection than a cycle), Eisler set poetry by his contemporaries – especially his long-term collaborator Berthold Brecht – as well as earlier authors, including Germans familiar to Schubert, such as Goethe. Despite its title, the *Hollywood Liederbuch* became a vehicle through which Eisler could express his feelings about being exiled from his homeland. There is a fleeting reference to the first phrase of *Winterreise*, "Fremd bin ich eingezogen," in Eisler's "Über den Selbstmord" ("On Suicide"), at the words "Und die ganze Winterzeit." (Eisler also dedicated a song to Schubert, a setting of Hölderlin's "Heidelberg," giving it the *Schwanengesang*-like title "An eine Stadt.")

Although the *Hollywood Liederbuch* acknowledges its nineteenth-century heritage, it would be inaccurate to say that *Winterreise* specifically was Eisler's primary reference point. Composers in the second half of the twentieth century similarly borrowed images or motifs that might be associated with Schubert's cycle but typically combined them with references to other works by him, or to works by other composers. Questions about influence then become less relevant than unpicking the historical significance of intertextuality. A notion of Romantic strangeness – hung, again, on the opening line of *Winterreise*, "Fremd bin ich eingezogen" – infiltrates Wolfgang Rihm's *Ländler* (1997), dedicated to his composer friend Wilhelm Killmayer.[12] Nico Muhly's *Good Night* (2017) takes as its texts fragments from both Schubert's essay, *Mein Traum*, and singer Ian Bostridge's book, *Schubert's Winter's Journey*, and borrows from Schubert's "Gute Nacht" what Muhly describes as its "hypnotic repeated chords":

> After a bell-like introduction, I tried to create similarly repetitive patterns but with hiccoughs in them in the piano, against a very simple vocal line. The piece ends with a memory of the delicious shift from minor to major in Schubert, which then dissolves into an echo of the bells at the beginning.[13]

Muhly's response, then, is a kind of textual-musical palimpsest, overlaying Schubert's autobiographical writing with Bostridge's commentary on *Winterreise* (thereby historicizing the cycle), and then loosely deriving its musical impetus from one of the songs.

There are several references to Schubert in Bernhard Lang's "Monadologies" cycle, which the composer describes as "meta-compositions," combining and manipulating musical cells from past centuries. The most substantial Schubert references are found in the thirty-second installment, *The Cold Trip* (2014–15). In part one, for voice and four guitars, Lang references the first half of *Winterreise*, with Schubert's second half providing material for Lang's part two, for voice, piano, and laptop. The latter uses samples of prepared piano that, Lang explains, create "palimpsests of Schubert's original textures. The voice in both parts traces the lost lines of the songs, sometimes touching them as if remembering." Müller's poems are rendered in punchy English translations and, as Frankie Perry observes, "it is instances of simple word-switching and brazen updating that are most memorable": thus, "Die Post" becomes "Mail," about waiting for messages to arrive in one's inbox.[14] Lang constantly explores the repetitive potential of Schubert's musical cells, looping vocal and piano phrases around themselves to intensify the feeling of anxiety. *The Cold Trip*, Perry points out, can be heard as a song cycle that "is both intrinsically indebted to and happily removed from its Schubertian origin . . . *The Cold Trip* might be understood on its own terms as Lang's winter journey, tagged with Schubertian graffiti that can be sought out, studied, appreciated, noted, or simply passed by." That a work so obviously derived from Schubert's *Winterreise* also can be taken on its own terms, without an awareness of its intertextuality, suggests that to search for Schubert in such music is to take the wrong path. The cycle's canonical status does not crumble as a result; if anything, composers' use of it to generate new music confirms its influence.

Literary Responses

Scott Messing's two-volume study of Schubert reception in the long nineteenth century contains strikingly few references to *Winterreise*.[15] A couple of individual songs – "Der Leiermann" and "Der Lindenbaum" – appear in novels, but the whole cycle does not really impinge on the literary imagination until later in the twentieth century. This absence reflects the performance history of *Winterreise*; as noted, the cycle was rarely heard in its complete form.

Literary references to *Winterreise* often mingle with other Schubertian tropes. In Romain Rolland's novel *Jean Christophe* (1903–1912), the titular character meets the reflected gaze of a countess, an old acquaintance, during a performance of "Der Lindenbaum." Messing claims that it is likely that Rolland was here nodding towards Schubert's supposed passion for Countess Caroline Esterházy. The song is also appropriate because the linden tree is a traditional place for lovers to meet, and in Müller's poem, of course, the wanderer reminisces about lost love. There is a hint of similar nostalgia in *Jean Christophe* – Philomela's "lovely voice" has an "elegiac warmth . . . and the pure music called up sad memories." Jean Christophe's romantic thrill at his potential reunion with Grazia is fleeting, for she is now married. Schubert's song was prescient.

"Der Lindenbaum" is also featured in perhaps the most famous novelistic description of listening to Schubert, Thomas Mann's *Der Zauberberg* (1924). Apparently the author owned a recording of "Der Lindenbaum" sung by Richard Tauber; Mann listened to it repeatedly, explaining that "[t]he song was for me the symbol of everything worthy of love and seduction, in which lurked the secret germ of destruction."[16] Similarly, the protagonist of *Der Zauberberg*, Hans Castorp, listens repeatedly to "Der Lindenbaum" on a gramophone. Mann goes into some details about the music of "Der Lindenbaum" but more important is what it means to Castorp:

> To him the song meant a whole world, a world which he must have loved, else he could not have so desperately loved that which it represented and symbolized to him. We know what we are saying when we add – perhaps rather darkly – that he might have had a different fate if his temperament had been less accessible to the charms of the sphere of feeling, the general attitude of mind, which the *lied* so profoundly, so mystically epitomized. [. . .]
>
>   What was the world behind the song, which the motions of his conscience made to seem a world of forbidden love?
>
> It was death.
>
> What utter and explicit madness! That glorious song! An indisputable masterpiece, sprung from the profoundest and holiest depths of racial feeling;
> a precious possession, the archetype of the genuine; embodied loveliness. What vile detraction![17]

Mann's account of Castorp's response to "Der Lindenbaum" presages significant strands of twentieth-century Schubert reception. First, a connection between the Lied and profound emotion. Second, the undermining of that profundity by technological mediation; the song could all too easily "degenerate to a piece of gramophone music played by electricity" – it was merely one of "Hans Castorp's favourite records." Third, a sense that Schubert's music embodied the Austro-German spirit. Finally, the inevitability of all this leading to death. As Castorp wanders wounded on the battlefield in the last pages of the novel, he sings lines from "Der Lindenbaum":

> A great clod of earth struck him on the shin, it hurt, but he smiles at it. Up he gets, and staggers on, limping on his earth-bound feet, all unconsciously singing:
> "Its waving branches whi—ispered
> A mess—age in my ear—"
> and thus, in the tumult, in the rain, in the dusk, vanishes out of sight.[18]

Castorp's tragic end – one shared by thousands of young men in the trenches – and its association with Schubert suggested a very different image of the composer from that familiar from popular hagiographical operettas such as *Das Dreimäderlhaus* (1916). Through the course of the interwar period, as a greater number of his Lieder became available from recordings and on the radio, scholarship on the composer flourished, and as performances of whole song cycles became more common, Schubert began to be taken much more seriously.[19] *Winterreise* was central to this new approach, for its scale, relatively sparse style, and existential poetic themes seemed more in keeping with the modern world, as is evident from the greater number of writers who invoked the cycle.

Samuel Beckett, in a letter to his cousin from 1965, described himself listening to recordings of *Winterreise* and "shivering through the grim journey again."[20] He had long been drawn to the cycle, returning repeatedly to Dietrich Fischer-Dieskau and Gerald Moore's version from 1955, and even claiming that he chose the actor Leonard Fenton for the role of Willie in the London premiere of *Happy Days* (1979) because he could sing some of it. Perhaps then it is unsurprising that Beckett's last play, *What Where?* (1983), contains an allusion to *Winterreise*. Each of the four actors – Bam, Bem, Bim, and Bom, virtually indistinguishable because all wear the same long grey gowns and have the same long grey hair – is interrogated about an unspecified violent crime. A small megaphone at head height projects the voice of Bam, who announces the passing of the seasons until finally the end is reached: "It is winter. Without journey. Time passes. That is all. Make sense who may. I switch off." Much as Youens argued about Mahler's *Lieder eines fahrenden Gesellen*, if Beckett is referring to Schubert here, it is through inversion and, indeed, negation: this is winter without a journey. Moreover, it seems that at the end of *What Where?* the reiterative voice is extinguished, unlike Schubert's equivalent, the hurdy-gurdy man.

Beckett's existential response to *Winterreise* has fed into productions of his plays and of the song cycle. In 2009, director Katie Mitchell presented an abridged version of Schubert's *Winterreise* (sung by tenor Mark Padmore, in a translation by poet Michael Symmons Roberts) interwoven with Beckett texts (recited by Stephen Dillane) and sound effects – dogs barking, wind blowing, gates closing, sobs, and footsteps crunching through the snow. Such "imaginative dialogues" between Schubert and Beckett have been pursued with other authors: for example, director Conall Morrison embedded songs from *Winterreise* into a performance of Georg Büchner's play *Woyzeck* to create *Woyzeck in Winter* (2017). Both works, Morrison reasoned, were by "a troubled genius who died young. Each narrates the course of one man's obsessive thoughts and his downward slide towards dissolution. The play is a collection of 24 scenes, the song cycle 24 songs. Placed side by side, playscript and lyrics could be said to be having a conversation."[21] Further integration of play and cycle was attempted by the actors singing the songs in translation. The critical reception of both of these productions has admittedly been fairly hostile; instead of appreciating the dialogue between *Winterreise* and the other texts as enriching each other, most reviewers have resisted disruptions to the musical cohesion of Schubert's cycle, feeling that neither Beckett nor Büchner gained much by the association.

Other writers have drawn from both Schubert and Beckett. Eva Figes's novel *Winter Journey* (1967) mirrors *Winterreise* (one of the author's favorite pieces of music) in its title. Janus Stobbs, the aging, traumatized protagonist, might resemble Schubert's wanderer or any of Beckett's lone voices. Silvia Pellicer-Ortin argues, though, that the more significant intertextual link for Figes was Robert Falcon Scott's *Journey to the Antarctic* (1901–1911), not least because Stobbs seeks out Scott's diaries.[22] The broad topoi associated with *Winterreise* – winter journeys and solitary figures – signal its cultural currency, and thus its canonical status, yet almost every link is compound, rarely representing "just" Schubert.

Elfriede Jelinek's play *Winterreise* (2011) represents a more historically sensitive response to Schubert. Tom Smith argues that Jelinek is attracted by the "emotional ambivalence" of Schubert's compositional response to Müller's poetry, that she is "drawn to music for its potential to articulate marginalized, isolated subject positions, and yet repelled by its easy co-option by those who would impose emotional norms."[23] Moments of "instability, dissoluteness and ambivalence" become means to "resist Schubert's co-option in discourses of nationalism," and a more personal, introspective relationship to the musical canon thereby can be established. In various scenes from Jelinek's play, glancing at Schubert serves to undermine or problematize the action on stage, much of which derives from recent Austrian history. An example involves the story of the kidnapped teenager Natascha Kampusch, who, on her escape in 2006 after eight years of being held hostage, became a minor celebrity, yet also attracted negative press from those who did not believe her tale. The opening lines from Müller's "Erstarrung," where the wanderer searches for traces of his beloved ("Ich such im Schnee vergebens / Nach ihrer Tritte Spur") are echoed in scene four's description of Kampusch's disappearance ("Da ist eine Schritte Spur, und jetzt ist sie weg . . . . Suche vergebens."). The subtle allusions in Jelinek's text are accentuated in productions through the use of Schubert's music: for instance, the director Johan Simons, in his version for the Munich Kammerspiele, punctuated the tirade against Kampusch with unison singing of phrases from "Mut!," thereby representing, according to Smith, "a judgemental society." Schubert is present in Jelinek's play as a kind of ghost, haunting the language. His music is almost surplus to requirements, but for those who are not well-versed in Müller's poetry, perhaps it is necessary to make explicit the lineage of an Austrian *Winterreise*.

Winterreise in Visual Media

At the start of Ingmar Bergman's film for television, *Larmar och gör sig till* (*In the Presence of a Clown*) (1997), the first eight measures of "Der Leiermann" are played repeatedly on a gramophone. The man lifting the needle is an inmate in Uppsala Psychiatric Hospital in the winter of 1925. Fifty-four-year-old Carl Åkerblom has been institutionalized, having attempted to murder his much younger fiancée. He is obsessed with Schubert, talking to his psychiatrist about the composer's illnesses and furtively listening to recordings, never getting further than those first eight measures of "Der Leiermann." Carl is visited in the night by the clown of the title, seemingly the figure of death; subsequently, he hatches a plan to make talking pictures, and decides that the film's plot should be a fictional relationship between Schubert and Mizzi Veith – a "Countess" who was forced into prostitution by her stepfather and whose suicide caused a scandal in Vienna in 1908. (Writers Karl Kraus and Peter Altenberg used Veith as an exemplar of moral hypocrisy.) In the end, the film is presented as a play, with Carl acting the role of Schubert. Music is the vehicle through which fantasy and reality are blurred: in the play's performance, the opening of "Der Leiermann" is heard again when the clown appears to Carl and when Schubert declines Mizzi's kiss. The music is a figment of Carl's imagination until the end of the play, when it becomes diegetic, accompanying the arrival of Count Veith at Schubert's deathbed to tell him that Mizzi has drowned herself.

Bergman explained that, for him, "Der Leiermann" is about death. In the film's narrative, it becomes a fragmented soundtrack to the ultimate demise of Carl, a "madman" who "identifies with Schubert and his destiny," according to the director.[24] Anyssa Neumann argues for a subtler approach than simply associating the song with the figure of death, and draws a comparison between Carl and the wanderer of *Winterreise*: both are "caught between past life, future death, and a musical stranger."[25] Bergman was unusually sophisticated in his selection of pre-existing music in his films, and in this instance, "Der Leiermann" adds to the portrayal of insanity. Yet, is one song alone enough to make *In the Presence of a Clown* about *Winterreise* as a whole? Can or should "Der Leiermann" serve as a synecdoche? It is an unusual song within the cycle in its deliberate musical simplicity and repetitiveness, and it is the only song directly addressed to another person. Its position as the last number has encouraged readings of the hurdy-gurdy man as a harbinger of death or as a potential imagined performer of the songs, the cycle being recycled. "Der Leiermann" is undoubtedly the most famous song from *Winterreise*, but it is not fully representative of its musical and emotional range; instead, it skews the image of the cycle towards the existential.

While some films sample songs from *Winterreise* (usually "Der Leiermann"), there have been a number of attempts to make films of performances of the full cycle. Some are fairly straightforward documentaries of concerts, with occasional nods towards the theatrical (such as Peter Pears in a deerstalker, in a version he made with Benjamin Britten for the BBC in 1970). Opportunities for close-ups and other camera angles that bring the audience closer to the performers have also been exploited (for example, Fischer-Dieskau and Alfred Brendel, 1979; Christophe Prégardien and Michael Gees, 2013). Other versions have taken more liberties to suggest alternative interpretations or framing narratives for the cycle. Swedish baritone Håkan Hagegård, who had played Papageno in Bergman's film version of Mozart's *The Magic Flute*, produced a version of the cycle for television directed by Måns Reuterswärd (1978). The story around the cycle was set in Gotland, with the songs sung in a free Swedish translation. Czech filmmaker Petr Weigl devised a film of *Winterreise* (1994) in which mezzo Brigitte Fassbaender sings the songs dressed as a nun, flanked by angels and devils (pianist Wolfram Rieger is never seen). The songs accompany a web of stories, loosely set in the nineteenth century, showing young couples frolicking in fields, a ballerina spooked on stage, and, inevitably, travelers in a wintry landscape. They might be enacting the nun's memories of her youth, but perhaps she is simply imagining lives different from her own, as art can help to do.

In 1997, director David Alden worked with Ian Bostridge and Julius Drake on a performance of *Winterreise* filmed in a deserted asylum. The piano being deemed a hindrance to creating a sense of drama, it remains out of sight, leaving Bostridge to sing while wandering through the empty rooms. Occasionally he is joined by silent characters in Biedermeier dress; at one point, he sits by the fire, contemplating the blade of a dagger. A more fantastical approach is taken for "Die Krähe," with Bostridge filmed from above, the tails of his long black coat becoming the wings of the crow as he circles through the white sky. "He's up there with the bird looking down, dizzy," Bostridge later explained, finding a synergy with Schubert's hallucinatory music.[26] A documentary accompanied the DVD release, showing Bostridge and Drake rehearsing with Alden; interestingly, both were somewhat resistant to trying to "act out" the cycle, arguing that there was enough drama in the music without additional histrionics.

The continued appeal of presenting *Winterreise* in a quasi-theatrical way partly reflects the cycle's ubiquity. It is, these days, the most frequently performed of Schubert's three cycles (*Schwanengesang*, compiled by the publisher after Schubert's death, being the third), and there is probably a need to find new ways to "sell" the various versions. *Winterreise* continues to represent a challenge for performers and audiences. It is, undeniably, a long work, with little timbral variety beyond the capabilities of singer and pianist. When performed with skill, it can be tremendously engrossing, but even then, providing visual stimuli alongside musical ones might help some audience members engage with the story, such as it is. One challenge for directors and designers is that the imagery of the cycle, while in some senses easily rendered, can come close to cliché.

The problem is apparent in responses to the cycle by visual artists. Singer Lotte Lehmann produced watercolours illustrating the songs of *Winterreise*, which she also performed and recorded. Each one captures a scene, such as a windswept tree, or the protagonist (in Lehmann's rendering, a rather gothic-looking gentleman) leaving town, or him later weeping. German-born artist Mariele Neudecker produced a film to accompany a live performance of *Winterreise* by bass-baritone Andrew Foster-Williams and pianist Christopher Gould (2003). Snowy landscapes and ice-skaters, all from the 60th parallel north, were projected behind singer and pianist on the concert platform. South African artist William Kentridge undertook a similar project for the Aix-en-Provence festival in 2014, producing stop-action films animating pen-and-ink illustrations responding to each of the songs performed by Matthias Goerne and pianist Markus Hinterhäuser. Apparently, the images Kentridge associated with the cycle came from his childhood in Johannesburg, watching his father listen to a recording of *Winterreise* by Fischer-Dieskau and Gerald Moore. As Kentridge did not understand German, Müller's texts appeared "like prayers," he explained: they were incomprehensible but elicited an emotional response. For "Die Krähe," the tools slung over a worker's back become the wings of the crow, which then flies over varied landscapes, at one point seeming to morph into the Reichsadler atop a domed building; in a more domestic setting, a man – Kentridge's father? – looks out of a window.

Confronting history has occupied many post-war German and Austrian artists, and while Schubert's music does not feature in their works as often as Wagner's or Beethoven's, one can occasionally glimpse the legacy of *Winterreise*. Of Gerhard Richter's series of paintings derived from photographs of the Baader Meinhof gang, *18 October 1977* (1988), T. J. Clark writes, "These are mugshots from an anarchist archive. Concealment. Obstruction. Fading. Take a look at the pseudo-poignant record player (a record player!) with *Winterreise;* or, 'Street Fighting Man' stopped on the time-turntable."[27] Schubert's presence here, in a terrorist's cell, alongside The Rolling Stones, suggests that his canonical status is assured. The range of reference within which *Winterreise* thrives, though, has escalated. A retrospective of Sigmar Polke's took travel as its theme, charting the artist's responses to everywhere from Lapland to Indonesia as well as abstract landscapes. Its title, almost inevitably, was *Eine Winterreise*. Instating the article allows the difference between Schubert's cycle and its historical derivatives to be clear: it is not one winter's journey, but one of many.

Notes

1. On the musical canon, see William Weber, *The Rise of Musical Classics: A Study in Canon, Ritual and Ideology* (Oxford: Oxford University Press, 1992); and Klaus Pietschmann and Melanie Wald-Fuhrmann (eds.), *Der Kanon der Musik: Theorie und Geschichte. Ein Handbuch* (Munich: Edition Text+Kritik, 2012).
2. The literature on influence, as it is for canon and adaptation, is vast: for an introduction to some of the key issues, see Joseph N. Straus, *Remaking the Past: Musical Modernism and the Influence of the Tonal Tradition* (Cambridge: Harvard University Press, 1990); and David Metzer, *Quotation and Cultural Meaning in Twentieth-Century Music* (Cambridge: Cambridge University Press, 2003).
3. On musical adaptation, see Linda Hutcheon, *A Theory of Adaptation* (New York: Routledge, 2006); and Peter Szendy, *Listen: A History of Our Ears*, trans. Charlotte Mandell (New York: Fordham University Press, 2008).
4. On the complexities of transcriptions, see Thomas Christensen, "Four-Hand Piano Transcription and Geographies of Nineteenth-Century Musical Reception," *Journal of the American Musicological Society* 52/2 (1999): 255–98; and Jonathan Kregor, *Liszt as Transcriber* (Cambridge: Cambridge University Press, 2012).
5. Reinhold Brinkmann, "Musikalische Lyrik, politische Allegorie und die 'heil'ge Kunst': Zur Landschaft von Schuberts *Winterreise*," *Archiv für Musikwissenschaft*, 62/2 (2005): 75–97 (82).
6. See David Owen Norris, "Liszt's *Winterreise*," *The Musical Times* 126/1711 (Sept. 1985): 521–25.
7. Jürg Stenzl, trans. Irene Zedlacher, "In Search of a History of Musical Interpretation," *The Musical Quarterly* 79/4 (1995): 683–99 (686).
8. Simon Emmerson, Review of Michael Talbot (ed.), *The Musical Work: Reality or Invention?* (Liverpool: Liverpool University Press, 2000), in *Journal of New Music Research* 31/4 (2002): 393–98 (396).

9. On the relationship between Uhland's/Kreutzer's and Müller's/Schubert's cycles, see *RWJ*, 30–34.

10. Elaine Kelly, *Composing the Canon in the German Democratic Republic: Narratives of Nineteenth-Century Music* (New York: Oxford University Press, 2014), 157–164 (161).

11. Susan Youens, "Schubert, Mahler and the Weight of the Past: 'Lieder eines fahrenden Gesellen' and 'Winterreise,'" *Music & Letters* 67/3 (1 July 1986), 256–68.

12. Wolfgang Rihm, "Wer sich am Grat aufhält, weiss um den Absturz. Notizen zu Wilhelm Killmayers 'Poèmes symphoniques,'" in Wolfgang Rihm and Ulrich Mosch (eds.), *Ausgesprochen. Schriften und Gespräche*, vol. 1 (Winterthur: Amadeus, 1997), 334.

13. Nico Muhly, program note to "Good Night" in the Tanglewood Music Center Yearbook, 2017. https://archive.org/stream/tanglewoodmusicc2017bost/tanglewoodmusicc2017bost_djvu.txt. Accessed May 6, 2019.

14. Frankie Perry, Review of Bernhard Lang: The Cold Trip. Sarah Maria Sun, Aleph Guitar Quartet; Juliet Fraser, Mark Knoop. Kairos 0015018, in *Tempo* 72 (2018): 101–3.

15. Scott Messing, *Schubert in the European Imagination*, 2 vols. (Rochester, NY: University of Rochester Press, 2007).

16. Thomas Mann, letter of 1943, quoted in Rodney Symington, *Thomas Mann's* The Magic Mountain: *A Reader's Guide* (Newcastle: Cambridge Scholars Publishing, 2011), 333, n. 1.31.

17. Thomas Mann, *The Magic Mountain*, trans. H. T. Lowe-Porter (London: Minerva, 1928), 652–53.

18. Ibid., 715.

19. See Laura Tunbridge, *Singing in the Age of Anxiety: Lieder Performances in New York and London between the World Wars* (Chicago: University of Chicago Press, 2018).

20. Noel Witts, "Beckett and Schubert," *Performance Research*, 12/1 (2007): 138–44.

21. Jenny Gilbert, "Woyzeck in Winter" at www.barbican.org.uk/read-watch-listen/woyzeck-in-winter. Accessed May 6, 2019.

22. Silvia Pellicer-Ortin, *Eva Figes' Writings: A Journal through Trauma* (Newcastle: Cambridge Scholars Publishing, 2016), 106.

23. Tom Smith, "Emotional Ambivalence and the Musical Canon: Elfriede Jelinek's Restaging of Schubert's Songs in *Winterreise* (2011)," *German Life and Letters* 71/3 (2018): 331–52.

24. Bergman in Stig Björkman, "My Only Guide is the Pleasure Principle: Interview with Ingmar Bergman," in Paul Duncan and Bengt Wanselius (eds.), *The Ingmar Bergman Archives*, (Stockholm: Taschen, 2003), 528.

25. Anyssa Charlotte Neumann, "Sound, Act, Presence: Pre-Existing Music in the Films of Ingmar Bergman" (Ph.D. diss., King's College London, 2016), 194.

26. *SWJ*, 345.

27. T. J. Clark, "Grey Panic," *London Review of Books* 33/22 (Nov. 17, 2011): 3–7.

Appendix

Texts and Translations

1. Gute Nacht	**1. Good Night**
Fremd bin ich eingezogen,	I came here a stranger,
Fremd zieh' ich wieder aus.	As a stranger I depart.
Der Mai war mir gewogen	May favored me
Mit manchem Blumenstrauss.	With many a bunch of flowers.
Das Mädchen sprach von Liebe,	The girl spoke of love,
Die Mutter gar von Eh', -	Her mother even of marriage -
Nun ist die Welt so trübe,	Now the world is so gloomy,
Der Weg gehüllt in Schnee.	The road shrouded in snow.
Ich kann zu meiner Reisen	I cannot choose the time
Nicht wählen mit der Zeit,	To begin my journey,
Muss selbst den Weg mir weisen	Must find my own way
In dieser Dunkelheit.	In this darkness.
Es zieht ein Mondenschatten	A shadow of the moon travels
Als mein Gefährte mit,	With me as my companion,
Und auf den weissen Matten	And upon the white fields
Such' ich des Wildes Tritt.	I seek the deer's track.
Was soll ich länger weilen,	Why should I stay here any longer
Dass man mich trieb hinaus?	So that people can drive me away?
Lass irre Hunde heulen	Let stray dogs howl
Vor ihres Herren Haus;	In front of their master's house;
Die Liebe liebt das Wandern -	Love loves to wander -
Gott hat sie so gemacht -	God made it that way -
Von einem zu dem andern.	From one to the other,
Fein Liebchen, gute Nacht!	My dearest, good night!
Will dich im Traum nicht stören,	I don't want to disturb your dreaming,
Wär Schad' um deine Ruh'.	It would be a shame to wake you.
Sollst meinen Tritt nicht hören -	You won't hear my step,
Sacht, sacht die Türe zu!	Softly, softly the door closes!
Schreib im Vorübergehen	I write in passing
Ans Tor dir: Gute Nacht,	On your gate: Good night,
Damit du mögest sehen,	So that you may see
An dich hab' ich gedacht.	That I thought of you.
2. Die Wetterfahne	**2. The Weathervane**
Der Wind spielt mit der Wetterfahne	The wind plays with the weathervane
Auf meines schönen Liebchens Haus.	On my lovely darling's house.
Da dacht' ich schon in meinem Wahne,	And I thought in my delusion,
Sie pfiff den armen Flüchtling aus.	That it mocked the poor fugitive.
Er hätt' es eher bemerken sollen,	He should have noticed sooner
Des Hauses aufgestecktes Schild,	The symbol displayed on the house,
So hätt' er nimmer suchen wollen	So he wouldn't ever have expected
Im Haus ein treues Frauenbild.	To find a faithful woman within.

Der Wind spielt drinnen mit den Herzen
Wie auf dem Dach, nur nicht so laut.
Was fragen sie nach meinen Schmerzen?
Ihr Kind ist eine reiche Braut.

The wind plays with the hearts inside
As it does on the roof, only not so loudly.
Why should they care about my grief?
Their child is a rich bride.

3. Gefror'ne Tränen
Gefrorne Tropfen fallen
Von meinen Wangen ab:
Ob es mir denn entgangen,
Dass ich geweinet hab'?

3. Frozen Tears
Frozen drops are falling
Down from my cheeks.
How could I have not noticed
That I have been weeping?

Ei Tränen, meine Tränen,
Und seid ihr gar so lau,
Dass ihr erstarrt zu Eise
Wie kühler Morgentau?

Ah tears, my tears,
And are you so tepid
That you freeze to ice
Like cool morning dew?

Und dringt doch aus der Quelle
Der Brust so glühend heiss,
Als wolltet ihr zerschmelzen
Des ganzen Winters Eis!

Yet you burst from the wellspring
Of my heart so burning hot,
As if you wanted to melt
The entire winter's ice!

4. Erstarrung
Ich such' im Schnee vergebens
Nach ihrer Tritte Spur,
Wo sie an meinem Arme
Durchstrich die grüne Flur.

4. Numbness
I search the snow in vain
For the trace of her steps.
Where she, arm in arm with me,
Crossed the green meadow.

Ich will den Boden küssen,
Durchdringen Eis und Schnee
Mit meinen heissen Tränen,
Bis ich die Erde seh'.

I want to kiss the ground,
Penetrate ice and snow
With my hot tears,
Until I see the soil.

Wo find' ich eine Blüte,
Wo find' ich grünes Gras?
Die Blumen sind erstorben,
Der Rasen sieht so blass.

Where will I find a blossom,
Where will I find green grass?
The flowers are all dead,
The turf is so pale.

Soll denn kein Angedenken
Ich nehmen mit von hier?
Wenn meine Schmerzen schweigen,
Wer sagt mir dann von ihr?

Shall then no momento
Accompany me from here?
When my pains cease,
Who will tell me of her then?

Mein Herz ist wie erstorben,
Kalt starrt ihr Bild darin;
Schmilzt je das Herz mir wieder,
Fliesst auch ihr Bild dahin!

My heart is as if dead,
Her image frozen cold within;
If my heart ever thaws again,
Her image will also melt away!

5. Der Lindenbaum
Am Brunnen vor dem Tore
Da steht ein Lindenbaum;
Ich träumt' in seinem Schatten
So manchen süssen Traum.

5. The Linden Tree
At the well by the gate
There stands a linden tree;
I dreamed in its shadow
Many a sweet dream.

Ich schnitt in seine Rinde
So manches liebe Wort;
Es zog in Freud' und Leide
Zu ihm mich immer fort.

I carved in its bark
Many a word of love;
In joy and in sorrow
I was always drawn to it.

Ich musst' auch heute wandern
Vorbei in tiefer Nacht,
Da hab' ich noch im Dunkeln
Die Augen zugemacht.

Und seine Zweige rauschten,
Als riefen sie mir zu:
Komm her zu mir, Geselle,
Hier find'st du deine Ruh'!

Die kalten Winde bliesen
Mir grad' ins Angesicht;
Der Hut flog mir vom Kopfe,
Ich wendete mich nicht.

Nun bin ich manche Stunde
Entfernt von jenem Ort,
Und immer hör' ich's rauschen:
Du fändest Ruhe dort!

6. Wasserflut
Manche Trän' aus meinen Augen
Ist gefallen in den Schnee;
Seine kalten Flocken saugen
Durstig ein das heisse Weh.

Wenn die Gräser sprossen wollen
Weht daher ein lauer Wind,
Und das Eis zerspringt in Schollen
Und der weiche Schnee zerrinnt.

Schnee, du weisst von meinem Sehnen,
Sag', wohin doch geht dein Lauf?
Folge nach nur meinen Tränen,
Nimmt dich bald das Bächlein auf.

Wirst mit ihm die Stadt durchziehen,
Muntre Strassen ein und aus;
Fühlst du meine Tränen glühen,
Da ist meiner Liebsten Haus.

7. Auf dem Flusse
Der du so lustig rauschtest,
Du heller, wilder Fluss,
Wie still bist du geworden,
Gibst keinen Scheidegruss.

Mit harter, starrer Rinde
Hast du dich überdeckt,
Liegst kalt und unbeweglich
Im Sande ausgestreckt.

In deine Decke grab' ich
Mit einem spitzen Stein
Den Namen meiner Liebsten
Und Stund' und Tag hinein:

Den Tag des ersten Grusses,
Den Tag, an dem ich ging;
Um Nam' und Zahlen windet
Sich ein zerbroch'ner Ring.

Again today I had to travel
Past it in the depths of night.
There even in the darkness
I closed my eyes.

And its branches rustled,
As if they called to me:
Come here to me, friend,
Here you'll find peace!

The cold winds blew
Right into my face;
The hat flew off my head,
I didn't turn around.

Now I am many hours
Distant from that place,
And I still hear it whispering:
You'd find peace here!

6. Flood Water
Many a tear from my eyes
Has fallen in the snow;
Its cold flakes absorb
Thirstily the burning woe.

When it's time for the grass to sprout
There blows a mild wind,
And the ice will break apart
And the soft snow melt away.

Snow, you know about my longing,
Tell me, where does your course lead?
If you just follow my tears,
The brook will soon receive you.

You will flow through the town with it,
In and out of the busy streets;
When you feel my tears burning,
There is my sweetheart's house.

7. On the River
You who thundered so cheerfully,
You clear, untamed river,
How quiet you have become,
Give no word of farewell.

With a hard stiff crust
You have covered yourself,
Lie cold and unmoving,
Outstretched in the sand.

In your covering I inscribe
With a sharp stone
The name of my sweetheart
And the hour and day, as well.

The day of the first greeting,
The day on which I left;
Around name and figures winds
A broken ring.

Mein Herz, in diesem Bache
Erkennst du nun dein Bild?
Ob's unter seiner Rinde
Wohl auch so reissend schwillt?

My heart, in this stream
Do you now recognize your image?
And under its crust
Is there also a raging torrent?

8. Rückblick

Es brennt mir unter beiden Sohlen,
Tret' ich auch schon auf Eis und Schnee,
Ich möcht' nicht wieder Atem holen,
Bis ich nicht mehr die Türme seh'.

8. A Look Backward

It burns under both my feet,
Even though I walk on ice and snow;
I don't want to catch my breath
Until I can no longer see the spires.

Hab' mich an jedem Stein gestossen,
So eilt' ich zu der Stadt hinaus;
Die Krähen warfen Bäll' und Schlossen
Auf meinen Hut von jedem Haus.

I tripped on every stone,
As I hurried out of the town;
The crows hurled chunks of snow and ice
On my hat from every house.

Wie anders hast du mich empfangen,
Du Stadt der Unbeständigkeit!
An deinen blanken Fenstern sangen
Die Lerch' und Nachtigall im Streit.

How differently you received me,
You town of inconstancy!
At your sparkling windows sang
The lark and nightingale in competition.

Die runden Lindenbäume blühten,
Die klaren Rinnen rauschten hell,
Und ach, zwei Mädchenaugen glühten. -
Da war's gescheh'n um dich, Gesell!

The bushy linden trees bloomed,
The clear streams murmured brightly,
And, oh, two maiden's eyes glowed -
Your fate was sealed, my boy!

Kommt mir der Tag in die Gedanken,
Möcht' ich noch einmal rückwärts seh'n.
Möcht' ich zurücke wieder wanken,
Vor ihrem Hause stille steh'n.

Whenever that day enters my thoughts,
I want to look back once more,
I want to turn back again
And stand still before her house.

9. Irrlicht

In die tiefsten Felsengründe
Lockte mich ein Irrlicht hin;
Wie ich einen Ausgang finde,
Liegt nicht schwer mir in dem Sinn.

9. Will o' the Wisp

Into the deepest mountain chasms
A will o' the wisp lured me;
How to find a way out
Doesn't worry me much.

Bin gewohnt das Irregehen,
's führt ja jeder Weg zum Ziel;
Uns're Freuden, uns're Wehen,
Alles eines Irrlichts Spiel!

I'm used to going astray,
And every way leads to the goal.
Our joys, our sorrows,
Are all a will o' the wisp's game!

Durch des Bergstroms trockne Rinnen
Wind' ich ruhig mich hinab,
Jeder Strom wird's Meer gewinnen,
Jedes Leiden auch sein Grab.

Through the mountain stream's dry channel
I wend my way calmly downward.
Every river finds its way to the ocean,
And every sorrow to its grave.

10. Rast

Nun merk' ich erst wie müd' ich bin,
Da ich zur Ruh' mich lege;
Das Wandern hielt mich munter hin
Auf unwirtbarem Wege.

10. Rest

Now I first notice how tired I am
As I lay myself down to rest;
Walking kept me going strong
On the inhospitable road.

Die Füsse frugen nicht nach Rast,
Es war zu kalt zum Stehen;
Der Rücken fühlte keine Last,
Der Sturm half fort mich wehen.

My feet didn't ask for rest,
It was too cold to stand still,
My back felt no burden,
The storm helped to blow me onward.

In eines Köhlers engem Haus
Hab' Obdach ich gefunden.
Doch meine Glieder ruh'n nicht aus:
So brennen ihre Wunden.

In a charcoal-burner's tiny house
I have found shelter;
But my limbs won't relax,
Their hurts burn so much.

Auch du, mein Herz, in Kampf und Sturm
So wild und so verwegen,
Fühlst in der Still' erst deinen Wurm
Mit heissem Stich sich regen!

11. Frühlingstraum
Ich träumte von bunten Blumen,
So wie sie wohl blühen im Mai;
Ich träumte von grünen Wiesen,
Von lustigem Vogelgeschrei.

Und als die Hähne krähten,
Da ward mein Auge wach;
Da war es kalt und finster,
Es schrien die Raben vom Dach.

Doch an den Fensterscheiben,
Wer malte die Blätter da?
Ihr lacht wohl über den Träumer,
Der Blumen im Winter sah?

Ich träumte von Lieb um Liebe,
Von einer schönen Maid,
Von Herzen und von Küssen,
Von Wonne und Seligkeit.

Und als die Hähne krähten,
Da ward mein Herze wach;
Nun sitz' ich hier alleine
Und denke dem Traume nach.

Die Augen schliess' ich wieder,
Noch schlägt das Herz so warm.
Wann grünt ihr Blätter am Fenster?
Wann halt' ich mein Liebchen im Arm?

12. Einsamkeit
Wie eine trübe Wolke
Durch heit're Lüfte geht,
Wenn in der Tanne Wipfel
Ein mattes Lüftchen weht:

So zieh ich meine Strasse
Dahin mit trägem Fuss,
Durch helles, frohes Leben
Einsam und ohne Gruss.

Ach, dass die Luft so ruhig!
Ach, dass die Welt so licht!
Als noch die Stürme tobten,
War ich so elend nicht.

13. Die Post
Von der Strasse her ein Posthorn klingt.
Was hat es, dass es so hoch aufspringt,
Mein Herz?

Die Post bringt keinen Brief für dich.
Was drängst du denn so wunderlich,
Mein Herz?

You, too, my heart, in strife and storm
So wild and so bold,
Feel first in the silence your serpent
Stir with burning sting!

11. Dream of Spring
I dreamed of many-colored flowers,
The way they bloom in May;
I dreamed of green meadows,
Of merry bird calls.

And when the roosters crowed,
My eye awakened;
It was cold and dark,
The ravens shrieked on the roof.

But on the window panes -
Who painted the leaves there?
I suppose you'll laugh at the dreamer
Who saw flowers in winter?

I dreamed of love reciprocated,
Of a beautiful maiden,
Of embracing and kissing,
Of joy and delight.

And when the roosters crowed,
My heart awakened;
Now I sit here alone
And reflect on the dream.

I close my eyes again,
My heart still beats so warmly.
When will you leaves on the window turn green?
When will I hold my love in my arms?

12. Solitude
As a dreary cloud
Moves through the clear sky,
When in the crown of the fir tree
A faint breeze blows,

So I travel my road
Onward with sluggish feet,
Through bright, happy life,
Lonely and unrecognized.

Oh, that the air should be so still!
Oh, that the world should be so light!
When the storms still raged,
I was not so miserable.

13. The Post
From the highroad a posthorn sounds.
Why do you leap so high,
My heart?

The post does not bring a letter for you,
Why the strange compulsion,
My heart?

Nun ja, die Post kommt aus der Stadt,
Wo ich ein liebes Liebchen hat,
Mein Herz!

Willst wohl einmal hinüberseh'n
Und fragen, wie es dort mag geh'n,
Mein Herz?

14. Der greise Kopf
Der Reif hatt' einen weissen Schein
Mir übers Haar gestreuet;
Da glaubt' ich schon ein Greis zu sein
Und hab' mich sehr gefreuet.

Doch bald ist er hinweggetaut,
Hab' wieder schwarze Haare,
Dass mir's vor meiner Jugend graut -
Wie weit noch bis zur Bahre!

Vom Abendrot zum Morgenlicht
Ward mancher Kopf zum Greise.
Wer glaubt's? und meiner ward es nicht
Auf dieser ganzen Reise!

15. Die Krähe
Eine Krähe war mit mir
Aus der Stadt gezogen,
Ist bis heute für und für
Um mein Haupt geflogen.

Krähe, wunderliches Tier,
Willst mich nicht verlassen?
Meinst wohl, bald als Beute hier
Meinen Leib zu fassen?

Nun, es wird nicht weit mehr geh'n
An dem Wanderstabe.
Krähe, lass mich endlich seh'n
Treue bis zum Grabe!

16. Letzte Hoffnung
Hie und da ist an den Bäumen
Manches bunte Blatt zu seh'n,
Und ich bleibe vor den Bäumen
Oftmals in Gedanken steh'n.

Schaue nach dem einen Blatte,
Hänge meine Hoffnung dran;
Spielt der Wind mit meinem Blatte,
Zittr' ich, was ich zittern kann.

Ach, und fällt das Blatt zu Boden,
Fällt mit ihm die Hoffnung ab;
Fall' ich selber mit zu Boden,
Wein' auf meiner Hoffnung Grab.

17. Im Dorfe
Es bellen die Hunde, es rasseln die Ketten;
Es schlafen die Menschen in ihren Betten,
Träumen sich manches, was sie nicht haben,
Tun sich im Guten und Argen erlaben;
Und morgen früh ist alles zerflossen.

Of course, the post comes from the town,
Where I once had a dear sweetheart,
My heart!

Would you like to take a look over there,
And ask how things are going,
My heart?

14. The Old-Man's Head
The frost has spread a white sheen
All over my hair;
I thought I had become an old man
And was very pleased about it.

But soon it melted away,
And now I have black hair again
So that I am horrified by my youth -
How long still to the grave!

From the sunset to the dawn
Many a head turns white.
Who can believe it? And mine
Has not on this whole journey!

15. The Crow
A crow has accompanied me
Since I left the town,
Until today, as ever,
It has circled over my head.

Crow, you strange creature,
Won't you ever leave me?
Do you plan soon as booty
To have my carcase?

Well, I won't be much longer
Wandering on the road.
Crow, let me finally see
Loyalty unto the grave!

16. Last Hope
Here and there on the trees
There's a colored leaf to be seen.
And I stop in front of the trees
Often, lost in thought.

I watch a particular leaf
And pin my hopes on it;
If the wind plays with my leaf
I tremble from head to foot.

Oh, and if the leaf falls to earth,
My hopes fall along with it.
I fall to earth as well
And weep on the grave of my hopes.

17. In the Village
The dogs are barking, the chains are rattling;
The people are sleeping in their beds,
Dreaming of things they don't have,
Refreshing themselves in good and bad.
And in the morning all will have vanished.

Je nun, sie haben ihr Teil genossen
Und hoffen, was sie noch übrig liessen,
Doch wieder zu finden auf ihren Kissen.

Bellt mich nur fort, ihr wachen Hunde,
Lasst mich nicht ruh'n in der Schlummerstunde !
Ich bin zu Ende mit allen Träumen.
Was will ich unter den Schläfern säumen?

18. Der stürmische Morgen
Wie hat der Sturm zerrissen
Des Himmels graues Kleid!
Die Wolkenfetzen flattern
Umher im matten Streit.

Und rote Feuerflammen
Zieh'n zwischen ihnen hin;
Das nenn' ich einen Morgen
So recht nach meinem Sinn!

Mein Herz sieht an dem Himmel
Gemalt sein eig'nes Bild -
Es ist nichts als der Winter,
Der Winter kalt und wild!

19. Täuschung
Ein Licht tanzt freundlich vor mir her,
Ich folg' ihm nach die Kreuz und Quer;
Ich folg' ihm gern und seh's ihm an,
Dass es verlockt den Wandersmann.
Ach ! wer wie ich so elend ist,
Gibt gern sich hin der bunten List,
Die hinter Eis und Nacht und Graus,
Ihm weist ein helles, warmes Haus.
Und eine liebe Seele drin. -
Nur Täuschung ist für mich Gewinn!

20. Der Wegweiser
Was vermeid' ich denn die Wege,
Wo die ander'n Wand'rer geh'n,
Suche mir versteckte Stege,
Durch verschneite Felsenhöh'n?

Habe ja doch nichts begangen,
Dass ich Menschen sollte scheu'n, -
Welch ein törichtes Verlangen
Treibt mich in die Wüstenei'n?

Weiser stehen auf den Strassen,
Weisen auf die Städte zu.
Und ich wandre sonder Massen
Ohne Ruh' und suche Ruh'.

Einen Weiser seh' ich stehen
Unverrückt vor meinem Blick;
Eine Strasse muss ich gehen,
Die noch keiner ging zurück.

21. Das Wirtshaus
Auf einen Totenacker
Hat mich mein Weg gebracht;
Allhier will ich einkehren,
Hab ich bei mir gedacht.

Oh well, they had their share of pleasure
And hope that what they missed
Can be found again on their pillows.

Drive me out with your barking, you vigilant dogs,
Don't let me rest when it's time for slumber.
I am finished with all my dreams.
Why should I linger among the sleepers?

18. The Stormy Morning
How the storm has torn asunder
The heavens' grey cover!
The cloud tatters flutter
Around in weary strife.

And fiery red flames
Dart around among them;
That's what I call a morning
That really fits my mood!

My heart sees in the heavens
Its own image painted -
It's nothing but the winter,
Winter cold and wild!

19. Illusion
A light does a friendly dance before me,
I follow it here and there;
I like to follow it and watch
The way it lures the wanderer.
Ah, a man as wretched as I am
Is glad to fall for the merry trick
That, beyond ice and night and fear,
Shows him a bright, warm house.
And a loving soul within -
Only illusion lets me win!

20. The Sign Post
Why then do I avoid the highways
Where the other travelers go,
Search out the hidden pathways
Through the snowy mountain tops?

I've committed no crime
That I should hide from other men -
What is the foolish compulsion
That drives me into desolation?

Signposts stand along the highways
Pointing to the cities,
And I wander ever further
Without rest and look for rest.

Before me I see a signpost standing
Fixed before my gaze.
I must travel a road
From which no one ever returned.

21. The Inn
My way has led me
To a graveyard;
Here I'll stop,
I told myself

Ihr grünen Totenkränze
Könnt wohl die Zeichen sein,
Die müde Wand'rer laden
Ins kühle Wirtshaus ein.

Sind denn in diesem Hause
Die Kammern all' besetzt?
Bin matt zum Niedersinken,
Bin tödlich schwer verletzt.

O unbarmherz'ge Schenke,
Doch weisest du mich ab?
Nun weiter denn, nur weiter,
Mein treuer Wanderstab!

22. Mut!
Fliegt der Schnee mir ins Gesicht,
Schüttl' ich ihn herunter.
Wenn mein Herz im Busen spricht,
Sing' ich hell und munter.

Höre nicht, was es mir sagt,
Habe keine Ohren;
Fühle nicht, was es mir klagt,
Klagen ist für Toren.

Lustig in die Welt hinein
Gegen Wind und Wetter!
Will kein Gott auf Erden sein,
Sind wir selber Götter!

23. Die Nebensonnen
Drei Sonnen sah ich am Himmel steh'n,
Hab' lang und fest sie angeseh'n;
Und sie auch standen da so stier,
Als wollten sie nicht weg von mir.
Ach, meine Sonnen seid ihr nicht!
Schaut ander'n doch ins Angesicht!
Ja, neulich hatt' ich auch wohl drei;
Nun sind hinab die besten zwei.
Ging nur die dritt' erst hinterdrein!
Im Dunkel wird mir wohler sein.

24. Der Leiermann
Drüben hinterm Dorfe
Steht ein Leiermann
Und mit starren Fingern
Dreht er was er kann.

Barfuss auf dem Eise
Wankt er hin und her
Und sein kleiner Teller
Bleibt ihm immer leer.

Keiner mag ihn hören,
Keiner sieht ihn an,
Und die Hunde knurren
Um den alten Mann.

You green mourning garlands
Must be the sign
That invites weary travelers
Into the cool inn.

What, all the rooms
In this house are full?
I'm tired enough to drop,
Have taken mortal hurt.

Oh, merciless inn,
You turn me away?
Well, onward then, still further,
My loyal walking staff!

22. Courage
If the snow flies in my face,
I shake it off again.
When my heart speaks in my breast,
I sing loudly and gaily.

I don't hear what it says to me,
I have no ears to listen;
I don't feel when it laments,
Complaining is for fools.

Happy through the world along
Facing wind and weather!
If there's no God upon the earth,
Then we ourselves are Gods!

23. The False Suns
I saw three suns in the sky,
Stared at them hard for a long time;
And they stayed there so stubbornly
That it seemed they didn't want to leave me.
Ah, you are not my suns!
Go, look into someone else's face!
Yes, recently I, too, had three
But now the best two have gone down.
If only the third would also set!
I will feel better in the dark.

24. The Hurdy-Gurdy Man
Over there beyond the village
Stands an organ-grinder,
And with numb fingers
He plays as best he can.

Barefoot on the ice,
He totters here and there,
And his little plate
Is always empty.

No one listens to him,
No one notices him,
And the dogs growl
Around the old man.

Und er lässt es gehen,	And he just lets it happen,
Alles wie es will,	As it will,
Dreht, und seine Leier	Plays, and his hurdy-gurdy
Steht ihm nimmer still.	Is never still.
Wunderlicher Alter!	Strange old man,
Soll ich mit dir geh'n?	Shall I go with you?
Willst zu meinen Liedern	Will you play your organ
Deine Leier dreh'n?	To my songs?

---

1   Translation by Celia Sgroi, 1998, gopera.com/winterreise/songs/cycle.mv. Use of this English translation is kindly permitted by Celia Sgroi.

Guide to Further Reading

Armitage-Smith, Julian. "Schubert's *Winterreise*, Part I: The Sources of the Musical Text." *Musical Quarterly* 60/1 (1974): 20–36.

Barry, Barbara R. "'Sehnsucht' and Melancholy: Explorations of Time and Structure in Schubert's *Winterreise*," in *The Philosopher's Stone: Essays in the Transformation of Musical Structure* (Hillsdale, NY: Pendragon Press, 2000), 181–202.

Baumann, Cecilia C. *Wilhelm Müller, the Poet of the Schubert Song Cycles: His Life and Works* (University Park: Pennsylvania State University Press, 1981).

Baumann, Cecilia C. and M. J. Luetgert. "*Die Winterreise*: The Secret of the Cycle's Appeal." *Mosaic* 15/1 (1982): 41–52.

Berlin, Isaiah. *The Roots of Romanticism* (Princeton: Princeton University Press, 1999).

Bingham, Ruth Otto. "The Early Nineteenth-Century Song Cycle," in James Parsons (ed.), *The Cambridge Companion to the Lied* (Cambridge: Cambridge University Press, 2004), 101–19.

Borries, Erika von. *Wilhelm Müller, der Dichter der Winterreise: Eine Biographie* (Munich: C. H. Beck, 2007).

Bostridge, Ian. *Schubert's Winter Journey: Anatomy of an Obsession* (London: Faber & Faber, 2015).

Brinkmann, Reinhold. "Musikalische Lyrik, politische Allegorie und die 'heil'ge Kunst': Zur Landschaft von Schuberts *Winterreise*." *Archiv für Musikwissenschaft* 62/2 (2005): 75–97.

Budde, Elmar. *Schuberts Liederzyklen: Ein musikalischer Werkführer* (Munich: C. H. Beck, 2003; 2nd ed. 2012).

Byrne Bodley, Lorraine and Julian Horton (eds.), *Rethinking Schubert* (New York: Oxford University Press, 2016).

(eds.), *Schubert's Late Music: History, Theory, Style* (Cambridge: Cambridge University Press, 2016).

Chailley, Jacques. *Le Voyage d'hiver de Schubert* (Paris: Alphonse Leduc, 1975).

Clark, Suzannah. *Analyzing Schubert* (Cambridge: Cambridge University Press, 2011).

Cone, Edward T. *The Composer's Voice* (Berkeley: University of California Press, 1974).

"Poet's Love or Composer's Love?" in Steven P. Scher (ed.), *Music and Text: Critical Inquiries* (Cambridge: Cambridge University Press, 1992), 177–92.

"Words into Music: The Composer's Approach to the Text," in Northrop Frye (ed.), *Sound and Poetry* (New York: Columbia University Press, 1957), 3–15.

Cottrell, Alan P. *Wilhelm Müller's Lyrical Song-Cycles: Interpretations and Texts* (Chapel Hill: University of North Carolina Press, 1970).

Cunningham, Andrew and Nicholas Jardine. *Romanticism and the Sciences* (Cambridge: Cambridge University Press, 1990).

Daverio, John. "The Song Cycle: Journeys through a Romantic Landscape," in Rufus Hallmark (ed.), *German Lieder in the Nineteenth Century* (New York: Routledge, 2010; 1st ed., Schirmer, 1996), 363–404.

Deutsch, Otto Erich (ed.), *Schubert: Die Dokumente seines Lebens* (Kassel: Bärenreiter, 1964; rev. ed. Wiesbaden: Breitkopf & Härtel, 1996), trans. Eric Blom as *Schubert: A Documentary Biography* (London: J. M. Dent & Sons, 1946); and as *The Schubert Reader: A Life of Franz Schubert in Letters and Documents* (New York: W. W. Norton, 1949).

(ed.), *Schubert: Die Erinnerungen seiner Freunde* (Wiesbaden: Breitkopf & Härtel, 1957; repr. 1983), trans. Rosamond Ley and John Nowell as *Schubert: Memoirs by His Friends* (London: Adam and Charles Black, 1958).

Dürr, Walther. "Schubert in seiner Welt," in Walther Dürr and Andreas Krause (eds.), *Schubert-Handbuch* (Kassel: Bärenreiter; Stuttgart: Metzler, 1997; 2nd ed. Bärenreiter, 2007), 1–76.

"Zyklische Ordnung und Liederzyklus. Schuberts 'Winterreise,'" in *Programmbuch Schubertiade Hohenems 1984*, s. l. [1984], 74–84.

Erickson, Raymond. "Music in Biedermeier Vienna," in Robert Pichl, Clifford A. Bernd, and Margarete Wagner (eds.), *The Other Vienna: The Culture of Biedermeier Austria* (Vienna: Lehner, 2002), 227–41.

"Vienna in Its European Context," in Raymond Erickson (ed.), *Schubert's Vienna* (New Haven and London: Yale University Press, 1997), 3–35.

Everett, Walter. "Grief in *Winterreise*: A Schenkerian Perspective." *Music Analysis* 9/2 (1990): 157–75.

Feil, Arnold. *Franz Schubert: Die schöne Müllerin, Winterreise*, trans. Ann C. Sherwin (Portland: Amadeus Press, 1988). (German original, *Franz Schubert: Die schöne Müllerin, Winterreise*, 1975.)

Fischer, Kurt von. "Some Thoughts on Key Order in Schubert's Song Cycles," in Tamara S. Evans (ed.), *Kurt von Fischer: Essays in Musicology* (New York: Graduate School and University Center, City University of New York, 1989).

Fisk, Charles. *Returning Cycles: Contexts for the Interpretation of Schubert's Impromptus and Last Sonatas* (Berkeley: University of California Press, 2001).

Giarusso, Richard. "Beyond the Leiermann: Disorder, Reality, and the Power of Imagination in the Final Songs of Schubert's *Winterreise*," in Barbara M. Reul and Lorraine Byrne Bodley (eds.), *The Unknown Schubert* (Aldershot: Ashgate, 2008), 25–41.

Gibbs, Christopher H. (ed.), *The Cambridge Companion to Schubert* (Cambridge: Cambridge University Press, 1997).

Gibbs, Christopher H. and Morten Solvik (eds.), *Franz Schubert and His World* (Princeton: Princeton University Press, 2014).

Gish, Theodore. "*Wanderlust* and *Wanderleid*: The Motif of the Wandering Hero in German Romanticism." *Studies in Romanticism* 3/4 (1963): 225–39.

Goldschmidt, Harry. *Das Wort in instrumentaler Musik: Die Ritornelle in Schuberts Winterreise* (Hamburg: Von Bockel, 1996).

Gramit, David. "Schubert's Wanderers and the Autonomous Lied." *Journal of Musicological Research* 14 (1995): 147–68.

Greene, David B. "Schubert's *Winterreise*: A Study in the Aesthetics of Mixed Media." *Journal of Aesthetics and Art Criticism* 2/29 (1970): 181–93.

Hafer, Edward Michael. "The Wanderer Archetype in the Music of Franz Schubert and the Paintings of Caspar David Friedrich." Ph.D. diss., University of Illinois at Urbana-Champaign, 2006.

Hallmark, Rufus (ed.), *German Lieder in the Nineteenth Century*, rev. ed. (New York and London: Routledge, 2010).

"The Literary and Musical Device of Apostrophe in *Winterreise*." *19th-Century Music* 34 (2011): 3–29.

Hamlin, Cyrus. "The Romantic Song Cycle as Literary Genre," in Walter Bernhart, Steven Paul Scher, and Werner Wolf (eds.), *Word and Music Studies: Defining the Field* (Amsterdam: Rodopi, 1999), 113–34.

Hanslick, Eduard. *Geschichte des Concertwesens in Wien*, 2 vols. (Vienna: Braumüller, 1869).

Hanson, Alice M. *Musical Life in Biedermeier Vienna* (Cambridge, Cambridge University Press, 1985).

"Vienna, City of Music," in R. Erickson (ed.), *Schubert's Vienna* (New Haven and London, Yale University Press, 1997), 98–118.

Hatten, Robert. *Interpreting Musical Topics, Tropes, and Gestures: Mozart, Beethoven, and Schubert* (Bloomington: Indiana University Press, 2004).

Heindl, Waltraud. "People, Class Structure, and Society," in Raymond Erickson (ed.), *Schubert's Vienna* (New Haven and London: Yale University Press, 1997), 36–54.

Holmes, Richard. *The Age of Wonder: How the Romantic Generation Discovered the Beauty and Terror of Science* (New York: Pantheon Books, 2008).

Howe, Blake. "Whose *Winterreise?*" *Nineteenth-Century Music Review* 13/1 (2016): 113–22.

Johnson, Graham. *Franz Schubert: The Complete Songs*, 3 vols. (New Haven and London: Yale University Press, 2014).

Kinderman, William. "Wandering Archetypes in Schubert's Instrumental Music." *19th-Century Music* 21/2 (1997): 208–22.

Korstvedt, Benjamin M. "'The Prerogative of Late Style': Thoughts on the Expressive World of Schubert's Late Works," in Lorraine Byrne Bodley and Julian Horton (eds.), *Schubert's Late Music: History, Theory, Style* (Cambridge: Cambridge University Press, 2016), 404–25.

Kramer, Lawrence. "The Schubert Lied: Romantic Form and Romantic Consciousness," in Walter Frisch (ed.), *Schubert: Critical and Analytical Studies* (Lincoln: University of Nebraska Press, 1986), 200–36.

Kramer, Richard. *Distant Cycles: Schubert and the Conceiving of Song* (Chicago: University of Chicago Press, 1994).

Kreutzer, Conradin and Ludwig Uhland. *Conradin Kreutzer's* Frühlingslieder *and* Wanderlieder, trans. Luise Eitel Peake, facsim. ed. (Stuyvesant, NY: Pendragon Press, 1989).

Leighton, John. "The Winter Landscape," in *Caspar David Friedrich: Winter Landscape* (London: National Gallery Publications, 1990), 34–51.

Leroux, Georges. "Wanderer: An Essay on Franz Schubert's *Winterreise.*" *Queen's Quarterly* 118/4 (2011): 499–516.

Lewin, David. "'Auf dem Flusse': Image and Background in the Schubert Song," in Walter Frisch (ed.), *Schubert: Critical and Analytical Studies* (Lincoln: University of Nebraska Press, 1986), 126–52. Also in Lewin, *Studies in Music with Text* (New York, NY: Oxford University Press, 2006), 109–33.

Lewis, Christopher. "Text, Time, and Tonic: Aspects of Patterning in the Romantic Cycle." *Intégral* 2 (1988): 37–73.

Lindmayr-Brandl, Andrea. "Es ist doch eine wahrhaft grosse, herrliche Stadt! Vertraute Briefe von Johann Friedrich Reichardt aus Wien." *Schubert-Jahrbuch, 2006–2009* (2009): 27–37.

Malin, Yonatan. *Songs in Motion: Rhythm and Meter in the German Lied.* Oxford Studies in Music Theory. (Oxford: Oxford University Press, 2010).

Marshall, H. Lowen. "Symbolism in Schubert's *Winterreise.*" *Studies in Romanticism* 12 (1973): 607–32.

Moore, Gerald. *The Schubert Song Cycles* (London: Hamilton, 1975).

Müller, Wilhelm. *Werke, Tagebücher, Briefe*, ed. Maria-Verena Leistner. 6 vols. (Berlin: Gatza, 1994).

Gedichte aus den hinterlassenen Papieren eines reisenden Waldhornisten II. Lieder des Lebens und der Liebe. Herausgegeben von Wilhelm Müller (Dessau: Christian Georg Ackermann, 1824), 75–108.

Homerische Vorschule: Eine Einleitung in das Studium der Ilias und Odyssee (Leipzig: F. A. Brockhaus, 1824).

"Wanderlieder von Wilhelm Müller. Die Winterreise. In 12 Liedern." In *Urania: Taschenbuch auf das Jahr 1823*, Neue Folge, 5. Jahrgang (Leipzig: F. A. Brockhaus, 1823), 207–22.

Muxfeldt, Kristina. *Vanishing Sensibilities: Schubert, Beethoven, Schumann* (Oxford: Oxford University Press, 2011).

Newcomb, Anthony. "Structure and Expression in a Schubert Song: Noch einmal 'Auf dem Flusse' zu hören," in Walter Frisch (ed.), *Schubert: Critical and Analytical Studies* (Lincoln: University of Nebraska Press, 1986), 153–74.

Parsons, James (ed.), *The Cambridge Companion to the Lied* (Cambridge: Cambridge University Press, 2004).

"'My song the Midnight Raven Has Outwing'd': Schubert's 'Der Wanderer,' D. 649," in Siobhán Donovan and Robin Elliott (eds.), *Music and Literature in German Romanticism* (Rochester, New York: Camden House, 2004), 165–82.

Peake, Luise Eitel. "The Antecedents of Beethoven's Liederkreis." *Music & Letters* 63/3–4 (1982): 242–60.

"Kreutzer's *Wanderlieder*: The Other *Winterreise.*" *The Musical Quarterly* 65/1 (1979): 83–102.

"The Song Cycle: A Preliminary Inquiry into the Beginnings of the Romantic Song Cycle and the Nature of an Art Form." Ph.D. diss., Columbia University, 1968. Ann Arbor, MI: UMI.

Pichl, Robert, Clifford A. Bernd, and Margarete Wagner. *The Other Vienna: The Culture of Biedermeier Austria* (Vienna: Lehner, 2002).

Ramalingam, Vivian S. "Arcadian Elements in *Die Winterreise*: Bringing Sidney's Sundogs to Light," in David Crawford (ed.), *Encomium Musicae: Essays in Memory of Robert J. Snow* (Hillsdale, NY: Pendragon Press, 2002), 693–715.

Reed, John. *Schubert: The Final Years* (New York: St. Martin's Press, 1972).
  The Schubert Song Companion (Manchester: Manchester University Press, 1985).

Reul, Barbara M. and Lorraine Byrne Bodley (eds.) *The Unknown Schubert* (Aldershot: Ashgate, 2008).

Richards, Robert J. *The Romantic Conception of Life: Science and Philosophy in the Age of Goethe, Science and Its Conceptual Foundations* (Chicago: University of Chicago Press, 2002).

Rosen, Charles. *The Romantic Generation* (Cambridge, MA: Harvard University Press. 1995).

Schaeffer, Erwin. "Schubert's *Winterreise*." *The Musical Quarterly* 25 (1938): 39.

Schall, Carl and Karl von Holtei (eds.), *Deutsche Blätter für Poesie, Litteratur, Kunst und Theater*, vol. 1 (Breslau: Grass, Barth, 1823).

Schochow, Maximilian and Lily Schochow. *Franz Schubert: Die Texte seiner einstimmig komponierten Lieder und ihre Dichter*. 2 vols. (Hildesheim and New York: Georg Olms, 1974).

Schubert, Franz. *Winterreise* (Vienna: Tobias Haslinger, 1828). Published in two separate volumes.
  Winterreise: The Autograph Score. With an introduction by Susan Youens. (New York: Dover, 1989).

Solvik, Morten. "Schubert's Kosegarten Settings of 1815: A Forgotten *Liederspiel*," in Christopher H. Gibbs and Morten Solvik (eds.), *Franz Schubert and His World* (Princeton: Princeton University Press, 2014), 115–56.

Stein, Deborah. "The End of the Road in Schubert's *Winterreise*: The Contradiction of Coherence and Fragmentation," in Lorraine Byrne Bodley and Julian Horton (eds.), *Rethinking Schubert* (New York: Oxford University Press, 2016), 355–82.

Suurpää, Lauri. *Death in* Winterreise: *Musico-Poetic Associations in Schubert's Song Cycle* (Bloomington: Indiana University Press, 2013).

Thorau, Christian. "'Und als die Hähne krähten': Zum Verhältnis von Traum und Wirklichkeit in Schuberts 'Frühlingstraum,'" in *"Der Flug der Zeit": Franz Schubert: Ein Lesebuch* (Tutzing: Hans Schneider, 1997), 32–51.

Thym, Jürgen (ed.). *Of Poetry and Song: Approaches to the Nineteenth-Century Lied* (Rochester: University of Rochester Press, 2010).

Tunbridge, Laura. *The Song Cycle*. Cambridge Introductions to Music (Cambridge: Cambridge University Press, 2010).

Turchin, Barbara. "The Nineteenth-Century *Wanderlieder* Cycle," *The Journal of Musicology* 5/4 (1987): 498–525.

Wolf, Friedrich August, Anthony Grafton, Glenn W. Most, and James E. G. Zetzel. *Prolegomena to Homer (1795)* (Princeton: Princeton University Press, 1985).

Wollenberg, Susan. *Schubert's Fingerprints: Studies in the Instrumental Works* (Farnham: Ashgate, 2011).

Wood, Gillen D'Arcy. *Tambora: The Eruption that Changed the World* (Princeton, NJ, and Oxford: Princeton University Press, 2014).

Wulf, Andrea. *The Invention of Nature: Alexander von Humboldt's New World* (New York: Vintage Books, 2015).

Youens, Susan. "'Der Lindenbaum': The Turning Point of *Winterreise*," in Gerald Chapple, Frederick Hall, and Hans Schulte (eds.), *The Romantic Tradition: German Literature and Music in the Nineteenth Century* (New York: University Press of America, 1992), 309–32.

"Retracing a Winter Journey: Reflections on Schubert's *Winterreise*." *19th-Century Music* 21/2 (1985): 128–35.

Retracing a Winter's Journey: Schubert's Winterreise (Ithaca and London: Cornell University Press, 1991).

"Schubert, Mahler and the Weight of the Past: 'Lieder eines fahrenden Gesellen' and 'Winterreise.'" *Music & Letters* 67/3 (1986): 256–68.

"'Wegweiser' in *Winterreise*." *Journal of Musicology* 5/3 (1987): 357–79.

Zbikowski, Lawrence M. "The Blossoms of 'Trockne Blumen': Music and Text in the Early Nineteenth Century." *Music Analysis* 18/3 (1999): 307–45.

Index

Printed in the United States
By Bookmasters